Praise for
THE 30-DAY SOBRIETY

The Experts

"If you are concerned about your drinking and looking for answers, look no further. *The 30-Day Sobriety Solution* will change your life. Dave Andrews and Jack Canfield have integrated powerful new tools and techniques for recovery, many of which have been inexplicably left out of current recovery programs, with what we know already works. And by tightly integrating a full-featured and interactive website, which includes multimedia content and is regularly updated with breakthroughs in the field of recovery, *The 30-Day Sobriety Solution* is a comprehensive program that works, all for the price of a book."

—*JUSTIN LUKE RILEY, president and CEO, Young People in Recovery*

"Disguised as a book, this is a brilliantly effective lifestyle makeover for anyone fighting the lonely battle with alcohol. Dave and Jack's dynamic program culls from the very best tools for personal change—mindfulness, EFT tapping, visualization, journaling, and more—to provide effective and commonsense solutions that can be implemented immediately. They don't judge, and they don't insist on permanent abstinence. They understand deeply, and with a compassionate and encouraging tone, show you how to "reboot" your body for a healthy relationship with alcohol. The multimedia program on the book's companion website, and the supportive community you'll find there, will support you in lasting change, even if you've failed with other approaches. Follow their coaching, and you can put your drinking problems behind you forever."

—*DAWSON CHURCH, PhD, author of the award-winning bestseller* The Genie in Your Genes

"*The 30-Day Sobriety Solution* is a great book. It combines the best techniques of the human potential (EFT Tapping, neurolinguistic programming, life purpose exercises, goal setting, meditation, guided visualization, affirmations, journaling), with the best approaches from recovery counseling and coaching in a comprehensive approach that works to overcome alcohol abuse and addiction."

—*John Gray, #1* New York Times *bestselling author of* Men
Are from Mars, Women Are from Venus; What You Feel
You Can Heal; *and* Staying Focused in a Hyper World

"Alcoholism and addiction are so complicated. Getting and staying sober is a monumental challenge for those struggling with the problem. Other diseases and afflictions usually bring sympathy and empathy to those suffering, but with alcoholism and addiction there is still an undercurrent of moral judgment, affecting not only the person suffering but also their family, friends, and colleagues—shame all around. *The 30 Day Sobriety Solution* by Dave Andrews and Jack Canfield provides an elegant, compassionate, and "easy-to-follow" road map to sobriety and a fulfilling life. This is all grounded in Jack Canfield's proven success principles. This book is the Apple computer for recovery and long-term sobriety!"

—*DAN MARKEL, CEO and founder of MyLife Recovery Centers*

"Since society reinforces drinking, being sober can be a huge challenge. *The 30-Day Sobriety Solution* offers a lifeline to those ready to take charge of their drinking behavior. Jack Canfield and Dave Andrews have created a practical guide that fills an important niche in the literature on recovery."

—*PAUL R. SCHEELE, PhD, cofounder of Learning Strategies; CEO
of Scheele Learning Systems; and author of* Natural Brilliance

"If you know anyone who is struggling with alcohol and addiction, please give them this book. It offers a breakthrough approach, combining the very best of the human potential movement with the very best of recovery programs. *The 30-Day Sobriety Solution* will take people beyond recovery, helping them experience deep and lasting happiness in life."

—*MARCI SHIMOFF, #1* New York Times *bestselling author of*
Happy for No Reason *and* Chicken Soup for the Woman's Soul

"*The 30-Day Sobriety Solution* is a classic book that gives the reader powerful tools to overcome any addiction. I highly recommend it."

—*TONY O'DONNELL, PhD, ND, addiction expert*
and author of Miracle Detox Secrets

"Finally, a book that combines the best of timeless success principles with potent recovery and therapeutic practices and coaching strategies, making it a comprehensive, inspiring, and powerful recovery resource."

—*JANET BRAY ATTWOOD,* New York Times *bestselling*
author of The Passion Test *and* Your Hidden Riches

"This is a wonderful, thoughtful book that will guide you and inspire you to get complete control over your drinking problem once and for all."

—*BRIAN TRACY, bestselling author of* No Excuses, Maximum
Achievement, *and* Change Your Thinking, Change Your Life

"*The 30-Day Sobriety Solution* brings the power of positive psychology to recovery, and by integrating it with other proven techniques and tools for life change, Jack and Dave have created the new standard for achieving sobriety."

—*SHAWN ACHOR, happiness researcher and*
bestselling author of The Happiness Advantage

The 30-Day Graduates

"Wine was always my drink of choice, and even after facing serious health consequences from drinking excessively, I still couldn't face quitting. After my last emergency room visit, I actually went to the liquor store on the way home, telling myself I needed alcohol to "relax." I've attended a six-week AA treatment facility in the past and have tried AA meetings. *The 30-Day Sobriety Solution* is the only thing that has helped. I felt like I was reading a program written specifically for me. Not only have I completely quit drinking, but I used the same methods to quit smoking. My nineteen-year-old daughter even told me how happy and proud she was of me, and for the first time since I can remember, I actually feel like a good role model."

—*NATHALIE, 30-Day Graduate from Winnipeg, Canada*

"All areas of my life started to slowly improve at the very beginning. I was very skeptical at first, but the more solutions I completed, the more clear things became. Within two months of starting *The 30-Day Sobriety Solution,* I was closer to my family, performing better at work, coping with stress much more easily, had lost thirty pounds, was training for a marathon, and, most interesting, my social life actually improved."

—*ROBERT, sales executive, 30-Day Graduate from Vienna, Austria*

"When I heard about *The 30-Day Sobriety Solution*, my interest was instantly piqued. The habit of a glass of wine with dinner had crept into my life, and that one glass was enough to diminish my motivation to work out, meditate, or even read. And being a doctor, I felt that this was a contradiction to what I believe and teach others. I also wanted to drop some extra weight, reduce toxicity, and explore my desire to drink that glass of wine in the first place. Not only did *The 30-Day Sobriety Solution* help me successfully navigate my initial goals, but as a result of doing each day's action steps, I really felt different. I became less stressed, more centered, and there was no longer a craving to "take the edge off" toward the end of my day. I was also thrilled about how so much of what I learned improved other areas of my life as well. I feel great, and highly recommend *The 30-Day Sobriety Solution*, whether your goal is to quit drinking completely or just to cut back on the nightly ritual of drinking wine."

—DR. LIZ ANDERSON-PEACOCK, author, professional speaker,
and coach, 30-Day Graduate from Ontario, Canada

"Having my doctorate in psychology not only meant that I was able to study some of the most celebrated psychologists in the field but also that I learned what really drives human behavior and how to change it. What was so exciting about *The 30-Day Sobriety Solution* was how effectively it "translated" and applied so many of these critical concepts, techniques, and teachings to cutting back and quitting drinking, as well as integrated countless other transformational tools taught by leading authors, trainers, and self-help experts. The end result is a comprehensive, holistic program that will become the new standard for sobriety— all for the price of a book."

—BYRON, PhD in psychology, 30-Day Graduate from Phoenix, Arizona

"When I started *The 30-Day Sobriety Solution*, I had one goal—to remove my desire to drink. In the past, I had been able to string together some continuous sobriety, but the desire to drink always remained. After recently turning fifty, I knew I wanted to live the rest of my life differently, and *The 30-Day Sobriety Solution* ended up being exactly what I needed to help me accomplish this. By the time I finished the program, the desire to drink was amazingly gone, and it continues to be to this day. In fact, when I think about drinking, I wonder why it ever seemed so important to me in the first place."

—LENORE, 30-Day Graduate from Dallas, Texas

"The solutions I learned from *The 30-Day Sobriety Solution* have been extremely effective in maintaining sobriety and thriving in it; they are the foundation upon which my sobriety is based."

—DAN, lawyer, 30-Day Graduate from Jackson, Wyoming

"*The 30-Day Sobriety Solution* did what I didn't think was possible: it made getting and staying sober fun. Prior to discovering this program, I tried many things, from AA to therapy to other recovery programs, but none of them freed me from the prison alcohol was holding me in like *The 30-Day Sobriety Solution*."

—MISSY, 30-Day Graduate from Grand Rapids, Michigan

"I am still amazed, looking back on the way I was when I first started *The 30-Day Sobriety Solution*, to see how far I've come. And all without Alcoholics Anonymous, without inpatient or outpatient rehabilitation, and even without anybody to cheer me on. It is truly amazing, and I just want to thank you for *The 30-Day Sobriety Solution*. It has given me everything I need to thrive in sobriety."

—JAMES, retired military, 30-Day Graduate from Istanbul, Turkey

"With eleven years of sobriety, I know that the key to ongoing happiness is embracing personal growth, whether it is related to creating more success in my career, developing and maintaining more fulfilling relationships, or being more emotionally and physically healthy. What surprised and excited me were the results I experienced when I completed *The 30-Day Sobriety Solution*. Not only did my life improve in each of these areas, but more importantly, it helped me have even more fun and passion in my life *without alcohol*. I believe that *The 30-Day Sobriety Solution* is a groundbreaking program that will help anyone who wants to get and stay sober and be happy in life without feeling the need to drink."

—SHEIRA MACKENZIE, speaker, trainer, and coach,
30-Day Graduate from Portsmouth, Rhode Island

"I might even venture to say that half of the value I have gotten out of this program has been outside of just controlling my drinking. Once I control the drinking, I have a fairly large amount of time in the evenings and on the weekends where I would have gotten blasted before, but now I have to fill that time with productive or enjoyable activities. A lot of the lessons *The 30-Day Sobriety Solution* taught during the 30 days were stuff that was applicable in terms of staying positive, ways to grow and expand your horizons, and how to basically crawl out of the small little tunnel I have been in for so many years with drinking."

—MIKE, engineer, 30-Day Graduate from San Diego, California

"I felt like *The 30-Day Sobriety Solution* was breathing life back into me. Every day, I learned new tools and techniques that actually worked. I was finally able to imagine a happy life without alcohol, something that had always escaped me. And one of the surprising results was that for the first time in my life, I felt like I was not alone, even though I was doing the program alone at home."

—HANNAH, business owner and life coach,
30-Day Graduate from Sydney, Australia

"When I started *The 30-Day Sobriety Solution*, I was skeptical because my past attempts to quit drinking using "conventional" treatment methods didn't work for me. So I doubted this book and the additional content and recordings on the companion website were going to result in the breakthrough I was searching for to finally overcome my excessive drinking. Within the first week, I experienced more progress than in all my other previous treatment attempts combined, and I can honestly say after completing the program that the positive impact it had in my life was phenomenal. For the first time in over a decade, I actually can see a happy and fun future that doesn't include drinking."

—JERRY, 30-Day Graduate from San Antonio, Texas

"In the past, I always connected drinking to immediate gratification, not realizing I was only trying to fill a void in my life. Now I clearly see that over time drinking guarantees I will always feel empty inside, where sobriety opens up the possibility to experience true happiness, joy, and fulfillment."

—SUSAN, business owner and entrepreneur,
30-Day Graduate from Philadelphia, Pennsylvania

"I tried willpower to quit drinking on my own. I tried switching to beer and wine. I tried Alcoholics Anonymous several times, but found the program was too ambiguous. However, *The 30-Day Sobriety Solution* was something I could sit down and do every night. And the "homework" not only helped keep me on track, it helped me get clear and understand how I was feeling and provided me with tools and techniques to change."

—MATT, IT project manager, 30-Day Graduate
from Kansas City, Missouri

"Taking an honest look at where I was at in my life was hard. I was in my midforties, divorced, and no matter how hard I tried or how many promises I made, my attempts to quit drinking over the last year never lasted for more than three days. My greatest accomplishment was my two teenage children, but I felt ashamed and guilty for not being the parent they deserved. *The 30-Day Sobriety Solution* helped me get to the "why" that always led me back to drinking. And once I uncovered that, and was able to use the various techniques in the program to resolve it, not only did I easily overcome the three-day sobriety "wall" I always ran into, but my desire to drink was gone."

—TAMARA, 30-Day Graduate from Kansas City, Missouri

"Some of my earliest memories were of being terrified of my father's drunken rages, and despite my childhood promises to never drink like my father did, I discovered I had an almost undeniable compulsion to drink excessively. After recently turning sixty, and my nightly drinking reaching an embarrassing fifth of scotch every night, I knew I had to change. I had always been a successful entrepreneur, and even maintained a healthy, active lifestyle, but I just couldn't seem to escape my addiction to alcohol. *The 30-Day Sobriety Solution* finally freed me from my decades of drinking. Working through the daily program was a wonderful journey, and the end result is I have complete confidence in my ability to live the rest of my life sober."

—BRIAN, *business owner, 30-Day Graduate from Trenton, New York*

"*The 30-Day Sobriety Solution* is really a powerful program that's targeted at taking a whole new approach to life."

—ANN, *MBA graduate, 30-Day Graduate from New York City*

"Sobriety has become second nature. I can't really explain it, other than that soon after completing *The 30-Day Sobriety Solution*, I just stopped thinking about drinking, even though I still go to the pub with friends."

—THOMAS, *teacher and aspiring author,*
30-Day Graduate from London, England

"For many years, I tried to give up drinking, both on my own and working with counselors, but nothing seemed to break the bond until I read and dedicated myself to working through *The 30-Day Sobriety Solution*. This fantastic program gave me a huge variety of tools to work with, and it has enabled me not only to find relief, joy, and happiness in sobriety, but also to find real meaning and direction in my life. I recommend this book to anyone who is serious about giving up problem drinking and waking up to experience life's true potential."

—CHRISTINA, *30-Day Graduate from Greece*

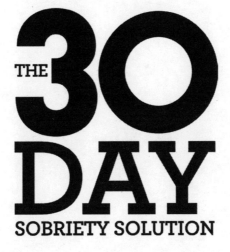

THE **30 O
DAY**
SOBRIETY SOLUTION

THE 30 DAY

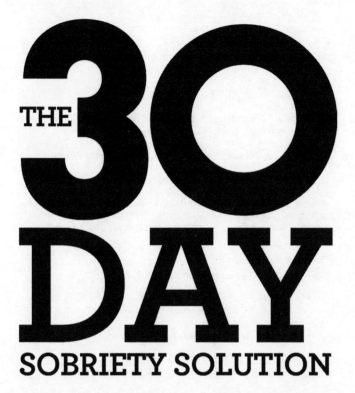

SOBRIETY SOLUTION

HOW TO CUT BACK OR QUIT DRINKING IN THE PRIVACY OF YOUR OWN HOME

JACK CANFIELD
and
DAVE ANDREWS

**SIMON &
SCHUSTER**

London · New York · Sydney · Toronto · New Delhi

A CBS COMPANY

First published in Great Britain by Simon & Schuster UK Ltd, 2016
A CBS COMPANY

1 3 5 7 9 10 8 6 4 2

Simon & Schuster UK Ltd
1st Floor
222 Gray's Inn Road
London WC1X 8HB

www.simonandschuster.co.uk

Simon & Schuster Australia, Sydney
Simon & Schuster India, New Delhi

The author and publishers have made all reasonable efforts to contact
copyright-holders for permission, and apologise for any omissions or errors in
the form of credits given. Corrections may be made to future printings.

A CIP catalogue record for this book
is available from the British Library

ISBN: 978-1-4711-4866-8
Ebook ISBN: 978-1-4711-4867-5

Text design by Paul Dippolito
Printed in the UK by CPI Group (UK) Ltd, Croydon, CR0 4YY

Sim⟨   ⟩ ⟨   ⟩er
that is made ⟨   ⟩ ⟨   ⟩s the Forest
Stewardship C⟨   ⟩ ⟨   ⟩organisation.
Our book ⟨   ⟩ ⟨   ⟩d paper.

NOTE TO READERS

This book is dedicated to the memory of Dr. Bryan Duke,
without whom this program might never have been written.

We hope The 30-Day Sobriety Solution *will help inspire*
and teach millions of people how to thrive in sobriety and
avoid years of unnecessary pain and suffering.

Bryan Jefferson Duke, 1966–2008

CONTENTS

Contents

PHASE IV

CULTIVATING COURAGE AND POSITIVE RELATIONSHIPS TO THRIVE IN MIND, BODY, AND SPIRIT

Contents

PHASE V

CREATING YOUR PERSONALIZED PLAN TO THRIVE IN LIFE

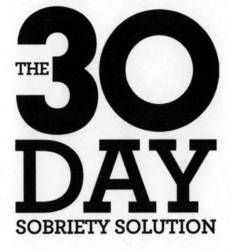

INTRODUCTION

I want to share with you why I devoted the better part of two years of my life to coauthoring this book.

Before I learned to read, I had learned the dark side of drinking. My earliest childhood memories are of my father's drunken rages—he could drain almost an entire bottle of whiskey in one evening. And when he drank too much, he always became angry and violent.

I can still remember in vivid detail being a terrified five-year-old, hiding in the bottom half of the console of an old stand-up radio that I could crawl into, praying that he wouldn't find me and hit me. But even though I had found the perfect hiding spot, I still had to listen in fear as he physically and emotionally abused my mother and my younger brother. And on the occasions when he found me before I was able to hide, he would severely whip me with a thick leather belt or a heavy pig-bristle hairbrush, which hurt and stung more than any bare hand ever could.

Thankfully, when I was six, my mother filed for divorce, and with that my life forever changed. I finally felt unafraid and free to be a child again. However, as she attempted to hide from the pain and embarrassment of her failed marriage and her inability to cope with the stress and anxiety of raising three kids by herself, my mother went from moderately drinking—primarily during multifamily picnics and other social occasions—to turning to alcohol as her daily way of coping.

It was all she knew to do. And to be fair, there weren't a lot of options at that time—but whatever options there were, such as Alcoholics Anonymous, they were public, and my mother was very private. In our family you didn't "air your dirty laundry in public." My aunt and my grandmother were also alcoholics, often passing out at dinner, but it was a family issue that was never openly discussed—or addressed.

The scary part is that this story of mine is not unique. Today more than seven million children in the United States live in a household where at least one parent is alcohol dependent or is abusing alcohol, and even though there is not always physical abuse as there was in my case, the result is all too often some form of childhood wounding that needs to be healed in later life.

If there is such a thing as an "alcohol gene," it skipped my youngest brother and me, but emerged in the next generation, gripping the lives of two of my three children. So I have seen firsthand the ravages of alcohol addiction and drug abuse—both on the alcoholic and on the extended family members. It is because of these very painful personal experiences that I am so committed to this book and to helping you, the reader.

While there have been great advances in personal development, psychology, and neuroscience over the past twenty years, most people are still not getting the help they need to overcome their abuse of alcohol. Society in general has failed to provide the proper tools and techniques for people to successfully overcome their problem drinking. David Sheff, in his book *Clean: Overcoming Addiction and Ending America's Greatest Tragedy*, states, "Prevention efforts have failed, and so too has what passes for a treatment system. Ninety percent of people who need help never receive it." Ninety percent!

A few years ago while I was conducting a workshop in Philadelphia, I met Dave Andrews. When I mentioned the devastating effects alcohol had had on my family, he excitedly told me about the extraordinary success he was having with an online coaching program he had developed called "The 30-Day Sobriety Solution." I was instantly intrigued, especially when he told me how much of my work on success principles he had integrated into his program.

In my Breakthrough to Success seminars, workshops, and trainings, I have taught these same principles to well over a million people of all ages, races, religions, and income levels in forty-seven different countries. I have had many participants in every country who were struggling with the negative effects of their drinking and wanted to cut back or quit. And when they learned the principles and participated in the exercises I taught, I consistently witnessed incredible breakthroughs, which were usually followed up by letters and emails expressing how those breakthroughs had led to long-term sobriety.

When I met Dave, I was thrilled to learn he was using these same principles and techniques to help people quit or cut back their drinking—and he was consistently seeing positive results. Once I reviewed the program and saw how brilliantly it was structured, I asked Dave to write a book with me so this revolutionary approach to sobriety or cutting back could reach more people.

Dave and I spent the next two years turning the program into a book. When *The 30-Day Sobriety Solution* was complete, we then tested it with a group of volunteers who were struggling with problem drinking or who were currently in recovery, and discovered that the book format—based on the most current research and insights gleaned from Dave's hundreds of hours of successful private coaching—was decidedly as effective. In fact, the most common feedback we received from the participants after they completed the program was that their desire to drink was *completely gone.*

Other affirming feedback from the book-only test group led us to implement a free complementary website with many of the features of Dave's original online program. This "companion" for your sobriety journey includes powerful tools such as soundtracks of guided visualizations and meditations, inspirational and instructional videos, and supplemental chapters.

I have dedicated my life to helping people change their lives. Now that I have seen the results of combining my success principles with Dave's effective approach to achieving sobriety, I am confident that *The 30-Day Sobriety Solution* is indeed a breakthrough program that will help you successfully create a life where alcohol is no longer in control.

I am honored and humbled that you have picked up this book, and I wish you all the best for a sober and fulfilling life!

—Jack Canfield

Getting Started

My recovery is the single greatest accomplishment of my life.
And without that, the rest of my life would have fallen apart.

—JAMIE LEE CURTIS
Award-winning actor and bestselling author[1]

The 30-Day Sobriety Solution is filled with life-changing, lasting ways to cut back or quit drinking. We developed these highly effective methods over eight years of research into cutting-edge scientific findings about addiction and through thousands of hours of working with people who wanted to stop drinking heavily. By combining timeless success principles with potent recovery and therapeutic practices and coaching strategies, we created the most comprehensive, inspiring, and powerful recovery resource ever published.

If you are not sure if this book is for you, answer these questions:

- Do you want to have fun and be naturally inspired and passionate about life without always feeling like you have to drink to be happy and fit in?
- Are you concerned about the effects of your drinking on your finances, family, relationships, health, weight, and/or career? Do you have legal problems as a result of your drinking?
- Are you frustrated because you have not lived up to promises that you made to yourself and to others to finally cut back or quit drinking? Are you discouraged that you have failed multiple times to cut back or quit?
- Are you a "work-hard, party-hard" type of person or a "weekend warrior"? Do you know deep down that your drinking habits

5

are holding you back from what you really want to accomplish in life?

- Do you want to cut back or quit drinking, but you're leery of some of the conventional "public" methods of recovery such as Alcoholics Anonymous (AA) and rehab? Are you looking for a more private solution that you can work on at home?
- Are you afraid that if people knew how much you *really* drank, they would no longer respect or like you?
- Are you concerned about what you are going to do when you go to the next office party or wedding, or when you go on your next vacation, and whether you will be able to get through it without alcohol?
- Are you in recovery but feel stuck? Are you wondering what you can do to create more passion and enthusiasm in your life and your sobriety?

If you answered yes to some or all of these questions, then you are in the right place! Throughout this book, you will find stories of people just like you who had these same questions and were able to get the answers they were searching for from *The 30-Day Sobriety Solution*, even after trying and failing with past attempts to cut back or quit drinking.

If you are still not sure if you have a problem with drinking, consider this recent finding. A US government report released in November 2014 found that 29.3 percent of the adult population—that's almost one out of every three adults—meets the definition for excessive drinking.[2]

The reality is that if you think you might have a problem, or if you think changing your drinking would benefit you, you are probably right.

Although this book is geared toward the problem drinker, excessive drinker, or alcoholic (whatever term you prefer to use), and people living in recovery, these solutions can be and have been used to recover from addictions to drugs (legal and illegal), gambling, sex, shopping, smoking, overeating, and other really self-destructive habits. Rather than attempt to address all of these in this book, however, we will focus solely on the problem drinker who is struggling to cut back or quit drinking and on the individual who is looking to be reinspired in recovery.

Last, we know some of you are ready to *get started now*, and we appreciate your enthusiasm. This "Getting Started" chapter includes relevant information that will help you understand the layout of this book and program. So feel free to quickly browse through it before getting right to Day 1 of the program.

The Inspiration Behind
The 30-Day Sobriety Solution

In this book, you are going to get to know us through our stories, including the challenges we have faced, our lowest points, and our greatest accomplishments. Jack Canfield is perhaps best known as America's #1 Success Coach; the author and editor of more than two hundred inspirational and self-help books, including *The Success Principles* and the Chicken Soup for the Soul® series (with over five hundred million copies sold and sixty *New York Times* bestsellers); a professional speaker; and a teacher to well over a million people around the world. Dave Andrews is best known for being a "sobriety expert" and America's #1 Sobriety Coach. As a recovered alcoholic, he knows firsthand what it is like to struggle with the fear and helplessness of trying to overcome the grip of alcoholism to eventually achieve the state of mind that he calls "thriving in sobriety."

We first met over five years ago, and it became instantly clear how much we had in common. We are both unabashedly enthusiastic about human potential and people's ability to transform their lives in a dramatic fashion. We are both committed to growing and learning, to serving others, and contributing to the greater good. We are both passionate about our families, maintaining balance, and being positive and inspirational role models to those around us. We teach those same principles, solutions, and techniques that have worked for us to anyone who wants to make profound changes, and we love doing this through coaching, training, and the written word. But most importantly, we both have been touched in profound ways by alcoholism and addiction.

Jack's mother, father, grandmother, aunt, sister, two of his children, and one of his stepchildren have struggled with alcoholism and addiction. Jack knows what it is like to be one of the more than a hundred million people in the United States whose lives have been turned upside down by a loved one struggling with alcohol abuse. Dave knows firsthand what it's like to struggle with alcoholism. He knows what it's like to desperately want to quit drinking, but to be terrified at the same time that a life without alcohol would be unhappy and boring.

Together we combine our personal experiences with our extensive collective knowledge of human potential and transformation to overcome addictive behaviors in a way that has never been done before.

We are absolutely convinced that applying the solutions taught in this program will enable you to live the life you've always dreamed of but deep down knew was impossible until you overcame your greatest challenge—your self-defeating relationship with alcohol.

The same solutions and techniques taught in *The 30-Day Sobriety Solution* have not only worked for us, they have helped our clients and students all over the world achieve breakthrough success in accomplishing everything they dreamed, including lasting sobriety; permanently cutting back on their drinking; propelling their careers to new heights; looking and feeling younger and sexier; and attaining greater financial wealth, greater health and fitness, greater passion and joy in their relationships, and greater overall happiness and fulfillment. When you work with the solutions in this book to finally cut back or quit drinking, you will be surprised at how easily you will also accomplish all of the rest of your goals.

These Solutions Work, Even if You Have Tried Before and Failed

Amazingly, as soon as I stopped drinking and drugging, I became a successful actor. Hollywood called. The rest is history.

—SAMUEL L. JACKSON

Actor whose films have grossed over $8 billion[3]

"He passed the sobriety test. Now I think he's just showing off."

You, too, can successfully cut back or quit drinking even if you have tried before and failed. Why? Because our experience with our clients has shown us that these techniques and solutions work—as long as you always work the solutions. That means you need to complete the exercises in each chapter and consistently practice the techniques you learn.

Take Chris's story, for example. Over four years ago, Chris found *The 30-Day Sobriety Solution* online. Like many of the people we have helped, Chris had already tried Alcoholics Anonymous, therapy, inpatient and outpatient rehab, and several other methods to get sober. He had come to the conclusion that nothing would work;

he was also afraid that sobriety would be boring and make him un-happy. However, he was about to lose his house and knew that he might lose his marriage and access to his two young children next. In a recent letter, he shared the following:

> For once, it felt like I found a program that spoke the same language I spoke that was able to remove the stigma of my addiction and find solutions that actually worked. And not only worked to help me get and stay sober, but worked in every aspect of my life. It was something that I could do on my own, privately, and the more effort I put into the work, the more positive results I gained in my life.
>
> In a nutshell, the program made sobriety easy and second nature for me. With that, my finances, health, and relationships all changed in dramatic fashion for the positive.

Today Chris is celebrating more than four years of sobriety. For the first time in his life, he broke the six-figure-salary barrier—not just once, but three years in a row. He is still married, and his rela-tionships with his wife and kids have changed in ways that he al-ways wanted but feared were impossible. Chris also went through a complete physical transformation and is in better shape than he has been in for over a decade—all of which he attributed to completing *The 30-Day Sobriety Solution.*

If Chris's story was the exception, you would not be reading this book. In fact, we have received countless letters and emails sharing inspiring stories of recovery from individuals with a range of sobri-ety goals: some quit for good and never looked back; some were able to return to moderate drinking; and some already in recovery be-came reinspired and excited about staying sober. We will share many of their stories with you.

The fact is that anyone can learn to consistently produce these same kinds of results. We know this because for over eight years, we researched, developed, tested, and improved the principles and techniques that we present in *The 30-Day Sobriety Solution*. We used them in hundreds of hours of coaching people who were struggling with problem drinking, and by integrating feedback from those sessions, we created a life-changing recovery program that works.

Throughout this book, we'll tell you the stories of some of the people we've helped who have struggled with the same issues as you. In many cases, their names and/or identifying details have been changed. However, the problems they faced and the solutions they implemented are real.

You will also find quotes from many high-profile individuals in recovery—actors, musicians, authors, and athletes—who have shared their stories of addiction and recovery in memoirs and interviews. The people we work with are often deeply inspired to hear that they are not alone in their struggles and that some of the most successful, well-known people also had issues with drinking and drugs and overcame them. Many of them share that some of their greatest accomplishments came only after they finally got sober.

Can I Become a Normal Drinker Again?

I found getting sober surprisingly easy with The 30-Day Sobriety Solution, *even after never going more than two days without alcohol for over fifteen years. As long as I did the solutions, it wasn't difficult.*

—THOMAS
30-Day Graduate from London, England

Without fail, almost every client asks us, "Can I become a normal drinker again?" We will cover this in greater depth in Day 1, but briefly, we do believe it is possible for *some* people to cut back their drinking to that of a normal—or social—drinker. These people can have one or two drinks and not want more—the defining characteristic of a "normal drinker." They get to the point in their sobriety where they can take it or leave it. *But this is true for only a very small percentage of problem drinkers.* And although numerous studies and other successful recovery programs advocate cutting back on drinking and provide case studies to prove that this option is viable for some people,[4] we know that this position is controversial. If you find yourself feeling frustrated or angry about this assertion, we just ask that you suspend judgment for now.

Even though many past graduates of *The 30-Day Sobriety Solution* have successfully cut back drinking, our experience has also shown us that everyone has to abstain from alcohol for at least 30 days. We will review this further in Day 1, including some options around when you can begin abstaining.

You are likely wondering if you are one of the few who can return to drinking after the program. At this stage, it is too early to know. But don't worry; we will cover this topic more thoroughly in Day 1 and Day 30.

How We Structured This Book

I've never seen an approach to getting sober that makes you enthusiastic about sobriety. In other programs, it seems like sobriety is a sentence into purgatory, but The 30-Day Sobriety Solution *is so attractive because not only does it actually work, it gets you excited about being sober.*

—ANN

30-Day Graduate from New York City

The 30-Day Sobriety Solution presents you with an easy-to-follow 30-Day plan to recover, reclaim, and reinvent your life. It is organized in a proven format that has regularly resulted in feedback from participants that each solution was "almost eerily" delivered at the exact time it was needed.

To help you effectively learn and assimilate these powerful solutions, we have organized the book into thirty chapters, to be read one per day. The chapters unfold in five phases. Most participants complete the program within 30 days. But you can decide to complete it in a 30-, 60-, or 90-day period. We will tell you how on Day 1. You'll be introduced to one solution each day, with exercises you can complete at the end of reading that day's content. As you take yourself through each phase of this program, you will learn how to thrive in sobriety, whether your goal is to cut back your drinking, quit drinking, or get reinspired in your recovery.

————

Let's review the content of the book and its organization to give you a sense of what to expect. Feel free to skim this section, as it is meant only to give you a brief overview of what you will learn.

The 30-Day Sobriety Solution begins with Phase I, which contains the absolute basics that you must master to get from where you are to where you want to be. This phase is covered in six days and is often completed during the first week of reading this book, with a review day on Day 7. However, if you have chosen the 60-day or 90-day option, you would complete this phase over the first two or three weeks. Here is some of what you will learn in Phase I:

- The magic of 30 days and the "30-Day Reboot," and why this specific time frame works.
- One of the fundamental principles of sobriety: how to create a belief and vision for your new sober self that makes it much easier to stick to your decision to change your drinking habit.
- How to apply the psychological drivers of pain and pleasure to move yourself toward your new thriving-in-sobriety vision.
- How to set your sobriety goals to ensure that they don't backfire.
- How to identify the real reasons for your drinking and why your addictive nature is actually your greatest gift.
- The art of forgiveness and how to let go of the past to embrace the present.

- Some basic nutritional guidelines and recommendations you can follow to reduce your cravings for alcohol and facilitate the physical and mental recovery process.

Phase II addresses the important inner work you will need to do to help remove the mental and emotional blocks and beliefs that prevent you from thriving in sobriety. This section is covered in Days 8 through 13 and is most commonly completed during the second week of the program, with a review day on Day 14. Here is some of what you will learn in the second week:

- The willpower illusion and how your willpower actually hurts your chances of cutting back or quitting drinking.
- How to align your values, thoughts, beliefs, and feelings to ensure that the actions you take are actually the right ones for long-term happiness and fulfillment.
- The lies you've been telling yourself that have kept you from achieving and thriving in sobriety.
- How your subconscious mind has been sabotaging your success for most of your adult life and how to reprogram your subconscious to make sobriety easier and more natural.
- The power of tapping and how to use this simple technique to help you overcome some of your greatest obstacles to cutting back or quitting drinking.

Phase III reveals the most effective methods for changing your thinking to create an unshakable belief in yourself and your dreams. This section is covered in Days 15 through 20 and is most commonly completed in the third week of the program, with a review day on Day 21. Here is some of what you will learn in the third week:

- How to harness the incredible power of visualization—a secret to the success of Olympic athletes, top entrepreneurs, world leaders, and people who have gone from excessive drinking to thriving in sobriety.

- The transformative effect of asking questions and how changing the questions you ask yourself can change your life.
- The power of the law of attraction and how "drinking thinking" has repeatedly tricked you into believing that you need alcohol in your life to be happy, and why the opposite is actually true.
- How and why affirmations can be one of the most powerful techniques to create positive change and lasting fulfillment.
- How to develop and cultivate an attitude of gratitude—a necessary component for achieving lasting sobriety.

Phase IV gives you the tools and techniques you need to more easily create physical health and wellness, along with mental and emotional balance. It concludes by teaching you how to build and maintain meaningful and fulfilling relationships. This section is covered in Days 22 through 27 and is most commonly completed during the fourth week of the program, with a review day on Day 28. Here is some of what you will learn in the fourth week:

- What creates your fears and doubts and how to overcome them so that you can live with courage every day.
- The incredible power of meditation to heal addiction and promote health and wellness.
- The five fundamentals of healing your physical body and how to eat and exercise to decrease your cravings and increase your energy and passion.
- The truth about "positive addiction" and how to get in touch with fun, inspiring, healthy, and confidence-building activities to make negative addictions disappear forever.
- What "crabs in a bucket" can teach you, and how your new team of friends, peers, alliances, and networks can build lasting success in sobriety and help you fulfill your dreams.
- How to heal the relationships that have been damaged by your drinking, and how to identify, change, and, when necessary, eliminate the relationships that continue to hold you back.

Phase V covers how you can apply what you have learned to customize your own plan for thriving in sobriety without feeling overwhelmed or stopped by a fear of failure. This section is covered in Days 29 and 30 and wraps up *The 30-Day Sobriety Solution*. Here is some of what you will learn in this section:

- How to create a powerful and inspiring vision for your future life thriving in sobriety, including proven techniques to help you implement and manifest this vision in your life.
- The mind-sets and strategies of people who have learned how to thrive in sobriety and life despite facing unbelievable challenges.
- Your answer to the question "Can I ever drink again?"

The Companion Website

One of the things I loved about The 30-Day Sobriety Solution *was the ease of learning and implementing the daily solutions. Past attempts to quit drinking had always led to delaying when I would stop drinking or rationalizing why I deserved to drink, but with this program I found myself naturally motivated to read each day's solution and complete the action steps. I also loved how each solution built on the previous ones, which all led to my finally happily embracing sobriety.*

—BRIAN

30-Day Graduate from Trenton, New York

This book comes with free access to *The 30-Day Sobriety Solution* companion website. Throughout the book, we will be referring you to the website. Not only will you find great supplemental content for every day's solution but also a forum where you can interact with past and present clients of *The 30-Day Sobriety Solution*. This website also includes critical recordings, such as guided visualizations related to the day's exercises. This has allowed us to dramatically extend the value of *The 30-Day Sobriety Solution*—enabling us to give you a comprehensive multimedia program all for the price of a book. You may want to visit the website now at www.The30DaySolution.com just to get a feel for what is there.

Lastly, we include four additional bonus solutions on the companion website that are integrated with the review days on Day 7, Day 14, Day 21, and Day 28. As we worked with people struggling to get and stay sober, we identified four solutions that virtually everyone on this path needs at some point or another.

- **Day 7—The Social Solution** covers the top 11 excuses that you can use to avoid drinking and feeling judged by others in any social situation. If you are planning to attend a party or a social event where people will be drinking, this is a must-read for you.
- **Day 14—The Relapse Solution** teaches you how to beat the odds of relapse and provides you with real solutions that work if you do relapse.
- **Day 21—The Frequently Asked Sobriety Questions Solution** includes the top questions that we have received from our sobriety coaching clients. It gives you answers to questions you did not even realize you wanted to ask, without having to pay the thousands of dollars others have paid for expensive coaching services.
- **Day 28—The Sobernomics Solution** teaches you the basics of what we call "sobernomics," a path to creating financial wealth and security with your newfound sobriety.

How to Read This Book

I was a trained coach, and successful at helping facilitate positive change in others, but I still turned to excessive drinking late in life to deal with some of my personal challenges. And no matter what I tried, I just couldn't seem to let go of alcohol as the answer. Then I found The 30-Day Sobriety Solution, *and I realized the answers were right in front of me. Although I was fa-*

miliar with most of the tools and techniques in the program, the unique way they had been adapted to quitting drinking, as well as the strategic order in which they were taught, led to the exact breakthrough I needed to finally overcome my drinking problem.

—TAMARA

30-Day Graduate from Kansas City, Missouri

Everyone learns differently, and you probably know how you learn best. Nonetheless, we would like to make a few suggestions that you might find helpful.

The solutions are presented in a specific order, and they build on one another. Think of them like the numbers to a combination lock—all of the numbers are needed, and they are needed in the right order. Remember, if you know the combination to a lock, regardless of your IQ, ethnicity, race, gender, or age, *the lock has to open for you.*

As you read each day's solution and complete the exercises, we strongly urge you to take notes in the margins, highlight on your tablet or smartphone, or underline or circle anything that stands out to you. Find things that are important to you and that you want to take action on. Then go back and review your notes or highlighted text as often as possible. Remember, repetition is absolutely necessary to the learning process. Most people have to hear or see things multiple times in order to remember them, so by repeatedly exposing yourself to the ideas and techniques in this book, you will begin to change the way you think and live in the world. Every time you go back and read something you've marked, you'll be reminded of what you most need to do to get from where you currently are to a life thriving in sobriety. Reading the additional material, listening to the audios, and watching the videos on the companion website will also help you accomplish this.

As you go through the program, you might find that some of the solutions presented in this book sound familiar. That's good! Even if they do sound familiar, don't skip over them. Make sure to take a look at your life to see if you are currently practicing them. If not, commit to take action today!

The solutions will work on you only if you work on them.

If you're hesitating to take action on some of the steps or feeling resistant, that's okay. Our experience has shown that the steps you most resist are the ones you most need to take. If you are only going to read this book and not do the exercises, you will not get the same transformational experience as you would from actually doing the work—not even close.

It Can Be Yours

Sober is sexy!

—DEMI LOVATO

Platinum-selling recording artist and founder of the
Lovato Treatment Scholarship Program[5]

As you embark on this journey, take a second to realize what can be yours in your new life if you just follow the simple steps laid out for you in this book:

- Whether it is having fun and excitement in your life without alcohol—it can be yours!
- Whether it is health and completely reversing the damage you have done with alcohol, finally losing the weight you always wanted, and looking younger and sexier—it can be yours!
- Whether it is finally feeling free from needing alcohol and waking up feeling naturally energized instead of tired and crappy—it can be yours!
- Whether it is taking your career to the next level and finding, embracing, and creating a new career in your life—it can be yours!
- Whether it is restoring your relationships with family and

friends, and becoming the parent and spouse you always dreamed of being—it can be yours!

- Whether it is getting that spark back that you had in early recovery but have lost over the years—it can be yours!
- Or whether it is simply going to a party or going on a vacation and having an awesome time without needing alcohol—it can be yours!

We will show you how you can do all of this, and we will prove to you that others just like you were able to change their lives from top to bottom and blow away every myth that they held on to about how being sober sucks.

Your New Life Awaits . . .

It's time to start living the life you've imagined.

—HENRY JAMES SR. (1811–1882)

American philosopher

It is completely normal if you feel both excited and afraid. In fact, we would be concerned if you were not a little afraid at this stage. Giving up or changing a habit that is as pervasive as drinking can be terrifying. After all, you may have been using alcohol daily for years just to get by. By quitting or changing your drinking habit, you put yourself out of your comfort zone, and fear is the natural reaction to such an act.

Take a deep breath and realize that we are here to guide you through this process. Millions of people around the world have already done what you want to do, and there is no reason that you cannot follow in their footsteps.

Your new life awaits—so don't hesitate. Turn the page and start Day 1 now.

Mastering the Absolute Basics to Get from Where You Are to Where You Want to Be

The beginning is the most important part of the work.

—PLATO (428–c. 348 BC)

Greek philosopher

We are excited to welcome you to Phase I of *The 30-Day Sobriety Solution*. This first phase is often completed over the first week of the program, and it will show you how to live a happy and fulfilling life without the desire to drink. These techniques have already worked for countless others just like you, who were either trying to cut back or quit drinking, or get reinspired in their recovery.

Before you turn the page (or swipe, tap, or click, if you are reading an ebook) to Day 1 of *The 30-Day Sobriety Solution*, it is important that you know this first solution sets the foundation for the whole program. It will hopefully address all of your questions, explain the tools and resources available to you and how to make best use of them, and, most importantly, start you along what most 30-Day Graduates consider a fun, exciting, and, of course, at times, challenging journey. We also want to give you advance notice that this first solution is the longest one in the book. This is just to make sure you have everything you need to successfully complete the program. We promise you the other solutions are much shorter, so hang in there. Let's get started now.

The 100% Solution

Building Your Foundation for Thriving in Sobriety

*Take the first step in faith. You don't have to see the whole stair-
case. Just the first step.*[1]

—DR. MARTIN LUTHER KING JR. (1929–1968)
Clergyman and civil rights leader

As the above quotation from Martin Luther King Jr. says, all you have
to do is take the first step. And congratulations—you have already
taken the first step by picking up this book and starting to read it.
Don't worry about how far you have to go or what you have to do.
You have just opened the door to a life full of unlimited potential
and possibility, and we invite you to walk through that door with
us now.

The Golden Buddha

We would like to start by having you read this story by Jack that appeared in the first *Chicken Soup for the Soul*[2] book:

In the fall of 1988, my wife and I were invited to give a presentation on self-esteem and peak performance at a confer-

ence in Hong Kong. Since we had never been to Asia, we decided to extend our trip and visit Thailand.

When we arrived in Bangkok, we decided to take a tour of the city's most famous Buddhist temples. Along with our interpreter and driver, my wife and I visited numerous Buddhist temples that day, but after a while, they began to blur in our memory.

However, one temple left an indelible impression in our hearts and minds. It is called the Temple of the Golden Buddha. The temple itself is very small, probably no larger than thirty feet by thirty feet. However, as we entered, we were stunned by the presence of a ten-and-a-half-foot-tall solid gold Buddha. The statue weighs more than two and a half tons and is valued at approximately $196 million. It was an awesome sight—the kindly and gentle yet imposing solid gold Buddha smiling down at us.

As we immersed ourselves in normal sightseeing tasks (taking pictures while oohing and ahhing over the statue), I walked over to a glass case that contained a large piece of clay about eight inches thick and twelve inches wide. Next to the glass case was a typewritten page describing the history of this magnificent piece of art.

Back in 1957, a group of monks from a monastery had to relocate a large clay Buddha from their temple to a new location. The monastery was to be relocated to make room for the development of a highway through Bangkok. When the crane began to lift the giant statue, the weight of it was so tremendous that it began to crack. Rain also began to fall. The head monk, who was concerned about possible damage to the sacred Buddha, decided to lower the statue back to the ground and cover it with a large canvas tarp to protect it from the rain.

Later that evening, the head monk went to check on the Buddha. He shined his flashlight under the tarp to see if the

Buddha was staying dry. As the light reached the crack, he noticed a little gleam of light shining back and found that strange. As he took a closer look at this gleam of light, he wondered if something was underneath the clay. He fetched a chisel and hammer from the monastery and began to chip away at the clay. As he knocked off shards of clay, the little gleam grew brighter and bigger. After many hours of labor, the monk stood face-to-face with the extraordinary solid gold Buddha.

Historians believe that several hundred years before the head monk's discovery, the Burmese army was about to invade Thailand (then called Siam). The Siamese monks realized that their country was about to be attacked and covered their precious golden Buddha with an outer layer of clay to keep their treasure from being looted by the Burmese. Unfortunately, the Burmese apparently slaughtered all of the Siamese monks, and the well-kept secret of the golden Buddha remained intact until that day in 1957.

As we flew back to Los Angeles on Cathay Pacific Airways, I began to think to myself, *Just like the clay Buddha, we are all covered with a shell of hardness created out of fear, anger, resignation, and self-doubt, and yet underneath that outer layer, each of us is really a "golden Buddha," a "golden Christ," or a "golden essence," which is our real self. Somewhere along the way, between the ages of two and nine, we begin to cover up our "golden essence"—our natural self. Much like the monk with the hammer and the chisel, our task now is to discover our true essence once again.*

What about you? What have you been using drinking to cover up or hide from? What "golden" parts of yourself have you let alcohol conceal? Today we will start to uncover the answers to these two important questions and help you get back in touch with the parts of you that may have become lost due to your problem drinking.

The 30/60/90 Day Plan

In the early eighties, Maine's legislature enacted a returnable-bottle-and-can law. Instead of going into the trash, my sixteen-ounce cans of Miller Lite started going into a plastic container in the garage. One Thursday night, I went out there to toss in a few dead soldiers and saw that this container, which had been empty on Monday night, was now almost full. And since I was the only one in the house who drank Miller Lite—Holy shit, I'm an alcoholic, I thought, and there was no dissenting opinion from inside my head—I was, after all, the guy who had written The Shining *without even realizing (at least until that night) that I was writing about myself. My reaction to this idea wasn't denial or disagreement; it was what I'd call frightened determination.*

—STEPHEN KING

Author of over fifty novels selling more than 350 million copies[3]

As we mentioned in "Getting Started," this book was designed for you to read and implement over 30 days. We have repeatedly found that people who are serious about cutting back or quitting drinking will experience the greatest likelihood of success by completing one solution a day for 30 consecutive days.

Mike, a graduate of *The 30-Day Sobriety Solution*, discovered how effective it was for him to have a solution a day to turn to. He would come home every day from work and have the urge to drink, but instead of giving in to that urge, he would dive into that day's solution. So instead of going to happy hour, he replaced that with doing the program.

We have also found that a couple of alternatives can work just as well, including completing a solution every two or three days. The key to being successful is to decide the frequency that works best for you, and then hold yourself accountable for following through with that discipline. In fact, research has shown that you are more likely to follow through with something if you have set up a structured plan of action.[4]

For example, if you plan to complete this program in 30 days, you need to set aside approximately forty-five minutes to an hour each day, which at first might sound like a lot of time. However, put it into perspective by thinking about the amount of time that you used to spend drinking every week. Often, the time you spent thinking about drinking, planning the next drinking event, doing the actual drinking, and then recovering from your drinking adds up to far more than an hour a day. Some of our graduates have shared that simply cutting out or cutting down their time spent on social media websites was more than enough to free up the necessary time to complete the program.

To help you succeed, we have created three email lists that you can join for free and that will help you complete *The 30-Day Sobriety Solution* in either 30, 60, or 90 days. For example, if you sign up for the 30-day list, you will receive an email every day for 30 days that briefly outlines that day's content and provides links to optional online resources. If you select the 60- or 90-day option, you will receive an email every second day or every third day. You can even track your progress and what you completed each day. We strongly recommend you use this free support system to keep you on track. To sign up for one of these email support systems, simply go to http://Day1.Solutions.

Can You Ever Drink Again?

I found myself drinking two bottles of wine on the couch and said, "Jada, I think we've got a problem here." From that day on, I went cold turkey. I haven't had a drink in eight years.

—JADA PINKETT SMITH
Actor and singer-songwriter[5]

We are always asked two questions when working with people in *The 30-Day Sobriety Solution*: "Can I ever drink again?" and "Do I need to quit drinking right now?"

Cutting back *is* a viable option for some people, as proven by past graduates who were able to achieve a take-it-or-leave-it attitude toward alcohol; in addition, numerous studies have confirmed that cutting back works for some people.[6]

Nonetheless, in order for you to become a social drinker, you will need to abstain from alcohol for at least 30 days. In a minute, we will discuss the magic of 30 days and why this minimum period of time is necessary for making any profound change in your life.

But you do not have to stop drinking completely today. In fact, we often tell people we work with to pick a time during the first week when they *will* stop drinking. However, the caveat is that you must *not* be under the influence of alcohol while reading this book and completing the exercises. For example, during the first week, many clients complete the program during the day, before having anything to drink.

Most importantly, depending on how much you drink, we must remind you that quitting drinking abruptly can be dangerous. Daily excessive drinkers, such as those who drink around a fifth or a liter of hard liquor a day, can experience life-threatening seizures when they quit drinking all of a sudden. So please be sure to consult a doctor before you quit.

If you decide to quit later in the first week, do not "go all out" in the days leading up to that moment. For instance, do not suddenly decide to drink twice as much as you usually do by making the excuse that you want to "make the most" of the last time that you drink. Anytime that you increase your use of a mind-altering substance, bad things can happen. You make poor decisions, drive when you should not, or drink so much that you pass out (and if you pass out lying on your back, you risk asphyxiation). Because no one knows your drinking habit like you do, be smart about how you go about quitting.

Also, our experience has shown us that *cutting back works for only a very small percentage of problem drinkers*. Don't worry today about whether or not you are in this minority because, right now, you cannot know. On Day 30 we will address this question in far more detail, but for now, simply understand that *you need to quit drinking completely for at least 30 days*, even if only cutting back is your goal. If you are doing this program to be reinspired in your recovery, you may find the mention of a cutting-back option upsetting. We understand and respect this point of view and ask only that you don't let your belief about this hold you back from moving forward with this program. *The 30-Day Sobriety Solution* can help you enrich your life in recovery and ensure your continuing success.

Last, we want to share with you a definition of sobriety: "moderation in or abstinence from consumption of alcoholic liquor or use of drugs."[7] We use the word *sobriety* throughout this program; however, we want to be clear that the use of this word does not exclude those who desire to only cut back. Although some dictionaries define *sobriety* as complete abstinence, we prefer this definition because it isn't important if you drink or abstain, as long as alcohol no longer has a negative impact on your life and you can drink responsibly.

The 30-Day Reboot

I haven't gone back to drinking, and the thought of ever having another hangover gives me chills. I feel great, and I can't believe that I wasted a lot of my life trying to avoid life.

—MATT

30-Day Graduate from Kansas City, Missouri

At this point, you may be wondering what is so special about 30 days. In their book *The Answer: Your Guide to Achieving Financial Freedom and Living an Extraordinary Life*, John Assaraf and Murray Smith describe an experiment conducted by the National Aeronautics and Space Administration that demonstrates why it takes 25 to 30 days to successfully reprogram the brain.[8] NASA was preparing to send astronauts into space and wanted to determine the mental and physical long-term effects of disorientation that the human brain and body experienced in zero gravity. It created goggles with convex lenses that turned everything upside down. Then it picked several subjects, who wore the goggles twenty-four hours a day for several weeks and attempted to function as normally as possible during this time, including eating, reading, and working, all while seeing the world upside down.

After 25 to 30 days, an amazing thing happened. One by one, the subjects started to see things right side up while still wearing the goggles. Effectively, their brains formed enough new neural connections to re-create reality in a more useful way.

The results of this experiment really are astonishing. The brain, after a few short weeks, "rewired" itself to ensure that one could not only survive but even thrive in a new environment. So, how long do you have to do something new to really change how you think—but not just to change how you think, but to actually change the neural connections in your brain to facilitate such a change in thinking? This study shows that such a change can occur in as little as three to four weeks.

Why does this matter? The bottom line is that you take *daily* action. We have outlined daily actions for you throughout *The 30-Day Sobriety Solution*, so that you can truly change the way you think and act for the long term. However, if you don't take regular, repeated action to implement the solutions in this book, you will greatly reduce your chance to succeed.

We call this concept the 30-Day Reboot. By taking the positive action laid out in this program, including 30 days of abstinence, you are essentially "rebooting" your system. Whether your goal is to cut back or quit drinking or simply to get reinspired in your recovery, this 30-Day Reboot will provide you with the foundation you need for sobriety.

Your Destiny Is the Consequences of Your Daily Decisions

It is in your moments of decision that your destiny is shaped.

—TONY ROBBINS

World-renowned speaker and author of *Awaken the Giant Within*

Our goal for this program and our promise to you is to provide you with all of the information, inspiration, tools, and techniques that you need to recover, reclaim, and reinvent your life without alcohol, or, as we like to say, to thrive in sobriety.

We want sobriety to become second nature to you, so that the idea of taking a drink rarely enters your mind. And even when the thought of drinking does occur, it will seem more like an echo from an old habit and time rather than a serious consideration. We also want to be clear: we cannot help you achieve this goal without your commitment and desire. We are here today asking to be your role models, coaches, and mentors on your road to reclaiming your life from alcohol. We are asking you to make the decision today to change your life and your self-destructive relationship with alcohol. Give yourself a gift today: the gift of making a clear decision to get and stay sober—the gift of committing to work for as long as it takes to learn how to thrive in sobriety.

This clarity in your decision making will give you the power to produce the results that you really want. Here's a little secret. When you fully commit to thriving in sobriety, the answers you seek come a lot more quickly than you could ever expect. Some of the greatest moments in life come when we make very clear, committed decisions. This is one of those moments.

Your destiny is the consequences of your daily decisions. Read this sentence a few times and make sure it really sinks in. Remember, even when you do not make a decision, you just made a decision. You decided *not* to decide. So why not make a decision that empowers you?

Today, make that choice to move toward your new future—one in which alcohol no longer defines who you are.

The 100% Solution

Ninety-nine percent commitment is not possible. We are either 100% or not committed at all. I was amazed to discover this, because I had made a lifestyle out of tepid commitments that turned out to be noncommitments. I was just conning myself that I was partly committed. I had adapted to the pain of early rejection with the decision "Don't play." If I didn't play, I wouldn't have to face losing. And if I were forced to play, I could always play halfheartedly. If I lost, I could say it didn't matter, because I wasn't trying. It took me many years to realize that I wasn't even in the game if I was not committed. My body might have been out on the field, but my soul was on the bench. Soulless play is worse than no play at all.

—GAY HENDRICKS

Author of *Conscious Living: Finding Joy in the Real World*

If you want to cut back or quit drinking, and if you truly want to thrive in sobriety and life, you must choose to take 100% responsibility for all your life experiences, including the quality of your relationships, your health, your accomplishments, your failures, your debts, your physical state, your feelings, and, most importantly, your drinking habits.

This is not easy! No one really wants to do it. It's easier and more convenient to blame someone else—the weather, your horoscope, your friends, your husband or wife, your parents, your children, your lack of finances, your boss, your colleagues, the economy, or even the people who make, serve, and sell alcohol. We are afraid to acknowledge the real source of our problem—ourselves.

The truth is that you, and *only* you, are responsible for the quality of your life. This is the core idea on which this book is built.

Many years ago, Dr. Robert Resnick, a psychotherapist in Los Angeles, taught us a very simple but very important formula that has had a profound effect on our lives and work. It is a core principle[9] we have taught to hundreds of thousands of people around the world that clarifies what 100% responsibility really means:

E (Event) + R (Response) = O (Outcome)

Every outcome you experience in life—sobriety or alcoholism, excessive drinking or "normal" drinking, financial success or poverty, health or sickness, happiness or dissatisfaction—is the result of how you have responded to an earlier event or events in your life. The formula states that if you don't like the outcomes you are experiencing in your life today, you have two options:

1. You can blame the event (E) for your lack of results (O). In other words, you can blame anything and everything else: the presence of a liquor store and bar on every corner, your lack of education, racism, not having enough money, your friends, your family's drinking history, your past failed attempts at quitting drinking, the death of a loved one, losing your job, and so on. Without a doubt, these factors exist. But if any one of them was so absolute in deciding how your life would unfold, nobody would ever succeed. Actor Robert Downey Jr. would never have finally gotten sober to star in the *Iron Man* movies, Jackie Robinson would never have become the first African American to play major league baseball, and Samuel L. Jackson would not have become one of the top-ten-grossing actors of all time after the age of forty (after he went to rehab and got sober).

For every difficult circumstance in which someone ended up failing, thousands of other people faced the same circumstance and succeeded. The external conditions and circumstances are not stopping you—you are stopping yourself!

2. Or you can change your responses (R) to the events (E)—the way things are—until you get the outcomes (O) you want. You can't change the past, but you can change how you respond to the past. To do this, you must regain control of your thoughts, your beliefs, your desires, and, ultimately, your actions. You need to stop responding to events by drinking, whether it is drinking to celebrate, drinking to forget, or drinking to socialize, and respond with thoughts and actions that are aligned with your values, goals, and purpose. Don't worry. We know this is easier said than done. We will give you the tools and techniques you need to regain control of your thoughts and choose more effective actions.

You Have to Give Up All Blaming

All blame is a waste of time. No matter how much fault you find with another, and regardless of how much you blame him, it will not change you.

—WAYNE DYER

Author of *Your Erroneous Zones*

As long as you continue to blame something or someone else for your lack of accomplishments in any area of your life, you will never become successful. This concept is particularly critical to your drinking. It is easy to outsource the blame to someone or something else because change is scary. It is far easier to place blame instead of taking responsibility and risking the uncertainty and discomfort of facing the unknown. Most importantly, blaming others takes away your power to make any lasting change.

If you are going to cut back or quit drinking for good *and* continue to stay inspired once you are sober, you have to acknowledge the truth—that you are the one who thought the thoughts, created the feelings, made the choices, and took the actions that got you to where you are now.

You Have to Stop All Your Complaining

The man who complains about the way the ball bounces is likely the one who dropped it.

—LOU HOLTZ

Legendary college football coach

Everyone complains, but why? If you complain about someone or something, you must believe that there is someone or something better. If you didn't actually believe that something better was possible in your life—more friends, more money, a larger house, a more fulfilling job or career, more joy, a more loving spouse—you wouldn't complain. In your mind, you have a picture or an image of what you prefer because it's better. And you know you would prefer that something better, but you aren't willing to take the risks that are required to create it.

Let this really sink in. *Every circumstance you complain about is something that you can change but have chosen not to.* Problem drinking is a perfect example of this. You have the ability to cut back or quit drinking; however, you have to accept that doing this requires you to change.

So why haven't you changed yet? It's because it involves risks—you run the risk of being bored, not being liked, being ridiculed and judged by other "normal drinkers," or not being able to deal easily with stress or the uncomfortable feelings that might come up. You also run the risk of failure, and of disappointing (yet again) your parents, your friends, your spouse, or your children if you fail.

Making a change might be a struggle and take extra effort, time, and money that you don't think you have. Making a change might be distressing, unnerving, and unpleasant. So, instead of experiencing any of these uncomfortable feelings, you avoid taking any risks and stay put and complain about your situation. And, of course, you drink. You drink and complain to anyone that will listen. You drink to numb out your uncomfortable feelings.

In order to grow, you need to make the decision to stop complaining and to stop spending time with complainers, and get on with creating the life of your dreams.

99% Is a Bitch, 100% Is a Breeze

There is a difference between interest and commitment. When you're interested in doing something, you do it only when it's convenient. When you're committed to something, you accept no excuses, only results.

—KEN BLANCHARD
Coauthor of *The One Minute Manager*

One of the most important components of the 100% Solution is the No-Exceptions Rule. This rule means that once you are 100% committed, there are no exceptions and no renegotiating. Not only does this rule make life easier and simpler, it frees you from inner conflict. Instead of internally debating over and over about whether you will or won't do something, like drinking, your decision is already made. The real power and value from this come from all the energy you can now redirect to focus on what you actually want to create and accomplish in your life.

However, the moment your commitment drops to 99%, you open the door for the internal debate to begin, and when it comes to alcohol, this is a debate that usually ends in a rationalization to drink again.

Think about this from another perspective. Have you ever been somewhere where you knew there was absolutely no way you could drink? For example, you went somewhere where no one was drinking and no alcohol was available, and the option was 100% closed off to sneak in any alcohol or even have a single drink. What was your reaction? Most likely, leading up to the event, you were annoyed; but when you got there, you accepted it and found that you were not obsessing about drinking. Why? Because you knew without question the option didn't exist, so you didn't even start down the "what-if" path of whether you should drink. When you commit 100%, you create "the-option-doesn't-exist" event in your life every day. But when you are less than 100% committed and times get tough, you end up giving in to your cravings.

Here's Dave's story of his last drink and how this led him to apply the 100% Solution to his life:

I remember the last time I drank as if it happened yesterday. It was a warm and humid day just outside of Seattle. I had just flown in from Denver for a week of technical training for my job. I had forty-two days of sobriety, was going to Alcoholics Anonymous, and even had a sponsor. As soon as I got into my rental car, I felt this overwhelming shift inside, and all of a sudden my craving for alcohol reached an all-time high.

I called my sponsor and was able to refrain from drinking that first night, but the obsession was growing. The moment I stepped out of that first day of training, I knew that I was going to find the nearest liquor store and start drinking. With a liter of Captain Morgan rum and a liter of Absolut vodka in hand, I planned to drink that night, without question, and likely every night that week. What I did not know was how life-threatening that week would end up being for me.

My first night of drinking was uneventful, and I made it to my training session the next day. But all I could think about during the training was my next drink. Once I returned to my hotel room, I immediately started drinking again. Because of my previous stint with sobriety, and the fact that

I was drinking more than usual because I wanted to "make the most of my drinking freedom," I woke up with a severe hangover and puked—something that I rarely did. I skipped the training that day, and by noon, I was feeling better and started drinking again. The previous two days seemed to be just a warm-up, because from noon to nine that night, I drank excessively. The last thing I remember from that evening was watching the television show *So You Think You Can Dance* while lying in bed, slightly propped up on my back.

The next morning, I awoke with vomit all over my clothes, the floor, and the bathroom. At that moment, I knew I was lucky to be alive. I suddenly recalled all the stories that I had heard about people who'd asphyxiated while intoxicated. I remember looking at myself in the mirror and barely recognizing the person staring back at me—overweight, face bloated, and puffy-eyed. I knew that if I did not commit 100% to getting sober at that moment, I might not have another chance.

The evening of August 15, 2007, was the last time I ever drank. That moment also marked the culmination of almost eighteen years of excessive drinking. This story represents the importance of the 100% Solution. Not until this last experience did I truly become committed to getting sober. I was finally ready to stop blaming and complaining about why I could not get sober, and I owned up to the truth—that I had complete control over my life and my decisions. It was also the first time in my life when I committed 100% instead of 99%. If I had been 100% committed to staying sober when I arrived in Seattle, the thought of drinking might still have entered my mind, and the craving might not have instantly disappeared, but the internal debate in my head never would have started because my decision would have already been made. That is the power of 100% commitment—while it might be challenging, it makes life far less complicated.

Today drinking represents to me total and complete pain,

and sobriety represents absolute pleasure. The thought of drinking is the equivalent of causing great physical and mental harm to myself. I know that you might find this difficult to believe, depending on the stage you are at, but this program will show you, step by step, exactly how I and others got sober and went on to be truly happy and successful.

The Myth of "Rock Bottom"

I was lost. Emotionally lost, physically lost, mentally lost. I didn't know where to turn or what to do. Part of my problem, although I didn't know it yet, was denial.

—JOSH HAMILTON

American League Baseball MVP, author of *Beyond Belief: Finding the Strength to Come Back*, and in recovery from alcohol and drugs[10]

You often hear about an alcoholic needing to hit "rock bottom" before getting sober. In reality, the rock bottom that everyone envisions—the homeless drunk begging for money on the street—is not close to the real meaning of hitting rock bottom. Have you wondered why some people can drink normally, but you don't seem to be able to? One reason is because others define their rock bottom very differently than you do. For example, "normal" drinkers might go out once every six months, drink too much, feel miserable, and say, "I will never do that again." That was their rock bottom, and they simply chose not to allow alcohol to play a more significant role in their lives.

By embracing the 100% Solution, you are acknowledging that you have reached your rock bottom and that you will no longer allow alcohol to play a controlling role in your life—you will no longer live in denial. Because "rock bottom" is whatever you decide to make it, you can decide now that you have suffered all of the negative consequences that you are ever willing to suffer from drinking—*that today you have hit your rock bottom.*

There is a great analogy we love to share. We often ask the people we work with if they shoplift. The answer is almost always no. We then follow up with the question "Do you have a debate with yourself about shoplifting when you are in a store and you see the perfect opportunity to get away with it?" Of course, the answer is still no, and the reason is simple. If you are 100% opposed to stealing, then you never engage in a debate on whether or not to steal. But if you did have a history of shoplifting and you had never committed 100% never to steal again, when the opportunity presented itself, the internal debate of whether or not to steal could start. And once the debate has started, especially when it's related to an addictive behavior, the ability to say no is much more difficult.

So when you decide that you have hit your rock bottom, you will have reached that empowered 100% attitude, and you will stop wasting time and energy debating about when, where, and how much you will be drinking. Instead, when the thought to drink enters your mind, you won't even entertain the debate because you are now 100% committed to not drinking.

Why Do You Drink?

No matter how many negative consequences I suffered or how many times I promised to quit drinking, I always returned back to my drink of choice—wine. The 30-Day Sobriety Solution finally changed all of that. Every solution seemed to bring me more clarity and wisdom about why I was drinking, and as I worked through the exercises, I was able to solve what was really driving me to drink.

—NATHALIE
30-Day Graduate from Winnipeg, Canada

We have some great news for you! Contrary to what you might believe, you do not have a problem with alcohol, which is exactly why we don't like to use the words *alcoholism* and *alcoholic*.

We use "problem drinker, "excessive drinker," and other terminology rather than *alcoholic* because this word has negative connotations for most people. Given what we know about the brain and self-actualization, labeling yourself an alcoholic can ultimately be counterproductive to thriving in sobriety.

So if your problem is not with alcohol, what is your problem? Simply put, drinking alcohol is the symptom of a deeper problem, or what is often referred to as a symptomatic behavior. The real problem is *why* you use. The deceased actor Patrick Swayze discussed this in his book *The Time of My Life*: "In all my life, I never drank for the sake of drinking; it was always a response to some kind of emotional difficulty I was going through. Drinking for me was a symptom of a problem, not the problem itself."[11]

Drinking alcohol is the symptom, and the real problem lies elsewhere. Although various programs and therapists discuss this point, they often do not state it as clearly as it should be stated. Alcohol abuse, drug addiction, overeating, and other compulsive negative behaviors are responses to one of a variety of factors in your life.

For example, the average American watches almost five hours of TV a day.[12] If you're watching too much TV, what is the real problem? The TV itself is not the problem; the *reason* you watch TV is the problem. You watch too much TV because you are bored, you want to live the lives of the people on the shows rather than your own life, or you believe it helps reduce your stress or distract you from your feelings. The same is true for your drinking. The alcohol itself is not the problem—the *reason* you drink is the problem.

Part of the challenge with cutting back or quitting drinking is that people often become too focused on stopping their drinking instead of understanding and identifying why they drink, and then changing that reason. Addressing the underlying causes of why you drink is a critical component to stopping your desire to drink in the first place or, equally important, your desire to switch your problem drinking to some other addictive behavior. If you simply attempt to cut back or quit drinking without addressing your *why*, you will only go down the path of manifesting other addictive behaviors. Even if you do manage to stop your addictive behavior but fail to work on the "why," you will likely not be very fulfilled in life.

"You Can't Hire Someone Else to Do Your Push-ups for You!"

Step 1: apply Miracle Cellulite Cream to problem areas. Step 2: run 10 miles a day.

If you want to see the benefits from doing anything of value in life, you have to do it yourself. As Jim Rohn, pioneering success coach and motivational expert, states, "You can't hire someone else to do your push-ups for you." No one else can do it for you. We can show you the way, but you will have to do the work. You can choose to embrace the solutions and the action steps, even if you have some doubt, or you can choose to always look for reasons and rationalizations for why what we are teaching won't work for you.

We are not saying that every single solution will be a perfect fit for you, and you may choose to disregard some of them; however, as one 30-Day Graduate shares below, you will find some solutions that will work wonders for you:

> What I love about *The 30-Day Sobriety Solution* is that it gives dozens, if not hundreds, of tools and techniques you can use to help you get sober. In Day 1 it acknowledges that everyone is unique, and that is why some solutions result in incredible breakthroughs for one person but not for another. I found this statement refreshingly honest, and logical, and experienced that most of the solutions really helped me to "thrive in sobriety." And the few that I didn't get as much value from, I simply didn't integrate into my life beyond the program.

Another 30-Day Graduate said that she felt like she opened up a "supercharged Craftsman tool kit of things to use for sobriety," and as a result, she started seeing amazing shifts happen within only the first two weeks. For the first time in her life, she was able to say, "I don't see myself drinking. I don't see choosing feeling the way I felt before when I know I can feel like this." The solutions that do work for you will change your relationship with drinking for the rest of your life, as long as you embrace them with passion, purpose, and a positive expectation.

A Vote for Living

The thing I really like about The 30-Day Sobriety Solution *is that it's focused on getting you to thrive in sobriety and getting you really excited about it. Up until I found* The 30-Day Sobriety Solution, *it always seemed like to conquer alcohol I needed to have a boring and somewhat painful life that would not involve much with social activities. And that I probably would be committing myself to life with not much fun. But* The 30-Day Sobriety Solution *actually got me excited about being sober.*

—ANN

30-Day Graduate from New York City

You are now ready for your first exercise, which we refer to as an **action step**. Assuming you've already gotten approval from your health care professional to quit drinking, this first one is optional, especially if you already have some extended sobriety. But don't get used to action steps being optional. We recommend that you schedule an appointment with your qualified health professional to get your standard blood work, weight, blood pressure, and other vital signs measured.

This is important for two reasons. First, the people we have helped often have two things in common: they are great at rationalizing that they do not have a problem with drinking—at least most of the time. Second, health-related consequences of excessive drinking are some of the most common and the most difficult to hide from because your blood work does not lie.

Dave's blood work tests showed the typical bad numbers for his liver, the fats known as triglycerides, and other indicators that go hand in hand with a drinking problem. Every time Dave got his blood work done, the doctor asked him the same question: "How much do you drink?" His temporary solution was to lie to the doctor about how much he was actually drinking, and then to eventually switch doctors—or to simply not go at all. He rationalized that drinking was okay, but ultimately he could not overcome his fears about his alcohol abuse cutting his life short, and particularly how that would affect his two young daughters.

Another reason for getting a physical is that by going to the doctor, you are taking a stand and telling the world that you want to survive and that you are making an effort in that direction, which is a *vote for living*. And this is one vote you don't want to miss. So as soon as you stop reading this, pick up the phone and schedule an appointment with your doctor or qualified health professional to get a complete physical and blood panel.

The photos of Dave below show him before and after sobriety, and indicate what is possible by completing *The 30-Day Sobriety Solution*. Our graduates consistently report very similar results, and these dramatic outer physical changes are a manifestation of the inner changes that also occur as a result of the program.

Dave Andrews in 2006 and Dave Andrews after getting sober and completing the Denver Marathon with Bill Phillips (bestselling author of *Body for Life: 12 Weeks to Mental and Physical Strength*).

The Heart of *The 30-Day Sobriety Solution*

Through the 30-Day solutions and action steps, I was able to deal with and overcome many issues in my life that in the past I had to mask with alcohol. Fully grasping the concept of being

*excited about life and having the gratitude for it propelled me
into areas of my life I had never been to or even knew were possible to reach within myself.*

—DESIREE

30-Day Graduate from Harare, Zimbabwe

The heart of *The 30-Day Sobriety Solution* can be summed up in one word: *action*.

When you read the solutions, we would love to be able to say to you, "Just think about the answer, and you will be on your way to thriving in sobriety." However, the reality is that you have likely spent years "strengthening" your dependence on alcohol. To reverse this, you must take the time to actually complete the action steps at the end of each day's solution, and, most importantly, this includes *writing down your answers*. Something happens when the ink (whether real ink or "electronic ink," if you are using a computer, smartphone, or tablet) hits the "paper."

Believe us when we tell you that our clients have tried to prove us wrong on this. However, once we convinced them to start journaling and writing down the answers to the action steps and their notes on the content covered, they began to see real change happen. Several powerful things happen when you put your thoughts on paper.

First, you remove ambiguity and gain clarity. Your thoughts can be unorganized and unclear, but putting them on paper forces you—in many ways—to get clearer, and clarity is incredibly powerful. Second, writing things down removes the thoughts from your head, essentially freeing your mind and reducing your inner conflict and clutter. Your brain knows it can now release some of those thoughts because you have written them down. Third, writing things down engages more of your senses, which is extremely powerful. When you write things down, you are physically taking action, and you experience visually what you have written. Simply, *writing is the doing part of thinking*.

You might be asking, "What if someone reads my personal thoughts without my permission?" Trust us, we understand your fears related to writing down the details of your personal thoughts and feelings, and how violated, ashamed, or embarrassed you might feel if someone discovered and read them. Our recommendation is to find a safe place to record and store your writing. For example, you can use Google or Hotmail documents, which allows you to create and store Word documents online that are protected by your user name and password. You can even set up a new account just for your writing activity. Alternatively, if you really like the touch and feel of a physical journal, you can get one just for this program and keep it hidden and locked. On the companion website,[13] we provide these various journaling solutions, as well as the results of a research study that proves the incredible value of journaling.

To further understand the importance of writing in your journal (*and* completing each day's action steps), look at the Cone of Learning, developed by American educationist Edgar Dale. The Cone of Learning shows the effects of different kinds of learning on human memory. Simply stated, the more you engage actively in the learning

The Cone of Learning

process, the more you will retain. If you only read the solutions but don't do the exercises and don't experience any of the material in any other way, you will end up remembering only about 10 percent of it two weeks later. That will not make a huge impact on your cutting back or quitting drinking.

We have therefore created a companion website for each solution that will help make sure the solutions work for you by involving you in written exercises, guided visualizations, supplemental audio content, and more. The bottom line is that the more fully you engage in this program with all of the exercises and resources, the more fully you will experience the transformations you are seeking. The impact will be much more powerful than if you only read the material. And here is the best part: it doesn't take a lot of time to do the writing exercises and other activities that are in the book and on the website. You can do all of this work in the same amount of time that you might have spent at happy hour or while partying over a weekend.

Day 1 Action Steps

The money I saved from not drinking well exceeded the cost of The 30-Day Sobriety Solution, *but the changes it helped me make in my life were priceless.*

—ROBERT

30-Day Graduate from Vienna, Austria

At the end of every day's solution, we will summarize the action steps that we covered. You can choose to do them as you go or wait until the end of the chapter. We recommend that you do them at a time when you will most likely follow through. For example, you may feel that stopping and doing the first action step when it is first presented for the day propels you forward to complete the other ones, or you might feel that you need to read the entire chapter before doing any of the action steps. *Unless we mention that an action step is optional, it is required because it is essential for your success in this program.* You may need to access the free companion website for some of these action steps; however, reading the additional content and resources on the site is optional. They are just there for additional support if you want to go deeper.

One of the benefits of the companion website is that it allows us to give you a wide range of content, such as new breakthrough research, additional success stories, specially recorded videos from experts, online tools and resources, and multimedia content that we otherwise could not deliver.

If you prefer listening over reading, we highly recommend purchasing the audio version of the book, which is integrated seamlessly with the companion website for ease of use. Many of our graduates have told us that listening to the material was effective and enjoyable for them because they could take notes easily and be more engaged in the content. If you are interested in finding out more about this, simply visit the companion website for today's solution at http://Day1.Solutions.

Now let's review today's action steps:

- **Start a journal.** Whether you keep an online journal using Google Docs or Hotmail SkyDrive or a physical journal, start one right now. In your journal, write down your answers to the exercises, your thoughts on the content for the day, and your progress and setbacks along your path to thriving in sobriety. Remember, you don't need to worry about grammar or spelling in your journal, but you do want to write in it every day, even when there isn't an action step that tells you specifically to do so. If you have chosen to do this in 60 or 90 days, you still need to write in your journal daily. The same is true for all "daily" action steps in future solutions.

- **Decide your time frame.** Choose whether you will finish this program in 30, 60, or 90 days and then sign up for a free email reminder on the companion website to help keep you accountable.

Then decide the day during the first week of this program on which you will quit drinking for at least 30 days. Write this date in your new journal. And decide right now that you are 100% committed to this plan and write it down in your journal.

- **Begin to use the equation E + R = O in your life.** Simply begin to pay attention to moments when you are complaining about or blaming an event rather than focusing on creating a new response that can change the outcome.

- **Capture the "before you."** Take a photo of yourself, or find a good recent "before" photo of yourself, and then schedule a visit to the doctor or health professional's office to get your blood work done (this last part is optional). You will be amazed at the end of 30 days how much sobriety can make your face look years younger and bring back the sparkle in your eyes.

- **Listen to the Time Travel Technique.** Through all of the coaching we have done and the feedback we have received, this guided exercise, which can be found on the companion website, has proven to create incredible leverage, clarity, and purpose. *It is critical you do this exercise.* One 30-Day Graduate shared with us, "In Day 1 of *The 30-Day Sobriety Solution,* I did the Time Travel Technique, which was life changing. This process gave me a level of clarity around my drinking that I had never experienced before. I finally knew, and accepted, that continuing to drink was going to keep me from everything I wanted in life, and sobriety was going to lead to true happiness and fulfillment." Immediately after you finish listening to the Time Travel Technique, write about your experience in your new journal.

Congratulations! You have just finished the longest chapter in the book. We promise the remaining solutions are much shorter. Be sure to access the companion website for the Time Travel Technique, to sign up for your free email reminders, and to find out more about the integrated audio version of this program at http://Day1.Solutions.

The Purpose Solution

*Identify, Acknowledge, and Honor
Your Thriving-in-Sobriety Vision*

Great minds have purposes, others have wishes.

—WASHINGTON IRVING (1783–1839)

American author

Each of us is born with a unique life purpose. Possibly the most important action you will ever take to cut back or quit drinking for good and truly thrive in sobriety is to identify, acknowledge, and honor your purpose. When you understand and know what you are here to do and pursue that with enthusiasm and passion, your desire to drink fades naturally. The Purpose Solution takes you through exactly how to do this.

Before we get started with identifying your life purpose, we have to ask an important question: Did you complete the action steps on Day 1 in the 100% Solution? If not, please stop reading right now and go back and complete them. If you completed them, congratulations! You have taken that critical first step, and you are on your way to creating a new and exciting life for yourself. Did you realize that completing Day 1 already puts you in the top 10 percent? Less than 10 percent of the people who buy a nonfiction book read past the first chapter.[1] By getting this far, you have proven already that you are willing to take more action than the other 90 percent, and with this continued action, you will inevitably reap the rewards you are seeking.

One Day at a Time

As I completed each day in The 30-Day Sobriety Solution, *I often found myself torn between wanting to spend more time focusing on that one solution rather than moving on to the next. What I quickly realized was that the future solutions built on the previous ones, as well as answered many of the questions that came up on those previous days. This organization of the solutions really helped me create a new, strong foundation for my sobriety.*

—LENORE

30-Day Graduate from Dallas, Texas

Yes, we know that "live your life one day at a time" is one of the most overused clichés of our time, but when it comes to overcoming an addictive habit, it couldn't be more appropriate. One day, one hour, one minute at a time—whatever it takes to help keep you moving forward.

As you go through *The 30-Day Sobriety Solution,* questions will inevitably come up. Questions about the content we included (and didn't include). Questions about certain action steps. And questions about your personal experience, and if others are experiencing similar challenges and breakthroughs like you. We assure you that most, or even all, of these questions will be answered by the end of the program. We can say this with confidence because we frequently receive this feedback from 30-Day Graduates. So as questions come up, feel free to make note of them in your journal, and if your questions aren't answered, you can use the companion website or the Frequently Asked Sobriety Questions Solution, which is a bonus solution on Day 21, to get answers.

As we mentioned on Day 1, you want to begin your 30 days

of continuous abstinence, or the 30-Day Reboot, sometime in this first week. One of the easiest ways to dramatically improve your odds of abstaining successfully is by removing all alcohol from your house. If you live with others who are not willing to do this, consider using a locked cabinet. For example, when one of Jack's family members was struggling with problem drinking, Jack added a lock to an existing cabinet and stored all liquor, beer, and wine in it.

This simple step will create an important barrier between you and alcohol—giving you some time to really consider your decision, rather than being able to react instinctively to a desire to drink. If you have already started your reboot, that is fantastic; just make sure you complete this step of removing all alcohol from your house. Otherwise remember to complete this step before starting your 30-Day Reboot.

Change Comes at the Edge of Your Comfort Zone

I will begin one of the most exhilarating, liberating, and exciting four weeks of my life. Scary, yes, and filled with unspeakable emotional discomfort, but for me it's an unquantifiable relief that I am being shown a different way to live. I am so tired of the lying, my inability to keep my word, the bullshit relationships, the hangovers, the cover-ups, and the helplessness to stop doing the things I truly want to stop doing.

—ROB LOWE

Actor and author of *Stories I Only Tell My Friends: An Autobiography*

Most people are initially fearful of cutting back or quitting drinking. This is because you are comfortable with drinking. It has become your trusted friend. And sobriety is a challenge for you and most likely not in your comfort zone. Fear is the natural reaction when you step out of your comfort zone. At this stage, a typical response that we hear from our clients is that they are afraid to quit drinking, yet at the same time, they are afraid to continue drinking. These conflicted feelings are completely normal.

For you to achieve your goal, you have to embrace fear and change. There is simply no other way around it. We will teach you what you need to know—you just need to be open to learning and applying these lessons and embracing change. The choices you make today, and every day, create your future, and real change comes at the edge of your comfort zone.

William James, a Harvard University psychologist, philosopher, and doctor, said, "It is our attitude at the beginning of a difficult undertaking that, more than anything else, will determine its successful outcome." Make the choice today to embrace a positive attitude about the journey on which you are embarking.

Remember, the only way that you can fail at cutting back or quitting drinking is to give up. If you don't give up, and if you keep searching for the solutions that best fit you, you will find the answers you seek. If you continue to take small steps right now, you will develop the momentum you need to build the life you most desire.

The Story of "The Alcoholic King"

A great irony exists among drinkers, one that Dave frequently experienced firsthand during his drinking days, and one that you might be able to relate to as well. Some refer to it as the "King's Reflection," although it is not usually used in relation to problem drinkers. We prefer to call it "The Alcoholic King."

A very common scenario exists—a ritual, in many ways—that is played out at the start of the "drinking day" for many problem drinkers. Somewhere in the neighborhood of two to five drinks, you often reach what may be referred to as an "optimal buzz." It is that moment in which the euphoria of drinking starts to manifest—the warm, tingling sensation in your stomach, the feelings of relaxation moving through your body, and the temporary letting go of all of your problems.

This peak state, one that you often "chase" the entire night to maintain, usually leads to daydreaming about all of the exciting and amazing accomplishments that you will achieve in life and how everyone will be so proud of you. During this peak state, problem drinkers dream of the life that they believe they are meant to live, including achieving financial goals, optimal physical fitness, various career accomplishments, and engaging in philanthropic efforts. *Can you remember having this experience when you drank?*

The ultimate irony is that this temporary state of mind is an alcohol-induced mirage that is virtually guaranteed to never manifest in your life. The reflection that you see during this peak state could not be further from reality. The sad truth is that the same thing that fuels this mirage is the same thing that ensures you will never accomplish these things—*alcohol*.

Just as this picture depicts, the image looking back at you from the mirror is a lie. Not only are you not that person looking back at you, but you never will be the person you want to be as long as alcohol continues to be in your life the way it is today. There simply isn't room in your life for drinking to excess *and* accomplishing all of your goals.

When you drink, you usually play out a very different story than what you really want. Problem drinkers start drinking and reach that peak state where they daydream about everything they want. Eventually they shift out of that peak state of mind but continue to try to regain it by drinking more. They eventually go to sleep, or pass out, only to wake up hungover and too tired and unenthusiastic to take any real action toward accomplishing their goals.

They get through the day, do the bare minimum they need to, and as they begin to feel better, they start to think, "Wouldn't it be nice to have a few drinks tonight?" or "I am so sick of my life, so maybe I will just have a drink to take the edge off." The process repeats itself, ensuring that the future will be the same as the past, bringing you no closer to your goals tomorrow than you were today. In fact, the opposite is often true, and you move further from the person you desire to be. At times, you may recognize how far you are from the person you want to be, which only creates more pain related to the choices you have made. So, in order to escape this reality, you drink more.

Deep down, do you know that you are meant for something better and that alcohol is keeping that "better life" from ever manifesting? Today you will discover how to create a powerful vision that will accelerate your desire to thrive in sobriety.

The Power of Vision

Throughout the centuries, there were men who took first steps down new roads armed with nothing but their own vision.

—AYN RAND (1905–1982)
Novelist and philosopher[2]

One of the themes of this book is how to get from where you are to where you want to be, or more specifically, how to cut back or quit drinking and thrive in sobriety. To accomplish this goal, you need to know where you are today and where you want to be in the future. And to get there you need a vision or a detailed description of what your destination looks and feels like.

Problem drinkers have several things in common. First, if they do have some idea of their vision, it often is not very clear. Second, they have never taken the time to write down their vision. Third, their vision is very different from the vision they are living, and alcohol has become the main coping mechanism for this disconnect. Today is all about clarifying and resolving these disconnects in your life.

Your Thriving-in-Sobriety Vision

The secret of getting ahead is getting started. The secret of getting started is breaking your complex, overwhelming tasks into small, manageable tasks, and then starting on the first one.

—MARK TWAIN (1835–1910)
Author of *The Adventures of Huckleberry Finn*

Figuring out a vision for your life is not as easy as it might sound, especially at the beginning of a new undertaking such as this one. When alcohol has played such a profound role in your life, uncovering your life's vision and purpose takes time and, most importantly, some extended sobriety.

At this stage, one approach works better than anything else, and that is simply to create a vision statement for yourself 30 days from today. These 30 days are setting the stage for a profoundly new and exciting life thriving in sobriety, and we know that if you can get through these 30 days, then anything is possible. This is your **first action step** for today.

The Vision Statement Guidelines

A dream is your creative vision for your life in the future. You must break out of your current comfort zone and become comfortable with the unfamiliar and the unknown.

—DENIS WAITLEY

Author of *The Psychology of Winning: Ten Qualities of a Total Winner*

Here are some basic guidelines that you need to follow when writing a vision statement:

- **Write it in the present tense.** Write your vision as if you are already living it. For example, "I am . . ."
- **Be as clear, concise, and specific as possible.** Ask yourself, "What will I be doing, experiencing, seeing, touching, and feeling?"
- **Write in the positive.** For example, do not write, "I do not drink every day." Studies have shown that your subconscious mind does not register the negative of a statement; it doesn't "hear" the *not*.[3] Therefore, when you say, "I do not drink," the subconscious mind receives this statement as "I do drink," and focuses on that. As Carl Jung, the founding father of analytic psychology, stated, "What you resist persists,"[4] which is why you need to always focus on what you *do* want rather than what you *don't* want. Instead, write, "I wake up every day feeling vibrant and excited about being sober."
- **Keep it short.** Some people prefer to keep their vision statement short, like a headline in a newspaper, while others prefer to add more details, as you'll see with the examples below.
- **Focus on the *what*, not the *how*.** Getting clear on your vision of sobriety is all that matters right now. The "how" will come later as a natural result of doing this and other exercises.

Writing Your Thriving-in-Sobriety Vision

If you want to change the fruits, you will first have to change the roots. If you want to change the visible, you must first change the invisible.

—T. HARV EKER

Author of *Secrets of the Millionaire Mind:*
Mastering the Inner Game of Wealth[5]

Here are some examples of vision statements from graduates of *The 30-Day Sobriety Solution*. As long as you get energized and inspired when you read your vision statement, the length is not important.

- Every day I wake up feeling excited, vibrant, and passionate about living a meaningful and fulfilling sober life.
- I am grateful to be solving my drinking dilemma and am excited to be creating a life of quality.
- Physically, spiritually, emotionally, and mentally, I am making decisions and choices that manifest sobriety every day in my life, and doing so allows me to live the life that I have always dreamed of—one of excitement, purpose, and giving back.
- I am full of life, love, and energy. I radiate as bright as the sun. I am strong, self-confident, healthy, and happy again. The more I fuel my body with the right things, the more alive I become. This is the best gift I am giving to life. Life is to be lived, and I am living it to the fullest—doing all of those things that used to be put off to the tomorrow that never came.
- I am vibrant, healthy, and energetic, like I was before the drinking thing, and what's amazing, it's even better than I imagined. I am happy and joyful and wake up with zest for each day.
- I am living my purpose, and my relationships are improving in ways that are amazing and will only get better. I am proud of myself, and it's so refreshing experiencing all the people who are so happy right along with me.

- I am full of gratitude for the immense learnings and beautiful gifts I have received from my "failures."
- I am healthy. I run without stopping and sometimes turn off the music just to be in the moment—fully aware and alive.

As you can see, these statements are written as if you have already turned your vision into reality. They are clear, concise, written in the present tense, and positive in nature. They also can vary in length—simply pick a length that feels right to you. We want you to know that the vision statement you write today is just for these 30 days and is not a vision statement for your entire life. We will help you discover and write that on Day 29. What is important now is that you focus on what you want to feel and what you want to be by the end of *The 30-Day Sobriety Solution*.

Once you have written your vision statement, review it several times a day, every day. For example, you can put your statement at the beginning of your journal, and every time you open your journal (whether physical or electronic), it will be the first thing you see, and you can quickly reread it. Or you can put your vision statement on an index card and tape it to your bathroom mirror, refrigerator, or near your work area. You can also print it and put it in your wallet and occasionally take it out to review. Or laminate it and tape it on the shower wall or on the inside cover of a notebook. You can even make your vision statement a screen saver on your computer, iPad, or smartphone. Dave puts his on the sill in front of the speedometer in his car, where he can easily flip it up and read it out loud when he is stopped at a red light. Get creative—the end goal is simply to consistently remind yourself of your vision so you are continually aligning with it.

What's the "Why" Behind Everything You Do?

Decide upon your major definite purpose in life and then orga-nize all your activities around it.

—BRIAN TRACY

Author of *Goals! How to Get Everything You Want—
Faster than You Ever Thought Possible*

Yesterday we addressed the fact that your problem is not with alco-hol, but rather that drinking alcohol is the symptomatic behavior of a deeper issue. One of the keys to cutting back or quitting drinking is identifying the reasons why you drink. One of the most effective methods to do this is to discover and embrace your life purpose.

Without a clear purpose as the compass to guide you, the achieve-ment of your goals and action plans may not ultimately fulfill you. As Stephen Covey writes in *The 7 Habits of Highly Effective People*, you don't want to get to the "top of the ladder" in life only to find out that the ladder was leaning against the wrong wall.

When Jessica found *The 30-Day Sobriety Solution*, she quickly dis-covered that her "ladder" was leaning up against the wrong wall. By most people's standards, Jessica was very successful. She had an undergraduate degree and a master's degree from highly regarded educational institutions and a successful career in which she was ex-celling and recognized for her invaluable contributions. She also had a boyfriend she loved and with whom she could see a bright future.

Even with all of that, Jessica was unhappy. She drank alone reg-ularly, binge drank on weekends, and experienced the occasional blackout. She constantly worried about her health, her safety when she blacked out, her relationship with her boyfriend, and her career. And every time she drank to escape those feelings, they only came back stronger when she sobered up. She felt like she was wasting her potential, and the easiest way to avoid her worries was by drinking.

As Jessica worked through *The 30-Day Sobriety Solution*, she started to really look at the "why" behind her drinking. One thing stood out above everything else—her career. She took time to look back over her life to analyze what had made her the happiest. She then thought about what her ideal day would look like if she could create it just the way she wanted, without getting caught up in the things that masked her true passion in life—things such as income, prestige, and what her parents thought was best for her. All of a sudden she gained clarity. As she reviewed the times in her life that had brought her the greatest joy, she realized she had a passion for fitness and a passion to help others achieve their goals, and that combining these two passions by becoming a fitness instructor and trainer excited her.

Buoyed by her new insight, she began to research a career in the fitness field. She talked to other trainers and looked into various certifications and training programs, and she realized that she was actually getting excited about her future for the first time. As a result, her whole life started to improve—her relationship with her boyfriend was better than ever, and she finally felt "authentic" in her life. She was much happier than before and, interestingly, her desire to drink faded quickly. For the first time, Jessica could envision a future without drinking. Sobriety became almost easy, and with every step she took toward creating this new life path, the universe seemed to respond by opening doors that previously had seemed closed.

Within eight months, Jessica became a Certified CrossFit Trainer, enrolled in a weight-lifting certification program, and was working on her certification as a group fitness instructor. Along with these new certifications and her passion about her opportunities in life, her existing job started to transform into one that she truly enjoyed and in which she found meaning where she was previously unable to. She was given opportunities at work that were not available to her when she was drinking, including a promotion. Although Jessica's dream is to eventually leave her existing job and pursue her life purpose, she no longer feels trapped in the life she is living. She has over two years of sobriety and, most importantly, is happy and excited in life without alcohol, and is even engaged to be married. Jessica's story is a testament to the power that clarity of purpose can create in your life.

What Were You Put on This Earth to Do?

There is one great truth on this planet: whoever you are, or whatever it is that you do, when you really want something, it's because that desire originated in the soul of the universe. It's your mission on earth. . . . And when you want something, all the universe conspires in helping you to achieve it.

—PAULO COELHO
Author of *The Alchemist*[6]

Now, let's figure out what it is that you *really* want, because without a purpose, you can easily get sidetracked. You can wander and drift, accomplishing little, and easily get pulled back into the desire to drink. However, if you have a purpose, everything in life seems to become aligned. When you are truly following your purpose, you are doing something you are good at, something that has the most meaning for you, something that has importance to you, and something that you love. As a result, the opportunities, people, and resources naturally move toward you. The world also benefits because when you are "on purpose," everything you do automatically serves others. And when you are on purpose, the desire to drink simply begins to fade away.

The goal of the Purpose Solution is to help you understand *why* you want to get and stay sober. When you understand the "why," you often also come to understand why you want to or need to cut back or quit drinking. For this reason, the Purpose Solution is broken down into two simple action steps that will each move you closer to discovering your life purpose.

The "Before You"

Getting my third DUI wasn't the miracle I was expecting, but it was the one I had been waiting for. It led me to The 30-Day Sobriety Solution *and ultimately freed me from the one prison I feared the most—the one I had created with alcohol.*

—BYRON

30-Day Graduate from Phoenix, Arizona

In this **second action step**, we want you to capture the "before you." Spend at least five minutes, or longer if you need it, to write down what caused you to want to cut back or quit drinking. This can include embarrassing or humiliating events (drunken arguments, making mean or hurtful comments, gossiping or sharing inappropriate information), ultimatums (from loved ones, employers, friends), legal challenges (DUIs, divorce, bar fights), health concerns (concerning blood work, weight issues, enlarged liver or heart), noticeable physical changes (bloated face, bloodshot eyes, skin discoloration), financial challenges (excessive bar expenses, poor decision making while drinking), or alarming changes in your drinking habits (increases in alcohol consumption, hiding your drinking, drinking alone more frequently).

For example, part of Dave's "before" story came during the holiday season. His in-laws were visiting, and while they were helping his wife move a bookshelf out of the guest bathroom, two empty bottles of vodka rolled out from underneath. Dave had hidden them there a year before when he was drunk and subsequently forgot. This was not only embarrassing to Dave but also led to his wife calling him at work and giving him an ultimatum not to come home unless he was serious about getting help. So Dave's "before" story included this event, as well as the other existing circumstances and challenges that drinking had created, including an emergency room visit for a heart attack scare, an enlarged liver, increasing debt related to spending money irresponsibly (on alcohol, going to bars, and unnecessary spending when under the influence), and drinking alone more frequently.

Use the following questions as you write down your "before you" story in your journal. If you need help getting started, we provide some additional questions as well as a guided audio version of how to capture this "before you" on the companion website at http://Day2.Solutions, so you can focus on writing your answers while listening to the questions. Remember, this is not an exercise in grammar or punctuation, but rather an exercise in writing down as much information as possible without self-judgment.

- Do you believe that you need alcohol to have fun in life, or that alcohol is necessary for you to feel like you fit in?
- Are you concerned with the consequences of your drinking, whether financial, legal, family related, health related, or career related?
- Are you sick of not living up to all of the promises that you made to yourself and to others about your plan to finally cut back or quit drinking, only to fail again?
- Are you the work-hard, party-hard or weekend-warrior type of person, but deep down you know that your drinking habits are holding you back from what you really want to accomplish in your career or your life?
- Do you want to be a better role model to your family and children? Do you want to attract a relationship that is not based on drinking or getting drunk to have fun? If the answer is yes, write down the ways in which you haven't been a good role model or how you have attracted the wrong kind of people in your life.
- Are you depressed? Have you been using drinking as the way to escape your depression?

As you go through these questions, be as specific as possible. Write about what keeps you up at night and what scares you the most about your drinking. Refer to the Time Travel Technique you completed yesterday—specifically, what you would become in the future and look like if you continued with your current drinking habits.

We know this can be a difficult exercise, and we wouldn't ask you to do it unless we felt it was critical in your path to recovery. After you complete it, you will be able to look back after 30 days and see how far you have come. Like many people, you are probably unjustly hard on yourself and don't recognize and acknowledge your accomplishments. Having a picture of this "before you" will help you see more clearly where you were when you started and enable you to appreciate your progress more fully.

This exercise also plants an important "pain point" regarding why you do not want to drink. For most of this program, you will be looking at what you *do* want instead of what you *don't* want. However, reminding yourself why you started down this path in the first place is important at times. Remember, you never have to be this person again. Consider this action step a good-bye ceremony to the old you. One that will open the door for the "new you" to shine through.

If you want to deepen the psychological impact of this ceremony of saying good-bye to your old self, you can turn it into a ritual by burning, shredding, or burying a *copy* of the "before you." The more energy you put into the ritual or ceremony, the more impact it will have.

The "New You"

I would complete a solution every day and know that I was becoming a better person—not just in relation to drinking but in every area of my life. I started to get my self-confidence back, and, more importantly, I started to see a happier, healthier, future version of myself that I could become.

—MATT
30-Day Graduate from Kansas City, Missouri

We now come to the fun part, and what the Purpose Solution is all about—to identify, acknowledge, and honor your purpose, or your "why" for cutting back or quitting drinking. Today's **third action step** is to write down what you really want in life and specifically what sobriety will give you and what doors it will open up for you. This is similar to the "before you" exercise you just completed, but instead of focusing on what you don't want and your concerns about drinking, you focus on all the things you do want in order to thrive in sobriety.

For example, Dave wanted to be a better husband and father, wanted to be fit and healthy, and wanted to be free from feeling like he needed alcohol in his life to be happy. He wasn't happy in his career as a computer systems engineer and wanted to be a positive role model and leader, and to inspire, teach, and coach others. But he knew this would never be possible with alcohol in his life. When he was finally able to see a future without drinking, he realized he had virtually an unlimited number of ways he could embrace a more meaningful and fulfilling path—from being a more present father, loving husband, engaged employee, and inspirational leader. He never imagined that his life purpose would be fulfilled by working in the field of recovery, but as thriving in sobriety became a reality for him, he realized his life purpose was to help lead others to do the exact same thing.

So let's discover your "why" for cutting back or quitting drinking, which will lead to your "new you." Write down your answers to the following questions in your journal. If you need additional questions or want to use the guided recording, remember to go to the companion website for today at http://Day2.Solutions.

- How will you really feel when you are thriving in sobriety? What will your energy level be like? How will you feel about yourself? What will going to bed sober and waking up without a hangover feel like and be like?
- What are you going to finally be able to accomplish now that you are not compelled to drink so frequently? Will you learn a new sport, take up a new hobby, learn how to speak a new language,

do rewarding volunteer work, or engage in new, enjoyable activities with your friends and loved ones?

- How will your career change? Will you look for a new career, start
  your own business, or simply start performing much better at
  your existing job? Will you be more upbeat, personable, and confident at work with your newfound attitude and energy level?
- How will your finances change? Will you be saving money from
  not drinking and not engaging in drinking-related activities? Will
  you be able to earn more money?
- Will you find a loving and supportive partner because your sobriety is attracting into your life people that you really want? Or will
  you be able to rekindle the passion and love in an existing relationship? Will you feel sexy or more attractive as a result of your
  newfound health and energy?

Be as specific as you can and use your notes from the Time Travel
Technique when you write down your answers to these questions.
You want to build the biggest "why" possible here, so that you can
begin to see why *drinking equals pain* and *sobriety equals immense pleasure*. The Purpose Solution works because it reminds you of the many
great things you are able to accomplish when you are sober, and it
helps you continue to take action, almost effortlessly.

Staying on Purpose

Now that you have written down what really inspires and excites
you—specifically, what becomes possible in life when you cut back
or stop your drinking and are thriving in sobriety—the **fourth action step** is to take some time *every day* to read what you wrote, pref-
erably in the morning. To be clear, we do not want you to reread
the "before you" notes, because completing that exercise has already
given you its intended value; however, we will refer back to it later.
We do want you to review your "new you" journal entry every day,

at least for the next three weeks, along with the vision statement that you wrote for these 30 (or 60 or 90) days.

You might find yourself becoming irritated with how often we use the phrase "thriving in sobriety," but we assure you that there is a very important reason for this, which we will explain in Day 12.

Day 2 Action Steps

I don't put pressure on myself. I let things happen how they should naturally. That's how I am today. I'm a recovering alcoholic and addict, and I don't drink and I don't do drugs. I live my life one day at a time.

—NAOMI CAMPBELL
Supermodel[7]

As we close the chapter on Day 2, we want to share a passage from *The Alchemist* by Paulo Coelho:

It's the thought of Mecca that keeps me alive. That's what helps me face these days that are all the same . . . I'm afraid that if my dream is realized, I'll have no reason to go on living . . . You're different from me, because you want to realize your dreams. I just want to dream about Mecca . . . I'm afraid that it would all be a disappointment, so I prefer just to dream about it.

Are you afraid to live the life of your dreams? It's not enough to simply dream about your ideal life. You have to take the necessary actions to create it. You have to stop dreaming and start living! Creating and pursuing your vision of thriving in sobriety takes courage, and the simple act of writing down your answers to the questions in today's action steps is an important first step in achieving this new vision for yourself. If you have not yet purchased a journal or started an online journal, stop reading and do so now.

- **Write your 30-Day Vision Statement.** Follow the guidelines and the sample vision statements we provided, and come up with your own statement that captures the "you" that you desire to be, thriving in sobriety, by the end of this program.

- **Capture the "before you."** Write down in your journal your thoughts about all of the driving forces that got you to look for ways to cut back or quit drinking. You can refer to the questions under the "before you" heading, use your notes from the Time Travel Technique, or use the guided recording from the companion website.

- **Capture the "new you."** Write down in your journal all the positive "whys" regarding what sobriety will bring to your life. You can refer to the questions under the "new you" heading as well as the thoughts and feelings that you experienced when completing the Time Travel Technique, or use the guided recording on the companion website.

- **Review your 30-Day Vision Statement and your "new you" journal entry.** Keep your vision statement visible and accessible so that you can read it often and review the "new you" notes every day for at least the next two weeks. One easy way to make sure you remember to do this is by adding a recurring private calendar meeting for every day (with your vision statement written into the meeting details) on your computer or smartphone.

As always, we have some fantastic additional content on the companion website, including the optional guided recordings to help you through the action steps. Go to http://Day2.Solutions.

The Pendulum Solution

Embracing Your Painful Past to Unleash
Pleasure and Joy in the Present

Everyone recognizes beauty only because of ugliness. Everyone recognizes virtue only because of sin.

—LAO TZU

Sixth-century BC Chinese philosopher and author of *Tao Te Ching*[1]

When Dave was eleven years old, he got sick with the flu. He experienced many of the typical symptoms, including high fever, vomiting, chills, body aches, and fatigue. But this time, when he got sick, he asked his mom a question that changed his perspective on life forever: "Mom, why do people get sick?" Without hesitation his mother responded, "If you never got sick, you would never know how great it is to feel healthy."

This simple story perfectly captures the essence of the Pendulum Solution: *you can understand your problem drinking or alcohol dependency only in the context of its opposite—sobriety.* We are going to show you how learning and applying this concept in your life will accelerate your ability to make and maintain not only sobriety but also countless other positive changes in your life.

All or Nothing

I can't remember drinking. When I stopped, I would look at a beer and think how great it would be. I'd get this pang in my stomach to go back out and have fun, but then I'd remember that I used up that right—that I did a full life's worth of drinking between fourteen and twenty-seven.

—GERARD BUTLER
Actor[2]

Most problem drinkers can relate to a lack of balance in life. In fact, you might operate from an all-or-nothing attitude. But this type of thinking can lead to a challenge we often see in early sobriety. In the first two days of this program, we asked you to start imagining what is possible in your life when you are finally thriving in sobriety. As you start to wake up and energize that part of you, we often find that you might get tempted to start setting all sorts of goals along with your goal to get sober. Don't do this! Even if you have been sober and are doing this program to get reinspired in your recovery, don't start setting other goals.

Inevitably, we see two negative outcomes when you set too many goals at once. First, your focus on sobriety wanes or disappears, and you slip back into your old tendencies. Second, you take on so much in your life that you become overwhelmed and begin missing deadlines. This last one is the most common and usually makes you feel like a failure, which often takes you right back to drinking, ensuring that none of your goals will be accomplished.

Therefore, do yourself a big favor and stay focused on your sobriety during this 30-Day program. You will have plenty of time to work on your other life goals later. And the great thing about accomplishing your sobriety goal is the domino effect that occurs afterward. This first domino of achieving sobriety can seem unmovable and insurmountable, but once you learn how to push it over, the rest of the dominos fall more easily, and you will be amazed at your new-found ability to overcome challenges that used to hold you back.

The Law of Duality

Life is a tennis match between polar opposites: winning and losing, love and hate, open and closed. It helps to recognize that painful fact early. Then recognize the polar opposites within yourself, and if you can't embrace them or reconcile them, at least accept them and move on. The only thing you cannot do is ignore them.

—ANDRE AGASSI
Tennis champion who overcame his crystal meth addiction[3]

At the core of the Pendulum Solution is the law of duality, which states that two different feelings, characteristics, or features cannot exist without each other. Common examples include good and evil, hot and cold, and right and wrong. When considering "good" in the context of "evil," the definition of "good" becomes clear.

So what does the law of duality have to do with your drinking? First, this law helps you understand sobriety because sobriety is typically defined *only* in the context of alcoholism or addiction. Without the existence of alcohol dependency, you would not be able to understand sobriety. It is the same thing with thriving in sobriety—you can understand what it means only through its opposite. Everyone has his or her own definition of what the opposite of thriving in sobriety is. For Dave, this was drinking despite knowing what it was taking from him—his health, his wife, his kids, his career, and his passion and purpose.

When you are able to finally cut back or quit drinking for good, you are given this gift of knowing what the exact opposite of thriving in sobriety is. You are able to experience and appreciate the highs of sobriety because you have experienced the lows of drinking.

Your Problem Drinking Is Your Greatest Gift!

I consider my journey in recovery to be
one of the greatest gifts of my life.

—BRENÉ BROWN

Author of *The Gifts of Imperfection: Let Go of Who You*
Think You're Supposed to Be and Embrace Who You Are[4]

When John found *The 30-Day Sobriety Solution*, everything seemed to be going well for him. He owned and operated a flourishing financial firm that he'd built from the ground up. At age forty-six, he could easily have sold his firm and never have to work another day in his life. He had an eight-year-old son, was happily married, and was a respected member of his community.

But John also had a secret. He drank more than a half liter of vodka every night. Over time, his drinking changed from being a social and enjoyable experience to a private and compulsive behavior. He tried acupuncture, hypnotherapy, willpower, counseling, and various supplements to help cure himself of his drinking compulsion, none of which worked. He felt isolated and alone, and doubted whether he would ever be able to quit drinking. He was terrified to quit, and he was terrified of what might happen if he kept drinking.

As John worked through *The 30-Day Sobriety Solution*, he began to see and experience a new life without alcohol, one in which he was actually happy. He completed one solution a day, embracing and applying what he learned with passion and perseverance, and he started to see his daily compulsions dissipate. He was able to stay completely sober using what he learned. At first, he found that staying sober became easy during the week; however, weekends remained a challenge. But as the weeks passed and the solutions continued to stack up and build in his life, he suddenly found it less challenging to stay sober on the weekends as well.

Enjoying extended sobriety for the first time in decades, he found that he was ready to start tackling new goals in his life. John was always passionate about health and fitness, even though over the years he had let his drinking take priority over his passion for taking care of his body. So as sobriety became easier, John decided to start P90X, an intense 90-day workout program that he had always dreamed of doing but never had the time or determination to pursue, given his nightly drinking habit. But this time he finished the program and regained a level of fitness and health that he had not experienced since college. He lost more than twenty-five pounds of fat and put on more than ten pounds of muscle.

For the first time in decades, John felt like the person that people saw on the outside matched how he felt on the inside. He felt a renewed passion for every aspect of his life and experienced firsthand how the power of perspective he had gained from his past excessive drinking allowed him to truly appreciate and embrace his new life in sobriety. John's story is a testament to the polar opposites that you can experience in life, all in a relatively short period of time.

These polar opposites are like two sides of a pendulum, as the image below depicts. Excessive drinking is like pulling the pendu-

lum all the way up to one side—to the "dark side," where depression, addiction, and unhappiness flourish. However, when you are able to finally let go of the pendulum, as John did, it naturally propels you to the top of the other, positive side, where you experience and appreciate being healthy and sober.

You might have heard that "pain is the currency of transformation." But perhaps for you, your *excessive drinking* is the currency of your transformation. With excessive drinking eventually come pain and hurt, and when you experience pain and hurt, ironically, you enable yourself to more quickly go to the opposite of those feelings— pleasure and happiness.

The graduates of *The 30-Day Sobriety Solution*, like John, regularly share how their problem drinking has been a gift in many ways. They share how today they spend much of their lives on the other side of the pendulum, thriving in sobriety, and even when they do experience pain and sadness, they are able to use the tools they learned in this program to deal effectively with these emotions. They are able to truly appreciate and value the lives they have today because they have such vivid memories and pain associated with the days when drinking was controlling their decisions and their relationships. The crazy mood swings they experienced during their times of excessive drinking are gone, and they are able to reach wonderful, natural highs without having to experience the incredible lows. The accomplishment of overcoming excessive drinking has propelled them forward in many other areas of their lives, and goals they once considered unattainable, or were too afraid to take on, all of a sudden became far less scary and overwhelming in the context of the changes they made getting sober.

We understand this can be hard to believe at this stage, so all we ask is that you remain open to the possibility—as John did, even though he had doubts initially. Today John has over two years of sobriety, and although he has faced his share of life challenges since getting sober, the tools he learned in this program have allowed him to do it without turning to vodka to cope.

What about you? When you think about actually being happy in sobriety, what do you think is possible in your life? American author, lecturer, and advocate for the blind Helen Keller, who certainly understood duality in life, said, "Character cannot be developed in ease and quiet. Only through experiences of trial and suffering can the soul be strengthened, vision cleared, ambition inspired, and success achieved."[5]

Whether you are aware of it or not, your past really has been perfect. What brought you to this exact point in your life is exactly what was meant to be. Over time, you will realize that it was a gift. What you do with this gift is up to you, but know that it is a gift that can keep on giving your entire life. Once again, we know this might be hard to believe right now, but we are asking you to trust us.

How the Greatest Gift Keeps On Giving

Sobriety was the greatest gift I ever gave myself. I don't put it on a platform. I don't campaign about it. It's just something that works for me. It enabled me to really connect with another human being—my wife, Sheryl—which I was never able to do before.

—ROB LOWE

Shortly after we signed the publishing deal for *The 30-Day Sobriety Solution*, Dave received a letter from his daughter that demonstrates the "greatest gift" concept from a completely different perspective. When you finally overcome your problem drinking and thrive in sobriety, you get to see the positive impact this has on your loved ones. Here is what Briana wrote:

Your words help me through times that are so difficult. You say the best things to make me feel special, wanted, and loved. I'm so proud to tell people that you're my dad. You are fun, brave, and adventurous. I am so happy that after all of your work you finally are out there doing it! It makes me feel overjoyed to think that you're finally getting your book published and you're helping others! I am so glad that you stopped drinking. And to be honest, I'm glad that you had a problem with it before. I am glad of this because you have taught me so much from it! I have learned that people can be one way and change in an instant, whether it's a good change or a bad one. I have to be honest to say that I was a little bit scared about your addiction, and after you stopped, even though I was young, I realized that by you overcoming it, I could/can do anything I want to in life. It must be hard to push through a "wall" that is so heavily bearing on you. Once you pushed through that "wall," I felt like I was also capable of pushing through walls that block me from my dreams.

At first you may understandably feel embarrassed or ashamed of your past and want to hide from it, or act like it never even happened. However, eventually this will change, and your shame and embarrassment will transform into confidence and pride, and you will become an inspiration to those around you.

The Pleasure Principle

Every negative event contains within it the seed of an equal or greater benefit.

—NAPOLEON HILL (1883–1970)
Author of *Think and Grow Rich*[6]

Every decision you make in life is to either avoid pain or gain pleasure. Sigmund Freud, the founding father of psychoanalysis, first described this phenomenon as the pleasure principle.[7] Right now you are probably trying to prove this statement wrong, but we challenge you to find any action that you take that cannot be traced back to this simple concept. Whether you are volunteering your time for a worthy cause, sitting in front of the TV, going to your job, or spending time with family, at the root of all of these actions is the desire to either avoid pain or experience pleasure. Similar to the previous examples, pain and pleasure are opposites of each other. More importantly, every decision that you make regarding whether or not to drink comes back to satisfying one of these two basic needs.

Why is this concept so important? Let's look at Dave's story again. Dave drank for many reasons. Early on, he drank to fit in and to feel connected to a group of friends. Later on, he drank because he wanted to hide from the painful things going on his life, as well as from the pain that he felt as the result of not following through with his dreams and goals. Drinking also allowed him to avoid the pain of knowing he was not being the husband, father, and son he wanted to be. The further along he got in his "drinking career," the more pain his drinking created in his life. Finally, he reached his bottom, where the pain was significant enough for him to act to avoid further pain and to finally get sober for good.

Dave finally created enough pain around his drinking to get sober, but it took him years longer than it needed to. All he, or anyone, has to do to get sober *now* is to make sure that enough pain is associated with drinking and enough pleasure is associated with staying sober. It really is that simple. Sobriety becomes second nature if you associate strong feelings of pleasure with sobriety and strong feelings of pain with excessive drinking.

Addiction Explained

Dr. William Glasser, known for pioneering reality therapy and choice therapy, offers one of the simplest and most powerful explanations of addiction. In his highly acclaimed book *Positive Addiction*, Glasser discusses negative addiction in depth and shares the following: "The reason addiction is powerful and difficult to break is that it alone of all the choices consistently both completely relieves the pain of failure, and provides an intensely pleasurable experience." Glasser goes on to explain, "It is this peculiar, unique combination of pain relief first and then, quickly, a 'rush' of pleasure that is necessary for an addiction."[8]

Consider this statement in relation to what we just covered. In the short term, drinking eliminates pain and provides pleasure— almost instantly. How many things are so effective at almost instantly relieving pain in your life, while adding pleasure (albeit short term) at the same time? When you consider your drinking in this context, are you surprised that you have a problem? You shouldn't be. The effect of drinking is powerful and quick acting, and tempts even the strongest-willed individual. But don't let this discourage you; *The 30-Day Sobriety Solution* shows you exactly how to remove pain and create lasting pleasure, all without alcohol.

Putting the Pleasure Principle to Work for You

In the end, some of your greatest pains become your greatest strengths.

—DREW BARRYMORE
Actor-director and author of *Little Girl Lost*[9]

If you want to thrive in sobriety, you have to make sure you link enough pleasure to staying sober and you link enough pain to drinking. During these first three days, our primary focus has been doing exactly this.

You have already done part of the **first action step** for today. On Day 2 in the Purpose Solution, you captured in your journal a snapshot of the "before you" and the "new you." We are going to build on this by first reviewing what you wrote yesterday. The reason we want to review the "before you" one more time is because we want to reinforce the link of pain to drinking. And not just pain, but *massive* pain. Studies show that you will do as much as two times more to avoid pain than to gain pleasure.[10] By reviewing your journal notes of your "before you" again, you are taking a powerful initial step toward linking pain to your drinking.

The key to doing so is not merely to reread what you wrote but also to experience it emotionally. It is one thing to recognize that if you drink, you might push away your loved ones. But it is a completely different thing to acknowledge the pain and feelings you experience when you push away your loved ones—the loneliness, the sense of failure, the disappointment, and the fear of potentially losing them from your life. When you really *feel* these feelings, you "anchor" the pain associated with your drinking.

Your **second action step** is to do the same exercise with your "new you" journal notes. Feel what it feels like to thrive in sobriety and to finally accomplish so many positive changes in your life. Really experience how it feels in your body, how you look, and the energy you have to move forward in so many areas of your life that you always dreamed of. One of our graduates told us how valuable this exercise was to his ongoing sobriety:

> I have always been a very visual person, but I never realized how useful this strength was until I started applying it in *The 30-Day Sobriety Solution*. Today I have two collections of images—one of the future me that kept drinking, and one of the future (and current) me thriving in sobriety—that I can easily recall in vivid detail. Whenever I am struggling, I simply recall these pictures and find I am naturally inspired to take positive action.

We recommend that you close your eyes while doing this, put on some relaxing music in the background, and focus on creating images and movies in your mind that really evoke your feelings. You can even play music that induces negative feelings while reviewing your journal notes for the "before you" and music that elicits passion and excitement while reviewing your journal notes for the "new you."

Breaking Through When Others Break Down

Wouldn't it be great if you could increase your odds of success two-fold? *New York Times* business reporter Charles Duhigg, in his best-selling book *The Power of Habit: Why We Do What We Do in Life and Business,* references one study that tells you exactly how to do this.[11]

Patients who were recovering from knee or hip surgery were each given a booklet with their rehab schedules and instructed to write their goals and a detailed action plan for each of the thirteen weeks of recovery. Three months later, the patients who had written out plans were walking well before those who had not, recovering almost twice as fast. They were also able to get in and out of their chairs without assistance almost three times faster than those who didn't write down their goals or action plan.

Those who recovered faster had written very specific, detailed plans for their recovery, including the exercises they would do, when and where they would do them, the places they would go, and the friends and family they would meet with and at what times. They wrote what they would do if the pain was too great, and specifically how they would deal with the movements they knew would cause pain (which was important because these were the times they would be most tempted to quit). They also defined rewards for certain milestones, no matter how small, such as being able to meet their spouse at the bus stop. One person put a bowl of M&Ms next to his bathroom door and rewarded himself with one M&M every time he walked into the bathroom and one M&M every time he walked out.

So, your **third action step** for today is to write in your journal a detailed plan for how you are going to overcome the temptation to drink. Include things like driving home along a different route to avoid bars and liquor stores, listing various activities you can engage in when the craving to drink is strongest, and deciding on a time of day that you are going to complete the solution and action steps for the day. List several people you will spend time with who are positive influences, and, of course, choose what kinds of rewards you can give yourself during the day or at the end of every day to celebrate abstaining from alcohol. Most importantly, focus on the time of the day you would usually drink and plan alternative activities for that time. This simple *written* plan of action works! It should take less than ten minutes to complete, but once you have written it down, refer to it daily and stick to it.

Day 3 Action Steps

The fallacy about drinking, however, is that when people say they drink to forget, all it does is magnify the problem. I would have a drink to banish the problem and then, when it didn't go away, have another one . . .

—ERIC CLAPTON
Singer-songwriter, author of *Clapton: The Autobiography*,
and founder of Crossroads Centre Antigua[12]

When you are tempted to drink—and the odds are high that you will be tempted to drink again—remind yourself of the pain you will experience by drinking and the pleasure you will gain by choosing to stay sober. Remember that how you feel drives the choices you make in your life. At some level, you believed that drinking equaled more pleasure than pain or was simply less painful than not drinking, which led you to drink.

Either way, because the balance was skewed in favor of drinking, you ended up doing just that. Shifting that pain-pleasure balance in your favor to match the new vision of yourself is not difficult and—guess what—in only three days, you have taken incredible steps to accomplish that. If you find yourself craving alcohol, simply come back to these action steps, or you can jump ahead to Day 13, the Tapping Solution, and use the tapping techniques to lessen or even completely remove your craving.

- **Review the "before you" journal notes from Day 2.** Remember, the key is to really *feel* what you wrote—not simply to read it. Experiencing the feeling creates a powerful link between drinking and pain. Imagine your experience with all five senses: what it feels like, sounds like, tastes like, looks like, and smells like. Feel free to add any additional insights to this list.

- **Review the "new you" journal notes from Day 2.** Once again, experience the positive feelings of this "new you" thriving in sobriety. Allow yourself to really feel amazing about the changes. Congratulate yourself out loud and tell yourself how great it is to be the person you knew you were always meant to be. Feel free to add any additional insights to this list.

- **Write down in your journal your quit-drinking strategy.** Make a detailed list of when you are going to complete *The 30-Day Sobriety Solution,* what you will do to overcome cravings to drink, activities you can do, good role models you can spend time with, people you can call, and small rewards you can give yourself for following through.

Be sure to visit the companion website, where we include an extremely funny and enlightening video of a famous late-night talk-show host sharing how absurd his drinking was before he got sober, at http://Day3.Solutions. We have also included on the website an optional guided version of today's first two action steps.

The Forgiveness Solution

*Embracing Forgiveness and Creating an
Abundance of Love and Happiness*

> *When we forgive, we set a prisoner free and discover that the
> prisoner we set free is us.*
>
> —LEWIS B. SMEDES (1921–2002)
> Author of *Forgive and Forget: Healing the Hurts We Don't Deserve*[1]

Some people live as if they have a heavy ball and chain tied to them. And if they could finally free themselves from this extra weight, their future would be full of promise and opportunity. Perhaps this rings true for you—maybe you are tied to past anger, fear, or pain, or are full of regret from not doing the things you said you would. Releasing this ball and chain is often the final step in completing your past so that you can embrace your future.

We have found that something as simple as forgiving a parent, best friend, or even yourself for past hurts and transgressions can be one of the single most effective solutions to cutting back or quitting drinking for good. The truth is, we need to let go of the past to embrace the future, and the Forgiveness Solution will provide you with proven techniques to finally accomplish this.

We Accept the Sobriety We Think We Deserve

I think we all wish we could erase some dark times in our lives. But all of life's experiences, bad and good, make you who you are. Erasing any of life's experiences would be a great mistake.

—LUIS MIGUEL

Singer-songwriter[2]

"We accept the love we think we deserve." Stephen Chbosky's quote from his book, and later the movie, *The Perks of Being a Wallflower*, is brilliant in its simplicity, yet it doesn't apply just to love. *You also accept the sobriety you think you deserve.* If you don't think you deserve to be sober or you don't think you deserve to thrive in sobriety, you will never attract it or accept it in your life. You might get close to reaching the coveted thriving-in-sobriety state of mind, but then self-sabotage will inevitably kick in.

As we said on Day 1 in the 100% Solution, alcohol is not the problem; rather, it is the symptom. To get and stay sober, or to successfully cut back on drinking, you need to solve the problem, or the "why," behind your drinking. One of the most common whys that problem drinkers struggle with are overwhelming feelings of guilt and shame. Guilt about things they have done when drinking and shame about not being able to cut back or quit drinking on their own. These feelings of guilt and shame keep the problem drinker coming back to alcohol to cover up the problem, which only adds to the guilt and shame.[3] When you are finally able to forgive yourself and heal this pain, you can move forward.

What are guilt and shame? Guilt is best explained as a feeling that occurs when you behave in ways that don't match your beliefs. For example, you believe you should stop drinking, you say you are going to stop drinking, but then you drink again, so you feel guilty. Shame is a much stronger feeling and is usually defined by a conscious or subconscious belief, at some level, that you are a "bad" person. Guilt comes from your behavior. Shame comes from a belief that you are somehow flawed. Often, shame is a constant negative feeling about yourself, an overall feeling of emptiness. Shame can manifest in your life in many ways, although quite often it comes from a traumatic event or series of events from your childhood and ultimately leads to an ongoing experience of suffering.

One of the greatest challenges of this suffering is that you can become addicted to it. You hold on to it like a close friend. Over time, it becomes a part of you that is hard to let go of. Today you will learn an effective technique that is at the core of the Forgiveness Solution— the Total Truth Process, a powerful emotional healing process we learned from bestselling authors John Gray and Barbara DeAngelis.[4]

The Total Truth Process

Originally I was a happy drunk. But later I was miserable because it's a depressant. I was just ashamed of myself, really.

—EWAN MCGREGOR
Actor[5]

This simple but powerful tool will help you release those ball-and-chain negative emotions from the past and return to your natural state of joy and love in the present. For many of you, finally freeing yourself from your past hurts, humiliations, guilt, shame, and resentments will be one of the most important things that you do in *The 30-Day Sobriety Solution*.

The reason this process is called the "total truth" is that when we're upset, we often don't communicate the totality of our true feelings—especially to the person we're the most upset with. We get stuck in the negative emotions of anger or hurt and are rarely able to move past those to a more complete emotional state. The Total Truth Process helps you gain access to a more natural emotional state that brings back the closeness, thoughtfulness, and caring you truly feel toward someone else. The intention of this process is not to purge or dump your negative emotions on another person but to move through those emotions, releasing them and returning to your natural state of being—one of love and acceptance. Creativity and joy can easily flow from you in this natural state. And it is only in this state of mind that thriving in sobriety can become a full reality in your life.

One of the reasons the Total Truth Process is so incredibly effective is because it includes *all* the stages of the natural process you need to go through to reach a true state of forgiveness. When you apply this process, you ensure that you don't get "stuck" on any one stage, especially the initial stage of anger or resentment, which can easily happen. When you get stuck at this stage, your desire to drink often increases because drinking helps you temporarily escape these negative feelings. Of course, drinking is an ineffective solution because it masks these feelings only momentarily—it cannot resolve or release them. When you use the Total Truth Process, you will clear all the feelings, so that you can be at peace with the issue.

The Stages of the Total Truth Process

As long as you don't forgive, who and whatever it is will occupy rent-free space in your mind.

—ISABELLE HOLLAND (1920–2002)
Children's book author[6]

You can do the Total Truth Process verbally or write it as a letter or a journal entry. However you decide to do the process, your goal is to communicate and release your anger and hurt, which allows you to move toward love and forgiveness.

In the early stages of cutting back or quitting drinking, you may find yourself on a bit of an emotional roller coaster. And when you are in an emotionally volatile state, it is best that you don't do the Total Truth Process verbally with another person. Instead, we recommend that you wait until after completing *The 30-Day Sobriety Solution* to do this particular process in person. You might also find that the simple act of writing down your emotions in the form of a Total Truth Letter—which you don't send to the person—is all you need to do in order to move yourself back into your natural state of love and joy.

Here are the six steps or stages of the Total Truth Process:

Acknowledge your anger and resentment.

I'm angry that . . . *I'm fed up with . . .*
I hate it when . . . *I resent . . .*

Acknowledge the hurt and pain that it created.

It hurt me when . . . *I feel hurt that . . .*
I felt sad when . . . *I feel disappointed about . . .*

Acknowledge the fears and self-doubts that it created.

I was afraid that . . . *I get afraid of you when . . .*
I feel scared when . . . *I'm afraid that I . . .*

Own any part that you might have played in letting it occur or letting it continue.

I'm sorry that . . . *I'm sorry for . . .*
Please forgive me for . . . *I didn't mean to . . .*

Express what you wanted that you didn't get and/or what you want now.

All I ever want(ed) . . . *I want(ed) . . .*
I want you to . . . *I deserve . . .*

Understand where the other person was/is coming from and forgive him or her.

Now put yourself in the other person's shoes and attempt to understand where he or she was coming from at that time.

Also acknowledge what needs that person was trying to meet—
however inelegantly—by his or her behavior.

I understand that . . .	*I forgive you for . . .*
I appreciate . . .	*Thank you for . . .*
I love you for . . .	

Get out your journal, whether it is electronic or paper, and start your **first action step** for today, right now. Think about the person you hold the most anger or resentment toward and begin with that one person. Don't be surprised if the first two stages are painful to work through. John Green, the author of the young-adult novel *The Fault in Our Stars*, captures this best when he writes, "That's the thing about pain. It demands to be felt."[7] As we mentioned yesterday in the Pendulum Solution, sometimes you have to feel those painful emotions to move forward.

In order to really have a breakthrough today, you, like most problem drinkers, need to focus on forgiving yourself. So you may want to do the Total Truth Process with yourself. Also, make sure to write a Total Truth Letter to each of your parents or the guardians who raised you. Make sure to address any feelings left over from your childhood—especially any that were traumatic.

Finally, if you are really ready to live a life of love, passion, and joy, make a list of everyone you have any anger toward and anyone who may have hurt you—family members, teachers, classmates, friends, employers, coworkers, ex-spouses and ex-lovers, the police, the military, or the legal system. Over time, work through that list. You don't need to do it all today. That's not possible, and even though you do want to work through your whole list eventually, this can be such an emotionally intense and time-consuming process that the most important thing is to just get started with at least one person today. And don't worry, because of the importance of this topic, we revisit some key parts of it on Day 27 in the Love and Relationship Solution.

Forgive and Move On

Life demands these hurtful experiences for you to learn how
forgiveness feels. It could be no other way. If there is anyone in
your life that you must forgive, instead of seeing them as some-
one who has hurt you, try to see them as someone who was
sent to teach you forgiveness and thank them for this precious
gift—then forgive them, and let it go.

—JACKSON KIDDARD
Author and philosopher[8]

In order to let go and move on, you need to come from a place of forgiveness and love, especially when dealing with your family, your individual relationships, and your career. Maybe your best friend lied to you. Maybe a coworker gossiped about you or took full credit for your project. Maybe your spouse had an affair and then treated you badly during the divorce. Or maybe a business partner made a bad decision and ruined you financially. You need to forgive each and every one of these people who hurt you somehow in the past. Forgiving someone *does not* mean that you need to forget what happened, condone the person's actions or behaviors, or ever trust him or her again, but in order to move on, you do need to forgive the person for whatever he or she did or didn't do, learn whatever lessons you can from the situation, and then let it go.

Forgive Yourself

In order to attain total freedom, you also need to forgive yourself. Forgive yourself for the pain and harm you may have caused others. Forgive yourself for continually telling your loved ones that you would cut back or quit drinking but never following through. Forgive yourself for the mistakes you might have made under the influence of alcohol. Forgive yourself for the harm you might have done to your body, your career, or your finances by drinking.

When you forgive yourself and others, you release the past and bring yourself back to the here and now. Tony Robbins, one of the most influential teachers of this generation, reminds us constantly that "the past does not equal the future."[9] You always have the opportunity to change your life—right this minute. The past is the past. It does not determine who you are or what you will be in the future. Your power is in the present moment. And if you are living in the present, then you are able to choose and attract good things into your life. You can focus on taking action now to create what you really want for the future—for yourself, for your family, and, of course, for your sobriety. If you are stuck in your story of how the past should have been different, your energy is stuck, and you can't move forward. You have to forgive and let go in order to reclaim the power and the energy that you need to move ahead and create the life that you really want—a life thriving in sobriety.

Thousands of people in our seminars and our coaching practice have experienced enormous and unexpected benefits when they finally, truly forgave someone. They've released migraine headaches they've had for years within minutes, found immediate relief from persistent physical ailments, slept through the entire night for the first time in years, and felt their overwhelming compulsion to drink fade away. Believe us, working on forgiveness is definitely worth the effort, as Desiree's story illustrates so beautifully.

Desiree's Story of Forgiveness

Even though it has only been three weeks, my whole life has turned around completely! I have been struggling almost all my life with this each and every day, and it is wonderful realizing when I wake up each morning that the way I used to live my life is in the past and I can greet each day with excitement instead

of the habitual cycle hanging over me . . . I am more energized,
happier, and healthier!

−DESIREE

30-Day Graduate from Harare, Zimbabwe

Desiree had her first drink when she was just eight years old. One of her earliest father-bonding memories was sitting with her dad, pouring him drinks, and having a special little glass to herself. As the youngest child of four, Desiree had to grow up quickly. When she was sixteen years old, her mother died in a car accident, and just two years later, her father, who had been a bedridden alcoholic most of his life, passed away from cirrhosis of the liver.

Desiree knew only one way to cope with all of this loss so early in her life—drinking. Even though she was drinking to excess nightly, she managed to stay employed, but the rest of her life was in shambles. Three broken marriages, two illegal abortions, and losing custody of her four-week-old son through an ugly divorce left her desperate and suicidal.

She knew that alcohol was only making things worse, but no matter what she tried, she couldn't quit. Desiree said, "I tried self-discipline, abstinence, willpower, AA, and so many other things that would last for a while, and then I was off the wagon again! AA may work for others, but it never did for me . . . I felt as though I was reduced to less of a person and had no right or place on the face of the earth, and was even more suicidal."

While Desiree was desperately searching online for an answer that would finally help her, she found *The 30-Day Sobriety Solution.* In early sobriety, she wrote to us, "Through the 30-Day solutions and action steps, I was able to deal with and overcome many issues in my life that in the past I had to mask with alcohol. Fully grasping the concept of being excited about life and having the gratitude propelled me into areas of my life I had never been to or even knew were possible to reach within myself."

Desiree has been sober for over three and a half years. In sobriety, with all the newfound tools and techniques she now has at her disposal, Desiree was finally able to forgive—not only all those people who had hurt her in life, but also herself. And not just forgiving, but actually starting to love herself. She discovered quickly that all of these changes propelled her forward in every other area of her life as well.

Desiree became recognized for her exceptional contributions at work. Her love life flourished, and her friendships and family ties became stronger. Instead of always being the "problem child" in her family, she became the one who encouraged, supported, and led others to make positive changes. Today she is considering becoming a full-time recovery coach and told us, "I am forty-five and feeling fabulous!"

The Forgiveness Affirmation

One final technique for helping you forgive is to recite this affirmation several times each day:

> I release myself from all the demands and judgments that have kept me limited. I allow myself to be free—to live in joy, love, peace, and sobriety. I allow myself to create fulfilling relationships, to have success in my life, to experience pleasure, to know that I am worthy and deserve to have what I want. I am now free. I release all others from any demands and expectations I have placed on them. I choose to be free. I allow others to be free. I forgive myself, and I forgive them. And so it is.

Just like the 30-Day Vision Statement you have already written, we recommend that you include this at the beginning of your journal and read it out loud at least once a day for the next two weeks. Many of our clients prefer to condense this affirmation so that they can easily memorize it, so feel free to edit it as you see fit.

Bryan Had It All

It's taken me years to let go of the terrible shame. I wouldn't change a thing, because it brought me here today—and without all that pain, would I be the same person? However, I speak to many addicts all the time, and what I probably tell them most often is: it's not your fault. I know it feels like your fault. I know everyone else tells you it's your fault. I know everyone's hurt and angry with you. I know you've done bad things. But the only thing within your control is seeking help to stop.

—KRISTEN JOHNSTON

Actor, author of *Guts: The Endless Follies and Tiny Triumphs of a Giant Disaster*, and founder of SLAM, NYC (Sobriety, Learning and Motivation)[10]

We would like to share with you a moving story that shaped Dave's life, demonstrates the power of guilt and shame, and played an enormous role in creating *The 30-Day Sobriety Solution.*

You know those people who seem like they have everything going for them? My friend Bryan was one of those people. Prestigious brain surgeon, great-looking, charismatic, beautiful wife, and two amazing kids. I was envious.

We met at a fantasy football draft party in 2002. We became casual friends, seeing each other at various parties and get-togethers. I met his wife and two kids, who were the same ages as my two kids.

Years later, there was one time we met up that I still vividly recall—it was just after receiving a disturbing phone call from my doctor. Dr. Lee sounded strangely somber as he said to me on the phone, "I have the results of your blood work, and there are some concerning numbers." There was an awkward pause as he followed up with the question "Dave, how much do you drink?"

This was not a new question to me. My response to doctors in the past was to lie—and then find a new doctor. But I knew something was different this time. I downplayed my drinking to Dr. Lee, agreed to not drink as much, and to come back in two months to get my blood work done again.

Then, after that concerning phone call, I reached into my big bag of coping skills and decided to go to the bar.

And Bryan was there—Bryan the prestigious brain surgeon. I thought, *Who better to ask advice from*? I shared my doctor's concern, and his response was simple and to the point. He said, "Dave, all of these people in this bar have a lot worse numbers than that; you don't need to worry about it."

What a relief! All I wanted to be told was that I had nothing to worry about. It didn't matter to me whether it was true. Of course, it didn't cross my mind that using the population of the bar might not be the best baseline for health and wellness.

About a month later, I walked into the same bar, and a friend came up to me. "Dave, you are not going to believe this. Bryan almost died. He had complete organ failure. He has been drinking vodka out of a Gatorade bottle in his car on a regular basis and taking all kinds of prescription medications without a prescription. He is going to be in the hospital for ten days and then is going to a 90-day rehab program."

I was speechless. Not only was Bryan's life never going to be the same, but this was also a wake-up call for me. Drinking was creating havoc in my life. I was having marriage problems and health issues, and even though I didn't even really enjoy drinking anymore, I couldn't imagine stopping.

As I was struggling to turn things around with my drinking, I watched Bryan come back from rehab—he was a new person. He looked amazing; he had that sparkle in his eyes, had lost some weight, and all the puffiness in his face was gone.

Once again, I was envious.

I had figured out enough to get some sobriety under my belt but just barely enough to keep my family off my back about my drinking. I reached out to Bryan for help, but, unfortunately, he chose to be private about it and was not willing to help.

About eight months later, on April 25, 2008, I got an email that would change my life forever—Bryan had relapsed and had taken his life with a shotgun.

Right then I knew that my future could easily mirror Bryan's. I knew that with the suicidal thoughts I was having, and with all my failed attempts at sobriety prior to that, my next drink really could be my last—just like it was for Bryan.

At the funeral, seeing his heartbroken wife and two kids, and watching the slide show of all the memories of Bryan with his family, I knew that it could be my family sitting there at my funeral.

In that instant, I made several decisions.

I decided that I would never forget the path that drinking and addiction can lead you down. I decided that I would never take my sobriety, or the sobriety of others, for granted. I decided that if anyone ever asked for help and I was in the position to help them, I would never turn them away. And I decided that if drinking for seventeen years had any kind of upside, it was that the firsthand experience would help me know how to help others.

A short time later, I made another decision that changed my life forever: I decided that there had to be other solutions for recovery—and that was the moment where the initial idea to research and eventually create *The 30-Day Sobriety Solution* came from.

Over the years, I have given a lot of thought to what might have been going through Bryan's mind in those final hours before he took his own life. It isn't hard for me to imagine the overwhelming guilt and shame that he must have felt after failing again—after letting down his wife, kids, family, and friends, and putting his career as a doctor in jeopardy.

In the end, I believe the reason he took his life was that he was unable to truly recover from the guilt and shame of his past, unable to truly forgive himself and others, and, therefore, unable to truly love himself.

If you asked me if I felt much guilt or shame over my drinking before I got sober, I would have said no. Overall, I didn't think that I was in denial about my drinking issues, but clearly I was in denial about how much guilt and shame I had.

Once I realized that so many other "normal" people struggled with drinking and addiction, I felt a light turn on inside of me as I heard their stories. I realized I had been dimming that light through my drinking years because of how much blame and shame I held on to. I felt like a failure because I couldn't get and stay sober.

Bryan's story helped me understand this. His tragic death helped free me, and I will always be grateful to him for the lessons he taught me, even though they came from such a heartbreaking incident that I would do anything to go back and change.

Love Your Addiction, Love Yourself

Holding on to anger and resentment is like drinking poison and expecting someone else to die.

—SOURCE UNKNOWN

This brings us to the final topic of the day—loving yourself. Poisoning your body with alcohol on an almost daily basis, judging yourself for your inability to quit or control your drinking, and beating yourself up for your mistakes all lead to one end result—you stop loving yourself, and, worse yet, you may even begin to hate yourself.

Loving yourself can sound a bit hokey, but don't let the importance of this concept slip by just because it sounds *woo-woo* or cliché. If you don't love yourself, how will you ever treat your body and mind with respect? If you don't love yourself, how can you ever truly reach the level of fulfillment and meaning in your life that you deserve? If you don't love yourself, how can you ever expect anyone else to truly love you?

You cannot change the fact that you spend every minute of every day of your life with yourself. Accept who you are, accept that you make mistakes, and decide right now to make a conscious decision to love yourself. Slipups in life are normal and are *not* unforgivable sins. *The only sin in your life is to spend time remembering and focusing on your sins.* You will find that as your love for yourself becomes more real, your thoughts will become more positive, and you will attract more people, places, and things that bring joy and prosperity into your life.

Remember, the "new you" is one that is thriving in sobriety, living a meaningful and fulfilling life, and inspiring and supporting your friends and family every day. What is not to love about the "new you"? Better yet, the old you that suffered from drinking and the old you that made selfish decisions offer a much-needed perspective to truly appreciate and celebrate the "new you." So take a second and thank that old you for validating and confirming how amazing it is to live this new life of sobriety and excitement.

You are empowered every time you choose love and weakened every time you choose hatred, anger, guilt, or shame. Love lifts you up. Hatred, anger, guilt, and shame bring you down, and there is no way that you can overcome addictive behavior when you are constantly feeling anger, resentment, guilt, or shame. Martin Luther King Jr. said that the only way to convert an enemy to a friend is through love, not through hatred or anger. You may have heard the saying "At the end of our lives, there will be only two things that matter: who we loved and who loved us." Yes, love really is the answer, and it all starts with loving yourself.

"I Love Myself"

Love loves people right where they are.

—MASTIN KIPP

Founder of TheDailyLove.com[11]

It is important to understand that your desire to drink actually comes from a positive intention—your desire to feel good. It is human nature to want to feel good. The problem is that using drinking as the solution to feeling good is flawed. Over time, drinking ruins your health, contributes to depression, and causes accidents. Rather than connecting you to others, it separates you from others. Most importantly, it disconnects you from loving and taking care of yourself.

The first way you can start to love yourself and others more is to stop judging yourself. Accept yourself right where you are. Not where you are going to be in 30 days, or where you were last year, but right where you are today—at this very moment. Which brings us to our **second action step** for today.

Many books over the years have taught techniques to love yourself where you are, but one book, *Love Yourself Like Your Life Depends on It*, by Kamal Ravikant,[12] focuses on how to transform your life by teaching just one powerful life-changing concept—loving yourself.

To do this, Ravikant teaches a simple technique—to repeat the three-word mantra "I love myself." Use this mantra in your daily life. Say it out loud when you are at home alone, in your car, or simply going for a walk. And better yet, when you look in the mirror over the course of the day, say, "I love you," as you look into your own eyes.

We know this sounds strange. We are asking you to trust us

and all the other people that have confirmed that this technique changed their life. And what do you have to lose by trying it? After you read this chapter, go into the bathroom, look in the mirror, and do it. As easy as it sounds, you might be surprised to find that it is harder than you think to say those three words to yourself and mean them. If you experience discomfort saying "I love you" to yourself, it only validates the importance of doing this. If it is awkward and uncomfortable at first (and it probably will be), keep practicing it and saying it to yourself in the mirror until it feels natural and normal. There will be a moment when you break through, and when you do, you will experience a dramatic shift in your life. This is an important action step to take—and repeat—until it feels natural and true to you.

Also ask yourself, *What would you do with your life if you were deeply and truly in love with yourself? What would you do if you loved yourself like a parent loves a child or like a child loves his or her mother? Would you want your child, spouse, or loved one to drink as much as you drink?* Close your eyes and consider this for a moment. Until we really think about it, we often don't even realize how little love we have for ourselves.

Day 4 Action Steps

In life, pain is inevitable but suffering is optional. There are no victims, only volunteers.

—TONY ROBBINS

What you need to take away from today is simple and powerful. You drink for many reasons, and, over time, these reasons undoubtedly include guilt, shame, and pain from past events. Every time you drink, guilt and shame weigh more heavily on you, and eventually alcohol stops working as a solution to mask your problems and instead amplifies them.

To thrive in sobriety, you need to accept and become aware of this, forgive yourself and others, and begin loving yourself again.

- **Complete the Total Truth Process.** Go through the six steps of the Total Truth Process to address at least one past resentment, guilt, anger, or shame you might have. Be sure to focus on forgiving yourself and forgiving others who are responsible for any traumatic events you experienced in childhood. Although you can eventually do this process with the person you are forgiving, you may want to wait until after you have attained more long-term sobriety. For now, just write a Total Truth Letter to the person (but do not send it), making sure to give all six steps equal attention. Create a list of all people you need to complete this process with for later.

- **Practice the forgiveness affirmation and the "I love myself" mantra.** Review these regularly. Post them at the beginning of your journal with the other key items to review for at least two weeks. Consider putting a reminder in your bathroom, such as a Post-it note or a string around your toothbrush that prompts you to say "I love myself," or, as you look into your eyes in the mirror, "I love you." Let go of any judgments that this technique is silly or any thoughts that it won't work, and just trust us that it does.

Be sure to visit the companion website at http://Day4.Solutions to review the additional supporting material, which includes the important topic of the stigma of alcohol addiction and how to overcome it, as well as information on a fantastic documentary film, *The Anonymous People*,[13] which examines the personal and societal value of recovery through the moving stories of people who are public about what their lives are like now that they're no longer using alcohol or drugs.

The Believe-in-Yourself Solution

Believing in Yourself and Believing It Is Possible

The thing always happens that you really believe in, and the be-lief in a thing makes it happen.

—FRANK LLOYD WRIGHT (1867–1959)
American architect[1]

If you are going to be successful in cutting back or quitting drinking and creating the life of your dreams, you first have to believe that it's possible—that you have what it takes to make it happen. Simply put, you have to believe in yourself. You can call this belief self-confidence, self-assurance, or self-esteem, and it consists of an absolute certainty that you have the ability and the inner means and skills to create whatever you want.

Believing in Yourself Is the Starting Point for All Achievement

I used alcohol as a friend, companion, and protector over the years. I made it into whatever it needed to be, whenever I needed it. I acted like it was the answer to my emptiness and loneliness, instead of realizing it was actually the source. In the end, it was all a lie that lasted well over a decade. Alcohol left me with self-doubt, guilt, shame, depression, anxiety, and fear. The 30-Day Sobriety Solution *helped me take off the mask I had been hiding behind, freeing me to finally thrive in sobriety.*

—BYRON

30-Day Graduate from Phoenix, Arizona

When you think about yourself, in particular about the "you" before you started this 30-Day program, what are the predominant thoughts or images that come to mind? Did you think of yourself as a drunk, alcoholic, or problem drinker? Did you think of yourself as someone who would never be able to figure out how to bring sobriety into your life in a positive way?

You have probably had thoughts similar to these, maybe quite frequently. Having a positive self-image is vital to your success. Psychology teaches us that a large portion of our behaviors are driven by how we see ourselves. When we have a healthy self-esteem, we take healthy risks, we are more goal-directed and driven, and we face fears head-on. When we have low self-esteem, we don't take risks, we stop when faced with the slightest roadblock, and we don't believe in ourselves.

Neuropsychologists say this is true because we spend our whole lives becoming conditioned.[2] Through a lifetime of events, our brain learns what to expect—whether it eventually happens that way or not. And because our brain expects that something will happen a certain way, we often create exactly what we anticipate.

To sum it up, believing in yourself is the starting point for all achievement, and today is all about making massive progress in shifting your beliefs about yourself and your ability to thrive in sobriety. When you have fully installed a new belief system of thriving in sobriety, your odds of accomplishing it are forever in your favor.

The Number One Reason You Are Not Sober Today

I felt like The 30-Day Sobriety Solution *was breathing life back into me. Every day, I learned new tools and techniques that actually worked. I was finally able to imagine a happy life without alcohol, something that had always escaped me. And one of the surprising results was that for the first time in my life, I felt like I was not alone, even though I was doing the program alone at home.*

—HANNAH

30-Day Graduate from Sydney, Australia

We have discussed this before, and certainly will again, *because it is that important.* If you have tried to cut back or quit drinking in the past and failed, part of the reason is due to the fact that on some level you don't believe it is possible. Maybe you don't believe it is possible for you to be sober *and* happy at the same time. Maybe you don't believe you can go more than a few days without craving alcohol to the point where you know you will give in. Maybe you don't believe you can be successful in life without alcohol. Or maybe you just don't believe in yourself. The bottom line is that if you don't believe you have what it takes to get sober, you won't. You must *choose* to believe in yourself!

When was the last time you wanted to do something but because you didn't believe that you could do it, you never even tried? Maybe a friend whom you don't consider as smart or talented as you accomplished that same goal, and you said to yourself, *If they can do it, I certainly can.* Then you actually went out and accomplished it.

What changed to make you do it? Maybe you learned something new. Maybe now you had a role model you could follow. However, the most likely answer is that you simply started to believe you were able to do it—you started to believe in yourself. And once you believe in yourself, everything changes. You overcome fear. You find solutions when you come up against challenges. And you naturally leverage your strengths and talents.

Does a Sober Vacation Seem Impossible?

People become really quite remarkable when they start thinking that they can do things. When they believe in themselves, they have the first secret of success.

—DR. NORMAN VINCENT PEALE (1898–1993)

Author of *The Power of Positive Thinking*

Can you imagine vacationing at a tropical resort in Mexico and not drinking? Diane certainly couldn't, yet that is exactly what she did after completing *The 30-Day Sobriety Solution*. And she actually had fun on the vacation, something she doubted would ever be possible. Diane started drinking the way most people start drinking—socially. Her entire social circle drank, and she believed that being an adult meant drinking alcohol. She also believed that being able to "hold your liquor" was an admirable trait. She was proud to excel at it.

Over the years, Diane had three daughters and managed to stay sober through her pregnancies; however, her two marriages were created and destroyed by alcohol. By the time she reached her midfifties, she was a widow and surrounded by people who drank heavily. She knew it was time for a change but wasn't quite ready—until she returned from a vacation and felt compelled to drink excessively. That night, she passed out, smashed her head on the floor, and almost bled to death.

Shortly after that, Diane found *The 30-Day Sobriety Solution* and felt like she had opened up a "supercharged Craftsman tool kit of things to use for sobriety." Within the first two weeks, amazing shifts started happening in her life. She was sober, and it wasn't a struggle. She connected with her children and used the tools she was learning to communicate more effectively with them, including helping them solve some challenges they were having. For the first time in her life, she said, "I don't see myself drinking. I don't see choosing feeling the way I felt before when I know I can feel like this."

Today she believes in herself like never before. She now has a sense of calmness and peace that previously eluded her. When she looks in the mirror, she sees a completely different image of herself—someone who is healthy and happy and has a radiant glow in her eyes.

In fact, when we recently reached out to Diane to see how she was doing, we found that she was able to return to "normal" drinking. Two full years after completing the program, Diane is able to have the occasional martini and not feel the urge to get drunk or go back to her previous excessive levels of drinking. She loves to do her own version of the 30-Day Reboot by abstaining for 30 days and reviewing her favorite solutions and exercises from the program.

Like many people in recovery, Diane found that some of her friendships had to change. Certain friends were not as funny or compatible when she removed drinking from the relationship. Today she is thriving in sobriety, spending time tutoring, volunteering for a local food bank and homeless shelter nonprofit organization, and maintaining wonderful relationships with her children.

Teetotalism

I don't drink. I've never tried a drug. It's just something that I genuinely don't have a desire for.

—BLAKE LIVELY

Award-winning actor[3]

The **first action step** today is simple and fun. It is all about shifting your beliefs so that you truly believe it is possible to thrive in sobriety. Whether your goal is to cut back or quit drinking, it is critical that you believe that *you* can do it. Part of this belief is also believing that sobriety will add joy and happiness to your life, not boredom and sadness.

By now it is highly likely that your beliefs about the benefits of *not* drinking have already shifted. With each sobriety success story and every quote from someone thriving in sobriety, you simply start to believe that changing your life is possible. And the powerful processes you have used this first week dramatically expand your self-awareness and help you let go of past guilt, anger, and resentments. To continue this progress, we are going to give you more examples of people who are actually thriving in sobriety. This brings us to the term *teetotalism*.

Teetotalism is the practice or promotion of complete abstinence from alcoholic beverages. And it will surprise you to know who is actually on this list. It includes past leaders of countries, rock stars, athletes, politicians, CEOs, and well-known TV personalities. People such as Jennifer Lopez, Jim Carrey, Warren Buffett, Natalie Portman, Brett Favre, Eddie Murphy, Diana Ross, Donald Trump, Muhammad Ali, and Albert Pujols. So take a minute right now to review this list on today's companion website: http://Day5.Solutions.

The next time you feel embarrassed about your drinking past, or you think that not drinking at a party makes you stand out negatively, remind yourself of this list of high-profile people. *You are not alone.* Whether you consider some of the people on this list role models or not, it is hard to ignore the accomplishments of these famous teetotalers.

The Placebo Effect

Hundreds of scientific studies have validated the placebo effect, or the benefit that results from a patient believing in a treatment that has no substance or active ingredients—in other words, a fake treatment. But the patient doesn't know the treatment is a sham. According to Dr. Irving Kirsch of the University of Connecticut, placebos are about 55 to 60 percent as effective as most active medications like aspirin and codeine for controlling pain.[4]

One study, for instance, tested thirteen people who were extremely allergic to poison ivy. Each person was rubbed with a harmless leaf on one arm and told it was poison ivy. Each was also rubbed on the other arm with poison ivy and told it was harmless. Interestingly, all thirteen people broke out in a rash where the *harmless* leaf was rubbed, whereas only two had a reaction to the poison ivy.[5]

In another study, surgeons performed arthroscopic knee surgery on patients with osteoarthritis, but only two-thirds actually underwent surgery. One-third of the patients' surgeries were faked. Their surgeons made the incisions but did nothing to repair the knees. All of the participants were aware that they might receive the placebo surgery, but no one was told if they'd actually received it until after the study was over. Two years after the surgery, the patients who had undergone the placebo surgery reported the same amount of relief as the patients who underwent the actual operation. Their brains had expected that "surgery" would improve the knee, so it did.[6]

In another story from early investigations into the placebo effect, in 1957 a patient was diagnosed with advanced cancer of the lymph nodes and had painful cancerous tumors throughout his body. "Mr. Wright" was given only a short time to live, but he had heard of an alternative cancer treatment whose creator claimed it worked on people as well as on animals, and begged to receive it. His own physician, after much persuasion, finally agreed to administer it. The patient received an injection on Friday afternoon, and by the following Monday, his tumors had shrunk by half. Ten days later, after further treatment, doctors could find no trace of cancer, and the patient was released from the hospital. Interestingly, no other cancer patients who received the treatment showed any improvement.

Two months later, however, Mr. Wright read reports that the treatment was quackery. He suffered a relapse immediately, with the tumors returning. His physician, to try to buy him more time, told him that a new, much stronger version of the drug had been developed, and the patient agreed to have another injection. However, his physician did *not* have a new version of the drug, which had been thoroughly disproved, and so he gave Mr. Wright an injection of distilled water. The injection worked again—the patient believed he had received an effective cancer treatment, and his tumors disappeared.

Two more months passed, and the patient read a definitive report that the treatment was ineffective. Mr. Wright died two days later.[7]

There is no question that your beliefs have a dramatic impact on your life. The placebo effect comes down to the power of expecting an outcome—really believing in it. When you expect results, your beliefs are in accordance with those expectations, and your thoughts, feelings, and actions align with them as well. When you believe it is possible to thrive in sobriety, and when you believe in yourself, sobriety will become a reality for you.

The Choice of What to Believe Is Up to You

You have to give up "I can't." The phrase "I can't" is the most powerful force of negation in the human psyche.

—PAUL R. SCHEELE

Cofounder of Learning Strategies Corporation, author of *Genius Code*

If you are going to thrive in sobriety, you have to stop saying "I can't" and all of its relatives, such as "I wish I were able to." When you say "I can't," these two disempowering words actually make you weaker. We use a technique called muscle testing to test the effect of thoughts on physical strength. A person extends an arm as he says a positive or negative phrase. A tester pushes down on the arm. Invariably, when the tester pushes down on the arm after the person says something negative, like "I can't sing," he *always* tests weaker. When he says something positive, such as "I can sing," as the tester pushes down on the arm, he always tests stronger.

This is your **second action step** today. We want you to test this out, though, over the course of this program. Every time you catch yourself using the word *can't*, rephrase the sentence. For example, if you were to think, *I can't quit drinking, because then I won't be happy*, you can simply shift to *I can stop drinking, and I am excited to learn how to be sober and happy*. We know it can be challenging to even catch yourself using this word at first, so one effective option is to recruit a friend, coworker, or spouse as a partner. You can both agree to point out to each other when you use the word *can't*.

We Believe in You

You have to believe in yourself when no one else does. That's what makes you a winner.

—VENUS WILLIAMS
Tennis champion

If having others believe in you was a requirement for sobriety, most of us would still be drinking excessively today. It is entirely possible that everyone around you gave up believing that you would ever get sober or permanently cut back your drinking. If you tried to cut back or quit in the past and made declarations to others about how you were going to change, only to go back to the way you were (or even worse), it is fair to assume that the people around you will stop believing in you. *That is okay!*

What they think about you has no impact on your ability to succeed. Too often we go through life letting the opinions of others hold us back. It doesn't matter what has happened up to this point in your life—the fact that you are still here and still reading says all we need to know.

We believe in you! Nothing in this book is too advanced or hard for you or anyone to do. It simply takes some dedication, commitment, and perseverance, which you have already demonstrated by getting this far.

If you have any people in your life who doubt your ability to cut back or quit drinking, decide this instant that you are not going to give their opinion any power. In fact, let their doubt fuel your desire to demonstrate how wrong they are.

Why Did I Wait So Long?

At the worst of it, I no longer wanted to drink and no longer wanted to be sober, either. I felt evicted from life. At the start of the road back, I just tried to believe the people who said that things would get better if I gave them time to do so. And I never stopped writing.

—STEPHEN KING[8]

People we coach through *The 30-Day Sobriety Solution* inevitably tell us, "I wish I hadn't waited so long to do this." They often say this after a breakthrough that makes them realize that being sober and happy is not as challenging as they had thought it was. *Don't worry, this is a normal feeling.*

In yesterday's solution, Dave shared his story about the time he went to the bar and discussed his worrisome blood work results with Bryan, who assured him that he was fine and had "nothing to worry about." That was exactly what Dave wanted to hear, but he didn't realize then that Bryan was giving him a perfect example of "confirmation bias." Confirmation bias is when you get the answer you *want* to a question, and you stop looking for other input. Most likely, you have practiced this. For example, you have a concern or worry, so you go to the internet and search for information. The first time you read something that validates that you have nothing to worry about, you stop looking, regardless of the source.

Confirmation bias is likely something that led you to wait before you even picked up a book like this. Dave wanted to deny the health impact of his drinking, so he listened to advice from someone who he knew was a heavy drinker—and a doctor, no less!

So, the **third action step** for today is to answer this question in your journal: *Where have you used confirmation bias to hold you back?* Here's how one 30-Day Graduate explained his experience with confirmation bias:

> There were moments in *The 30-Day Sobriety Solution* that led to incredible clarity, and one of those for me was the concept of "confirmation bias." It was clear that despite all my education and knowledge about addiction, when it came to looking in the mirror, I only let in the information that confirmed I didn't have a problem. Once I changed this, everything started changing.

Another example might include searching online for "proof" that drinking red wine is healthy, even if you are drinking four or five glasses a night. Or you're always looking for validation that cutting back is actually possible for you, even though you drink a fifth of liquor a day. Most qualified experts would agree that drinking four glasses of red wine a day is *never* healthy, and that going from a fifth-a-day drinker to a "normal" drinker is not possible. As you continue your journey to sobriety, be sure to recognize when you are *looking for the answer you want to hear rather than really seeking out the truth*.

To end the day on an inspirational note, and to build your believing-in-yourself muscles, we want to share some stories regarding supersuccessful people and what they had to overcome to create success.[9] While their stories may not involve overcoming problem drinking, they did have to overcome tremendous challenges.

- Walt Disney, the founder of Disney World, was fired by a newspaper editor because he "lacked imagination and had no good ideas." He was told by MGM studios that the idea to put a giant mouse on the screen (Mickey Mouse) would terrify women.

- J. K. Rowling, billionaire author of the *Harry Potter* series, was a divorced single mother on welfare while writing the first book in the series, which was rejected by twelve publishers. She was told not to quit her day job.
- Oprah Winfrey was told she was "unfit for TV" and fired from her job as coanchor on a local news station.
- Sidney Poitier, Oscar-winning actor, was told by a casting director, "Why don't you stop wasting people's time and go out and become a dishwasher or something?"
- Steven Spielberg, one of the most successful directors in Hollywood, was rejected from the University of Southern California School of Theater, Film and Television three times.
- The Beatles, looking for a record deal in 1962, were turned down by Decca Records, which said, "We don't like their sound, and guitar music is on the way out. They have no future in show business."
- Elvis Presley was fired by the manager of the Grand Ole Opry, who told him, "You ain't goin' nowhere, son. You ought to go back to drivin' a truck."
- Ronald Reagan, the fortieth president of the United States, didn't take office until one month before his seventieth birthday.

It is never too late, regardless of your age, how many setbacks you have had, or your drinking history—you, too, can overcome almost any obstacle life throws at you and live the life of your dreams.

Day 5 Action Steps

You can be anything you want to be, if only you believe with sufficient conviction and act in accordance with your faith; for whatever the mind can conceive and believe, the mind can achieve.

—NAPOLEON HILL

The Believe-in-Yourself Solution can be summed up in three short sentences:

Believe it is possible. Believe in yourself. Go for it!

When Jack wrote *The Success Principles,* he interviewed hundreds of people. Almost all of them reflected that they weren't the most gifted or talented in their fields, but they chose to believe that anything was possible. They studied, practiced, and worked harder than the competition, and that's how they got to where they are today.

It really is that simple. When you decide what you want, believe it is possible, believe in yourself, and then work hard to get it, you take 100% control of your destiny. Not only does cutting back or quitting drinking become easier to achieve, but you'll also start to see what you want in the rest of your life falling into place right alongside it. Your dreams really do start coming true.

Along with completing these action steps, we want to remind you that you should be writing in your journal every day, even if you limit it to just a few bullet points.

- **Review the list of famous teetotalers.** If you haven't done so already, visit the companion website and review the list of teetotalers.

- **Stop using the word *can't*.** Remove the word *can't* from your vocabulary. Instead, substitute more empowering words and phrases. For example, if you find yourself saying, "I can't go to a party and have only a couple of drinks," change it to "I can find ways to have a ton of fun at this party and still not drink, or I can have only two drinks." Consider doing this with a friend or loved one you regularly spend time with, so you can point out to each other when you hear the word *can't*.

- **Write down examples of using confirmation bias with your drinking.** Think about times in the past you have used confirmation bias to avoid dealing with your drinking. Maybe you spent time with people who drank more than you, so you could believe your drinking wasn't an issue. Or maybe you exercise, eat well, and have healthy blood work in spite of excessive drinking, so you tell yourself that you must not have a problem.

On the companion website, you will learn more about the science behind the placebo effect and find the list of famous teetotalers, as well as some other great resources. Go to http://Day5.Solutions.

The Outcome Solution

*The Power of an Outcome-Focused,
Purpose-Driven, Goal-Setting Strategy*

*Man is a goal-seeking animal. His life only has meaning if he is
reaching out and striving for his goals.*

—ARISTOTLE (384–322 BC)

Greek philosopher

You have committed 100% to thriving in sobriety, determined your 30-Day Vision, and learned how to forgive yourself and believe in yourself. Now you are ready to leverage the incredible power of goal setting.

The human brain is designed as "a goal-seeking organism."[1] Once you set a specific and measurable goal, your subconscious mind will work day and night to achieve it. This is true for any goal in your life, including cutting back drinking, quitting drinking, or simply completing the 30-Day Reboot.

The Test

*I got sober. I stopped killing myself with alcohol. I began to think,
Wait a minute—if I can stop doing this, what are the possibilities?
And slowly it dawned on me that it was maybe worth the risk.*

—CRAIG FERGUSON

Talk-show host and author of *American on Purpose*

Before we jump into goal setting, let's take a moment to address some common experiences and challenges that often come up during the first week, especially after you've stopped drinking. In every problem drinker, there live two "people" or identities—the thriving sober person and the problem-drinker person. This week, you have been empowering your identification with the sober person and disempowering your identification with the problem drinker, which ultimately leads to an internal conflict. Before this program, the problem drinker part of you usually "won," and you would drink. Now that is no longer the case. However, sometimes the problem drinker part will essentially fight for its life. That part of you is afraid of disappearing after being in control for so many years, and this can lead to a temporary increase in the desire to drink. For now, just know that if you are actually experiencing an increased desire to drink, it is normal—and most importantly, short lived!

Another experience during the first six days is that "when it rains, it pours." You start making these wonderful changes in your life, and then you are suddenly faced with more challenges, including relationship issues, changes in your health, financial setbacks, work-related stresses, or a combination. For our clients on the cusp of making a breakthrough change in their life, one that will have positive ripple effects all around them, it's almost as if they're being tested one last time. If they pass this test, their lives change forever. If they don't, their old habits and self-defeating behaviors come back as strong as ever.

Trust us: if you are experiencing this, it means you are on the doorstep of something amazing, and all you need to do is push through. The truly wonderful life that awaits you on the other side is worth the effort and the discipline.

And remember, the initial desire to drink is often very intense when it is first triggered—say, by the smell of stale beer in a bar or the sight of your favorite liquor store—but that intensity usually drops significantly in as little as fifteen seconds. If you feel these urges, don't fight them. Simply accept that you are experiencing them and take a few deep breaths. This alone is often enough to move you beyond the initial temptation. If the deep breaths aren't effective enough, and you feel you need more reinforcement, we recommend you skip ahead to the tapping exercise, which you will find on Day 13 in the Tapping Solution.

The Power of Goal Setting

If you want to be happy, set a goal that commands your thoughts, liberates your energy, and inspires your hopes.

—ANDREW CARNEGIE (1835–1919)
American industrialist and philanthropist

Goal setting is one of the most powerful tools at your disposal. Virtually every successful coach, trainer, and motivational expert teaches goal setting as a key component of creating a successful life.

Surprisingly, goal setting is underutilized in most recovery programs. The Outcome Solution addresses this oversight by teaching you the right techniques for goal setting, so that you actually get the results you desire. Today you will learn how to use an outcome-focused, purpose-driven method of goal setting to ensure that the 30-Day Thriving-in-Sobriety Vision you wrote on Day 2 in the Purpose Solution becomes a reality.

The Outcome Solution not only applies to accelerating your achieving your goal to cut back or quit drinking, but can also be used to set and accomplish goals in every area of your life, including losing weight, starting a new career, achieving financial freedom, making new friends, finding true love, excelling at sports, and mastering a new hobby.

The Short-Term Trap

I just realized that drinking was counterproductive to what I was trying to do. Acting is very difficult in weird ways. You'd have to get to class by 8:00 a.m., work all day, rehearse all night, and it's not really good to do when you're hungover. I'd wanted to be an actress my whole life, that was my goal, that was all I cared about. Something had to go, so I chose drinking to go. Has it been difficult? Oh yeah. Sometimes it would be nice to just have some red wine with dinner, but it's not worth the risk. I have a great life, a great situation. Why would I want to risk self-destructive behavior?

—KRISTIN DAVIS

Actor who has been sober for over twenty years[2]

Satisfying your short-term desires is often in conflict with accomplishing your long-term goals. This is one of the most important concepts we want you to take away from the Outcome Solution. Today you will identify and commit to at least three specific goals that, over time, will have a profoundly positive impact on your life—and that you can accomplish only through the choice to stay sober.

And let's be honest—it isn't easy to stay sober when you are used to drinking frequently. The temptation to satisfy your short-term desire to drink can feel overwhelming, but you will be less willing to give in to that temptation when you clearly know that doing so undermines achievement of your longer-term goals.

Take a second and think back to the greatest accomplishments in your life. Now ask yourself, *What sacrifices did I have to make, especially in the short term, to create that success?* Maybe you wanted to get an A in a class in school, make a sports team, break a record, become the top salesperson in your company, save money for a car, lose weight, get fit, perform in a play, create a rock band, become a cheerleader, or raise money for a favorite cause. Whatever it was, most likely you had to make some short-term sacrifices—working hard, getting up early, staying up late, giving up desserts, and saying no to distractions like television, video games, and socializing.

The question now is: *Are you willing to forgo the short-term satisfaction that drinking brings to ensure the longer-term happiness and fulfillment you desire in your life?* Every time you feel overwhelmed by the desire to drink, ask yourself that question. Consider the costs you will face from choosing to drink, in both the short term and the long term, and the benefits you will gain by choosing not to drink, especially in the long term.

The Power of Positive Pressure

The pursuit of a goal brings order in awareness because a person must concentrate attention on the task at hand and momentarily forget everything else. These periods of struggling to overcome challenges are what people find to be the most enjoyable of their lives. . . . By stretching skills, by reaching toward higher challenges, such a person becomes an increasingly extraordinary individual.

—MIHALY CSIKSZENTMIHALYI

Psychologist and author of *Flow: The Psychology of Optimal Experience*[3]

In his book *Eat That Frog!: 21 Great Ways to Stop Procrastinating and Get More Done in Less Time*, Brian Tracy, one of America's leading authorities on the development of human potential and personal effectiveness, writes: "Only about 3 percent of adults have clear, written goals. These people accomplish five and ten times as much as people of equal or better education and ability but who, for whatever reason, have never taken the time to write out exactly what they want."[4]

As we said on Day 1 in the 100% Solution, your destiny is the consequences of your daily decisions. Along with your purpose and your beliefs, your goals will help you set the standards for these daily decisions. Remember, in every situation, there are only two choices. Your decision will either take you toward what you want or take you away from what you want. So always ask yourself, *Is this action going to take me toward my goal or away from my goal?*

Setting a goal means that you acknowledge, in your conscious and subconscious minds, that where you are is not where you want to be. Simply put, having goals creates positive pressure in your life.[5] In virtually every study, written, time-bound goals are a key component of attaining high performance. Remember back to Day 3, the Pendulum Solution, where we shared with you the study of patients recovering from hip and knee surgeries, and how setting goals for their recovery helped them walk almost twice as fast as those that did not set goals. The same principle applies to you and your goal of thriving in sobriety.

SMART Goals

You want to set a goal that is big enough that in the process of achieving it you become someone worth becoming.

—JIM ROHN (1930–2009)
Author of *The Art of Exceptional Living*

Zig Ziglar, one of the all-time great motivational speakers, once said, "What you get by achieving your goals is not as important as what you become by achieving your goals."[6] As you move toward achieving your goals, you become the person you were meant to be—a healthy, vibrant, passionate, successful person who doesn't need alcohol to get through the day or the weekend. You become a person who is a great role model to peers, friends, family, and coworkers. A person who no longer needs to drink to fit in, have fun, or feel successful.

Here are some basic guidelines for writing your goals that will significantly improve your success in achieving them. A popular acronym used to remember the criteria for setting goals effectively is SMART, which is commonly attributed to the work of management consultant Peter Drucker.

- **Specific**—Who, what, and where. Be as specific as possible.
- **Measurable**—The criteria for measuring your goal should be clear to you and others.
- **Attainable**—The goal should stretch you while still being attainable.
- **Realistic**—You should be willing and able to achieve the goal. It needs to be believable.
- **Time-bound**—The goal should be bound to a specific time frame. By what specific date and time will you achieve it?[7]

In short, you have to state specifically *how much* and *by when* in a way that an outside observer could verify that you have achieved it.

While this is just a brief overview of the key attributes of setting a SMART goal, you can find more information on setting your SMART goals on today's companion website.

Goals and Thriving in Sobriety

In the past, I always connected drinking to immediate gratification, not realizing I was only trying to fill a void in my life. Now I clearly see that over time drinking guarantees I will always feel empty inside, where sobriety opens up the possibility to experience true happiness, joy, and fulfillment.

—SUSAN

30-Day Graduate from Philadelphia, Pennsylvania

On Day 2 we asked you to create a 30-Day Vision Statement for yourself. If for any reason you didn't do this, stop and go back and do it now. This book is not like a novel you simply read. It's a program you *do*. These solutions are all important, and they are designed strategically to build on one another, leading to a powerful transformation in just 30 days. *The solutions always work for you if you always work the solutions.* But if you skip over reading the content or doing the exercises, you are cheating yourself of the opportunity to experience the full power of this program.

It is important to write down your goals because they will support you as you take the steps to fulfill your life purpose—something we will talk about more on Day 29. Today, we are going to work with the 30-Day Vision Statement.

Let's say that your 30-Day Vision Statement is "Every day I wake up excited, vibrant, and passionate about living a meaningful and fulfilling sober life." Some SMART goals that support your vision might include the following:

- I will have stayed sober for 30 days in a row by January 31, [year], at midnight.
- Every night by 10:00 p.m., I will have completed that day's reading assignment for *The 30-Day Sobriety Solution*, finished that day's action steps, and spent five minutes or more writing in my private journal until I have completed the program by 11:00 p.m. on April 21, [year].
- After I have immersed myself fully in all of the content and solutions in *The 30-Day Sobriety Solution*, I will have manifested passion, purpose, and 30 days of continuous sobriety in my life by July 15, [year], at 5:00 p.m.
- I will be a "normal drinker," thriving in life with a take-it-or-leave-it attitude toward drinking, by November 1, [year], at 7:00 p.m.
- I will have an amazing group of friends that are supportive of my sobriety, and regularly find creative, healthy, and fun activities to do that make thriving in sobriety a reality in my life, by January 31, [year], at 9:00 a.m.

Each of these goals, in one way or another, supports your 30-Day

Vision Statement and incorporates the SMART goal-setting recommendations. These goals are written from the perspective of what you want, *not* what you don't want. One of the most ineffective and self-destructive phrases you could use when setting your goals is "quit drinking" or "cut back drinking." The reason is that the subconscious mind does not hear negative words like *no, not, never, don't, stop,* or *quit.* What it hears is the word *drinking.* It then creates an image of drinking, which it then wants to fulfill through the action of drinking. If you say, "I am not thinking of a tiger," what image comes to mind? A tiger. So if you don't want to think of tigers, you'd say, "I am thinking about airplanes or a sunset in Hawaii"— anything but tigers.

Your **first action step** today is to start writing the goals that will support your 30-Day Thriving-in-Sobriety Vision. Feel free to use our examples or create ones that speak more powerfully to you. In any case, remember that right now we are focused on one key vision— thriving in sobriety—and you should write down three or more goals that support this.

At least one goal should be similar to the first four examples we gave, but you can also write one or two other goals, such as what your career, friends, family, health, and love life might look like when you are thriving in sobriety. These should not be what you consider big goals outside of thriving in sobriety, like becoming the president of your company or going on an African safari; when you focus on accomplishing too many big goals at once, you often end up failing at all of them. By concentrating on this one main goal of thriving in sobriety, you set yourself up for long-term success. This strategy of focusing on three goals that support this one main goal works! Time and time again, we see our clients get to the end of these 30 days having fully accomplished their goal of thriving in sobriety, and then go on to manifest other achievements in virtually every area of their lives.

How Military Veteran James Embraced Goals

I am still amazed, looking back on the way I was when I first started The 30-Day Sobriety Solution, *to see how far I've come. And all without Alcoholics Anonymous, without inpatient or outpatient rehabilitation, and even without anybody to cheer me on. It is truly amazing, and I just want to thank you for* The 30-Day Sobriety Solution. *It has given me everything I need to thrive in sobriety.*

—JAMES
30-Day Graduate from Istanbul, Turkey

James is one of our heroes. When he was fresh out of high school, he knew he wanted to serve his country, so he joined the United States Air Force. James was surprised by his own success in this new environment, and was recruited by a highly selective, prestigious unit in the air force. As he served his country, his pride and self-worth reached an all-time high. When it came time for James to retire, at first he was excited about having new career opportunities, and he had a great sense of accomplishment from his military career. But he hadn't realized how much of his identity and self-worth were tied to his air force career, and before long, even though he became successful in his new job, drinking had become a nightly routine.

By the time James reached his early fifties, he was shocked to realize he had been drinking excessively for thirteen years. Somehow he believed, like many military retirees, that "the best days of my life were in the past." And because his postmilitary career required frequent traveling and gave him a lot of autonomy, he couldn't imagine what it would be like to travel sober.

James tried Alcoholics Anonymous and other recovery options that didn't work for him, but when he came across *The 30-Day Sobriety Solution*, he recognized some of the same principles and techniques that had helped him be successful in the military and his current career. When he completed the program, he told us, "The program took every positive characteristic and every personal strength I have succeeded with in the past, improved them, and applied them in positive ways to live a sober and happy life."

Because so many of the 30-Day solutions helped James create breakthroughs, he was surprised that he had never considered applying the simple act of goal setting to his sobriety. After all, in the air force and his later career, setting and accomplishing goals was a fundamental technique he used to create success. As he continued to focus on his vision of thriving in sobriety and setting supporting goals to accomplish this, his life changed. James said, "Your program absolutely cured me. That's the best way to put it. The thought of drinking might enter my mind—rarely—just like any other thought would, but there was an instantaneous reaction, and in less than a second, I was thinking, *Why in the world would I ever do that?* And that's the end of it—no internal debate."

James was sober for almost a year before he decided to experiment with drinking again. He quickly realized that being a "normal drinker" was not something that would work in his life, so he decided to go through *The 30-Day Sobriety Solution* a second time. Once again, he discovered that he was able to have new insights and breakthroughs. Today he is truly thriving in sobriety, and recently emailed, "I'm happier than I've ever been in my whole life."

Stupid Juice

One day, while James was at a restaurant with a friend who was drinking, he looked at his friend's beer and internally referred to his beer as "stupid juice." It surprised him, as he had never used that phrase before, and it led to a profound realization:

Alcohol makes you do stupid things. You make stupid decisions, say inappropriate things, and offend people. The more you drink, the dumber you get. And what's really crazy about it is that you don't realize how stupid you are. And you keep drinking more of it and become stupider and stupider. It wears off, and the next day you look back and feel stupid because of the things you did.

Anytime that James thought of drinking or heard a radio commercial for one of his favorite drinks, he just referred to it as "stupid juice," and any desire he had to drink vanished. He realized that, over the years, the multimillion-dollar advertising campaigns for his favorite liquors had created strong associations with pleasure, freedom, and "good times." As James put it, "You might say I created my own brand image for alcohol, one that was personal to me. And believe me, there's no pleasure attached to it."

We recommend that you try out this powerful way to attach "pain" to the idea of drinking.

Why You Set Goals and Sometimes Nothing Happens

If you are bored with life, if you don't get up every morning with a burning desire to do things—you don't have enough goals.

—LOU HOLTZ

Have you ever set a goal that you failed to achieve? You're not alone. Even though we often want something better, we often fail to produce it. Here are a few of the most common reasons.

- You are not fully committed to the goal and attempt to accomplish it only if it's convenient.
- You don't have a big enough reason *why*—why it will be painful not to accomplish the goal and why it will be pleasurable and rewarding to accomplish it.

- You don't feel you deserve to achieve the goal—that you are not worthy or good enough.
- You don't believe it's possible—or you believe it is possible only for someone else.
- You are somehow different—a special case.
- You don't know what to do or how to go about it—you don't know whom to ask, or you are too proud or scared to ask.

Can you relate to any of these reasons? Can you identify any of these reasons behind past goals you failed to accomplish? You can set all the goals in the world and have every intention of accomplishing them, but if you haven't addressed these internal roadblocks, you will fail. That is the reason the Outcome Solution is on Day 6 and not on Day 1 or 2. Everything in *The 30-Day Sobriety Solution* before today has set you up for success in setting and accomplishing your goals. And everything that follows will reinforce and build on today's solution, including removing the blocks and limiting beliefs listed above.

On Day 1, the 100% Solution, you committed fully to let go of blaming and complaining. On Day 2, the Purpose Solution, you created a 30-Day Vision for your life and a powerful emotional connection to that vision to help keep you moving forward despite obstacles and challenges that will inevitably come up. On Day 3 in the Pendulum Solution you leveraged and applied the power of pain and pleasure in your life, so that the thought of drinking equals pain and the thought of sobriety equals ultimate joy and pleasure. On Day 4 in the Forgiveness Solution you forgave others—and most importantly—yourself, so that you could accept the love and sobriety you deserve in your life. On Day 5 in the Believe-in-Yourself Solution you chose to shift your beliefs and believe in the possibility of living in sobriety *and* to believe that you *can* do it.

That is why the goals you set today will be unlike any goals you have ever set. You have set yourself up for success, and the "magic" of this program is that each day, each solution, builds one upon the other to create massive positive change in just 30 days.

Using Your New Goals

Goals. There's no telling what you can do when you get inspired by them. There's no telling what you can do when you believe in them. There's no telling what will happen when you act upon them.

—JIM ROHN

Once you've written down your goals, your **second action step** is to review your list at least two to three times a day, which will activate the power of your subconscious mind. If you are in an appropriate place, read your goals one at a time *out loud with passion and enthusiasm*. Otherwise read them silently. After you read each goal, close your eyes and picture each goal in your mind as if you had already achieved it, and then visualize what your life will look like when you accomplish your thriving-in-sobriety vision. Fill in as many details as you can. Then take a minute to feel, as deeply as you can, everything you would feel if you had already accomplished this vision. It doesn't matter if your visualization appears fuzzy or in high definition, as long as you make the effort to picture it as best you can.

If you do this as a daily discipline, it will activate what psychologists refer to as "structural tension"[8] in your brain, which naturally wants to reconcile that tension between your vision and your current reality. By constantly repeating your goals and visualizing them as already accomplished, you will increase the structural tension, which your mind will work to resolve by making your vision come true. It does this by strengthening your motivation, boosting your creativity, and opening up your awareness to all the people, resources, and things around you that are there to help you attain your one main goal of thriving in sobriety, but that you may not have seen as accessible before.

You can use creative ways to constantly review your goals. For example, Jack puts his on three-by-five-inch index cards and keeps them by his bed to review every morning and evening. He also places his most important goal in his wallet where his driver's license would normally appear through the little plastic window, so he sees it every time he opens his wallet. Find something that works for you, so you are forced to habitually review your goals along with your 30-Day Thriving-in-Sobriety Vision. Also, we know these might be private, so find a way that protects your privacy while still enabling you to review them, such as keeping the list on your tablet or smartphone. This kind of repetition creates greater clarity, focus, and motivation to act, all of which will accelerate the accomplishment of your goals.

Day 6 Action Steps

Getting sober was one of the three pivotal events in my life, along with becoming an actor and having a child.

—GARY OLDMAN

Actor

The Outcome Solution is all about creating an outcome-focused, purpose-driven, goal-setting, and reinforcement strategy to ensure that your thriving-in-sobriety vision becomes a reality in your life.

- **Write down three goals that support your 30-Day Thriving-in-Sobriety Vision Statement from Day 2.** Write these goals following the SMART guidelines and examples we gave, without using the words "quitting drinking" or "cutting back drinking."

- **Determine a plan to review these goals, along with your vision, at least two times a day.** Figure out a daily strategy for reviewing your goals. Read them (out loud when possible), visualize having accomplished them, and create the feelings you would feel if you had already accomplished them. *Feeling the feelings is key.*

- **Optional: review the "new you" brainstorming notes from Day 2.** To help you follow through, review what you wrote regarding the solutions from Day 2. This will remind you what you stand to gain by accomplishing these goals.

As always, you can visit the companion website for today's solution, where we have included more studies and strategies to supercharge your goals and underline the importance of having intrinsic goals, at http://Day6.Solutions.

The Review Day and Bonus Solution

*Embracing the Power of Repetition
to Master the Basics*

*Any idea, plan, or purpose may be placed in the mind through
repetition of thought.*

—NAPOLEON HILL

Congratulations! You have completed Phase I, "Mastering the Absolute Basics to Get from Where You Are to Where You Want to Be." Take a minute and celebrate your dedication. As Babe Ruth used to say, "It's hard to beat a person who never gives up." And by completing Phase I, you have proven that you are committed to doing the work to get from where you are to where you want to be.

Days 7, 14, 21, and 28 are review days. The significance of repetition in your life has been enormous. *Repetition helped create your drinking problem; now it will help create your solution.* Before moving on to Phase II, please trust us and make that little extra investment of time right now; the rewards that you will gain from doing this will far exceed the amount of time it takes. And don't worry, we never give you additional action steps on the review days.

In Phase I you learned why a 100% commitment is critical to your success in *The 30-Day Sobriety Solution*, and you wrote a 30-

Day Thriving-in-Sobriety Vision Statement to accelerate your desire to get and stay sober. You learned about the law of duality and the role of pain and pleasure in your life, and why embracing forgiveness and letting go of guilt and shame are essential to your happiness. You explored the power of believing in yourself, and learned a proven process for writing empowering and exciting goals. On the companion website, we review each of these key concepts further, as well as share a special video from us.

You will also find access to your first bonus solution, the Social Solution, which covers the top 11 excuses you can use when you want to not drink and not feel judged in any social situation. If you are planning to attend a party or a social event where people will be drinking, this is a must-read for you. You will find all of this on the companion website at http://Day7.Solutions.

But before you visit the website, we have some information that we know you will find important as you are completing Phase I.

The Foggy Brain

I hated every minute of training, but I said, "Don't quit. Suffer now and live the rest of your life as a champion."

—MUHAMMAD ALI

World champion heavyweight boxer

There is a common expectation that people have in early sobriety. After a few days or weeks of continuous sobriety, people tend to believe that they should feel great physically—have more energy, feel clearheaded, and be more alert. If you were drinking three to four glasses of wine a night or were the weekend-warrior type drinker, then this might be true. However, if you fall into the heavier-drinking category, you might experience "foggy brain"— where your energy is low and you are unable to think clearly. It can feel like you're driving down a curvy road on a foggy night—

no matter how hard you concentrate on the road ahead, you struggle to see it clearly.

Please know that this can be completely normal at this stage. In fact, you may also find yourself feeling more irritable and becoming angry and frustrated more easily.

Remember, you are taking away an emotional and physical coping mechanism, and your body and mind need time to adjust. You are making a dramatic change in your life. If you were drinking heavily, your brain almost certainly stopped producing natural chemicals (like the neurotransmitters dopamine and serotonin) that are key to creating a good mood. But don't worry; the human body is amazing at self-healing. After some time, your body *will* resolve this imbalance on its own, and as that happens, your brain fog will lift and your mood will improve. If you would like to expedite this process, we have some basic nutritional recommendations.

Serotonin and Dopamine

I don't drink anymore. I don't want to get old, and drinking really makes you old. I just got fed up with feeling slightly groggy in the morning when I went out and had too many drinks. Now I can go out until two or three in the morning and leap out of bed the next day and feel great.

—JEMIMA FRENCH
Fashion designer[1]

Dopamine and serotonin have played critical roles in your drinking. Sometimes referred to as the "happiness hormone," serotonin helps regulate your mood and prevent depression. Dopamine also affects your mood, the brain's reward and pleasure centers, and your ability to focus.[2] Drinking generally stimulates the release of these brain chemicals, so you feel good at first. You might have a feeling of euphoria, well-being, and reward, but, over time, heavy drinking will deplete the amounts of dopamine and serotonin, leading to a low or depressed mood. By drinking often, you become conditioned to believe that alcohol will improve your mood, even though it no longer does so.[3]

This explains why many problem drinkers say that drinking eventually "stopped working." Even though you have stopped drinking, your brain's production of serotonin and dopamine does not immediately return to normal levels. In fact, some studies show that your brain may need up to 90 days—and in some cases, even longer—to return to normal levels of dopamine and serotonin production.[4] During this time, your desire to drink in order to reexperience that good feeling can be heightened.

However, there are other natural and healthy ways to stimulate the brain's production of serotonin and dopamine. We will cover many of them throughout the rest of this program, but here are some you can start today. We have consulted several nutritional experts to find out which foods and nutritional supplements provide the greatest support for an easier journey, but we recommend that you consult your own doctor or health care professional before adding supplements to your diet. We will cover this topic in more depth on Day 25 in the Mind and Body Solution. Also, for supplement recommendations, we like to visit Consumer Lab's website (www.consumerlab.com). This independent lab has been testing supplements since 1999, and posts its results—much like a *Consumer Reports* of the unregulated dietary supplement industry.

- **GABA supplements.** Gamma-aminobutyric acid (GABA) acts as a serotonin reuptake inhibitor (it alters the balance of serotonin in the brain, often improving mood) and has often been used in early sobriety to help alleviate withdrawal. But do not take GABA supplements while drinking. You can also get GABA naturally from cherry tomatoes, shrimp, bananas, and kefir (a drink that contains probiotics—the "good" bacteria that help keep your digestive system healthy).
- **Omega-3 fats.** Omega-3s raise the brain's dopamine level by 40

percent, which increases alertness, focus, and mood. Fish is your best source, specifically wild-caught (not farm-raised) salmon, sardines, herring, anchovies, and mackerel. You can either eat two servings per week or take 2 grams of omega-3 fish oil with eicosapentaenoic acid (EPA) and docosahexaenoic acid (DHA) per day. EPA and DHA are two types of omega-3 fatty acids that are found in fish and fish-oil products.

The Sugar Connection

Not only do you have a dependency on alcohol, but also you have a dependency on sugar, because alcohol is essentially fermented sugar. Sugar itself is extremely hard on your system and dangerous to your health, but we have found that for most people, quitting drinking while also dramatically cutting back on sugar is a recipe for failure, so generally we don't recommend it this early in sobriety. Regardless, we would be remiss not to address this topic and give some basic advice, because changing your diet can curb alcohol cravings. We will revisit and elaborate on this topic in Day 25.

The overall goal is to keep the amount of glucose found in the blood (your blood sugar levels) stable, which will help curb cravings for alcohol. Here are seven tips to help maintain stable blood sugar:

1. Never go hungry.
2. Eat at least every five hours.
3. Eat three healthy meals a day.
4. Always eat breakfast.
5. Never skip meals.
6. Ideally, get your vitamins and nutrients from food rather than supplements.
7. Fruit is a great alternative to candy bars and sweets to satiate sugar cravings.[5]

On today's companion website, we have included a recipe for a wonderful alcohol detox smoothie you might want to try. Last, we want to remind you that by abstaining from alcohol, you are perhaps making one of the biggest changes to your diet in years or even decades. Your goal is to quit drinking, and many of our clients simply find it easier if they allow themselves to have some sweets during the transition phase, because by the end of *The 30-Day Sobriety Solution*, you will be far better prepared to embrace a more comprehensive and healthy nutritional strategy.

Be sure to visit the companion website right now to finish your Phase I review and watch the special video we've created for you at http://Day7.Solutions.

Removing the Mental and Emotional Blocks That Prevent You from Thriving in Sobriety

Every great work, every big accomplishment, has been brought into manifestation through holding to the vision, and often just before the big achievement, comes apparent failure and discouragement.

—FLORENCE SCOVEL SHINN

Welcome to Phase II of *The 30-Day Sobriety Solution*. This phase is often completed during the second week of the program, unless you have chosen the 60- or 90-day option. Like so many of our clients, if you continue forward, you will accomplish what you set out to do when you started this program. In fact, most graduates find that they actually exceed their original expectations. Just as spiritual teacher Florence Scovel Shinn says, it is all about holding to the vision, no matter what challenges and setbacks you face. Which leads us to an important question. Are you reviewing your 30-Day Vision Statement and goals several times a day? If not, you do need to make this part of your daily recovery process.

As you start Phase II, it is important to remind you of the 30-Day Reboot. When you work through the solutions and observe

30 days of abstinence, you are rebooting your mind and body. The end result is a surge of personal growth and transformation in a short period of time. On Day 1, we asked you to pick a time during the first week to quit drinking, as long as it was approved by your doctor or health care professional. We expect that you have already done that if you're this far along in the program, but if not, be sure to start today. This 30 days of abstinence is imperative for your success.

So You Slipped. Now What?

Whether you have already started the 30-Day Reboot or are starting it today, the reality is that you may give in to your desire to drink before completing 30 days of abstinence. *This does not mean you have failed!* The most important thing to do is to forgive yourself and then continue forward with the program. However, we do have a few recommendations if you slip.

First, go back to Day 1, the 100% Solution, and listen to the Time Travel Technique on the companion website. This will help remind you of the pain you will experience if you keep drinking, and it will reconnect you to your *why*—what you really want in life and how sobriety will help you accomplish it.

Second, on the companion website for Day 14, you can access the Relapse Solution, which specifically addresses this topic in depth and explains how to make sure you don't slip again. Although we recommend you review this solution if you relapse, it is optional.

Third, your best chance for successfully quitting or cutting back drinking is to keep making progress in the program. With each additional solution you complete, you will gain valuable new personal insights and learn powerful tools to create last-ing change. Often one solution will result in the exact breakthrough you need to finally succeed, so by continuing with the program, you allow this to happen.

Before we jump into Day 8, let's briefly discuss dreams.

The Drunk Dream

I still dream, twice a week at least, that I've taken cocaine, and I have it up my nose. And it's very vivid, and it's very upsetting, but at least it's a wake-up call.

—ELTON JOHN
Singer-songwriter in recovery[1]

Have you ever woken up in a panic after having a dream that you got drunk? For weeks, months, and even years after getting sober, it is not uncommon to dream about getting drunk—and for a moment when you wake up, you feel the disappointment of having actually relapsed. If this happens, use it as an opportunity to remind yourself of the inevitable pain that comes from drinking. The feelings you experienced in that drunk dream were real, even though you didn't actually get drunk. The best way to move forward is to be thankful that you didn't drink and realize that the negative emotions you experienced in, or after, your dream are very similar to how it will feel if you *do* drink. Now let's get started with the first solution in Phase II.

The "Why Can't You Just Quit?" Solution

The Truth About Willpower

Willpower can produce short-term change, but it creates constant internal stress because you haven't dealt with the root cause.

—RICK WARREN

Author of *The Purpose Driven Life: What on Earth Am I Here For?*[1]

Willpower is often considered one of the greatest predictors of individual success, but it's not always your greatest asset for sobriety. The "Why Can't You Just Quit?" Solution explains the importance of willpower and how you can build and leverage it. It also reveals the truth about why strong willpower can actually stop you from thriving in sobriety.

What Is Willpower?

Willpower is defined as a "strong determination that allows you to do something difficult (such as lose weight or quit smoking)."[2] Isn't it telling that even the published dictionary definition of willpower includes an example of overcoming addictive behaviors? However, we prefer this definition from *The Life You've Always Wanted*, by

John Ortberg: "Willpower is trying very hard to not do something you want to do very much."[3] We're sure you can relate to that.

How many times have you decided that you were going to cut back or quit drinking? Dave can't even count how many times he said he was going to quit before his first sincere attempt. It was almost ten years later when he was actually able to accomplish long-term sobriety. During those years, he tried all kinds of ways to cut back and quit drinking; however, they all ended the same way—he went back to drinking at the same level or more within weeks or months.

The interesting thing is that everyone who knew Dave thought of him as someone who had incredible willpower and persistence, always being able to follow through with what he set out to accomplish. But when it came to changing his drinking, he always failed. He was unable to leverage his willpower to quit drinking as he had used it to power through other goals. This was hard for him to understand, and it also baffled his wife, who knew that Dave could accomplish anything when he set his mind to it.

After Dave had been sober for over two years, his wife asked him a question that plagues most loved ones of problem drinkers and alcoholics: "Why weren't we—me and our daughters—enough for you to quit drinking sooner?"

As any problem drinker or alcoholic knows, there is no easy answer. The truth is that unless you have struggled with highly addictive behaviors, it is almost impossible to explain. It is an addiction, an obsession, a habit, a way of life, and somehow you become convinced that the only life worth living is one that includes drinking.

And although today's solution is about willpower, we call it the "Why Can't You Just Quit?" Solution because this is the question that a hundred million or more family members, friends, and loved ones of alcoholics (just in the United States alone) ask over and over again. And at the center of the answer to this question lies willpower, both as part of the cause *and* the solution.

The Truth About Willpower

I tried willpower to quit drinking on my own. I tried switching to beer and wine. I tried Alcoholics Anonymous several times, but found the program was too ambiguous. However, The 30-Day Sobriety Solution was something I could sit down and do every night. And the "homework" not only helped keep me on track, it helped me get clear and understand how I was feeling, and provided me with tools and techniques to change.

—MATT

30-Day Graduate from Kansas City, Missouri

There are certain days in *The 30-Day Sobriety Solution* that are going to create an "Aha!" moment for you. This is one of those days.

Take a minute right now and think about some of the times in your past when you decided to quit or cut back drinking. Maybe you had an embarrassing or frightening incident related to your drinking, or you were sick and tired of the emotional roller-coaster ride that alcohol takes you on, or you had a drunken confrontation with family or friends. Whatever the reason, you were ready to make a change. This is where your willpower kicks in.

The problem is that willpower alone will always fail over time. To understand why, first you have to look at what you are feeling the moment you decide to make this change. Your decision always has a common theme: you are cutting back or quitting drinking because you perceive that drinking is holding you back in some way or creating specific problems or challenges in your life. Or, as we discussed on Day 3, you associate more pain than pleasure with drinking, so you stop. The best way to explain this is by using a numbered rating system.

Willpower and the Pain-Pleasure Balance in Your Sobriety

Imagine that you wake up one morning feeling miserable from a night of heavy drinking. Your head is pounding, and you can feel the blood pulsing in the veins in your forehead, making it hard to think clearly. Later that morning, your doctor calls to tell you that he is concerned about your blood work and that the numbers indicate some early signs of liver damage. At that moment, you feel disgusted with yourself, wondering, *How could I have let it go this far?* On a scale of 1 to 10, with 10 being the highest, your desire to drink is at an unusual low of 2. And your concerns and fears about the health implications of your drinking are at an all-time high of 9.

Right now, what these initial ratings mean is that you have more pain associated with drinking than you do with *not* drinking. The pain of staying sober is less than the pain of drinking, so you choose not to drink.

You stay sober for a couple of days, and an internal shift starts to occur. The more distance you have from the reason you decided not to drink in the first place, the further removed you are from the pain that led you to make that change. In fact, with the alcohol out of your system, you are feeling healthier, more confident, and more clearheaded. The pain that drove you to make that initial change is all but a distant memory—and now the desire to drink is starting to kick back in.

With your recent hiatus from drinking, your concern with your health has dropped from a 9 to a 5. At the same time, your desire to drink, which was down to a 2 because of your bad hangover and the call from your doctor, has risen to a 6. And with the weekend approaching, this number is quickly escalating as you start thinking about all of the fun things you can do over the weekend while drinking, and all the fun you'll miss if you don't.

This is where your willpower really starts to show up (or doesn't). Depending on how strong your willpower is, your sobriety may last through the weekend and beyond, or you might simply give in to the desire to drink, restarting the whole cycle again. Nevertheless, no matter how strong your willpower is, when there is greater pain associated with staying sober than there is with drinking, you will eventually give in to the desire to drink again—*unless* you have changed at a deeper and more fundamental level, which is what you are doing by going through *The 30-Day Sobriety Solution*.

Willpower can help initiate and sustain significant short-term changes in your life, but without doing the other, deeper work—the work you are doing in this program—willpower alone will never get you where you want and need to be.[4] We all have limited willpower. It doesn't matter who you are. People who appear to have incredible willpower appear that way only because they have also set themselves up *on the inside* for "success."

What Is Willpower in Your Life?

Think about something positive you do well that others struggle to do. Maybe it's eating healthy, or always showing up on time for meetings, or just being well organized. What separates you from the people who also want to be successful at these things but never seem able to? Willpower is certainly one factor, but the key difference is your beliefs. You have decided, consciously or unconsciously, that eating healthy equals pleasure, energy, and longevity, and that not eating healthy equals inflammation, pain, and illness.

When you go from not eating healthy to eating healthy, you'll often experience pain at first—the pain of eating foods you might not like as much, the pain of having to learn how to cook and prepare new meals, and the pain of going out with friends and not being able to enjoy the same unhealthy appetizers and desserts as everyone else. This is where using willpower is essential to your short-term success. However, long-term success only comes from truly changing yourself at a deeper level, and those who have successfully completed this transformation believe that eating healthy eventually equals ultimate pleasure—the pleasure of having more energy, the pleasure of looking and feeling better, and the pleasure of feeling more self-confident.

The 30-Day Sobriety Solution is about transforming yourself so that you no longer need willpower to stay sober in the long term. Sobriety should *not* be difficult to achieve and maintain, at least in the long term. Sobriety should not feel like a sacrifice or a curse; rather, it should simply be a choice you make because it is what you want. However, if you keep trying to quit and stay sober by using willpower alone, you will *always* ultimately fail. The only way to succeed and maintain that success over time is to change on the inside, which is what you are doing in this program.

Don't get us wrong. You need to use willpower early and often on your path to sobriety, but you also have to diligently continue with the inner work to make sure that you can overcome the urges to drink when willpower alone stops working. Rick Warren's quote from *The Purpose Driven Life* at the start of this chapter bears repeating. "Willpower can produce short-term change, but it creates constant internal stress because you haven't dealt with the root cause."[5] *The 30-Day Sobriety Solution* is all about dealing with this root cause.

If you experienced significant emotional trauma in your childhood, for example, to some degree this is probably one of the root causes for your desire to drink. When you do the personal work necessary to heal from this past pain, such as the Total Truth Process that you learned on Day 4, you are dealing with the root cause. Doing this inner work is what makes long-term positive change a reality in your life.

We have seen many high-functioning alcoholics quit drinking

for 30 days simply by leveraging their remarkable willpower, only to falsely "prove" to themselves and others that they don't have a drinking problem. Not only do they not do any personal growth work to deal with the root causes of their drinking, but also they actually spend a great deal of time during each of those 30 days thinking about and planning in detail when, where, and how much they are going to drink on Day 31.

So your **first action step** for today is to explore the role of willpower in your past attempts to quit drinking. Answer the following questions in your journal: *Have you previously tried to quit or change your drinking without seeking any help or using any outside resources? If so, how did it work?* Write down, as best as you can remember, the past times you quit drinking without support or without also doing the inner work. Address specifically how long you stayed sober, how your experience changed day by day, and, if you returned to drinking, what happened. The awareness you gain from this exercise often results in a greater willingness to do the personal-growth work necessary for long-term change.

The Willpower Illusion

Depending upon where you are on the "drinking continuum," willpower has likely created another challenge for you. It takes an incredible amount of willpower to ignore that you actually have a problem with drinking—to ignore all of the problems that have occurred in your career, your financial life, and your relationships as a result of your drinking—and to ignore the fact that your drinking alcohol most nights will dramatically affect your health and shorten your life. We call this "the willpower illusion."

Your drinking mind constantly tricks you into thinking that drinking is not a problem, that you can drink "normally," and that you can quit whenever you want.

Your "Movie Moment"

My heroes are the ones who survived doing it wrong, who made mistakes, but recovered from them.

—BONO

Twenty-two-time Grammy Award–winning musician

To really capture this, we want to share with you an analogy that we call the "Movie Moment." Think back to a movie where you were really invested in the main character—one you identified with and whose story you were really engrossed in. And then the character does something unbelievably dumb. Maybe he cheats on his girlfriend, who is clearly a perfect match. Or he walks into a dark house, ignoring many warning signs of danger. Or he lies about something that he has no chance of getting away with, making the situation far worse.

Whatever it is, you might find yourself getting emotionally triggered. In your mind, or even out loud, you might yell at the screen, "How can you be so dumb and not see what is going to happen next?! You have everything you ever needed, and now you are throwing it all away!" To you, the mistakes they are making are obvious, but they seem oblivious to their poor judgment.

The question we have for you is, what is *your* Movie Moment? What would someone in the audience yell at you if he or she were watching you starring in your current movie? Or, even more to the point, what would *you* be yelling at the screen if you were watching yourself in your own movie? Would you be yelling about your drinking and how much it negatively affects your life? The goal of this process is not for you to feel ashamed or embarrassed but to look at your life from a different and more neutral perspective—one that will help free you from any denial that might still be holding you back.

When you are a problem drinker, your mind is amazingly effective at creating the illusion that you do not have a problem. It is no coincidence that high-functioning alcoholics are the best at this, as they are some of the strongest-willed people you will ever find. High-functioning drinkers pride themselves on being able to do the work that many others give up on, pushing through challenges with their incredible willpower. Ironically, that same willpower keeps them from accepting their problem with drinking until they can no longer ignore it—and, tragically, for many that realization comes too late.

Your **second action step** for today is to act like you are watching a movie of your life that you are starring in. *What about your character's actions, or inactions, upsets you the most? Is he or she clearly in denial? What if one of your trusted loved ones, such as a parent, sibling, good friend, or child, were to watch it? What would that person say? If you could pick any person in the world to mentor you, but he or she had to watch your movie first, what would he or she see that you are pretending not to see?* Our experience is that this exercise is more effective and powerful when you can relax and let someone else take you through it, so we've provided a guided version of the Movie Moment exercise on today's companion website.

Willpower and Decision Fatigue

In their book *Willpower: Rediscovering the Greatest Human Strength*, psychologist Roy Baumeister and journalist John Tierney share an important study about willpower and *decision fatigue*.[6] After analyzing 1,100 decisions regarding prisoners' legal appeals over the course of one year, researchers uncovered a pretty amazing statistic: prisoners who appeared in front of the parole board early in the morning received parole 70 percent of the time, while those who appeared late in the day received parole less than 10 percent of the time. After analyzing the data and all the cases, researchers concluded that decision fatigue affected the judges' rulings. The mental effort necessary for deciding case after case simply wore down the judges as the day went on.[7]

This is relevant to your drinking, because most people drink at night, even though many begin their day planning not to drink. When the evening comes around, their willpower drops, and decision fatigue kicks in. Your **third action step** for today is to think about how your willpower fades as your day goes on and to decide how you are going to avoid decision fatigue and successfully complete this 30-Day program.

Here are two options that we find work well. The first is to decide that from now on, you'll begin your day by reading that day's solution and doing the action steps *before* decision fatigue has time to set in. If, for any reason, that is not possible, the other highly effective approach is to read the solution and do the action steps immediately upon getting home from work—that time when you would have regularly started drinking or gone to happy hour.

The Comparison Game

Despite all my education and knowledge about addiction, when it came to looking in the mirror, I only let in the information that confirmed I didn't have a problem. Once I changed this, everything started changing.

—BYRON

30-Day Graduate from Phoenix, Arizona

Have you ever looked at someone and thought, *I don't drink as much as he does.* Or, *I might occasionally drink too much, but I am not an alcoholic like my [friend, cousin, parent, sibling].* Or, *Look at what a great person she is; if only I had her life, all my problems would be solved.*

Comparing yourself to someone else is a "sobriety killer." This brings us to the **fourth action step**. When you compare yourself to others, you get caught up in focusing on your differences rather than on your similarities. And often these differences go something like, "I don't have a problem with alcohol like they do," or "Look at how much Jen [or Eric] drinks." When you focus on the differences, you stop noticing the similarities. You tell yourself you are different and that you don't have a problem.

In fact, a common scenario in the recovery world is that someone will go to rehab and be surrounded by alcoholics and addicts who are much farther down the path of addiction than he or she is, and so the person focuses solely on those differences and leaves rehab believing that he or she must not have a problem because he or she is not like "those people." In David Sheff's book *Clean: Overcoming Addiction and Ending America's Greatest Tragedy*,[8] Dr. Michael Pantalon, cofounder of the Center for Progressive Recovery, in New Haven, Connecticut, says, "Less severe people say that rehab made them feel their drug use was not that bad when compared to others in rehab and that this comparison led them back to use."

But when you focus on the similarities instead of the differences, you are less likely to get caught in denial. If you look for similarities, you can hear parts of your story in everyone else's story. That simple change has a profound impact on your awareness. You can better see your greatest challenges, which greatly helps you to quit or cut back drinking. So the next time you hear yourself saying that so-and-so is different from you, change your point of view and focus instead on what you have in common.

There are always going to be people better off and worse off than you, no matter where you are or what you're doing. Even though you are unique, and your story and your journey are different from everyone else's, you can embrace your individuality without getting caught in the illusion that those differences mean you don't have a problem. We have seen clients, friends, and even our own family members get stuck in this self-delusion. Everyone has to get over it in order to proceed with recovery.

Day 8 Action Steps

Whether you have willpower or not, you have to be willing to change and not rely solely on your willpower to get yourself through these 30 days. Dr. James Gordon, a Harvard-educated psychiatrist and founder-director of the Center for Mind-Body Medicine, in Washington, DC, says that it isn't that "some people have willpower and some don't, but that some are willing to change and some are not."[9]

Let yourself be open to the information in this program. Make time every day to do the action steps—especially the ones that make you a little uncomfortable. Just reading about the solutions won't get it done. As one of our friends said recently, "You can't get wet reading about the ocean." And you can't stay dry just reading about sobriety.

Don't let your willpower convince you that all you need is 30 days of sobriety to "cure" yourself from alcohol. Recognize that, during these 30 days, you are also becoming the person you have secretly dreamed of becoming—your true self. You are steadily transforming yourself into someone who can fully embrace all of life and thrive in sobriety.

Be sure to refer back to the text earlier in this chapter if you need to refresh your memory on the steps, as we only summarize them below:

- **Write down in your journal what role willpower has played in cutting back or quitting drinking.** Have you tried to quit drinking using only willpower? How, specifically, have those experiences worked out?

- **Write down your Movie Moment.** What bothers you the most about your actions, or inactions, as you watch an imaginary movie of your life from the perspective of an unbiased third party? Is your character clearly in denial about the negative impact of drinking on his or her (your) life? To really achieve a breakthrough in this action step, we highly recommend that you listen to the guided version on the companion website.

- **Decide how you are going to avoid the negative impact of decision fatigue.** What can you do differently now that you know your willpower weakens throughout the day? When will you read that day's solution and do the action steps? Is there something self-nurturing you can easily do at the same time you used to start drinking, like going for a walk?

- **Get out of the comparison trap.** Write the answers to the following questions in your journal. Do you regularly comment internally on other people's drinking habits? Do you believe that you do not have a problem like theirs? Do you regularly compare yourself to others, because you want what they appear to have or you want to reassure yourself that what you have is better? Think back to a time where you might have judged someone else for drinking or substance abuse. What similarities can you acknowledge you have or had with that person if you are completely honest?

As always, there is additional support material on the companion website at http://Day8.Solutions, including our top tips for building your willpower and the guided version of your Movie Moment.

The Action Solution

Getting Out of Your Head and Into Action

When you quit drinking, you stop waiting.

—CAROLINE KNAPP

Author of *Drinking: A Love Story*[1]

There's a lasting adage of success that says, "The universe rewards action." Yet despite the simplicity and truth of this principle, it's amazing that so many of us seem to get hung up by continually planning, organizing, and considering all of our options rather than just taking action.

By taking action, you activate other dynamics that move you toward sobriety. When you take action, others around you know that you are sincere and determined with your intent. You start actively learning from *your own* life experiences instead of just learning from books. You become more receptive to the feedback you are receiving as the result of the actions you are taking, and all of a sudden you have more information on how to improve things in an easier, quicker, and more efficient manner. Things that puzzled you before suddenly become clear, and things that seemed impossible now seem possible. You attract people who reinforce your path and encourage you. Once you take action, support flows your way.

Quite simply, taking regular action toward your goal of cutting back or quitting drinking, like we have strategically set out for you in each solution, all but guarantees your success at thriving in sobriety.

Take Action, Avoid Distraction

Over the years of teaching and coaching people, we have found that action is the one thing that separates those who successfully overcome problem drinking in the long term and those who don't. Those who are thriving in sobriety, even after having failed many times, are thriving because they took action and did what had to be done.

We can give you solutions for change and share inspirational stories of people who overcame seemingly impossible odds. We can convince you that you are no different from anyone else who has successfully quit drinking or achieved the "normal drinker" lifestyle. But none of this matters if you don't take action and do what has to be done.

We know you might be thinking, *Wait, I have taken action every day. I have read the material, done the action steps, and reviewed the companion website.* If so, that is fantastic. We applaud your accomplishments, and you should feel great about what you have done so far.

However, the Action Solution goes beyond just these 30 days. If you have found taking action in this program easier than usual, that is great and exactly what we intended. On the other hand, if you have found it challenging to take action so far, or if you are concerned about taking action beyond these 30 days, today will help you to take positive action, and avoid distraction, for the rest of your life.

And now it's time for you to take action.

Your Bridge to Thriving in Sobriety

I don't drink anymore. I don't smoke anymore. I don't do drugs anymore. All of those come with an "anymore." I used to do everything and a lot of everything.

—KELLY PRESTON
Actor[2]

Action is best explained as the bridge between your inner world and your outer world. Your outer world is a manifestation of your inner world, and, as you change on the inside (your thoughts, feelings, and beliefs), you also change on the outside.

Your inner world drives your actions, or inactions, to manifest in your outer world. Inaction is actually a kind of action because if you are not working the solutions, you are doing something else, even if that is just sitting in front of the TV.

So far in this program, we have been working primarily on your inner world, so that it changes your outer world. Results might include improved health, weight loss, better relationships, and a promotion at work or a new job, as well as your primary goal of cutting back or quitting drinking. At the end of these 30 days, if you do the solutions, you will find your inner world has changed so dramatically that the actions you take will become second nature in supporting your thriving in sobriety.

The Definition of a Hero

The most successful people are long-term thinkers. They look into the future as far as they can to determine the kind of people they want to become and the goals they want to achieve. They then come back to the present and determine the things that they will have to do—or not do—to achieve their desired futures.

—BRIAN TRACY[3]

When Dave's oldest daughter made the sixth-grade honor roll, he attended a school celebration. The principal gave a speech acknowledging the students and defining a hero as "somebody who does what needs to be done." His point was that a hero doesn't have to save lives or have some special superpower that no one else has—all heroes have to do is what they already know needs to be done. When you do what needs to be done, you, too, are a *hero*—and anyone who has curbed an addictive behavior such as drinking would readily agree.

The opposite of heroic action is inaction and procrastination—delaying something that you know should be done now. If you are like most problem drinkers, you have delayed addressing your drinking many, many times in the past. The bottom line is that we all procrastinate, but people who have mastered how to quickly overcome procrastination are happier, healthier, and more successful.

In a study published in *Psychological Science* in 1997,[4] researchers rated college students on an established scale of procrastination and then tracked their academic performance, stress, and general health throughout the semester. Initially, there seemed to be some benefit to procrastination, as students put off work for more enjoyable activities, but the eventual cost of procrastination far outweighed the temporary benefits. Procrastinators earned lower grades and reported higher cumulative levels of stress and illness. The study concluded that procrastination is a self-defeating behavior with long-term costs.[5]

This sounds similar to the "short-term trap" discussed on Day 6 in the Outcome Solution. By giving in to your short-term desires, you pay the ultimate price of never accomplishing your long-term dreams and goals. Focusing on the short term not only costs you your dreams, it creates more stress and illness in your life. When you choose to focus on the long term and make decisions based on *those* desires, however, you can more easily overcome procrastination and move toward your dreams, including thriving in sobriety.

Sobriety Anxiety

If something is worrying you, always do something about it. It doesn't have to be the big thing that will make it disappear. It can be any small thing. But the positive effect it will have on you will be enormous.

—STEVE CHANDLER

Author of *100 Ways to Motivate Yourself: Change Your Life Forever*[6]

Think back to a time when you decided to quit drinking or change how you drink. Perhaps you decided to drink only on the weekends, not drink any hard liquor, or never have more than two glasses of wine. What were some of your initial thoughts right after deciding to make the change? Most likely they included thoughts such as:

- Maybe I will make one exception for the party next weekend, so I can have fun.
- If I quit drinking completely, my coworkers won't want to hang out with me, and that might cost me the upcoming promotion.
- If I stop at two glasses of wine, I should be fine, even if I drink every night.
- I will be too stressed if I can't get drunk at least once a week.
- I have too many challenges and concerns to do this right now, but maybe next month will be a good time.

Behind all of these thoughts is WORRY—worries about the bad timing of making this change, about not enjoying an upcoming party, about it being a career-limiting decision, and about not knowing how to deal with stress without alcohol. These worries, on top of the legitimate worries about your health and relationships that problem drinking brings, can completely paralyze you.

Worries are "sobriety killers." When you become consumed by worrying, the only action you may take is to escape through drinking. We refer to worry as sobriety anxiety: you have become accustomed to dealing with your worries and anxiety by drinking, so eventually your continued worrying pushes you past your breaking point, and you decide to drink.

Even though worrying does tell you that you need to do something, that is the only value it serves. To take action, you need to stop all the worrying. You have to *decide* to stop worrying. The easiest way to do this is to ask yourself one simple question: *What can I do about this right now?* And then take action—any action, however small, that moves you forward.

In the book *Constructive Living*, David Reynolds writes, "The mature human being goes about doing what needs to be done regardless of whether that person feels great or terrible. Knowing that you are the kind of person with that kind of self-control brings all the satisfaction and confidence you will ever need. Even on days when the satisfaction and confidence just aren't there, you can get the job done anyway."[7] As Reynolds writes, taking action will give you the satisfaction you seek. Even if you are "not in the mood" to take action, the best way to change your mood is to do what you know needs to be done—you act like a hero does.

Overcoming Resistance

At age thirty-nine, Mike felt that his life was on hold. He was a successful engineer, often recognized as a high performer, yet every night he came home unsatisfied. The only way he knew how to deal with this feeling was to drink. He would arrive home and immediately open a beer or pour a quadruple bourbon, and drink until he passed out, which was usually his only stopping point once he started drinking.

Mike knew there must be more to life, and he did have some dreams, but as his fortieth birthday neared, he started to doubt whether he would ever accomplish them. That is when he found *The 30-Day Sobriety Solution*. Mike was a little skeptical, but at the same time, he was inspired by the success stories, so he decided he had nothing to lose.

Instead of having a drink after work, he came home and immediately started the solution for the day even though he was usually *not in the mood*. He quickly realized that all he had to do was push through a little bit of resistance at first, and by the time he was done with the solution for the day, he found that his mood had improved completely. He felt encouraged and even excited at times about what he was learning. And more importantly, he was surprised to discover that his desire to drink was gone.

Mike cruised through the 30 days—not drinking once—something he hadn't done in many years. Shortly after completing *The 30-Day Sobriety Solution*, Mike gave us the following feedback:

> I might even venture to say that half of the value I have gotten out of this program has been outside of just controlling my drinking. Once I control the drinking, I have a fairly large amount of time in the evenings and on the weekends to fill with productive or enjoyable activities.

Mike changed the course of his life over those 30 days. Within months of completing the program, he was promoted at work, something he knew would not have happened before doing the program. He became clear about what he really wanted in life, which was to work as an engineer at an amusement park and find a girlfriend. And now he had the time and motivation to go after those dreams.

It's been three years since Mike completed the program, and he has celebrated his one year anniversary at his dream job, working for one of the biggest amusement parks in the United States. He also has a serious girlfriend and told us recently, "I can't say that I'd change much about the transformation in my new life. I got pretty much everything I wanted."

Mike is one of our graduates who is able to have just one drink when he wants to and has a take-it-or-leave-it attitude about drinking. And it all started because he took that one simple step when he got home from work—pushing through the initial resistance he had and doing the work in the program instead of fulfilling his short-term desire to drink.

The **first action step** for today is to write down your top three worries related to your problem drinking, whatever they are. Then note anything you have done in the first nine days of this program that will help address those worries and anything you plan on doing for the remainder of this program. For example, one common worry is about the impact of your drinking on your health, so you might write down that abstaining from alcohol for 30 days will address this worry. The most important thing to do is to acknowledge your worry and then quickly move on to acknowledge that you are doing something, no matter how small, to deal with it.

Ready Fire Aim[8]

I knew I was lucky, and somehow I knew that if I didn't stop, everything would go tits up—my career, my family, my everything.

—EWAN MCGREGOR[9]

You may have heard "Ready, aim, fire!" before. It's a familiar term for clearly focusing on your target before you shoot, but when you apply it to your life, the problem is that you might spend your entire life aiming at the target, but never firing. Do you know people who are always planning, preparing, or having to get things perfect before they even start? If you want to hit any target in the quickest way possible, you need to fire first, notice where the bullet ended up, and then modify your aim appropriately. If the bullet landed three inches above, aim lower and fire again. Where did it land now? Fire again and keep modifying. If you do this, you'll soon find yourself hitting the target square on. This same approach is true for everything in life.

Most successful people we know have a low tolerance for excessive planning. They are excited to get going. *The 30-Day Sobriety Solution* was developed with your success in mind. All the preparation and planning have already been done for you. All you need to do is read each chapter and complete the action steps for the day you are on in the order we provided. It's that simple. Just keep *firing*. And remember that there is rarely a "perfect" time or way to do anything. As long as you keep taking action and keep moving, you will experience profound changes over these 30 days.

Sir Isaac Newton's first law of motion, sometimes called the law of inertia, states that "objects in motion tend to stay in motion and objects at rest tend to stay at rest."[10] This is true about the actions you take and don't take. If you wake up on Saturday morning and immediately wash the dishes, straighten the house, and work out, how do you think this will affect your mood for the rest of the day? But if instead you wake up on Saturday morning and plop down on the couch in front of the TV for several hours and eat junk food, how will your mood, and your day, differ?

We often find that people who struggle with problem drinking also struggle with an all-or-nothing mentality—the notion that something isn't worth doing unless you go all out at it. This couldn't be more false. Don't discount or ignore taking a step because it seems too insignificant or like it is "not enough." The forward momentum you get from even a small step is undeniable and worth the effort.

This takes us to the next action step of the day—"tiny habits" that can totally transform your ability to make and maintain significant changes in your life.

"tiny habits"

A bicycle maintains its poise and equilibrium only so long as it is going forward toward something. You have a good bicycle. Your trouble is you are trying to maintain your balance sitting still, with no place to go. It is no wonder you feel shaky.

—MAXWELL MALTZ (1889–1975)
Author of *Psycho-Cybernetics: A New Way
to Get More Living out of Life*[11]

In 2007 the Hershey Company wanted to sell more Kit Kat bars. The marketing strategy it deployed was simple and brilliant. The company wanted to link eating Kit Kat bars to drinking coffee, since coffee was already a habit for much of its desired target market. This gave birth to the marketing message "a break's best friend" and an extensive radio and TV ad campaign repeatedly linking coffee with Kit Kat bars. The result? The $300 million brand grew to $500 million.[12]

This campaign was so effective because it linked a new behavior to an existing behavior that was already firmly rooted. The best thing about this simple, brilliant, and proven marketing strategy is that you can implement it in your life to create amazing breakthroughs.

B. J. Fogg, PhD, the founder and director of the Persuasive Technology Lab at Stanford University, knows the power of tiny habits[13] and developed a simple three-step method to create any new desired habit.

1. Start small. To defeat procrastination, you need to start small. In his book *Time Warrior: How to Defeat Procrastination, People-Pleasing, Self-Doubt, Overcommitment, Broken Promises and Chaos*, Steve Chandler writes, "Keep your life creative and simple: What needs to be done now in these three minutes? That's all you ever need to ask, and you'll never have anything like procrastination bother you again."[14] Whatever needs to be done, make it easy and quick. Fogg notes that the new habit should seem like no big deal when beginning.

2. Find an anchor. Pick an existing routine or habit to act as a trigger for the new habit you want to create. Your life is full of routines, so just pick one. For example, Fogg began doing push-ups right after going to the bathroom. He started with just two each time, but today he does more than a hundred throughout the day. Other routines to link to a new habit might be brushing your teeth, washing your hair, getting in your car, hanging up the telephone, closing the refrigerator, checking your email, or turning on the TV.

3. Celebrate immediately. Whenever you find yourself doing your new behavior, give yourself kudos right away, whether it is a thumbs-up, saying "Good job!" out loud, affirming yourself in the mirror, or doing a fist pump. This simple acknowledgment acts as a very powerful reinforcement.

Implementing this tiny-habits method is the **second action step** for today. The key to succeeding with this method is to start small, so let's apply it to your 30-Day Vision Statement you wrote on Day 2. Pick a routine or behavior that you currently do at least five times a day as a trigger and reviewing your 30-Day Vision Statement as the new tiny habit. For example, after you use the restroom, immediately read your vision statement, or say it out loud or silently in your head if you have memorized it. The third step is to acknowledge your success immediately following the behavior. Soon it will become a new habit.

Now that you know this simple, effective technique, you might be tempted to use it to develop more than one new habit—and maybe even use it for a new habit that isn't directly related to your goal of quitting or cutting back drinking. Please don't do this. We know that we sound like a broken record on this topic, but trust us that you need to remain focused on these 30 days and your vision from Day 2. This focus will reap you incredible results in the long term.

Day 9 Action Steps

The Action Solution is all about taking action and avoiding procrastination, not just throughout these 30 days but also for the rest of your life. When you replace worrying with action directed toward meeting the challenge or solving the problem, your life will start to improve, you'll achieve more of your goals, and you'll find yourself thriving in sobriety.

- **Write down your top three worries related to problem drinking.** Then write what you have done in this program to date, and what you will do over the remaining 30 days, to address these worries. The goal is to give yourself permission to stop worrying, since you are taking positive action that addresses those concerns. And when you find yourself worrying, come back to the question "What can I do about this right now?" And then take action—any action, however small, that moves you forward in addressing the issue you were worrying about.

- **Start a tiny habit.** Using the start-small strategy, link repeating your 30-Day Vision Statement (out loud when possible) to an existing routine in your life that you do at least five times a day. And to make it even more powerful, take twenty seconds to experience the feelings you will feel when you have made your vision a reality. Then remember to give yourself some sort of acknowledgment for completing it: a thumbs-up, a thank-you in the mirror, a fist pump, or just saying, "Good job!" out loud.

On the companion website, there are two fantastic, free online tools that we have found instrumental in helping you to take action and celebrate your successes. So be sure to visit http://Day9.Solutions.

The Core Values Solution

Discovering Your Core Values

When we honor our values, we feel an internal "rightness." It's as if each value produces its own special tone. When we live our values, the various tones create a unique harmony.
—From the book *Co-Active Coaching: Changing Business, Transforming Lives*[1] by Henry Kimsey-House, Karen Kimsey-House, Phillip Sandahl, and Laura Whitworth

Integrity. Passion. Freedom. Honesty. There are hundreds of core values, and we each have our own personal set. When we let our lives be guided and directed by our values, we feel happy, fulfilled, and a deep sense of connection with others and ourselves.

We develop our core values throughout our lives. Your ability to cut back or quit drinking and to thrive in sobriety is related directly to whether you make decisions that align with your core values. When your actions express your values, you will achieve a state of inner and outer balance that will bring you peace, clarity, and joy. And when they don't, you will experience tension, confusion, guilt, shame, dissatisfaction, and even depression or chronic disease.

Core Value Contradictions

Anyone who can't go five minutes without a cigarette, or can't stop drinking, or is strung out on drugs knows that after awhile there develops an attachment to the ritual of using it that has little to do with your original motive. The original impetus was to feel its effect, and the effect seemed positive at the time.

—ROBERT DOWNEY JR.
Actor in recovery[2]

What are your core values? We rarely find people that can answer this question with any real clarity. We also know that when your behavior is out of alignment with your core values, it creates a deep disturbance in your psyche that can lead to lack of passion and loss of energy in your life.

When you look at someone who struggles with problem drinking, this issue becomes even more pronounced. Excessive drinking can numb your awareness of your core values and often leads to bad decision making, whether it's prioritizing your drinking over visiting a friend who needs your help, not finishing a task you promised to complete, or simply choosing to spend time at the bar instead of spending time at home with your family.

Dave's core values include honesty, generosity, success, passion, love, and fun. When Dave compared this list to his behavior when he was drinking heavily, it became clear why he was abusing alcohol. His decisions and his behavior contradicted almost all of his core values, except, at times, fun. When your life doesn't match what you say you care about, you're uncomfortable and unhappy. You look for a way to escape. Drinking was Dave's escape.

His excessive drinking kept him from living his core values. Honesty? Dave lied about his drinking and hid bottles of alcohol from his family. Generosity? Because of the time and money it took to support his habit, he never had the time or the money to be as generous toward others as he wanted—except for sometimes paying for a round of drinks at the bar. Success? Dave and everyone around him knew that he was never going to be truly successful when he was drinking almost every night of the week. Love and passion? Over time, drinking had drowned out most of the passion and love in his life—and eventually even the fun of drinking disappeared. Dave was trapped in a horrible state of imbalance, stress, and discomfort. *Can you relate to any of this?*

Today is about rediscovering and aligning with your core values so that you will never feel like you need alcohol to escape. Legendary civil rights leader Dr. Martin Luther King Jr. reminds us, "If we are to go forward, we must go back and rediscover those precious values."[3]

The Sobriety System

The Sobriety System, and specifically identifying my core values and the lies I have been telling myself, was a revelation for me. I didn't realize how out of alignment my actions were from my core values, and how many beliefs I was holding on to that were keeping me from ever getting sober. The action steps for these two days significantly changed my life—increasing my self-confidence, improving my self-worth, and ultimately making me believe that a life thriving in sobriety was possible.

—COURTNEY

30-Day Graduate from Newark, New Jersey

The 30-Day Sobriety Solution is based on the Sobriety System, a model of how your core values, thoughts, beliefs, feelings, emotions, and behaviors affect one another. You can see this dynamic in the diagram below. Over the next three days, you will learn how valuable this system is in helping you make sobriety second nature. This model is an effective tool for quickly identifying the predominant challenges and obstacles that are holding you back from accomplishing your goals.

Let's explore each component of the system. We'll work through it using a common limiting belief that many problem drinkers

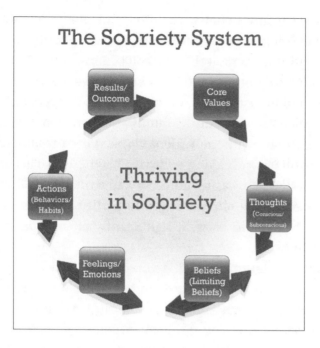

have—the belief that *a sober life will be boring and unexciting.* Be sure to refer back to the diagram above as you read through this. For additional examples, visit the companion website.

- **Core Values.** Core values are the guiding principles—such as honesty, integrity, loyalty, respect, love, fun, family, faith, success, balance, creativity, and justice—that dictate your behavior and action. So if you hold the belief that a sober life is a boring and unexciting life, and one of your core values is "fun," this will inevitably result in your going out drinking and partying in order to fulfill your value of fun.
- **Thoughts (Conscious and Subconscious).** When you believe that a sober life will be boring and unexciting, your thoughts gravitate to all the various ways that drinking can be fun (drinking games, tailgate parties, uninhibited play and humor). And you think that a life without drinking will not be fun (feeling anxious, inhibited, and left out).

- **Beliefs (Limiting Beliefs).** The limiting belief is that sobriety is boring and unexciting. Note the double-sided arrows in the diagram above, which indicate that your beliefs affect your thoughts, and your predominant thoughts create your beliefs. For example, when you first started drinking, you probably didn't believe that being sober was boring, but as you went out drinking and had good times with your friends, you started to link fun with drinking and not drinking with not having fun. This created a new belief, which was reinforced by advertisements linking fun to drinking, or by role models who partied frequently. Once a limiting belief is in place, it significantly affects your thoughts and feelings.

- **Feelings and Emotions.** What you believe determines much of what you feel and experience, and your feelings contribute to and reinforce your beliefs. So once again, if you believe being sober is boring, and you think about going out with others and not drinking, you will likely feel disappointed, anxious, afraid, and resentful. These negative emotions reinforce your belief that not drinking is boring, represented by the double-sided arrow in the diagram. However, if you think about going out and drinking with friends, and remember the positive experiences you had doing this in the past, you will feel excited and happy.

- **Actions (Behaviors and Habits).** Predominant feelings (such as love, joy, fear, and anger) lead you to act and form habits. Your actions, in turn, also affect how you feel. However, after a certain point, you act automatically and unconsciously in response to your thoughts, beliefs, and feelings.

- **Results and Outcomes.** Your actions create outcomes, which can affect your core values. If one of your core values is fun, then drinking, *at least in the early stages*, reinforces this value. You are being run by thoughts, beliefs, and feelings that you are no longer aware of and that are reinforced by the results of your actions. You can get stuck in an endless loop of self-reinforcing, self-destructive thoughts, beliefs, feelings, and behaviors. But with the intervention of tools and processes like these in *The 30-Day Sobriety Solution*, you can change. By changing any part of the system (new thoughts, new beliefs, new images, new feelings, new behaviors), you can change the whole system.

Reviewing the Sobriety System may lead you to some "Aha!" moments, shedding light on why you do what you do. It may also lead to some scratch-your-head moments, stirring up more questions than answers. Although the system is simple, it can seem complicated initially. That is why today's focus is mainly on core values.

Core values are the starting point of the Sobriety System. If you don't clarify your core values, you cannot leverage the full value of this system. Lisa, a 30-Day Graduate from Minneapolis, Minnesota, shares how today's solution helped her to regain peace and happiness:

> In revisiting the Core Values Solution, I have realized it is probably the most effective and powerful solution for me. When going through my journal, I noticed how I had slowly "slipped down the slippery slope" away from some of my core values, and this, in turn, created terribly uncomfortable negative emotions, which, of course, could only be temporarily relieved by a few glasses of wine. Welcoming back and embracing my core values has been the tipping point for me. When I am living in support of my core values, I experience inner peace and happiness, and the desire to drink in order to escape from negative emotions literally evaporates. I'm also feeling grateful today that I did not attend the "wild" Christmas party, which is a big step for me because it angered the hostess and I received a curt and cold email in response, but thanks to *The 30-Day Sobriety Solution,* I had the resolve to stay on purpose with my core values.

How Robert Rediscovered His Freedom, Spirit, and Creativity

The 30-Day Sobriety Solution *worked miracles for me.*

—ROBERT

30-Day Graduate from Vienna, Austria

Robert's father was a workaholic who didn't get home most nights until ten o'clock. And as much as he loved his mother, she was strict, and he couldn't wait to be on his own. Once he turned eighteen, four years after he started drinking socially, Robert moved out.

Like many young adults, Robert was fearless. He knew there was a lot more to life, and his courage, passion for knowledge, and curiosity led him to explore an exciting, diverse world. He studied philosophy, and was drawn to Taoism and Buddhism. He trained in tai chi and kung fu, traveled to other countries and cultures, and discovered a strong spiritual connection to nature. He also embraced his creativity by writing and composing songs and performing.

Then one day, as he neared thirty, everything changed. He got involved with a woman, who got pregnant. Robert knew it was time to "grow up," and they married. His most influential role model was his workaholic father, so Robert's career in sales became his top priority. But his drinking, which had increased throughout his twenties, became a growing concern.

Over the next ten years, Robert worked during the day and drank eight to twelve high-alcohol-content beers (5.5 percent) every night. His occasional attempts to quit would last no more than three days, and whenever he went on business trips, which were frequent, he really let loose.

By the time Robert turned forty, he had two young children and knew he needed to change. He was drinking excessively almost every night, almost completely in private. Robert found *The 30-Day Sobriety Solution*, and even though he was uncertain and afraid, he was encouraged by some of the changes he made early on in the program. Before the program, the longest he had stayed sober was ten days; after starting the solutions and reconnecting with his passion for learning, he had two months of sobriety and shared this with us:

> All areas of my life started to slowly improve at the very beginning. I was very skeptical at first, but the more solutions I completed, the more clear things became. Within two months of starting *The 30-Day Sobriety Solution*, I was closer to my family, performing better at work, coping with stress much more easily, had lost thirty pounds, was training for a marathon, and, most interesting, my social life actually improved.

Robert also shared that today, Day 10, was his favorite solution, because he rediscovered his core values of freedom, spirituality, creativity, health, and variety. He realized that when his life had abruptly changed by becoming both a husband and a father in less than a year, he had stopped expressing these core values. As he started to reconnect to them again, he became happier and more fulfilled, and his need to escape by drinking was reduced significantly.

Our last update from Robert is a great example of the power of perseverance. Robert has been sober for over two of the last two and a half years. He left his job in sales and has been working toward his MBA. Today he considers his drinking to be moderate. He doesn't get drunk and is excited about all the positive changes he has made. He also used his favorite solutions to give up caffeine and quit smoking. Even though Robert has had a couple of setbacks along the way, he is optimistic and committed to thriving in sobriety.

Defining Your Core Values

The solutions I learned from The 30-Day Sobriety Solution *have been extremely effective in maintaining sobriety and thriving in it; they are the foundation upon which my sobriety is based.*

—DAN

30-Day Graduate from Jackson, Wyoming

Our lives are in harmony when we make decisions in line with our core values. But drinking to excess virtually ensures that our Sobriety System is broken and that many decisions will contradict our core values. When you have the self-awareness and courage to align your actions with your core values, you make better decisions, live a more fulfilling and purposeful life, and thrive in sobriety. Zig Ziglar says, "You cannot consistently perform in a manner which is inconsistent with the way you see yourself."[4] Today is about getting in touch with your true identity and letting it shine through all you do.

That means it is time to rediscover *your* core values—the ones that will empower you in every aspect of your life. You can refer to your core values to help you make difficult decisions, choose a particular lifestyle, select a new career, or parent your children. Let's get started.

Day 10 Action Steps

I was drinking quite often, and when I drank, it gave me permission to do things that I normally would not do. I had a moral frame of reference. I never played around or anything except when I drank.

—MARTIN SHEEN

Actor in recovery

The following four-step process is one of the most effective methods we have discovered for helping you get in touch with the core values that deep down you want to live by. Be sure to complete this process in your journal. You might enjoy listening to some relaxing music while you work through each step.

Action Step 1: Core Values Discovery Process

- **Review and write down the core values that stand out in the list below.** First, read through the values listed below. If one feels important to you, write it down. Be sure to trust your instincts. You can always eliminate it later if you decide it isn't a fit. You might find it valuable to view the much longer list on the companion website at http://Day10.Solutions. However, you do not want to add values to your list that you think you *should* have, *want* to have, or *need* to have. This is about only what *actually* matters to you.

accountability	achievement	appreciation
authenticity	comfort	courage
creativity	dependability	excitement
fame	family	freedom
friendship	fun	generosity
happiness	health	honesty
humor	influence	integrity
joy	justice	love
loyalty	openness	passion
patience	peace	power
privacy	recognition	reliability
security	self-reliance	spirituality
status	strength	success
tolerance	truth	vulnerability
wealth	wisdom	

- **Think of situations, people, movie, or TV characters that really upset, offend, or anger you.** This might include coworkers, friends, family members, public figures, or other people in the public eye. You can also include situations or experiences you have had such as driving in heavy traffic, waiting in line, or a pet peeve. As you think of each one, write down which of your values was compromised in each situation. For example, someone who cuts in line might upset you because he violated your values of respect for others and fairness. Or someone who doesn't tip the waiter might upset you because she violated your values of generosity and appreciation. Take a minute to write down any values that apply.

  The values you identify in this step are crucial for two reasons. First, these might include your core values, although that is not always the case. Second, and more likely, these are values that you are most guilty of violating, either now or in the past. If this is true, make sure you note which values you might be violating. If you are still doing this action today, underline it; if you were guilty of doing it in the past, put a star by it or boldface it. But be sure you make a note to revisit any actions you identify here that you are still doing. You want to change them.

- **Think of the people (dead or alive) whom you admire the most.** Include interactions that impressed you or touched your heart. You might include people like Oprah Winfrey, Tony Robbins, Mother Teresa, Taylor Swift, Bill or Melinda Gates, Tom Hanks, Michael Jordan, Nelson Mandela, Bono, Princess Diana, Pope Francis, John F. Kennedy, or a family member or friend. What experiences or activities do you admire? Mentoring others? Taking care of children? Kind teachers? Community activists? Charitable actions? Creative acts? Write down the values or emotions you respect most about these people or situations. For example, Dave and Jack both have had mentors, and some of their values included passion, discipline, love, integrity, and generosity.

The important thing is to make note of what values you see, not what values you think others might see in that person or situation.

- **From your list, pick ten values you identify with most and write down how your drinking has played a role in contradicting or violating each of these.** If you don't have ten or more, that is fine; just use the ones you have written down. For at least three minutes, make a list of every way your drinking helped make sure that you did *not* fulfill these values. You might be surprised to discover that drinking has compromised, to some degree, virtually every one of your core values. Here are some examples we have heard from our clients:

  - **Passion.** "I am unable to have passion and enthusiasm in the morning when I am hungover, which sets the tone for the whole day and often has me craving to drink again that night."
  - **Success.** "How can I be successful if I feel like I need to drink to be happy? Would I consider a great leader to be 'great' if he or she depended on alcohol as much as I do?"
  - **Happiness.** "I feel a false sense of happiness when I drink, but in the morning, I realize that drinking only *seems* to fill this emptiness in my life. I know real happiness is finding my life purpose, but my drinking ensures I won't accomplish that."
  - **Honesty.** "When I drink, I often exaggerate, lie, drive drunk, and make other choices that I find reprehensible."
  - **Responsibility.** "I like to wallow in self-pity and negativity sometimes when I drink, and the mornings after I get really drunk, I feel sorry for myself and act like I am somehow the victim."

Action Step 2: Integrating Your Core Values

Now it is time to use the core values you identified. Update your 30-Day Vision Statement (Day 2) and goals (Day 6) with some of your core values. By integrating your core values into your vision and goals, you instantly create a more authentic and meaningful connection to them, which will dramatically accelerate your successful accomplishments. Please take a minute and complete this now in your journal. For example, if passion is one of your values, see where you might be able to add the words *passion, passionate,* or *passionately* into your 30-Day Vision Statement or goals.

————

In *The 7 Habits of Highly Effective People*, Stephen Covey says, "As you live your values, your sense of identity, integrity, control, and inner-directedness will infuse you with both exhilaration and peace. You will define yourself from within, rather than by people's opinions or by comparisons to others."[5] And it is exactly the same for thriving in sobriety—you need to start making decisions that are in alignment with your core values.

Excessive drinking and core values don't mix! If your actions constantly contradict what you care most about, your attempts at getting sober won't last, and thriving in sobriety will be impossible. So, over the next twenty days, when you are presented with any important decision to make, we challenge you to think about which choice is most in sync with your core values. As this becomes a habit, you will make better decisions, and—most importantly—you will experience more inner peace, happiness, and joy.

On the companion website, you will find additional examples to help you understand and integrate the Sobriety System into your life, as well as the longer list of core values. You can find the site at http://Day10.Solutions.

The Lie Detector Solution

Confronting Your Limiting Beliefs

> *The biggest obstacle to creating a wonderful life is self-limiting
> beliefs. A self-limiting belief is an idea you have that you are lim-
> ited in some way, in terms of time, talent, intelligence, money,
> ability, or opportunity.*
>
> —BRIAN TRACY

We all have beliefs that influence and often limit our lives. You
have beliefs about your capabilities, what success means, how
to relate to other people, and why you need alcohol in your life.
Moving beyond the beliefs that limit you and hold you back is a
critical step toward cutting back or quitting drinking. Today you
will learn how to identify the limiting beliefs—the lies you tell
yourself—and replace them with positive beliefs that support your
path to sobriety.

Your Beliefs

*A core belief is defined as something you assume as true about
reality, and as long as you hold on to it, your belief will hold your
body's informational fields to certain parameters. You will per-*

ceive something as likable or unlikable, distressing or enjoyable, according to how it fits your expectations.

—DEEPAK CHOPRA

Coauthor of *Freedom from Addiction: The Chopra Center Method for Overcoming Destructive Habits*[1]

Let's revisit the Sobriety System diagram and focus on today's solution—identifying and clearing limiting beliefs that are holding you back.

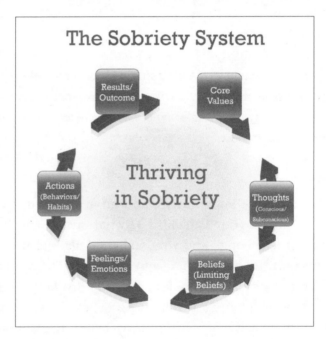

Beliefs are ideas that you hold to be true. You have beliefs about yourself and the world, whether you are aware of them or not. Your beliefs determine your decisions and your behavior, which, in turn, create your future. A belief can be so powerful that if you are exposed to information that contradicts that belief, your brain will actually filter it out.

A part of your brain called the reticular activating system (RAS) acts as a filter for all incoming sensory data (sounds, sights, smells, taste, and touch). There are about eleven million bits of information per second vying for your attention. It's impossible to attend to all of that, so your RAS filters out most of it. The information that gets through the filter into your awareness includes your strongly felt needs, your stated goals, and your conscious (and unconscious) beliefs.

Just to get a feel for how this works, focus right now on what you are feeling in your right foot. You can feel that, right? But until we directed your attention to it, your RAS was filtering it out because it wasn't relevant to your reading, which was your focus. This filter is useful because it allows you to ignore most unimportant stimuli so that you can focus on the task at hand. The problem is that the RAS may also filter out important information, such as opportunities and resources that could help you achieve your sobriety goals, because that information does not match your dominant belief: *I need alcohol to be relaxed, confident, funny, and fun in social situations,* or *I need alcohol to relax at the end of a long, hard workday.*

From the Sobriety System, you can see how thoughts and beliefs are connected. Your thoughts create your beliefs, and your beliefs direct your thoughts. Your thoughts and your beliefs are constantly interacting, and the important point here is that they have a *huge* impact on your life, your state of mind, and—in particular—your ability to cut back or quit drinking.

Since your beliefs control your RAS (the doorway to your perception), if you are going to change your life, you first have to change the beliefs that are keeping you stuck.

Believing in Yourself

Your worst enemy cannot harm you as much as your own unguarded thoughts.

—THE BUDDHA

As you learned on Day 5, what you believe about yourself shapes your life. Whether a belief is positive or negative, it affects how you see the world and determines your actions. Ask yourself this: *If you believed that something was not possible, would you attempt to do it?* For the majority of people, the answer is no, and the stronger your belief that you cannot do something, the more likely you never will. Of course, the opposite is also true. The greater your belief that you can accomplish something, the more likely you will. Why? The answer is simple. Your belief that you can accomplish something will lead you to take the action you need to take. In other words, if you believe you can, you will try. If you believe you can't, you won't.

Limiting beliefs are lies that hold you back. They are lies that you have told yourself, often unknowingly. They constantly conflict with what you really want. Today's solution will help you identify the lies about drinking that have stopped you from successfully cutting back or quitting drinking—until now.

Change Your Limiting Beliefs, Change Your Life

A human being always acts and feels and performs in accordance with what he imagines to be true about himself and his environment.

—MAXWELL MALTZ[2]

Here are some examples of common limiting beliefs:

- I'm not (intelligent, attractive, rich, old or young, happy) enough.
- Nothing I do is ever good enough.
- I'm not worthy of love (success, money).
- I need more education to be able to get a better job.
- I don't have enough experience.
- I never have the time (or the money) to do what I want to do.

- I'm not safe.
- I don't have what it takes.

Do any of these beliefs sound familiar to you? You most likely have some of these limiting beliefs, but there is another list of lies that may also be holding you back from cutting back or quitting drinking.

The Lies That Limit You

Unless you become aware of limiting beliefs or lies you tell yourself, and then release them, they will virtually guarantee that you won't be able to cut back or quit drinking. Here are the 11 lies that will keep you from getting sober. We will start with number 11 and work our way up to number 1. As you read them, be sure to note which ones are applicable to you—we will come back to those in your action steps for today's solution.

11. Sex and sobriety suck.

"You reek of crackers!"

Drinking lowers your inhibitions, so the perception is that sex is better with alcohol. When you drink, you have the false belief that you are braver, more confident, and more sexually open. The truth is that alcohol just lulls you into a false reality in which you often make bad decisions based on poor judgment. Drinking can also result in sloppy sex, poor hygiene, the inability to perform, and unsafe sex, which can lead to sexually transmitted diseases (STDs) and unwanted pregnancies.[3] The bottom line is sober sex can be fantastic. Sobriety is a lot sexier than drunkenness. Sober people are healthier inside and out, maintain a better body weight, and have an attractive, natural energy and vibrancy that make sex much more appealing, enjoyable, and fulfilling.

10. Drinking reduces stress.

How many times have you come home from work thinking that you needed a drink to relax from the long day? We have all been programmed by TV, movies, and commercials to believe that drinking equals relaxation, fun, and reduced stress. The reality is that you create *more* stress in your life by excessive drinking. You put stress on your relationships and your family, stress on your health, stress on your career, and stress on your finances. Maybe you don't experience problems in every one of these areas of your life, but if you take an honest look at your drinking, we're sure it will be obvious where your drinking is creating more stress rather than reducing it.

9. I have to reach rock bottom to quit drinking.

Millions of people around the world quit drinking every year, and many of them did not wait until they lost their job, marriage, health, or wealth to finally quit. You can choose to quit drinking at any time. As we discussed in Day 1, you can choose your own rock bottom. All it takes is for you to make a clear decision and take action to make a lasting change in your life.

8. Alcoholics are losers.

We've avoided using the word *alcoholic* as much as possible in this program, but this label and its associated limiting belief often extend to excessive drinkers and problem drinkers. People struggling with addictive behaviors, whether they are full-blown alcoholics or "just" problem drinkers, are stigmatized and they feel embarrassed, guilty, and ashamed. Yet a US government report released in November 2014 found that 29.3 percent of the US adult population meets the definition for excessive drinking.[4] Many are high achievers. This reminds us of a famous Harvard Law School address to incoming students: "Look to your left, look to your right; one of you will not be here by the end of the year."[5] Thinking about it this way, you could say to an audience of US adults: "Look to your left, look to your right; one of you is an excessive drinker." Recovered alcoholics include presidents of countries and corporations, Grammy and Oscar winners, and very likely some of your neighbors and friends. See the list on the companion website.

7. Drinking wine is healthy.

Some drinkers like to quote studies that claim wine is healthy for the heart. More recent research indicates that these benefits are significantly overstated.[6] But if you are honestly only drinking one or two glasses of wine a couple of nights a week (eight-ounce glasses, not a whole carafe of wine), then we would not readily classify you as a problem drinker. But the fact that you are reading this tells us that you are probably drinking a lot more. The truth is that alcohol is a poison—in fact, the word *intoxicate* originally meant "to poison"[7] someone. Alcohol is used to fuel cars, and as a preservative, disinfectant, and anesthetic. Don't kid yourself into thinking that putting this poison into your body on a regular basis will somehow have a healthy impact. And by the way, you can get resveratrol (the healthy compound in red wine) from supplements.

6. I have an addictive personality.

Problem drinkers may rationalize their drinking by saying they have an addictive personality and can't do anything about it. Studies show that some people do have a genetic predisposition to addiction,[8] but you are not born an addict, and you do have the choice and ability to live a nonaddicted lifestyle. Being human comes with a great gift—the gift of being able to make choices in your life.

5. I can't have a successful career without drinking.

This common myth is held by drinkers who work in sales or any job that requires a lot of networking. They believe that drinking socially with clients is key to establishing a relationship and winning a sale. Many people also believe that socializing with coworkers over drinks is invaluable for building positive and beneficial relationships at work. However, the truth is that drinking negatively affects your job performance by decreasing your ability to focus and your productivity. Would you want your surgeon to operate on you while nursing a hangover? Trust us, your manager, your business partner, your clients, and the accounts you handle do not want their reputation and their success in the hands of someone who drinks excessively. Even if you do need to socialize with clients or colleagues, you can always order a nonalcoholic beverage like a club soda and lime, or even get one that looks like an alcoholic beverage, like cranberry juice and tonic water. Refer back to the bonus solution on Day 7, the Social Solution, for ways to avoid drinking and being judged at parties and networking events.

4. I have a disease.

Many people embrace the concept that their alcoholism is a disease and that, therefore, they cannot change. But if you have diabetes, high blood pressure, or heart disease, you change your diet. You can do the same for alcoholism or excessive drinking. Do not undermine your ability to change your relationship with alcohol by holding on to the belief that you have a disease and cannot change your behavior or recover from it.

3. I am not fun or likable without alcohol.

When you first got drunk, did you feel like you belonged for the first time in your life? Did you feel like a switch had turned on inside of you that made you funny and more interesting, and like you finally belonged? Drinking might *seem* to make you feel this way, but this is a false perception. Over time, most people no longer find your excessive drinking amusing; instead, they feel sorry for you. They judge you for having a drinking problem, although they will rarely tell you about it. Trust us, when you do get sober, you will hear what many of these people really thought about your drinking. Your drinking was not as hidden, under control, or acceptable as you thought it was.

2. Getting sober is too hard.

Maybe you constantly feel overwhelmed by the desire to drink and plan your next drink—convinced that you will never be free from your compulsion to drink. We know, all of this is scary. If you weren't afraid, you wouldn't be human. Cutting back or quitting drinking requires a dramatic change in your life, and that evokes fear. Think about your greatest accomplishments. They, too, required you to overcome fear, take courageous risks, and push through some tough challenges. If getting sober were easy, you would have done it already. It is hard, and it can be a struggle, but it will also ultimately lead to greater success in virtually every area of your life. We can promise you one thing—you are no different from the countless others who have overcome their addiction or abuse of alcohol to live meaningful, productive, and happy lives. You *do* have what it takes to accomplish your goal of sobriety. Keep reminding yourself of that no matter how hard and challenging it might seem to you right now.

1. It is not possible to be sober *and* happy and excited in life.

This lie is the most pervasive among problem drinkers. You believe that you cannot get sober, and even if you could, you wouldn't love life sober. Out of the countless people we have worked with, we have never heard anyone say that he or she had no concerns about being able to enjoy life sober. Dave recalls in his very early sobriety looking into the eyes of people in disbelief as they shared that they were truly happy sober and that even the idea of drinking no longer burdened them. We know this truth can be hard to believe, but we ask you to trust us. You can be sober *and* have a life filled with incredible joy, meaning, and passion.

The **first action step** for today is to write down which of these top 11 limiting beliefs/myths/lies you have believed up until now. Then take a moment to add to this list. Think of any other limiting beliefs you might have that keep you from getting sober that are not on this top 11 list. Have you embraced any other limiting beliefs that are directly tied to your drinking? Here are a few more to consider and see if they fit:

- Drinking gives me freedom, and if I stop drinking, I will lose my freedom. I don't like anyone telling me what I can and cannot do.
- There is no way I can become a "normal" drinker because complete abstinence is the only thing that works for problem drinkers.
- What makes me successful in my career is the "reward" of drinking at the end of a long day or week.
- I just never thought I could be someone who didn't drink.
- It is going to be too physically painful to quit drinking.
- I need to drink to feel love and be connected.
- Not only do most people drink, they also drink at the same levels I do.

Go ahead and add any of these limiting beliefs that fit to your list, as well as any new ones that might occur to you. We will come back to them soon.

How an MBA Graduate Learned to Cut Back Drinking

Ann couldn't imagine a life without alcohol, at least not a life where she was happy. She was in her early thirties, had an MBA from a prestigious Ivy League university, and was living in New York City. With no kids, she was enjoying the fast-paced life the city offered her. She was working hard, building her career, and going out with friends many nights of the week.

Ann started drinking in high school. It helped her feel like she fit in, she had more fun, and she felt more confident and independent. In college, she drank frequently and at times to excess, but so did her peers, so she wasn't concerned. But as she reached her midtwenties, she started to realize she was different—that her drinking had become a problem.

Before Ann found *The 30-Day Sobriety Solution,* she had already been to a therapist to deal with her drinking concerns and made attempts to quit and cut back, but nothing lasted. She continued to drink and continued to see it consume more and more of her life and her free time. But with *The 30-Day Sobriety Solution,* she started to see what her new life could look like, and realized that sobriety and having fun were not mutually exclusive.

Ann worked on the 30-Day solutions with the same tenacity with which she earned her MBA. Within weeks of starting the program, she found she was able to start socializing, and although it wasn't easy at first, she started having fun going out with friends and not drinking. And not just going out once a week, but going out as often as she did when she had been drinking. She even enjoyed the process of deciding which new nonalcoholic concoctions she would order.

After only a couple of months, Ann celebrated her first sober birthday in eighteen years. For the first time in her life, she was excited about sobriety. Fast-forward almost a year and Ann found that she was one of the few who was able to drink occasionally. She could go out and have a drink or two without any negative consequences. Ann's story is a testament to the fact that you can actually be happy and sober at the same time. And that for some, you might be able to return to a life of normal drinking.

What Do You Think About Sober People?

The **second action step** for today is to consider what you see and believe when you imagine sober people. What are their predominant traits and characteristics? Do you think they are happy or sad? What do you think they do to have fun? Do you think they are boring? Do you think they would judge or dislike you? Go ahead and take a minute to write down your answers before moving on.

Now ask yourself the following question: *Do you like the representation you have created in your mind of these sober people?*

You probably don't. And how can you ever get sober if you don't even like the image of what sobriety represents to you? If you believe that being sober equals being unhappy, you will never take the steps to thrive in sobriety. Your beliefs create your future because ultimately we all are well-oiled self-fulfilling-prophecy machines.

This list may have similarities with the limiting beliefs you identified in the last action step, and it may help you identify some additional limiting beliefs that you overlooked. Be sure to add any new beliefs to your list.

Now that you have awareness of your limiting beliefs, you're ready for the next step, which is shifting those beliefs. In order to shift the limiting belief that you are not fun and likable without alcohol, you need positive models of sobriety. Think of all the people you know, or know of, who don't drink or drink very little and are positive role models. Most likely, even though your initial image of a sober person isn't positive, when you actually consider these specific people, you will realize how wrong your belief or image was regarding sober people. Now let's take a look at some high-profile examples.

What Do Seven of the Top Ten Grossing Actors of All Time Have in Common?

I just decided that I pretty much got everything I could get out of it. I investigated wine and spirits thoroughly, and they certainly investigated me as well, and we found out that we got along beautifully, but maybe too well.

—JOHNNY DEPP
Actor

Consider the following statistic that shatters many of the top 11 lies that problem drinkers tell themselves. As of the writing of this book, at least seven of the top ten grossing actors of all time are either in recovery (Morgan Freeman, Samuel L. Jackson, Robert Downey Jr.), have talked openly about a history of alcohol abuse and either cut back dramatically or quit (Bruce Willis, Johnny Depp), or have chosen not to drink at all (Eddie Murphy, Tom Cruise).[9]

Think about this for a minute. Seven of the top ten actors of all time don't drink. Yet they work in an incredibly stressful and competitive industry—one that requires lots of socializing and networking to be successful. If you are concerned with how you might be perceived by others for not drinking, remember this list. Do you think their peers judge them for their choice not to drink? Hardly!

And guess what the following celebrities all have in common: Jennifer Lopez, Jim Carrey, Natalie Portman, Warren Buffett, Brett Favre, Diana Ross, Andy Murray, Donald Trump, Elton John, Tobey Maguire, Muhammad Ali, Prince, and Shania Twain. *None* of them drinks![10]

As you might recall from Day 5, teetotalers abstain from alcoholic beverages completely, and the list above contains just a few of the people who consider themselves teetotalers. And almost every one of them never had a problem with alcohol—they simply decided that sobriety made them happier and more fulfilled.

Where Do Your Limiting
Beliefs Come From?

I was afraid that I wouldn't be able to work anymore if I quit drinking and drugging, but I decided (again, so far as I was able to decide anything in my distraught and depressed state of mind) that I would trade writing for staying married and watching the kids grow up. If it came to that. It didn't, of course. The idea that creative endeavor and mind-altering substances are entwined is one of the great pop-intellectual myths of our time.

—STEPHEN KING[11]

Before we show you how to change your limiting beliefs, let's look at where they come from. Limiting beliefs are created in many different ways, but mostly they are created during an emotionally powerful event that happened in your childhood. For example, the belief "I don't fit in" or "I am not good enough" may have stemmed from being made fun of, or losing your best friend to someone else, or getting picked last for the team in gym class. But when you had your first drinking experience and suddenly felt like you belonged, you felt, even if only temporarily, like you were good enough. Through these experiences, you created—and then reinforced—a strong belief that drinking alcohol meant having friendships and feeling connected to others, and that not drinking meant not being as funny or interesting, or being isolated and lonely.

When Dave took the time to look for the source of his belief that it was not possible to be sober *and* happy in life, he quickly found it. Throughout junior high and high school, Dave was unhappy, but when he got to college and made good friends, he started having lots of fun. He suddenly became happy. But all of this happened only after he started drinking, so he created a strong association (and ultimately a self-destructive belief) that being happy, having friends, and having fun all came from drinking. This belief was continually reinforced over most of his "drinking career," until he finally became aware of it and changed.

Another common experience is divorce, which shapes children's beliefs about love, self-worth, relationships, marriage, and success, which can all affect your tendency to drink. If you felt abandoned or unloved, or somehow blamed yourself for the divorce, then alcohol may help you feel connected and loved. Alcohol also might help you mask the pain of traumatic events from your childhood, giving you a sense of relief and pleasure. But that underlying pain still exists, waiting to resurface again and again until you face it, feel it, and heal it.

Here's the interesting thing about limiting beliefs—they form in response to an event that happens in your life, but the event itself has *no* inherent meaning. The only meaning any event has is the meaning *you* give it. It is how you uniquely interpret the event that gives it its meaning. That is why two people can experience the same thing and respond to it completely differently. You each form a different interpretation of the event and therefore attach a different meaning to it. The problem is that most of us assign negative meanings about ourselves or about life to events that don't turn out as we hoped. *It is this negative interpretation or meaning that we assign to the event that creates a limiting belief.* Here are some examples:

"I lost the race—I am not a good athlete."

"I got a bad grade on that test—I am not good at math."

"I failed at quitting drinking again—I will never be able to get sober."

"Jean broke up with me—I must not be lovable."

"I didn't get that promotion—I must not be good enough to deserve it."

Once you change the interpretation or meaning that you assign to the event, you empower yourself.

"I lost the race—I need to train harder next time."

"I got a bad grade on that test—I know I am as smart as the people that aced it. I just didn't prepare as much as I should have."

"I failed at quitting drinking again—I know I can beat this if I just persevere long enough. What can I learn from that experience and do differently in the future?"

"Jean broke up with me—we must not be well suited for each other. I'll keep dating and searching for my ideal mate."

"I didn't get that promotion—I know I have what it takes. I just need to learn some new skills and develop myself personally."

You can change the meaning of any event to something positive. Just like the examples above, you always have a choice. You can interpret the event in a negative context and create or reinforce a belief that will hold you back, or you can create a positive, empowering belief that will propel you forward.

Now we will look at the limiting beliefs you just uncovered, determine the source of those beliefs, and create new beliefs by giving new and more positive meanings to the events in your life. *Imagine how your life would change if you started giving positive interpretations and meaning to the events in your life rather than negative ones.*

The Cross-Examination!

Both behavior and feeling spring from belief. To root out the belief which is responsible for your feeling and behavior, ask yourself, "Why."

—MAXWELL MALTZ

Let's do a quick review. The first action step for today was to note which of the top 11 lies were most prevalent in your life. Then you added to this list any that you uncovered by reviewing other common myths. Next, you captured what the characteristics and traits of a sober person look like to you, and you acknowledged how they might be in conflict with your goal to thrive in sobriety. And last, you acknowledged some positive sober role models.

Your **third action step** is to look at your own personalized list of lies and circle the top five that you think could hold you back the most from getting and staying sober. Then cross-examine each one, just like a lawyer would do. Make a strong case as to why that particular belief is not true and how it stops you from living a life that embodies the core values that you uncovered yesterday.

Alan Cohen, author of *Why Your Life Sucks . . . and What You Can Do About It*, suggests approaching it this way. "Imagine two lawyers in a courtroom inside your head. One is arguing for your possibilities and you achieving your goals. The other is arguing for your limits and why you don't deserve what you want. Who will win? The lawyer whom you pay the most. The way you pay these lawyers, however, is not with money; it is with your attention."[12]

One of Dave's limiting beliefs was that he couldn't be successful in his career without drinking. When he started to question this belief, he came to some important realizations. He was more present on the job and was a better employee when he wasn't hungover.

dear WINE,

we had a deal.
you were to make me funnier, sexier, smarter, and a better dancer.

I saw the video.

we need to talk.

He recognized how consumed he was during the day with thinking about and planning when he would drink again. He realized that he overestimated the quality and depth of the relationships he developed with coworkers and clients while drinking; in fact, when he spent time with them and didn't drink, he realized how consumed he had been with his own drinking and hadn't noticed that they drank a lot less than he did. And those who drank as much as or more than he did were so into their drinking that they didn't really care about him. Those who did care had their own issues with alcohol, which eventually had an impact on their ability to succeed at their jobs. Ultimately, Dave realized that what every manager and coworker cares about most is the quality of your work and your ability to work well with others. He clearly saw that his drinking was hurting him more than helping him.

The bottom line is that when you begin to take an impartial point of view, it becomes painfully clear how false and limiting your old beliefs are and why you need to change them.

Now consider what will happen if you continue to let your old beliefs guide your choices. *Where will you be six months, one year, or five years down the road? What will have happened to your health, your finances, and your relationships?* Continuing to embrace your old beliefs will only create more pain. It also means you won't be living by your core values. You won't be a positive role model to your family, friends, and peers. You won't live a long, healthy, fulfilled life. The list of negatives is endless. Take the time to honestly recognize and acknowledge the pain in your life that comes from hanging on to your limiting beliefs.

New Beliefs for Your New Life

If you believe you can, you probably can. If you believe you won't, you most assuredly won't. Belief is the ignition switch that gets you off the launching pad.

—DENIS WAITLEY

Now comes the fun part. It's time to create new beliefs to replace the lies that have been holding you back. New beliefs that support you thriving in sobriety. Beliefs that capture the way you want to be, act, and feel. Beliefs that support your core values, which you identified yesterday. Here are examples of new beliefs that address some of the limiting beliefs or lies we discussed today. You can use these or write your own.

Old Belief. It is not possible to be sober and still be happy and excited.

New Belief. It's easier to experience ultimate happiness, excitement, and fulfillment when I am sober. *Or:* It's easier to be happy and excited when I am sober.

Old Belief. I am not fun and likable without alcohol, and drinking reduces my stress.

New Belief. My sobriety makes me more fun, authentic, and present with my friends, family, and coworkers. Being sober gives me all the time and energy I need to manifest my goals.

Old Belief. Getting sober is too hard.

New Belief. I have everything I need to create a happy and fulfilling sober life.

Old Belief. I can't have a successful career without drinking.

New Belief. I can create a more successful career when I am sober because I am more awake, clearheaded, and focused.

As you can see, this is pretty straightforward. Write your new beliefs in a positive way (avoid negatives like *no* and *not*) and write them in the present tense. Follow the same guidelines from Day 2 that you learned in the Purpose Solution.

Once you have written your new beliefs, which support your values and goals, you are on your way to making some big changes. Hopefully you see how every solution builds on the previous solutions. Now recall the pleasure principle from Day 3 and the Pendulum

Solution. The best way to make sure that these new beliefs stick is to link so much pleasure to them that you are highly motivated to act on them. And yes, we know we have asked you to do this before, but repetition is one of the keys to your success in this program.

So take a moment to close your eyes and dream about this "new you." Allow yourself to get excited and really feel what it will be like to be the "new you," as if it were happening right now. How are your friends, family, and coworkers responding to you? Have you lost weight? Are you in better physical shape? Are you more successful in your career? Have you saved more money or rewarded yourself with something you have always wanted but couldn't afford before? Really see it, feel it, and believe it. The more you can picture yourself acting on these new beliefs, the more the "new you" becomes real, which will cause you to make changes more easily and effortlessly. So stop reading now and take a few minutes to do this visualization exercise.

When you are done, be sure to put the list of your new beliefs somewhere where you will see it and review it every day.

Day 11 Action Steps

For about ten years, I've been pretty much not drinking. I went through a normal kind of late-teens, early twenties drinking, but it was a choice I made, because I didn't think it was very good for my life.

—CHRISTINA RICCI
Emmy Award–nominated actor[13]

Here is a brief review of today's action steps. Be sure to refer back to the text if you need help remembering how to complete each one.

- **Capture your limiting beliefs.** Review the 11 myths/lies/limiting beliefs and write down which ones you believe. Then add to this list any other beliefs that have held you back from getting sober. The best way to uncover these is to think about why you drink and what scares you most about not drinking, and then ask yourself if those fears are real or if they are simply limiting beliefs.

- **Write down the characteristics and traits of a sober person.** Be sure to note if any of these traits is also limiting beliefs that you overlooked in the first action step. Then list any friends, family members, or public figures that you respect who are sober or are "normal drinkers," and review the list of celebrity teetotalers on today's companion website.

- **Cross-examine your limiting beliefs.** Pick the top five limiting beliefs that have been keeping you from getting sober. Next, write down how each of them limits you and what your life will look like if you allow these limiting beliefs to continue to run you. Then approach each limiting belief like a lawyer and create a strong case for why it is not true. Be sure to write this down in your journal.

- **Write new beliefs to replace your limiting beliefs.** Capture the way you really want to be, act, and feel. And then take a minute to imagine how it will feel to be living your life in alignment with those beliefs. Keep a list of these new beliefs in a place where you can easily review it daily for the next nineteen days.

Be sure to visit the companion website for today at http://Day11.Solutions, where we walk you through additional examples for each of today's action steps.

Day

The Subconscious Mind Solution

Leverage the Power of Your Subconscious Mind

I discovered that when we compete the conscious and the sub-conscious, the subconscious always wins. So we're functioning 95 percent of the day with a more powerful mind that was pro-grammed by other people with limitations that will prevent us from going someplace, yet we can't see it unless we purposely become aware of it.

—DR. BRUCE LIPTON
Author of *The Biology of Belief*[1]

Have you ever driven a car, arrived at your destination, and then realized you don't remember any of the details of driving there—the turns, lights, or traffic you just went through? This is one of the most common examples of the power of your subconscious mind.

Your subconscious mind is *far* more powerful than your con-scious mind. Your subconscious mind directs your choices and your drinking habits more than your conscious mind does. Today, with the Subconscious Mind Solution, we conclude our deep dive into the Sobriety System by teaching you how to use the power of your sub-conscious to thrive in sobriety.

The Recording of Your Life

The diagram of the Sobriety System illustrates how we want our life to be in harmony with our core values. When you contradict those values, you experience internal conflict, which contributes to your desire to drink. Yesterday we covered the importance of your beliefs and how they drive the decisions you make that either support or conflict with your core values. However, many of your beliefs are hidden in your subconscious—and are therefore harder to become aware of and change.

The subconscious is defined as "the mental activities [ideas, impressions, urges] just below the threshold of consciousness."[2] It is a part of the mind that we are not fully aware of, but that influences our feelings, judgments, and behavior. Your subconscious contains all of your "programming."[3] Like a video recording device with unlimited storage, it keeps a record of everything that happens to you and around you; however, it plays back only the most powerful recordings or programs from your past.[4]

The most powerful programs in your subconscious are your beliefs. When you have a strong belief system that is in sync with your core values, the benefits are extraordinary. Strong limiting beliefs, like the ones you uncovered yesterday and others that are still buried in your subconscious, impede your ability to cut back or quit drinking. The Subconscious Mind Solution will teach you the power and significance of the subconscious and how to work with it to thrive in sobriety.

Most of Your Behavior Is Unconscious

Your subconscious mind does not argue with you. It accepts what your conscious mind decrees. If you say, "I can't afford it," your subconscious mind works to make it true.

—DR. JOSEPH MURPHY (1898–1981)
Author of *The Power of Your Subconscious Mind*

Research suggests that most of your behavior is unconscious.[5] Think of your consciousness like an iceberg, where the conscious mind is just the tip, and the rest of the iceberg below the water, which is most of it, represents your subconscious. The amount of mental activity occurring outside your conscious awareness is massive.

It is understandable to be a little skeptical about how much your subconscious directs the decisions you make every day. Up until recently, the study of the unconscious was often dismissed as pop psychology; however, recent science has proven that the influence of the subconscious in our life is immense.

Dr. Bruce Lipton, a leading researcher in psychology and the best-selling author of *The Biology of Belief*, explains that our subconscious is "more than a million times more powerful than the conscious mind."[6] The subconscious mind can handle twenty million bits of information per second compared with the conscious mind, which can handle only forty bits of information per second.[7]

Think about when you first learned to drive a car. The amount of information you had to absorb all at once was overwhelming, especially if you learned to drive a stick shift. You had to keep your eye on the road in front of you, regularly look in your rearview mirror, pay attention to the traffic around you, watch for traffic signs and traffic lights, stay under the speed limit, and follow the rules of lane changing, turning, yielding, and merging with other traffic.

Having a conversation with a passenger, changing the radio station, or drinking coffee was virtually impossible when you were learning to drive. Now fast-forward to today. When was the last time you went on an errand and didn't even remember the details of driving? Maybe you were "lost" in a great song or were in the middle of an important conversation, and the next thing you knew, you were at your destination. That happened because your subconscious took over. It had been programmed countless times over the years to drive safely. There is too much going on for your conscious mind to process it all, so when your focus shifts, your subconscious kicks in. And most of the time, you are not even aware it is happening.

You may believe that your conscious thoughts are creating your reality and that by changing your conscious thoughts, you can learn to thrive in sobriety. However, your behavior is far more representative of your subconscious than your conscious. Dr. Drew Pinsky, addiction expert and producer and star of the reality-TV show *Celebrity Rehab*, says that addiction "operates outside of consciousness."[8]

Remember, your beliefs lead to your actions and behaviors, so until you can change your subconscious limiting beliefs, you will sabotage your efforts to become and remain sober. And you might not even know how or why you're sabotaging yourself, because just like when you are driving, your subconscious takes over without you consciously deciding when and where.

Lottery Winners Going Bankrupt

According to a recent study,[9] lottery winners declare bankruptcy at twice the rate of the general population. How is this possible? It's because the subconscious, which includes your limiting beliefs, sabotages you. Your subconscious works much like a thermostat—if you set the thermostat at 70 degrees, and the temperature goes up or down, your air-conditioning or heat will turn on. Similarly, if you are programmed to believe you don't deserve to have a lot of money, then when you come into a sudden windfall, your subconscious will kick in and bring you back to where it believes you should be—your comfort zone.

This operates the same way with sobriety. If deep down your self-concept and self-image are of being a "drunk" or high-functioning alcoholic, your subconscious will always work to bring you back to this core identity. If you don't first change these limiting beliefs and images in your subconscious, you will have a hard time making progress and staying sober.

In his book *Subliminal: How Your Unconscious Mind Rules Your Behavior*, bestselling author and physicist Leonard Mlodinow captures

the importance of understanding the interaction between our awareness and subconscious when he writes, "Our subliminal brain is invisible to us, yet it influences our conscious experience of the world
in the most fundamental of ways."[10]

Mlodinow mentions an interesting study[11] on how the subconscious can influence our actions, totally outside of our awareness.
Ironically, this study was done on wine purchases.

In the study, four French and four German wines were placed in
an English supermarket, and French or German music was played
in the background on alternating days. On the days when French
music was played, 77 percent of the wine sold was French. And on
the days when German music was played, 73 percent of the wine
purchased was German. This is a powerful example of how our subconscious can be influenced and how it can exert influence over our
decisions without our conscious awareness.

Bill Wilson, the cofounder of Alcoholics Anonymous, writes,
"How shall our unconscious, from which so many of our fears, compulsions, and phony aspirations still stream, be brought into line
with what we actually believe, know, and want! How to convince
our dumb, raging, and hidden Mr. Hyde becomes our main task."[12]
We agree. When you get your subconscious synchronized with what
you really want—your conscious desires and dreams that you have
started to identify during these first two weeks—it becomes much
easier to achieve and maintain your desired results.

Your First Six Years of Life

Many psychologists believe that the first six or seven years of a
child's life completely form his or her personality,[13] especially the
most powerful beliefs, because during this time, the subconscious is
easily programmable. Think of this programming as if you are writing notes with a pencil and you can use only one sheet of paper.
The first time you write something, it's clear and easy to read, but

once you fill up the page, you have to erase what you wrote earlier in order to write more. The more often you write on the paper, the harder it is to erase the previous writings. This is one of the reasons why early childhood is the best time to teach children languages and how to play instruments,[14] and also why, as we explained on Day 4 in the Forgiveness Solution, traumatic events from your childhood leave such a lasting negative impact.

But don't worry; all of this can be changed. The great news is that a lot of the previous days' solutions have already started to reprogram your subconscious, and over the next two weeks, you will learn many other solutions that work at the subconscious level as well as at the conscious level. Let's look at the Sobriety System one last time.

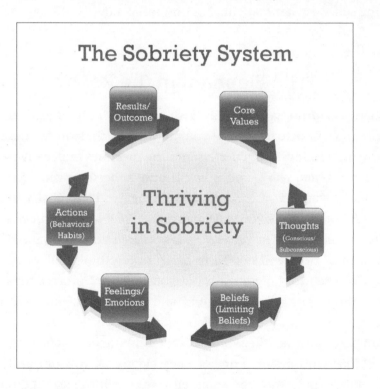

Even though we have placed the subconscious under thoughts, the subconscious really serves as the "engine" that powers both your thoughts and your beliefs.

For example, when Dave was five years old, his eight-year-old brother showed him a gallon jug of wine (with a screw cap) that was stored in a lower cabinet in the kitchen. His brother told Dave that if he wanted to "feel good," he could drink some of the wine. One night after Dave's parents had put him to bed, they discovered him in the kitchen, drinking from the wine jug. He doesn't know how many times he did this, but you can see how Dave's subconscious created a strong belief linking drinking to feeling good. While this is a common belief for many of us, the fact that this programming was formed at an early age made it much harder for Dave to break. However, once he understood this, he used the same techniques you are learning here to reprogram his subconscious with the belief that being sober is what really makes him feel good.

The Elephant in the Room

When you wrote your 30-Day Vision Statement on Day 2 and set goals on Day 6, we instructed you not to write them in the negative. The conscious mind *can* understand the meaning of negative words such as *no*, *not*, *don't*, and *won't*. It also understands the meaning intended by the phrases "*quitting* drinking" and "*cutting back* drinking." *However, numerous studies have proven that the subconscious mind does* not *understand negatives*.[15] So if you are saying to yourself, "Do not drink," or "I will not go to bars," or anything that you do *not* want yourself to do, your subconscious does not process the *not*. It hears those statements as "Drink" and "Go to bars," and will sabotage your intention to cut back or quit drinking.[16]

When you read the words "Don't think about elephants," you most likely just pictured one or more elephants in your mind. (You did, didn't you!) And when you tell young children not to do something, quite often they do exactly what you told them not to do. This isn't necessarily because they are trying to defy you; it's because the prefrontal cortex (the part of the brain that is responsible for analyzing thoughts and regulating behavior) is not yet fully developed and they did not process the *not* or the *don't*. Think of it this way. If you tell a two-year-old *not* to slam the screen door, the subconscious forms a picture of slamming the screen door, and that's what the child does. Instead, you could say, "Please close the screen door gently."

Once you stop focusing on and talking about how to *cut back drinking* or *quit drinking* and put more energy into deleting old programming and installing new programming with the focus on the positive thoughts and images of a sober and happy life, you experience a dramatic shift in your desire to drink.

Changing Your Subconscious

The solutions in The 30-Day Sobriety Solution *have changed me in ways I never imagined possible. On a conscious level, the changes are easy for me to recognize, but the most unexpected and powerful result of this program is that I finally feel like I have changed my subconscious programming and limiting beliefs that were always sabotaging my ability to get and stay sober. Today my life and my new story are exciting, and I know these great changes are going to last.*

—HANNAH

30-Day Graduate from Sydney, Australia

Whatever you consciously and repeatedly think about, accompanied by strong emotions, will reprogram your subconscious over time. It really is that simple. And throughout this entire program, we are teaching you the most effective techniques for accomplishing this.

For example, you might be sick of the phrase "thriving in sobriety." We use it a lot, but there is an important reason why. Although cutting back or quitting is the goal you started with, that is just a step toward the larger goal of living a happy and fulfilling sober life, or thriving in sobriety. And we want to continually activate that positive image and desire. On Day 1, we defined sobriety as "moderation in or abstinence from consumption of alcoholic liquor or use of drugs." So when we use the word *sobriety*, even if your goal is to cut back, this still applies. *The strategy behind using the phrase "thriving in sobriety" repeatedly throughout each solution is to reprogram your subconscious to focus constantly on that outcome.*

Day 12 Action Steps

If there is one solution that can put thriving in sobriety on cruise control in your life, it is the Subconscious Mind Solution. And yet today we are not going to give you a lot of exercises to complete. Rather, we just want to stress the importance of working to reprogram your subconscious and the role that plays in creating and sustaining a life of thriving in sobriety.

- **Reprogram yourself for success before bed.** While you are lying in bed at the end of the day, spend five minutes focusing on your goals, dreams, and desires, including your thriving-in-sobriety goals. Doing this before you fall asleep is a very effective way of helping to reprogram your subconscious overnight, because unlike your conscious mind, your subconscious never sleeps. Simply take time to visualize all your dreams and goals as already completed. What would you be seeing, hearing, and feeling?

- **Complete all of the guided recordings.** On the companion website, we have included guided imagery exercises for many of the past solutions that are perfect for reprogramming your subconscious. If you haven't done them yet, please do so today. In addition, we review some past solutions and explore more deeply how they are already helping to reprogram your subconscious.

- **Identify your subconscious drinking links.** Set aside a few minutes to write in your journal the situations, times, places, and emotional states (happy, sad, angry, bored) you were in when you used
to drink, and also note if any of those situations were times when
you really *craved* drinking. Then take a minute and see if you can
recall any incidents from your childhood that helped create these
links. For example, maybe every night when your dad came home
from work, he would have a drink to "take the edge off." Or maybe
no one ever watched a football game on TV without a six-pack of
beer. Or maybe someone in your home would become abusive
when he or she drank. Or maybe the only times that your parents
seemed to have fun and relax were when they drank. Or maybe
Saturday night was always party night with lots of alcohol.

  Take the time to acknowledge these subconscious "lessons"
you learned as a child. They can reveal the source of the deep programming that has been causing your greatest struggles. However, don't worry if you can't recall any childhood events—just the
process of consciously looking for those events now can lead to
remembering some of them in the following weeks or months.

Be sure to visit the companion website at http://Day12.Solutions,
where we address hypnotism, one of the concepts that relates directly to the topic of the subconscious—why it works for some, why
it doesn't for others, and how we are all hypnotized.

The Tapping Solution

Tapping Away Your Desire to Drink

> *EFT tapping can make the entire recovery process both easier and shorter, potentially preventing relapses and giving addicts a way to treat themselves on a day-to-day, even moment-to-moment, basis.*
>
> —DAVID ROURKE
>
> EFT tapping practitioner who specializes in addiction recovery

Cutting back or quitting drinking is not easy, but thanks to Roger Callahan, Gary Craig, and others, there is now a technique that can make it much easier. That technique is popularly known as EFT, Emotional Freedom Techniques, or tapping.

First developed as the Five Minute Phobia Cure by Dr. Roger Callahan[1] to cure phobias, fears, and anxieties, it was later further developed and popularized by Gary Craig, Dawson Church, Nick Ortner, and others[2] to relieve stress, release negative emotions, make physical symptoms (including pain) disappear, dissolve and replace limiting beliefs, and reduce or eliminate cravings and addictions.

Gary Craig called this new system of emotional healing EFT Tapping, or simply tapping, because it combines focused thought with gentle tapping with your fingers on a series of seven to twelve acupuncture points. These acupuncture points lie on a set of meridians, or pathways in the body where vital energy is thought to flow. It is simple to learn and easy to perform on yourself, and it can radically accelerate the process of recovery. Today we will teach you exactly why tapping works, share with you some breakthroughs that others have experienced using it, and show how you can use tapping to thrive in sobriety.

The Stupidest Thing You'll Ever Do?

When we first introduce tapping to people, most of them think it's weird, too simple to actually work, and not something you would want anyone else to catch you doing. In the following excerpt from *The EFT Manual* by Dawson Church, a patient named Kari Reed describes her experience with—and her initial impressions of—the therapy:

> Tapping is probably the stupidest thing you'll ever do. Think about it—there are "special places" all over your face and body, and if you bang on those long enough, while saying some words and imagining some stuff, all your problems will go away. And let's face it, you know that when you're sitting there, your eyes closed, trying to picture your inner four-year-old, touching your face like a crazy person with a nervous tic, and mumbling that you truly and deeply love and accept yourself anyway, you probably look pretty stupid. In fact, we can go ahead and remove the "probably"—you look stupid. The problem with this stupid thing is that it actually works.[3]

Like many others, we were skeptical about tapping at first, but once we tried it on ourselves and with our families and friends, we were blown away by its speed and effectiveness. Since then, we have used it with thousands of people in both individual coaching sessions and large group trainings to release fears, anxieties, limiting beliefs, traumatic memories, and cravings. Almost everyone we have used tapping with experiences major breakthroughs in just minutes—results that would have previously taken hours, and even years in some cases. Jack became so impressed with the technique that he even teamed up with tapping expert Pamela Bruner to coauthor the book *Tapping into Ultimate Success: How to Overcome Any Obstacle and Skyrocket Your Success*.

How Tapping Is Changing Recovery

Tapping is a technique that can help you successfully quit or cut back drinking in as little as 30 days. Breaking an addiction or a strong habit no longer has to be painful or require the same constant effort as it did just a few years ago. You don't have to rely solely on your willpower or confessional meetings. Tapping combines focused thought with gentle finger tapping on a few key acupuncture points on the hand, head, and chest to reduce cravings, reduce the physical symptoms of withdrawal, clear emotions such as guilt and shame, replace limiting beliefs, and resolve any original underlying emotional issues that led to the alcohol abuse in the first place.

Here's an example of how powerful tapping can be. A patient named Cath visited Mair Llewellyn-Edwards, a master at tapping, as a last resort in her fight against her alcohol addiction. At that time, she was only just managing to hang on to the threads of her life as a professional and a mother of two young children. Two months before her visit, she had been on Antabuse, a medication that makes alcohol unpalatable, to help her abstain. However, her problems and cravings remained, and without alcohol, she had no way of tranquilizing her anxiety. She was in an emotionally volatile state.

During her first session with Mair, she learned the basic tapping procedure, focusing on getting rid of a slight headache. After two rounds of tapping, Cath said her mind felt clearer and her headache felt different. On the third round, her headache was completely gone. Cath went home with the instruction to use tapping on every concern before her next appointment the following week.

At Cath's second session, she was exuberant. She had used tapping to reduce her anxiety about everything and everyone! Tapping made her calm and confident each time she used it. And it helped her realize that she had been masking her anxiety with alcohol, which is why she would drink on her way home before facing her family at the end of a hectic day.

Tapping throughout her busy day as well as on her way home enabled Cath to reduce the buildup of stress at its source. It gave her confidence to face situations she had previously feared.[4]

How It Works

When you experience emotional or physical pain, your brain's stress response kicks in. Whether you're upset by a current event or an old memory, the emotional part of your brain releases a cascade of stress hormones like cortisol and adrenaline, which then communicate the stress to your entire body in a matter of seconds.

But by gently tapping on a series of eight acupuncture points on your body when you feel stressed, a second signal travels to your brain, telling it that you're safe. This signal that you're safe breaks the brain's association between the bad event and the stress response. And once that link is broken, it usually stays broken.

Here's how it works in relation to reducing cravings for alcohol—when you get a physical craving, your body becomes stressed, and you feel anxious. In the past, drinking was a way to relieve that stress and anxiety. But by tapping, you can calm your anxiety more easily and with fewer harmful side effects than drinking. Specifically, you calm a part of your brain called the amygdala, which disrupts production of the stress hormones that were flooding your body, so your body and mind can relax. And when your body and mind relax, your "need" for a drink disappears.[5]

Gloria Arenson, author of the book *EFT for Procrastination*,[6] specializes in helping people overcome compulsive behaviors. She has found that people struggling with an addiction or abuse problem usually struggle with a kind of "superstress." This occurs when they feel totally powerless about something in their life and reflexively tell themselves, *It's really awful, and there's nothing I can do about it!*

Superstress creates an imbalance in the feel-good brain chemicals dopamine and serotonin, which produces a craving for any substance (such as alcohol) that will make you feel good by raising the level of those neurotransmitters. The problem is, the relief is only temporary, and when the stressful situation continues, the craving returns. The cool thing about tapping is that it replenishes your levels of dopamine and serotonin, and so the craving stops.

A good deal of scientific research shows that tapping is effective for reducing cravings and addictions. For a study published in the journal *Integrative Medicine*, Dawson Church and Audrey Brooks examined cravings among 216 health care workers before and after tapping.[7] In the study, trays of alcohol, cake, and candy were brought into the room, so that the participants could get fully in touch with their cravings. The participants then identified childhood events linked to their cravings, such as "Mommy always gave me ice cream after my piano lesson" and "Dad always had a beer with me on weekend days after I turned fifteen. He died when I was eighteen, and I miss him so much." After about thirty minutes of tapping on the emotional intensity related to those childhood events, their cravings dropped by an astonishing 83 percent, and symptoms of anxiety and depression dropped by an average of 45 percent.

Five Ways You Can Use Tapping

People have all kinds of reasons for drinking, but most involve unresolved emotions, including stress, anxiety, and fear. Drinking is one way to tranquilize difficult emotions and keep them under control. What we're discovering with EFT is that it's possible to eliminate stress, anxiety, and other damaging emotions altogether, so the need for self-medication simply disappears.

When an addictive behavior serves no useful purpose, the be-havior disappears too.

—GARY CRAIG

Founder of EFT and author of the first edition of *The EFT Manual*

Using tapping can help you accelerate your recovery process in the following five ways:[8]

1. Reduces your desire to drink or your craving for alcohol. Tapping can often provide fast relief for cravings, which allows you to stop your use of alcohol with less pain.

2. Reduces your symptoms of withdrawal. Tapping can help free you from any physical or emotional side effects of alcohol withdrawal.[9]

3. Releases any feelings and limiting beliefs about cutting back or quitting drinking. On Day 11, in the Lie Detector Solution, we asked you to make a list of all your limiting beliefs, including the lies you have told yourself about drinking. You can use tapping to clear these and any other limiting beliefs that you uncover.

4. Releases any painful feelings that are associated with drinking or trying to quit. Cutting back or quitting drinking can bring to the surface a wide range of emotions, such as guilt, shame, embarrassment, self-hatred, fear, anger, or low self-esteem. If these are not cleared properly, they can keep you "stuck" and eventually lead you back to drinking.

5. Identifies and resolves the original events, emotional issues, and underlying feelings that caused your problem drinking. Alcohol abuse is often the result of painful or traumatic experiences from your past and unresolved feelings that you have not dealt with. Tapping can help you identify and resolve those experiences.

The true cause of addictions is anxiety, an uneasy feeling that is temporarily masked, or tranquilized, by some substance or behavior.

—GARY CRAIG

How Jose Tapped Away His Alcoholism

Jose was an alcoholic who drank four large bottles of beer, or the equivalent of eleven 12-ounce bottles, every night. He began at six o'clock, while he was still at the auto paint shop he owned, and continued at home until he eventually passed out.

Then Jose met EFT practitioner Javier Gomez, who was able to identify in only one session that drinking wasn't Jose's real issue. Rather, it was the loss of both his father and his brother, with whom he had been very close, about seven years earlier. Jose had not been able to let go of the pain from losing two of his closest family members. Javier decided to use a very simple tapping technique to help free Jose from his sadness and loneliness, which took less than twenty minutes. After this short tapping session, Jose reported feeling "liberated" as he headed back to work.

As he got ready for bed, Jose suddenly realized that he hadn't needed a drink that night—and hadn't even thought about it! He couldn't believe it. And each of the following three nights, he didn't drink either. On the fifth night after his first tapping session, some of his drinking friends showed up with lots of beer, which usually would have meant that Jose would drink even more than usual. But he declined their offer easily. He still had no desire to drink.

This story might sound unbelievable, but we have consistently seen these kinds of results with tapping. Jose dealt with his alcoholism by tapping on—and tapping into—his core issue, which was his grief over losing his father and brother.[10]

By now you know that the key to thriving in sobriety is dealing with the root cause of your drinking—your unresolved emotional issues. If you went through a painful experience, such as flunking out of school, being passed over for a promotion, losing your job, declaring bankruptcy, discovering that your spouse cheated on you, getting divorced, or losing a loved one, you will ultimately need to deal with those feelings of loss, betrayal, unworthiness, or low self-esteem. Tapping is a perfect solution. In fact, tapping can free you from these painful feelings in a fraction of the time it would take with more traditional methods of therapy.

So let's get started.

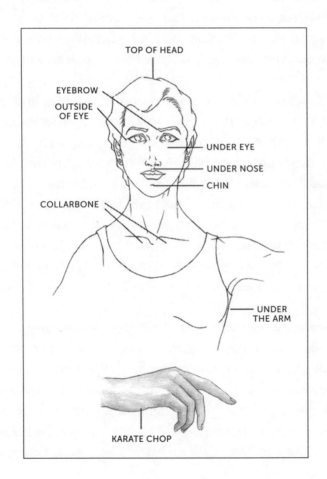

The Basic Tapping Protocol

The great thing about tapping is that it's easy. You can learn the basic protocol in under ten minutes. You can also learn how to tap by going to the companion website at http://Day13.Solutions and watching the *Introduction to Basic Tapping* video. As you watch the video, you may want to refer to the steps below as well as the diagram of the tapping points.

Start by practicing on yourself, but once you learn the basic protocol, you might want to practice it with your friends or family. When Dave first learned this basic tapping process, he used it with his daughters to help them overcome their test-taking anxiety and a fear they had of bad people hurting them or their family. Both of them thought it was weird at first, but when Dave checked in with them a week later, they acknowledged that it had actually worked.

1. Decide what issue you want to tap on. In tapping, the issue you're working on is sometimes referred to as your Most Pressing Issue, or your MPI. Decide if you want to tap on a craving, a physical discomfort, an uncomfortable or painful emotion, or a limiting belief that you would like to clear (let go of). Give it a name such as "This craving for a glass of wine," "My headache," "My fear of rejection," "My being upset with my husband," or "My belief that I can't relax without alcohol." We'll demonstrate the rest of the steps in the basic tapping protocol using the following fear or limiting belief: "I'm afraid that people will judge me and make fun of me if I don't drink with them."

2. Determine your level of discomfort—the intensity of the feeling or belief. Close your eyes and focus your attention on the MPI you have chosen to clear with tapping. For example, you could heighten your concentration on your fear that people will judge you if you don't drink by imagining being at a party with your friends where everyone is drinking. As you focus intently on the belief or fear, scan your body and notice what you are feeling and where. Determine on a scale of 0 to 10—0 meaning "no intensity at all" and 10 meaning "extremely intense"—the intensity of the discomfort you feel in your body when you focus on your craving, feeling, pain, or belief. By establishing a number before you begin to tap, you can measure any reduction in intensity after a few minutes of tapping.

3. Create your "setup statement." Now that you know your intensity level, the next step is to craft the "setup statement." The basic setup statement goes like this:

"Even though [fill in the blank with your MPI], I deeply and completely love and accept myself."

For example, you might say, "Even though I'm afraid people will judge me if I don't drink with them, I deeply and completely love and accept myself."

- If you were tapping to get rid of your headache, you might say, "Even though I have this headache, I deeply and completely love and accept myself."
- If you were tapping to get rid of a limiting belief, you might say, "Even though I have this belief that I can't relax without alcohol, I deeply and completely love and accept myself."

Once you have your setup statement, you can begin tapping. Looking at the diagram of the tapping points above, find the location of the karate chop point on the heel of one hand. (Either hand is fine.) With the other hand, using two or three of your fingers, start tapping on this spot firmly enough to feel it but not hard enough to bruise your hand, while you focus on your fear of being judged. While tapping on your karate chop point, say your setup phrase out loud three times.

4. Choose a "reminder phrase." Your reminder phrase consists of just a few words to remind you of your MPI, which you will say out loud as you tap on the sequence of the eight points in the tapping sequence. It can be as simple as "This urge to drink" or "This feeling of shame." Working with the MPI from above, your reminder phrase could be "This fear of rejection."

5. Tap through the points. We recommend that you begin by tapping on just one side of the body, using whichever hand is most comfortable for you. Using the index and middle finger, tap on each one of the eight points five to seven times while saying your reminder phrase out loud one time at each point before moving on to the next one. You have completed a "round" of tapping when you've tapped on each of the eight points. We recommend that you watch the video so that you're clear on the points, but don't worry about being too precise; tapping is very forgiving. Tap lightly but firmly. If you can't tap a certain point due to an injury, just skip that point. Tap on the eight points in the following order:

- *Top of the Head:* This fear of rejection.
- *Eyebrow:* This fear of rejection.
- *Outside of the Eye:* This fear of rejection.
- *Under the Eye:* This fear of rejection.
- *Under the Nose:* This fear of rejection.
- *Chin:* This fear of rejection.
- *Collarbone:* This fear of rejection.
- *Under the Arm:* This fear of rejection.

After three or four rounds of tapping on the points, stop, close your eyes, take a deep breath, and check to see what the level of intensity of the feeling (fear of rejection) is now. If your level is a 0, you can stop. If it is not yet a 0, keep tapping some more rounds until you bring it all the way down. Another option is to add in several "positive choice" rounds when the level of intensity is down to a 4 or below. We explain this in the next step.

6. Add a positive choice statement. When the intensity level drops to 4 or less, you can create one or more statements affirming a positive thought or action you could take. Use this structure:

"Even though [fill in the blank with your MPI], I choose to [fill in the blank with a positive action]."

For example, "Even though I'm afraid of being rejected if I don't drink with my friends, I choose to go and have a good time anyway."

A positive choice round might look like this:

- *Top of the Head:* Even though I'm afraid of being rejected if I don't drink . . .
- *Eyebrow:* I choose to go and have a good time anyway.
- *Outside of the Eye:* Even though I'm afraid of being rejected if I don't drink . . .
- *Under the Eye:* I choose to believe nobody will even notice, if I don't make a big deal about it.
- *Under the Nose:* Even though I'm afraid of being rejected if I don't drink . . .
- *Chin:* I choose to drink club soda and be myself.
- *Collarbone:* Even though I'm afraid of being rejected if I don't drink . . .
- *Under the Arm:* I choose to be happy knowing I don't have to worry about drinking and driving.

Now that you have learned the basic steps for tapping, let's look at a couple of different ways you can use it to help you cut back or quit drinking. Your **first action step** for today is to practice the basic tapping protocol and tap on one of your limiting beliefs that you identified on Day 11 in the Lie Detector Solution. Or try it with some cravings or negative emotions that you may be experiencing, using the following examples.

Tapping Away Your Cravings

One of the most valuable uses of tapping is to reduce your desire or craving for alcohol. Using the basic tapping protocol, your tapping session might look like this:

1. Rate the intensity of your craving from 0 to 10.

2. Create a setup statement like the following and say it three times while tapping on the karate chop point: "Even though I really desire a drink so badly that I am not sure that I can control myself, I totally and completely love myself."

3. Tap three or four rounds as you get in touch with your craving, how much you want to drink, and how good you think it will make you feel. As you tap on each point in the order below, state your reminder phrase ("This desire to drink") out loud. (Notice that it is okay to change the wording of your reminder phrase as long as it keeps you focused on the same issue.)

- *Top of the Head:* This desire for alcohol.
- *Eyebrow:* This desire for alcohol.
- *Outside of the Eye:* This desire for alcohol.
- *Under the Eye:* This desire for alcohol.
- *Under the Nose:* This desire to have a drink.
- *Chin:* This desire to drink.
- *Collarbone:* This craving for a drink.
- *Under the Arm:* This desire for alcohol.

4. Stop and rate the intensity of your craving again. Is it the same, lower, or higher? Keep tapping until you reach 0 and the craving is gone. Or once you reach an intensity level of 4 or lower, add in a few rounds with a positive choice statement.

- *Top of the Head:* Even though I have this desire for alcohol . . .
- *Eyebrow:* I choose to be free from it.
- *Outside of the Eye:* Even though I want a glass of wine . . .
- *Under the Eye:* I choose to be free from it.
- *Under the Nose:* Even though I have this urge to have a drink . . .
- *Chin:* I choose to have a glass of club soda.
- *Collarbone:* Even though I have this craving for a drink . . .
- *Under the Arm:* I choose to be totally free from this desire.

Be aware that when you tap on a craving, troublesome thoughts and feelings might come up. Here are some common thoughts that often arise:

If I don't have a drink, I'll feel too deprived.

I don't have the strength to refuse a drink.

Overcoming my alcohol addiction is impossible.

I can't live without alcohol.

I can't be relaxed and happy without alcohol.

I cannot sleep without having a drink.

I don't know how to socialize without a drink.

I won't have any friends if I don't drink.

A drink is my reward for working hard all day.

I can't stop drinking because I have a lot of stress.

I don't like anyone telling me what I can and cannot do.

Even if tapping does work, I am afraid it won't last.

If thoughts like these do surface, take a few moments to tap on those as well. For example:

Setup phrase: "Even though I've lost all my money through my drinking, I deeply and profoundly love and accept myself."
Reminder phrase: "This sense of loss."

Setup phrase: "Even though I believe a drink is my reward for working hard all day, I totally and completely love and accept myself."
Reminder phrase: "This belief that drinking is my reward."

Tapping Away Negative Emotions Associated with Your Drinking

As you work through the solutions in this 30-Day program, you might feel some of the following emotions: guilt or shame (because of your addiction), fear (that you won't be able to get a drink), anxiety (when you don't know what to do), unhappiness (because you don't have what you want), and anger (because you are not "allowed" to have a drink). Use the same tapping procedure to tap on these feelings as well. Here's an example:

> **Setup phrase:** "Even though I feel ashamed because I'm addicted to alcohol, I totally and completely love myself."
> **Reminder phrase:** "This shame."
> **Positive choice rounds:** I choose to be free from this shame. I choose to be free from this desire for a drink.

Tapping Away Pain and Discomfort

When physical symptoms or pain arises, you can use tapping to get them to subside. For example:

> **Setup phrase:** "Even though I have this terrible tension in my chest when I don't have a drink, I deeply and profoundly love and accept myself."
> **Reminder phrase:** "This tension in my chest."

Identifying and Finally Resolving Your Core Issues

If someone can be traumatized in thirty seconds, why can't they be healed in a day, an hour, a minute?

—RICK WILKES

EFT expert

As they often say in psychology, "The problem is not the problem." In other words, for problem drinking or excessive drinking, drinking is not the problem. As we talked about several times in the first few days, drinking is a symptom of an earlier emotionally laden "problem" that you need to clear in order to truly be free.

Underlying any self-destructive habit are unresolved emotional issues that almost always stem from unmet needs and traumas that were experienced in childhood. Painful events such as excessive teasing, emotional shaming, bullying, physical or sexual abuse, abandonment (due to work, drug or alcohol addiction, divorce, or death), severe accidents, catastrophic illnesses, witnessing a violent crime such as a rape or a murder, being kidnapped, failing a class in school, or dropping the ball that caused the team to lose the game can leave a mountain of unexpressed and unresolved emotions: guilt, shame, grief, betrayal, anger, resentment, fear, low self-esteem. You are trying to cover up or numb these feelings with alcohol, but you need to neutralize or release them. Your **second action step** is to go back to your Day 4 list of people whom you need to forgive and practice tapping to neutralize and release your feelings.

For example, Emily, one of Jack's coaching clients, is a high-level executive in a bank in Paris. She drank heavily to relieve the pressure of her highly stressful life, and she was also a workaholic. In their first session working together, Emily described her intensely over-committed life. In addition to her job, she was on several boards of directors, was a consultant to other financial institutions, and was planning her own wedding. As a perfectionist, she had to do everything at the highest level of excellence, which added more stress to her overly busy life.

When Jack began to explore where this pressure to do so much and do it so perfectly came from, Emily remembered an incident when she was five that occurred in the kitchen of her family's Paris apartment. The economy was in a recession, and her father blurted out to her mother, "I am not sure we are going to have enough money to feed all of the children." In Emily's five-year-old mind, she took her father's statement literally, and decided in that moment that she would become the perfect child in order to be one of the children who didn't go without eating. She would keep her room clean, say yes to every parental request, always do more than what was asked of her and do it perfectly, look for ways to contribute without being asked, and never express her own needs for fear of being a burden. Later, she also got straight A's in school, participated in every extracurricular activity she could, and was always "nice," never causing trouble.

When Emily tapped on her fear of being abandoned and not having enough food if she wasn't always perfect and overproducing, she neutralized the fear that had been driving her. She was able to reduce her perfectionism while still maintaining her excellent job performance, resign from two boards, reduce her consulting load, and hire a wedding planner. And, having eliminated the anxiety that had been her constant companion since she was five, she stopped drinking.

Tapping on cravings themselves is often successful, but identifying and clearing specific childhood events that underlie your drinking is the deepest, most thorough way to apply tapping to cravings and addictions.

Day 13 Action Steps

- **Practice the basic tapping procedure.** Simply practice the tapping sequence using the diagram every day until you no longer need the diagram and the examples to guide you. The easiest way to begin is to watch the *Introduction to Basic Tapping* video on today's companion website to guide yourself through this basic tapping process.

- **Revisit Day 4, the Forgiveness Solution.** If you are still holding any judgments, anger, or resentment toward yourself or anyone else, tap to neutralize and release those feelings.

On the companion website at http://Day13.Solutions, you'll find more suggestions and examples of how you can use tapping to cut back or quit drinking, including tapping on negative thoughts that might come up when you are repeating your 30-Day Vision Statement or your affirmation from Day 4. You'll also find a fifteen-minute audio recording by Jack that will guide you through a powerful transformational process to help you identify *and resolve* any underlying emotions and unconscious limiting beliefs that may have been motivating and driving your excessive drinking. Lastly, you'll find some guided tapping sessions led by tapping experts.

The Review Day and Bonus Solution

*Acknowledging, Celebrating, and
Reviewing Your Accomplishments*

> *We are what we repeatedly do. Excellence
> then, is not an act, but a habit.*
>
> —ARISTOTLE

Congratulations! Reaching the end of Phase II is a huge accomplishment, so close your eyes, take a few deep breaths, and really appreciate yourself for taking such massive positive action. Reaching Day 14 represents a significant milestone in your journey. You are well on your way to thriving in sobriety.

By completing Phase II, "Removing the Mental and Emotional Blocks That Prevent You from Thriving in Sobriety," you have learned and applied some critical concepts, including the Sobriety System. The Sobriety System can be life transforming, because when you reconnect with your core values, uncover and change your limiting beliefs around drinking, and utilize the power of your subconscious mind, you can make significant progress toward thriving in sobriety.

You uncovered the importance of your willpower, and why your past attempts to quit drinking might have failed. You learned specific solutions to overcome procrastination and take action. And you discovered the breakthrough technique of tapping to quit drinking.

Please make sure to visit the companion website for a quick review of each of these key concepts, as well as a special video from us that we have created for you.

Today's companion website also contains your second bonus solution—the Relapse Solution. This teaches you how to beat the odds of relapse and what to do if you find yourself returning to your excessive drinking habits. You can read this solution along with today's review content at http://Day14.Solutions, or you may prefer to save it for a rainy day—when you are feeling a little down or when you find yourself seriously considering drinking again.

Be sure to complete the Phase II review, as it is truly a critical component of your ongoing success. Before you know it, you will be on Phase III.

Creating an Unshakable Belief in Yourself and Your Dreams

Whatever the present moment contains, accept it as if you had chosen it. Always work with it, not against it. Make it your friend and ally, not your enemy. This will miraculously transform your whole life.

—ECKHART TOLLE

Author of *The Power of Now: A Guide to Spiritual Enlightenment*[1]

Welcome to Phase III. This phase is often completed during the third week of *The 30-Day Sobriety Solution*, unless you have chosen the 60- or 90-day option. As you head into Phase III, we want to take a minute to review the ongoing action steps we have asked you to do daily. Let's be honest. We have asked you to do a *ton*. When we have participated in intense programs like this (and rest assured we have), we know how annoying and overwhelming it can feel. We get it! Our advice is to simply do your best.

We know you've been working hard when we hear feedback like, "Do you realize how many ongoing action steps you have given us?" Yes, we do. We put a huge amount of attention and effort into the design of this program, and we have been receiving and integrating feedback from people like you for years, all to make sure that what we are asking you to do gives you the greatest amount of value in the shortest amount of time. Still, we know it is a lot to ask. But we also know that what we are asking is very doable, given the feedback from our graduates who are now thriving in sobriety. So let's take a look at them.

The Top 11 Ongoing Action Steps (in Order of Importance)

I found getting sober surprisingly easy with *The 30-Day Sobriety Solution*, even after never going more than two days without alcohol for over fifteen years. As long as I did the solutions, it wasn't difficult.

—Thomas
30-Day Graduate from London, England

1. Journaling. We really can't overstate the importance of this ongoing practice in your early sobriety (Day 1).

2. Review your 30-Day Vision Statement, which now includes some of your core values (Day 2 and updated in Day 10).

3. Review your three goals supporting your 30-Day Vision Statement, which were updated with some of your core values (Day 6 and updated in Day 10).

4. Continue to work through your list of people you need to forgive or let go of with the Total Truth Process. Although this doesn't have to be a daily exercise, it is critical for you to get through your whole list eventually. For some people, this process turns out to be their highest priority (Day 4).

5. Use tapping to clear your cravings, negative feelings, and limiting beliefs. You can use tapping to address many different challenges (Day 13).

6. Use the forgiveness affirmation and the "I love myself" mantra (Day 4).

7. Review your new beliefs (Day 11).

8. Continue using the "tiny habit," anchoring your 30-Day Vision Statement to an existing behavior (Day 9). (This step could easily be combined with step 2.)

9. Stop using the words "I can't" (Day 5).

10. Have a short nightly ritual before bed where you focus on your vision, goals, dreams, and desires. This accomplishes several steps listed above at once (Day 12).

11. Review your "new you" notes (Day 2).

Whoa, that can make you tired just reading it. Do we honestly expect you to do every one of these every day? Not necessarily, but the more of these action steps you do consistently, the more you set yourself up for breakthrough success. Rest assured, we practice what we preach. Both of us read our vision statements, repeat our affirmations, and visualize our goals daily. We regularly use the tiny-habit technique and the Total Truth Process, and we have almost completely removed the word *can't* from our vocabularies. We use the "I love myself" mantra. Dave journals every day, and Jack uses tapping every day.

To make it easier for you to follow through, we recommend that you combine some of the action steps. For example, start a tiny habit to review your 30-Day Vision Statement, goals, new beliefs, "new you" notes, and the forgiveness affirmation. With this new habit alone, you will accomplish six of these top eleven action steps every day! Okay, enough said.

You are going to love Phase III. Many consider this set of solutions the most fun, effective, and easy to implement in the program. But before we get started, let's talk about the monkey trap.

Avoiding the Monkey Trap

A monkey trap is a glass jar that contains a piece of fruit under a lid with a hole in it. The hole is just large enough for a monkey to put its paw into. When the monkey grabs the fruit, his fist is too big to pull out through the opening. The only way to get it out is by dropping the fruit. But instead of giving up the fruit, he keeps holding on to it because he wants it. Now that he has that food in his possession, he treats it like it is actually part of him. He would rather suffer the consequence of being stuck than let go of it and look for food elsewhere.

In many ways, your behavior might be like that of the monkey—you have grabbed on to the habit of drinking, and you believe and act like you can't let it go. You may get caught up in justifying and rationalizing it, not realizing that all you have to do is just let go.

One of the reasons that most people don't let go is explained by what psychologists refer to as *learned helplessness*, which describes how we take on an attitude that we are helpless to change. So even if you are presented with a solution to a major problem, you have become so helpless that you will never recognize the solution or take action to change.

You are *not* helpless, and hopefully by today, you have fully accepted this fact. You have complete control of your life, and what you choose to hold on to and what you choose to let go of are totally up to you. The solutions in this next phase of the program will help you exercise that choice in regard to your drinking.

The 4-Minute-Mile Solution

Using the Power of Creative Visualization

> *Imagination is everything. It is the preview*
> *of life's coming attractions.*
>
> —ALBERT EINSTEIN (1879–1955)
> Physicist

Visualization has always been around, but it didn't really become popularized until the 1980s.[1] Now, even though it isn't taught in school, almost all athletes—professional and Olympic—as well as leading entrepreneurs and business leaders use visualization. When you visualize doing something, your brain functions as if you are actually performing the task.[2] In other words, the brain doesn't distinguish between actually doing something and visualizing it. Performance experts and sports psychologists agree that this technique can greatly speed up the process of reaching your goals. And it's easy. You just close your eyes and imagine vivid, detailed pictures in your mind.

Visualization, like so many other solutions in *The 30-Day Sobriety Solution,* has rarely been used in the recovery process. In the 4-Minute-Mile Solution, you will learn not only how to use visualization to make thriving in sobriety a reality, but also how to accelerate the achievement of all your other goals in life.

The 4-Minute-Mile Barrier

Experimental and clinical psychologists have proved beyond a shadow of a doubt that the human nervous system cannot tell the difference between an "actual" experience and an experience imagined vividly and in detail.

—MAXWELL MALTZ[3]

On May 6, 1954, Roger Bannister did what most people believed was physically impossible—he became the first person to run one mile in under four minutes.[4] How did Bannister do it? First, he *believed* he could do it; he did not listen to all the doubters. Second, he visualized the race in incredible detail over and over again. He pictured everything— where he would accelerate and vary his pace, how he'd round the curves, and what his time would be at every point in the race. He did this so many times that when he entered the race, he was crystal clear on what he had to do and how he would do it, and he believed without a doubt that he would break the four-minute mile.

His time that day was 3:59:40. That accomplishment alone is amazing, but others soon followed in his footsteps. Within a few weeks, John Landy had accomplished the same "impossible" feat. Within three years, sixteen runners had.[5] How was it possible to go from no one running a four-minute mile to sixteen people doing it within three years?

It wasn't new shoes, a new track, or a new running style. It was simple—Bannister broke a limiting belief. Most limitations are mental, not physical. And once Bannister disproved this belief, other athletes thought, *If he can do it, I can do it, too.*

You can use the same technique that Roger Bannister used to break the four-minute mile to accelerate the manifestation of your goals—including to cut back or quit drinking for good and make thriving in sobriety a reality in your life. In fact, later today we will show that you can use visualization in almost every solution we have presented to accelerate its life-changing impact.

Today we will teach you the science behind this powerful technique and how to utilize it most effectively.

See What You Want, Get What You See

I would visualize things coming to me. It would just make me feel better. Visualization works if you work hard. That's the thing. You can't just visualize and go eat a sandwich.

—JIM CARREY
Actor[6]

When you envision a goal as already accomplished, the image (sobriety) and your current reality (abusing alcohol) don't match. This creates a conflict, or structural tension, in your mind. In order to resolve the tension, your mind either has to give up the vision of your accomplished goal or come up with a solution (ideas and behaviors) to make the vision a reality.

When you consistently visualize your goal as already accomplished, this image intensifies the structural tension, and three things begin to happen:

1. Your brain's reticular activating system (RAS)[7] is programmed to bring to your awareness anything that will help you attain your goal.

2. Your subconscious mind's creative aspect is activated and starts developing solutions for accomplishing your goal. You'll find yourself frequently coming up with new ideas—upon waking up in the morning, while taking a shower, when you're waiting in a line at a store, and even when you're watching TV or a movie.

3. Your motivation increases. You'll suddenly and unexpectedly find yourself doing things and taking actions to move toward your goal because you want to, and not because you feel like you have to.

You might remember that we also covered some of this on Day 11 in the Lie Detector Solution. To determine what you will be aware of, the brain's RAS filters about eleven million bits of information per second. Another study even found that the RAS can filter nearly four hundred billion bits of information per second that enter your brain.[8] Your RAS will let in anything that will help you achieve the goals that you constantly affirm and envision. It will also let in anything that matches and reinforces the beliefs and images you have about yourself, other people, and the world.[9,10] Just think about when you started a new project, whether personal or professional, and how soon after that you started to notice things that had always been there but that you had previously filtered out. For example, if you decide to buy a new car, you will start noticing all kinds of different cars and what you like and don't like. You will naturally remember to ask others who know a lot about cars for advice. However, before that, you were probably oblivious to noticing cars, and would never consider initiating a conversation about them, because your RAS filtered it out, since you were not interested in that data.

So how does all this apply to your efforts to thrive in sobriety? It turns out that visualization is the most effective way to reprogram your RAS. When your brain has detailed, colorful, and vividly convincing pictures, it will seek out and capture all the essential information to make those pictures a reality.[11] If you give it pictures of yourself thriving in sobriety, such as being in great physical shape, or laughing and smiling while spending time with close friends while drinking an iced tea, your RAS will be programmed to become aware of things that can help you do that. Your subconscious will also go to work on achieving this.

However, if you are constantly feeding your brain negative, fearful, and anxious images, such as drinking at a bar or sneaking alcohol at home, it will help you make those a reality, too. Unfortunately, most people often feed their brains images of what they don't want instead of what they do want. This is why it is so important to have a daily practice of visualization to plant positive mental images in your brain of you thriving in sobriety.

The Process for Visualizing Thriving in Sobriety

Formulate and stamp indelibly on your mind a mental picture of yourself as succeeding. Hold this picture tenaciously. Never permit it to fade. Your mind will seek to develop the picture. . . . Do not build up obstacles in your imagination.

—DR. NORMAN VINCENT PEALE[12]

Visualizing yourself thriving in sobriety is really simple—you close your eyes and imagine your goal as already complete. While a vision of a still picture is great, creating a short mental movie or scene can be more powerful. See yourself saying no to an alcoholic beverage that you're offered at a party. Or envision a whole weekend of fun activities without alcohol. Think about your 30-Day Vision Statement and supporting goals from Day 2 and Day 6. Create a detailed mental picture of exactly what you would be seeing through your eyes while you are already thriving in sobriety.

Vividly imagine all of the details—large and small—that you would see. Here are some questions you might want to focus on "seeing" the answers to:

- What does the thriving-in-sobriety version of you look like?
- What are you wearing?
- What is your weight?
- Who is with you, and what are you doing?
- What job do you have? How are you performing?
- How has your self-confidence changed?
- Are you more present and available for deep and meaningful conversations?

- How are people responding differently to you?
- Are you helping others more and giving back more to your community?
- How do you respond when people offer you a drink?

Your vision of thriving in sobriety will likely include multiple images or movies, such as one of you at work, where you feel alive and energetic while talking to your coworkers instead of being hungover. You see yourself with your spouse, kids, or family, doing something that represents how healthy and happy you are sober and how wonderful and fulfilling your relationships with them have become. You can create a scene with friends where you are doing an activity that you have always wanted to do, but drinking made it impossible. Or you even see yourself at a bar or party, having fun while sober, and when a friend offers you a drink, you see and hear yourself say—easily and confidently—"No, thanks" (or one of the excuses for not drinking that we shared in the Social Solution on the companion website for Day 7).

If you have trouble picturing what you would look and feel like when you are thriving in sobriety, you may find it helpful to review your 30-Day Vision again or go back to a time when you were not addicted to or abusing alcohol, even if you have to go back as far as your childhood. You can draw upon a positive memory and the positive feelings of pure joy and happiness you had without alcohol, such as when you were waiting in line to get on an exciting amusement park ride or having a pillow fight with your friends or family.

Supercharging Your Images and Movies

Not only did visualization have a huge impact on helping me thrive in sobriety, I was also able to apply this technique to creating success in my job, my writing, and my relationships.

—THOMAS

30-Day Graduate from London, England

To deepen the impact of your visualization practice, add sounds, smells, tastes, and feelings to your pictures.[13] What sounds, smells, and tastes would you experience, and—most importantly—what emotions and bodily sensations would you feel if you had already achieved your sobriety goals?

Focus on the smells and tastes that might replace the smells and tastes around drinking alcohol. For example, if one of your thriving-in-sobriety visualizations is of a sober you at a bar having fun with friends, then you would add the smells and tastes of your ginger ale or preferred nonalcoholic beverage.

Include in your visualizations the sensations you would feel—such as the satisfaction and pride at finally having achieved your goal of cutting back or quitting drinking, the warmth of the sun on your face as you look out over the ocean at a beautiful sunset and drink a fresh-squeezed lemonade, or the joy of waking up clear-headed and refreshed on a Sunday morning.

By creating these emotions in your mind and imagination, you provide fuel to propel your vision forward. Because your subconscious mind responds more to physical sensations and feelings than to logic, the stronger the feelings you create, the stronger the impact they will have. Research has shown that images or scenes that are tied to intense emotions become locked into your memory.[14]

To validate this fact, you only have to think about some of the major events in your life, especially the traumatic ones, and then think of all the specific details you can still easily remember. For example, when the Twin Towers at the World Trade Center collapsed on September 11, 2001, most likely you remember where you were, what you were doing, whom you were with, and maybe even the clothes you were wearing.

You have a detailed memory of tragic events because of the intense emotions attached to them. Intense emotions stimulate the brain to create stronger and deeper neural connections, which firmly lock a memory.[15] So add the sensations of strong emotions—joy, excitement, enthusiasm, pride—to your visualization. It will seal it in your mind.

You can also deepen the emotional intensity of your visualizations by hearing uplifting music, deeply feeling your passion for succeeding, and adding movement. In seminars, we have people stand up, spread out around the room, close their eyes, and then act out their visualization; for example being at a party, dancing, requesting a ginger ale at the bar, or being the designated driver. The more senses you engage, and the more you include your body in your visualization, the more your mind will retain it, and the quicker your results will be.

Byron's 4-Minute Mile

The 30-Day Sobriety Solution helped me accomplish so many goals and "firsts" in my life, such as my first sober birthday as an adult. This success helped me believe that I don't need alcohol to celebrate special occasions, even New Year's Eve and the Fourth of July—two holidays I was certain I needed to drink to enjoy.

—BYRON

30-Day Graduate from Phoenix, Arizona

There are certain moments in life we never forget. For Byron, it was his third DUI, which he had promised himself would never happen. Details of that morning are forever etched in his memory. The cold sensation of the steel handcuffs being secured around his bony wrists; the jarring noise of the jail cell door slamming shut, and the terrifying silence that followed; the cold concrete of the cell; and the emotional heaviness that enveloped him as the gravity of his mistake set in.

Throughout high school, Byron struggled with panic attacks and depression, in spite of his good grades. All he really wanted was to feel "normal," and he would have gladly traded his academic aptitude to feel like he belonged. After he graduated from high school, Byron discovered that drinking alcohol made him feel normal. In college, he was still able to get good grades, but now he actually had friends and felt happy—like he belonged. His panic attacks lessened dramatically, and he rarely felt depressed. Byron also realized he wanted to pursue a career in psychology. His mother had struggled with mental illness most of his life, and he wanted to help her.

Even though Byron drank heavily during college, he excelled and was awarded a scholarship to a graduate school for psychology. But as Byron continued his studies, he started drinking alone and got his first DUI, which hardly fazed him. In fact, when Byron took his first graduate class on addiction, he realized that his mom didn't have just mental health issues, she was also an addict. But as he studied more about addiction, he convinced himself that if he was getting his PhD in psychology, he couldn't be an alcoholic.

As Byron continued working toward his career as a doctor of psychology, he worked with a therapist. This alleviated most of his panic attacks, although general anxiety and depression still plagued him. His heavy drinking was no longer helping. Eventually Byron got a second DUI, but he still wouldn't accept that he had a drinking problem. After he graduated with a doctorate, he continued drinking, sometimes heavily and only on weekends, and other times every night. Then, in his early thirties, Byron got his third DUI and could no longer hide from the truth. A concerned family member recommended *The 30-Day Sobriety Solution* to Byron, which led to a breakthrough on the first day. "In Day 1 of *The 30-Day Sobriety Solution* I did the guided Time Travel Technique, which was life changing. This process gave me a level of clarity around my drinking that I had never experienced before. I finally knew, and accepted, that continuing to drink was going to keep me from everything I wanted in life, and sobriety was going to lead to true happiness and fulfillment."

As Byron no longer lived in denial, every solution led to additional insights and progress toward sobriety. He recognized many of the concepts in *The 30-Day Sobriety Solution* from his education in psychology and was excited to apply them in a unique, powerful way. Byron discovered that he was particularly good at visualization, and he could create and recall images in his mind with a high level of detail. He hadn't realized how valuable this ability was until he started using it to attract the life he wanted. "Today I have two collections of images—one of the future me that kept drinking and one of the future (and current) me thriving in sobriety—that I can easily recall in vivid detail. Whenever I am struggling, I simply recall these pictures and find I am naturally inspired to take positive action."

Today when Byron thinks of alcohol, or sees a commercial for alcohol and drinking, it no longer has any power over him. He has been able to restore his self-confidence, learn new coping mechanisms, and for the first time he is truly excited about what the future holds. As Byron shared recently, "Getting my third DUI wasn't the miracle I was expecting, but it was the one I had been waiting for. It led me to *The 30-Day Sobriety Solution* and ultimately freed me from the one prison I feared the most—the one I had created with alcohol."

The Exploding-Through Visualization

One of the most powerful techniques I did in The 30-Day Sobriety Solution *was the guided visualization of the healthy, vibrant, thin, energetic, and excited version of me exploding out
of the old, bloated, overweight, lethargic, and drunk me. To this
day, every time I find myself struggling with the desire to drink, I
just repeat this visualization in my head, and it leaves me feeling
confident and back in control. And most importantly, my craving
for alcohol diminishes.*

—TESS
30-Day Graduate from Denver, Colorado

There is a very simple but powerful visualization technique that we
recommend you use, especially in your early sobriety. Close your
eyes and picture yourself as a problem drinker. Fill in all the details, which might include what you're wearing, your antagonistic
or withdrawn demeanor, your slurred speech, and anything else that
applies. Briefly hold that image in your mind's eye. Then vividly
picture the sober, healthy, vibrant, and happy version of yourself
nestled inside the problem drinker. Again, fill in all the details. Now
clearly see the sober you explode from inside the alcoholic you, shat-
tering the alcoholic you into a thousand little pieces, and leaving the
thriving-in-sobriety version of you proudly and confidently standing tall—beaming with light and positive energy.

Now picture that thriving-in-sobriety version of yourself inside
a large, clear bubble. Picture the bubble floating up into the sky, radiating a glowing white light and attracting everything you need in
your life to fulfill your sober vision. You can even imagine yourself
inside the bubble, multiplying and spreading out all over the globe
until there are millions of them, each bubble of you on a mission to
serve you and your vision of thriving in sobriety.

Make a Vision Board

Once you have decided on the images that represent your goal of thriving in sobriety, you can also place them on a vision board. A vision board is a collage of various pictures, photos, outcome statements, motivational images, and phrases usually pasted or taped together on a bulletin board or poster board. You can even use Pinterest or one of the many digital vision board apps and software programs you can find online to create a vision board on your smartphone, tablet, or computer. These images are powerful reminders of what you want, and looking at them helps program your reticular activating system, accelerating the accomplishment of your goals.

Making and using vision boards are one of those things that people usually either love or hate, yet we are convinced of their power to speed up the process of achieving your goals. Using a vision board, along with the other solutions in this program, will lead to remarkable results.

You can create a vision board in many ways. Google "vision board" and click on the images tab along the top to find some examples you like. You can also use Google Images to find and copy a picture of almost anything you want to add to your vision board.

On the next page is a photo of a vision board that Dave created several years ago. This five-foot-by-four-foot vision board depicts goals on the left side and accomplishments on the right. On the goals side is a list of 101 goals he wants to accomplish in his life, and on the accomplishments side is a list of his greatest accomplishments to date. The accomplishments side also serves as a powerful expression of gratitude.

Use your board for all your goals—not just your goals for thriving in sobriety. Include work, play, family, financial, relationship, and service goals, because all of them are related to your sobriety in one way or another. If you are not sure what all your other goals are yet, don't worry. We'll explore this topic further on Day 29, and you can update your board as often as you like.

The more realistic you can make the photos of your ideal self, the better. For example, you can paste or Photoshop a picture of your head onto the ideal body you desire. You can include a photo of the company headquarters where you want to work. You can go to your local auto dealer and take a picture of yourself sitting in the car you want to own someday. But only include pictures of what you *do* want. For example, you don't want a picture with a bottle of wine crossed out.

We are so enthusiastic about the effectiveness of this technique that we have even hired graphic designers to create custom images that represent our most important goals. In fact, we paid a designer to create mock-up images of this book before the first version of the program was even released. And by the way, having custom images designed doesn't have to be expensive. Check out the websites Fiverr and Elance. You'll be surprised what you can get for five or ten dollars. We use them all the time.

Lines, Traffic, and Meals

A large part of my successful career was due to my ability to really see, or visualize, that success. The 4-Minute-Mile Solution was eye-opening for me because I realized I could use this same technique to thrive in sobriety—simply by picturing the future person I desired to become, and seeing it as my current reality.

—BRIAN

30-Day Graduate from Trenton, New York

Perhaps the best thing about visualization is that it doesn't take any extra time. You have time every day that goes underutilized. Whenever you are sitting on the subway or as a passenger in a car, or when you are waiting—waiting on hold, waiting in lines, waiting to see a doctor, waiting for a friend or family member, or waiting for your food to be delivered—you can use this time to your benefit. Rather than being annoyed with someone in line who is taking too long, or feeling impatient about the time it is taking for your takeout food to be delivered, or feeling antsy about what you have to get done, visualize your goals. This will make you happier, and you will feel like you are accomplishing something (which you are!). It will also help you to accomplish your goals faster.

After you practice visualization for a while, you'll find you can do it even with your eyes open, which means that you can do it anytime and anywhere.

The two best times to visualize are right before you go to bed at night and right when you get up in the morning. When you visualize just before falling asleep, you are programming your subconscious to focus throughout the night on how to create that goal.[16] You may wake up with insights and inspirations. When you watch a scary movie or the news right before bed, your dreams will often be related to what you watched or heard before you went to sleep. It is much more productive to "seed" your consciousness with positive, goal-oriented images rather than ones of violence and mayhem.

Connecting the Solutions

As we have stated, all the solutions in this program are carefully sequenced and build upon one another. And when you visualize yourself thriving in sobriety, you are reinforcing and integrating many of the past solutions, which is a big reason why you are able to experience such a significant transformation in just 30 days. Let's quickly take a closer look at how using visualization can enhance the impact of the earlier solutions.

- **The 100% Solution (Day 1).** When you continually visualize what you want, your ability to maintain a 100% commitment to your new life is much easier.
- **The Purpose Solution (Day 2).** The images you use in your visualizations and on your vision board represent the fulfillment of your true purpose.
- **The Pendulum Solution (Day 3).** Your visualizations create a powerful emotional and psychological association between sobriety and pleasure.
- **The Forgiveness Solution (Day 4).** First visualizing having a successful conversation working through the Total Truth Process with a loved one is an effective way to prepare for an actual conversation.
- **The Believe-in-Yourself Solution (Day 5).** Visualizing yourself as the person you want to be and achieving your sobriety goals helps strengthen your belief in yourself and your ability to succeed.
- **The Outcome Solution (Day 6).** By purposely creating structural tension between your current reality and what you are picturing in your mind, visualization facilitates the achievement of your goals.
- **The "Why Can't You Just Quit?" Solution and the Action Solution (Days 8 and 9).** Your willpower is naturally stronger and action comes more easily when you have a clear mental

image of what you want and why you want it. When your subconscious becomes deeply imprinted with your goal images, you will naturally take the actions you need to take.

- **The Sobriety System (Days 10, 11, 12).** Visualization combined with affirmations is one of the most rapid, effective methods for replacing limiting beliefs with powerful new thriving-in-sobriety beliefs.
- **The Tapping Solution (Day 13).** When limiting thoughts come up, you can tap on those limiting beliefs and let go of them.

Day 15 Action Steps

- **Create three to five mental images or movies to visualize.** Get clear on your thriving-in-sobriety mental images or movies. Write them down in your journal and visualize them at least once a day. Include all five senses (touch, sight, taste, smell, and hearing). Always create the feelings and emotions you will feel when you have achieved this goal. Visualize an experience in your past where you had a great time sober, even if you need to go back to a time in your childhood, before you drank. Do this when you are waiting in line or sitting in a waiting room. Review the previous action steps and use visualization with them.

- **Listen to the two guided visualizations on today's companion website.** The first one guides you in creating powerful thriving-in-sobriety images, and the second one guides you through the Exploding-Through Visualization.

- **Create a vision board.** Take time to create a vision board in the next month, perhaps at night or on the weekends. But make sure to get started *today* by creating, cutting out, or printing out at least one image you can focus on that inspires you about your goal of thriving in sobriety. Schedule the date and time when you will complete your vision board. You might want to invite a friend or family member to make one with you. It can be a lot more fun.

The companion website at http://Day15.Solutions has additional content on visualization, including more studies and success stories that illustrate the power and effectiveness of this technique. There is also a short interactive video demonstration of the power of visualization, which we think will blow your mind.

The Quality Question Solution

Change Your Questions to Change Your Life

> *A major stimulant to creative thinking is focused questions. There is something about a well-worded question that often penetrates to the heart of the matter and triggers new ideas and insights.*
>
> —BRIAN TRACY[1]

All day long, you ask yourself questions. *What do I have to do at work today? What errands do I need to run? I haven't heard from Denise in months; is she okay? Is tonight the season finale of my favorite TV show? What am I going to eat for dinner? Can I find something to "celebrate" tonight so I can have an excuse to drink?*

Asking questions is part of being human, but most of the time, the questions we ask ourselves keep us stuck in our current reality—including self-destructive patterns of drinking. However, there are a lot of questions that can help you break free from your current limitations and accelerate your transformation from a problem drinker to a person thriving in sobriety. The Quality Question Solution will teach you how to ask the right kinds of questions.

The Roller Coaster of Life

I'm loving sobriety. I've been sober for forty-nine days now, and it feels like second nature. And just as you wrote in the program, pushing down that first domino seemed like a huge challenge, but now the dominos fall easily.

—JAMES

30-Day Graduate from Istanbul, Turkey

Before we jump into the Quality Question Solution, let's take a moment to address what you might be experiencing at this point in your 30-Day journey. As you know, life can be an emotional roller coaster. When you drink, you experience highs, and then you face challenging lows. The great thing about thriving in sobriety is that it removes the frequency and depth of those lows. During these 30 days, especially the first few weeks, you might still experience some emotional waves. At one moment, you might feel amazing— like you finally have your drinking issue handled, and you can't wait to impress everyone with your phenomenal turnaround. And then all of a sudden, you might get hit with a huge craving, or a letdown, and you feel sad, angry, or scared. Or maybe you even slip and drink, breaking your promise to quit—at least for these 30 days. If this does happen, remember the recommendations we made at the start of Phase II: listen to the Time Travel Technique again on the companion website for Day 1; consider reviewing the bonus solution on Day 14, the Relapse Solution; and continue the program where you left off.

If getting and staying sober were easy, you wouldn't have bought this book—you would have already accomplished your goal. The path to sobriety is a journey, and sometimes a difficult one. And even though at certain times thriving in sobriety might seem challenging or even impossible, when you do get beyond that point— and you will—it will have an incredible domino effect on every other area of your life.

The reality is that some people do slip along the way—some quite a bit. Others don't slip at all. Regardless, and even though this may sound clichéd, it's how you respond to these slips or setbacks that defines you and your ultimate outcome. If you pick yourself up and get back to doing the work, you will accomplish your goal of happiness and sobriety. But if you give up, you will have the opposite outcome. And since you've read this far, it is clear that you are committed to thriving in sobriety.

The fact that you showed up again today is another reason to celebrate your success. Problem drinkers love to beat themselves up when they feel like they are not making as much progress as they had hoped to or they're not recovering quickly. Problem drinkers also tend to overlook or downplay the personal growth they have made. Don't let this be you! Fully appreciate and celebrate that you have made it this far. And if you doubt that you have made any progress, go back and read your journal entries from Day 1.

Okay, let's look at today's solution and lock in another way to keep making progress.

The Einstein Solution?

Albert Einstein, winner of the Nobel Prize in Physics, wrote, "The important thing is not to stop questioning. Curiosity has its own reason for existing."[2] Einstein was not talking about questions such as "What am I going to wear today?" but about questions with answers that can dramatically change your life.

You see, Einstein knew something about questions that many people don't. The process of frequently asking questions engages your subconscious mind, which searches endlessly for an answer.[3] In his book *How to Think Like Leonardo da Vinci: Seven Steps to Genius Every Day*, Michael Gelb writes, "Neuroscientists estimate that your unconscious database outweighs the conscious on an order exceeding ten million to one. This database is the source of your creative potential. In other words, a part of you is much smarter than you are. The wisest people regularly consult that smartest part."[4]

When you put your subconscious to work by asking it the right questions, you will soon discover the answers that can change your life. As you might recall from Days 11 and 15, the right questions reprogram your brain's reticular activating system to allow information into your conscious awareness that might help you with the answer.[5]

At some point, you have most likely experienced this by asking yourself a question and then, soon after, noticing something in your environment—a book, a song lyric, a newspaper headline, a picture—that had been right in front of you all along, but now you could see it in a way that sparked a new thought or association that led to an answer to your question. For example, maybe you want to start exercising more, so you ask yourself, *What type of workout program should I do?* A little later that same day, as you are quickly scanning your feed on Facebook, you notice a friend who lives nearby and you suddenly remember that he had posted about a great new

gym he joined. Because you asked the question, your mind was able to connect the photo of that person to his previous post and bring it to your attention.

When you ask the right questions, your conscious and subconscious work together to provide you with answers. Today you will learn how to create better questions that will help you achieve your sobriety goals.

Presuppositions: The Guaranteed Alcohol Attractor

If you ask the wrong question, of course, you get the wrong answer. We find in design it's much more important and difficult to ask the right question. Once you do that, the right answer becomes obvious.

—AMORY LOVINS

Physicist named by *Time* magazine as one of the world's one hundred most influential people[6]

Have you ever asked yourself, *Why can't I quit drinking?* Or *Why can't I drink normally?* Or, in extremely frustrating times, maybe even *Why am I a "loser drunk"?* The problem with this type of question is that it contains presuppositions that keep you stuck. When you ask, *Why can't I quit drinking?* the question is already based on the presupposition (or assumption) that you *can't* quit drinking, which results in your mind searching for answers that confirm and reinforce that limiting belief. The answers your subconscious might respond with include *Because you will never be able to succeed without alcohol*, and *Because if you didn't drink, your life would be boring*. These "answers" are not helpful. They just reinforce your limiting belief that you can't change.

The Quality of Your Life Equals the Quality of Your Questions

In *The Biggest Loser*—the reality TV show that helps contestants lose a large amount of weight in a relatively short time—a distraught contestant said she had asked herself thousands of times, *Why am I so fat?* Let's take a look at her question.

By asking "Why am I so fat?" she is confirming that she is *too fat*. She is creating negative feelings. Her question keeps her mind focused on being fat instead of on being or becoming healthy. She is telling her subconscious to keep focusing on being fat. This question will never yield a useful answer; she will just receive reasons and justifications for why she is fat. These answers will ultimately only reinforce her self-image as a "fat" person, so even if she does make progress in losing weight, her subconscious will most likely sabotage her because, deep down, she still identifies with a "fat" self-image. In addition, her asking this same question "thousands" of times made sure her focus was always on being fat, instead of on what she could do to be healthy and fit.

Imagine if, instead, she were to ask herself many times a day, *How can I achieve my ideal weight?* Or better yet, *How can I eat healthy, exercise, and achieve my ideal weight while absolutely loving the process?* This simple change in questions would have a dramatic impact because now she'd be focused on what she wants instead of what she doesn't want. She is instructing her conscious and subconscious minds to search for the answer of how to achieve her goal rather than to explain her unwanted condition.

It's easy to see that these two questions create radically different feelings. The question "Why am I so fat?" is likely to make you feel shame, resignation, and hopelessness, while the other question, "How can I achieve my ideal weight?" is likely to make you feel optimistic and hopeful because it presupposes that achieving your ideal weight is possible.

Your questions determine how you feel. And as you know from

the Sobriety System diagram in Days 10, 11, and 12, how you feel determines the actions you take and the results you get. If you feel discouraged, sad, or angry, the actions you take will be completely different than if you feel optimistic, hopeful, and inspired.

One of the most important ideas to take away from today is this: *The quality of your life is dramatically affected by the quality of the questions you ask yourself on a daily basis.*

Dave used to constantly ask himself questions like, *Why am I not able to be happy without drinking? How can I be so effective at accomplishing other goals, but when it comes to drinking, I can never quit or change?* One day while he was journaling, it dawned on him that he had been asking all the wrong questions. He immediately stopped asking self-defeating and disempowering questions and replaced them with one life-changing question—*How can I be sober and really happy and excited in life?* From then on, whenever he caught himself asking the old self-defeating questions, which was still often at first, he would replace them with his new empowering question.

Within weeks, Dave started to experience astonishing changes. Just by changing the questions he asked and asking the new one numerous times a day, he began to get valuable answers. Even more exciting, he would simply ask the question and not consciously try to come up with an immediate answer, knowing his subconscious would take on that task. Before long, he was constantly finding answers and insights about exactly what he needed to do. Sometimes the answer was to reach out to a past friend, join a recreational sports league, or not watch a certain television show that triggered negative emotions.

In each case, the answers were clear and taking action was easy. And, even more interesting, he started noticing that he had naturally stopped doing some self-defeating behaviors, which he didn't even realize until much later because it never felt like he'd made a conscious decision to stop. The changes were unconscious and effortless. *This is part of the dynamic we are constantly referring to when we talk about how this program eventually makes thriving in sobriety easy and effortless.*

Now *you* can start asking the right questions to direct your subconscious.

Why Do You Drink?

But if years down the road you are still saying, "Baby, I do it because it makes me happy," you don't really mean it.

—ROBERT DOWNEY JR.[7]

You might have noticed that we *don't* want you to ask questions that start with the word *why*. This is a general rule in most types of therapy and coaching—do not ask "why" questions about a bad habit or something you want to change. When you ask "why" questions, the initial responses are usually rationalizations and justifications. The answers you get to "why" questions are booby prizes—they are just not useful.

So pay attention. When you hear yourself asking "why" questions, take note. If the question is, *Why am I so unhappy when I am sober?* then you need to change the question. If you *are* going to use a "why" question, change it to *Why am I so amazing, loving, and smart when I am sober?* That would be a great question to keep asking yourself. But you'll see in a moment that asking *how* is almost always better than asking *why*.

Asking the Right Questions

Great minds ask great questions. The questions that "engage our thought" on a daily basis reflect our life purpose and influence the quality of our lives. By cultivating a Da Vinci–like, open, questioning frame of mind, we broaden our universe and improve our ability to travel through it.

—MICHAEL GELB[8]

Virtually all spiritual traditions have a variation of this phrase: "Ask and you shall receive." But first you must know *how* to ask.

Just as there are guidelines for setting goals and writing effective affirmations, there are also guidelines for asking questions that empower you instead of disempower you. Here are the key guidelines for asking questions that will liberate you instead of imprison you:

- **Ask "how," not "why."** Always ask how you can achieve what you want rather than why you are stuck or don't already have it. Instead of asking yourself, *Why can't I ever find the love I want?* or *Why do I always end up being rejected?* you can ask *How can I be sober while finding and falling in love with my soul mate?*
- **Ask frequently.** Keep asking the question silently in your mind—*and* out loud when appropriate—until you get an answer. We have asked ourselves certain questions hundreds and even thousands of times over a long period. The repetition keeps your conscious awareness aligned with your desired outcome, and reprograms your subconscious to come up with answers and solutions to support your goals.
- **Don't try to consciously answer the question.** The answer will come to you when you are ready, and often when you least expect it. You can ask the question and then let it go, with complete confidence that your subconscious is hard at work seeking your answer, which it will often reveal to you at times when your conscious mind is less focused, such as when you are taking a shower, washing dishes, or walking in the park. Or as Dave often experiences, an answer will come to him right as he is falling asleep.
- **Emotionally charge the question.** Add empowering vocabulary to make the question engaging and exciting. Specifically, go back to Day 10, the Core Values Solution, and include some of your core values. For example, if you identified love as a core value, add the word *love* into the question where appropriate. Such as, *How can I experience incredible love and joy in my sobriety?*

Today we want you to write down one question in your journal that captures your 30-Day Vision Statement. Let's use the first example from Day 2. "Every day I wake up feeling excited, vibrant, and passionate about living a meaningful and fulfilling sober life." Now let's change it to a question. "How can I wake up every day feeling excited, vibrant, and passionate about living a meaningful and fulfilling sober life?" If excitement and passion are two of your core values, then this is the perfect question. Be sure to turn your updated 30-Day Vision Statement from Day 10 into a question that includes some of your core values.

Then ask your question multiple times a day, especially before you go to bed at night, which is the perfect time to "task" your subconscious with answering the question. Remember, whatever you focus on right before you fall asleep will actually get more attention from your subconscious than other things that occurred during the day.

Day 16 Action Steps

There is one key takeaway for today—*ask questions that will empower and excite you, and avoid questions that keep you focused on what you don't want.*

- **Make a list of the questions you ask yourself that contain negative presuppositions.** Write down the questions you ask yourself that contain negative presuppositions about your problem drinking. These might include some of the examples we have just given you. You might want to also review the top five limiting beliefs you uncovered on Day 11 in the Lie Detector Solution. Most likely you are asking questions that contain presuppositions that reinforce those limiting beliefs. For example, if you believe you have an addictive personality, you might be asking yourself, *How am I ever* *going to quit drinking if I have an addictive personality?* This question presupposes that you have an addictive personality and (if that is even true) that it is permanent and unchangeable.

- **Write empowering questions.** Using the guidelines for asking quality questions, write down an alternative question to any presuppositions you identified, such as, *How can I leverage my unique strengths and talents to thrive in sobriety?* When you catch yourself asking a question with a limiting presupposition, simply re-ask the question in a way that doesn't presuppose you are stuck and can't change. Ninety percent of the time, you can simply change a "Why" question to a "How can I" question.

- **Write your 30-Day Vision Statement question.** In your journal, write your updated 30-Day Vision Statement in a question format using our guidelines. Ask yourself this question several times during the day, out loud when appropriate, and especially before you go to bed at night. In Day 2 we asked you to review your 30-Day Vision Statement and your "new you" journal entry for at least two weeks. Since today marks the end of those two weeks, you can stop doing this and simply replace that step with this question.

On the companion website at http://Day16.Solutions you'll find a questioning technique that you can use by yourself, and with others, to accelerate the accomplishment of your goals.

The Eternal Optimist Solution

Practicing Positive Expectation and Optimism

If you think in negative terms, you will get negative results. If you think in positive terms, you will achieve positive results.

—DR. NORMAN VINCENT PEALE[1]

The quality of your thoughts determines your happiness, your feelings, and ultimately the actions you take and the results you experience.[2] Today's focus is on how to harness the power of your thoughts to help you thrive in sobriety. When you think more positively and limit your negative self-talk, you greatly improve your ability to permanently cut back or quit drinking.

Negativity Explained

I would say about 80 to 90 percent of most people's thinking is not only repetitive and useless, but because of its dysfunctional and often negative nature, much of it is also harmful. Observe your mind, and you will find this to be true. It causes serious leakage of vital energy.

—ECKHART TOLLE[3]

The opposite of optimism is pessimism, or negativity. Negative thoughts such as complaining, blaming, worrying, and judging others result in feelings of anxiety, fear, anger, resentment, guilt, and shame. When you are caught up in negative thoughts and the negative feelings they create, you are not living in the present moment.

You might be thinking, *No, that isn't true. I get angry in the present when I am stuck in traffic or when my boss gives me a project I hate.* What is really bothering you in these examples? Have you ever been in bad traffic or been given projects you didn't like, yet you were still in a good mood? The difference was your interpretation of the situation—in particular, your interpretation of what was going to happen in the future because of this.

If you are listening to a great song in the car and have nowhere you need to be, the traffic might not bother you at all. In fact, you might even enjoy the time alone. But if the traffic is going to make you late, you might get angry or frustrated because you assume that being late is going to cause you future pain. The same goes for the project you hate. You make assumptions about the pain you are going to experience in the future when you work on that project.

Here's a story of three people that illustrates this. One person agreed to go outside with a coworker for a smoke break first thing in the morning, something she had never done before noon. Another overslept after staying up late watching football the night before. The third person was about to transfer from a local subway train to an express, as he did every morning, but he noticed how crowded it was and decided to stay on the less crowded local train and just be a little late for work. Each of these people worked at the World Trade Center, and because they were not in the towers on September 11, 2001, when terrorists flew planes into the buildings, they all survived, while their coworkers who were in the buildings did not.[4]

We can't predict the future or change the past. Just because something might appear bad or good to us in that present moment, we really have no idea how to judge a single event without knowing the whole story. And we will never know the whole story.

But you *can* learn to control your thoughts in the present moment. You can choose to interpret everything that happens as a good thing and be optimistic about it. How much happier would you be if you didn't get caught up in the negativity around the perceived "uncontrollable" and "bad" things that happen to you every day? Would you be as likely to drink?

Negative Drinking Thinking

Optimism is the faith that leads to achievement. Nothing can be done without hope and confidence.

—HELEN KELLER (1880–1968)[5]

Today we are going to explore positive versus negative thoughts. Unfortunately, this topic is boring, hard to grasp, and most people don't find it useful.

How does reading that make you feel? Probably not too excited to keep reading. And if this chapter contained the single most effective solution that could help you achieve a huge breakthrough, you would probably miss it because your expectations were so negative.

Your expectations change how you feel in the present moment, as well as how you will feel in the future, as you do the thing you have expectations about, whether it is reading this book, going for a jog, or attending a party knowing that you won't be drinking. But many people have been conditioned to have negative expectations more often than positive. (By the way, this topic is not really boring.)

Problem drinkers often get caught up in what we call "negative drinking thinking." They focus on the problems and challenges of drinking, and not on the desire and ability to thrive in sobriety. With negative drinking thinking, your thoughts often come back to complaining, blaming, and resenting, instead of being grateful for all the good things in your life. Mark Twain, the celebrated American author, captured this concept when he said, "I am an old man and have known a great many troubles, but most of them never happened."[6]

What about you? When this insight became really clear to Dave, he was newly sober and had decided to coach his daughter's first-grade basketball team. Five weeks after practices began, the league let a new girl, who had never played basketball before, join the team. And then the girl's mother informed Dave that her daughter would be able to make one of the two basketball practices before the first game. Dave decided to bench her for the first game because he didn't feel she would be prepared after only one practice, and because he thought that it wasn't fair to the rest of the players.

The girl's parents objected to this decision and contacted the league office to complain. It was the holidays, and there were delays in the league responding, which led to a lot of time for Dave to speculate on the eventual outcome. Fortunately, Dave had an insight during this time that dramatically changed his life.

Dave realized that he was being judgmental and resentful of the parents, and was also complaining about the situation. He even thought about how nice it would be to "fall off the wagon" and go drinking with friends and complain about it. He found himself playing out a variety of scenarios about what might happen, like how the league would respond or how the parents would respond, but he realized that *all* of these were negative. Not once did he think, "The league will support my decision, and the parents will be understanding."

Dave had always thought of himself as a positive person—a true optimist—but he realized now that this was a common theme in his life. When there was a potential conflict, instead of having an attitude of positive expectation, he focused on negative outcomes. This awareness was all Dave needed to change, and he found that once he had freed himself from this bad habit, it created a dramatic shift in the level of happiness he experienced.

Can you relate to this? Do you spend time thinking about negative outcomes or how things can go wrong before they even happen?

The more you do this, the more you will have a desire to drink, and the more likely the negative outcomes you envision will happen.

Negative Thinking Traps

The Eternal Optimist Solution opened my eyes to the fact that I am in control of the amount of negativity I let into my life, and that as long as I keep letting these negative thinking traps lead me back to feelings of self-loathing and anxiety, and ultimately back to drinking, I will never be happy. By implementing the action steps in today's solution, I was finally able to recognize and change my inner voice to support my goals and dreams of living a sober, happy life.

—COURTNEY
30-Day Graduate from Newark, New Jersey

Most everyone has some negative self-talk. To change it, you first need to identify what it sounds like to you. You may hear negative self-talk in interior dialogue in your own voice or in the voice of someone from your past or present who has put you down. Note the tone of the voice in your negative self-talk. The tone is far more important than the actual words. When self-talk is in the negative voice of someone who criticizes you, the overall impact of that self-talk is much more negative and hurtful. It can reinforce false beliefs and trigger a desire to drink. But you can change these negative messages.

The process of identifying and changing these destructive thought patterns or negative thinking traps, which can lead you back to drinking, is used in cognitive therapy, sometimes called talk therapy. This process has been successfully used to treat addiction. In many ways, the action steps for today are similar to the work a cognitive therapist would do with you. The action steps will help you see that your thoughts, feelings, and behavior are all connected. They will help you identify where your thinking is holding you back, and then help you shift that thinking. So if you find today especially valuable, we have included some additional cognitive therapy resources on the companion website, which you may want to check out.

When you actively stop negative thoughts and substitute positive thoughts, you also change negative, self-limiting beliefs and feelings that can trigger low moods and anxiety, which can trigger a desire to drink. Eventually positive self-talk leads to more positive behavior and experiences.

The first step in this process is to review the following list of negative thinking traps for many problem drinkers. Pay attention to the tone and voice of the self-talk in order to identify which traps are familiar to you and hurt your chances for thriving in sobriety.

- **Perfectionism.** When you are a perfectionist, you constantly judge and critique yourself. Instead, you want to acknowledge that, for most things, "good enough is good enough." Nothing will ever be perfect, so you are setting yourself up for an inevitable failure.

- **Negative Labeling.** When you define yourself or others with negative labels, such as "I'm a drunk" or "I'm a loser," it only strengthens your attachment to that label and makes it harder for you to change your behavior or your perspective. Avoid labels. You are not a drunk. Drinking is something you do, not who you are. A failure is something you experience, not who you are.

- **Generalizing.** This is the all-or-nothing trap. It is easy to say "I always" or "I never." You don't always do *anything*. For example, you don't drink when you are asleep. Instead, focus on specifics: for instance, exactly where and when do you feel uncomfortable, get anxious, and drink? Then use that information to better understand how to shift that behavior. Do you "always get drunk" when you have a drink, or are there times when you have just one or two drinks? Another form of generalizing is to use the words *everything* and *nothing,* as in "Nothing ever goes my way" or "I've tried everything, and nothing has worked." The truth is, you haven't tried *everything.* If you had, you'd already be sober. Generalization also uses the word *only,* as in "Drinking is the *only* way I can cope with stress." Of course it is not the only way. You can cope by exercising, dancing, meditation, massage, breathing techniques, tapping, and many more ways.

- **Deletion.** Deletion shows up with problem drinkers as "euphoric recall," which is the tendency to recall only the positive experiences of drinking and ignore the negative experiences and consequences. You delete all the negative experiences, so the idea of drinking becomes even more enticing.

  When we are coaching someone, we generally ask this question: "When you think of some past times drinking, what comes to mind first?" Their answer usually contains mostly positive memories. But when we ask clients specific questions to elicit their bad experiences and the negative consequences of their drinking, they realize that euphoric recall plays a major role in this deletion trap. Euphoric recall also relates to why willpower alone doesn't work—the farther away you are from the pain of drinking, the harder it is to abstain, because you remember the good times and forget the bad times. This is why your journal is a fantastic tool. You can go back and read what *really* happened, like the "before you" that you wrote about on Day 2.

- **Jumping to Conclusions.** You jump to negative conclusions and assume that things will turn out badly, or you see something that starts out the way other negative experiences or failures have started out, and you immediately play out the rest in your head. It is important to recognize that every event or situation is unique and different, and to stay open to what is happening in the moment.

- **Exaggeration/Minimization.** You exaggerate the importance of the "bad" things in your life ("This is the worst thing that's ever happened to me" or "I'm ruined") and minimize or fail to celebrate the significance of good things. Flip this around! Exaggerate the positive and minimize the negative.

- **Emotional Reasoning.** You get caught up in negative emotions and assume that they reflect the way things really are. Acknowledge that emotions are temporary and can be changed. Notice how you are feeling and ask yourself how you might have come to feel that way. What thoughts are you thinking? What pictures are you imagining? Once you recognize what makes you feel the way you do, it is much easier to identify and change the false logic that created those feelings.

- **"Should" Statements.** When you say "I *should* stop drinking," part of you responds by resisting with an "I don't want to, and you can't make me" kind of energy. Replace the word *should* with the word *want*, as in "I *want* to stop drinking." Or "I *want* to be in control of my drinking." Drop the word *should* from your vocabulary. Nobody likes to be "should on," *including you!*

- **Personalization.** This is when you view yourself as the cause of events that may have nothing to do with you. If you come home to find that your spouse or partner is upset, don't immediately assume it is about or because of you. Ask. Likewise, if he or she is getting ready to go out and says, "Well, I guess the reason you can't go to the party with me is because you're working on that important project for work," you could also end up personalizing this statement by thinking, *Why are you always so critical of my work when I'm just trying to make a living and support the family?* In fact, your spouse or partner might actually have been feeling compassion and empathy for you.

- **Mind Reading.** You guess what someone else is feeling or thinking without asking. So just ask. You might be surprised how wrong your assumptions are. Remember: "When in doubt, check it out!"

All of these negative thinking traps, which most problem drinkers struggle with at one time or another, contribute to low self-esteem and cause feelings of overwhelm, disconnectedness, hopelessness, and anxiety—all of which increase the likelihood that you will drink to numb out those feelings. But when you recognize, challenge, and replace your negative thinking patterns with positive ones, you dramatically reduce your desire to drink. So let's look at how you can break out of these repeating patterns of self-defeating thoughts.

The Power of Awareness

It is our desire that you become one who is happy with that which you are and with that which you have—while at the same time being eager for more. That is the optimal creative vantage point: to stand on the brink of what is coming, feeling eager, optimistic anticipation—with no feelings of impatience, doubt, or unworthiness hindering the receiving of it—that is the Science of Deliberate Creation at its best.

—ESTHER AND JERRY HICKS
Authors of *Ask and It Is Given: Learning to Manifest Your Desires*[7]

It all starts with awareness. You can't change what you aren't aware of. When you are not conscious of what you're doing, you just keep repeating the same self-destructive habits. The best way to expand your awareness is by journaling every day. That is why we sound like a broken record about writing in your journal—it is a critical component of creating the personal awareness that will lead you to a breakthrough.

Successful people are optimistic. Even in the face of great challenges, they are almost always able to reframe a problem or "failure" as an opportunity to learn and grow. People who struggle usually get caught in negative thinking traps, unable to break the pattern once it begins.

For example, have you ever temporarily cut back or quit drinking, only to disappoint yourself and go back to your old drinking habits? When this happened, did you feel like a failure and revert to negative thinking traps, such as making generalizations and exaggerations ("I'll *never* be able to stop drinking"), or jumping to conclusions and using emotional reasoning ("I'll never be able to *deal with stress without drinking*")?

These negative thinking traps will lead you back to drinking, so you want to recognize that those thoughts don't work, and then ask yourself what you need to do differently. For example, ask yourself, *How did I handle stress in my life before I started drinking?* or *What have I done to deal with stress when drinking wasn't an option, such as while at the office?* Most likely you will discover that one, or several, negative thinking traps led you back to drinking. Matt's story is a perfect example of how identifying the negative thinking traps in his life led to the breakthroughs he needed to thrive in sobriety.

Breaking Through Matt's Traps

I haven't gone back to drinking, and the thought of ever having another hangover gives me chills. I feel great, and I can't believe that I wasted a lot of my life trying to avoid life.

—MATT

30-Day Graduate from Kansas City, Missouri

In his early fifties, Matt had a successful career, beautiful wife, two smart and talented kids, and was a respected member of the community. Even though his career success had afforded him the freedom to never have to work another day in his life, he was terrified of not working. At the same time, no matter how successful he was at work, he never believed or felt he was "good enough." So Matt drank almost every night. He recalls how he felt toward the end of his drinking:

> I was anxious, depressed, and unhappy, and alcohol helped me cope with my feelings—until it didn't. At that point, I

felt desperation setting in, and I remember asking myself, *Now what?* I started going to Alcoholics Anonymous, where I was told, "Just quit drinking, and things will get better, but it might take a long time." I remember how scared I was to hear this. It painted a gloomy picture of my future—with months or even years of continued anxiety and depression. I knew there had to be a better approach for me, and that's when I found *The 30-Day Sobriety Solution.*

Within days of starting the program, Matt's life changed for the better. He said, "I would complete a solution every day and know that I was becoming a better person—not just in relation to drinking, but in every area of my life. I started to get my self-confidence back, and more importantly, I started to see a happier, healthier future version of myself that I could become."

During *The 30-Day Sobriety Solution*, Matt recognized his negative thinking traps, including perfectionism, exaggeration/minimization, jumping to conclusions, personalization, and making "should" statements.

- Since Matt believed he had to be perfect to be enough, he was constantly driving himself to do more and be better. Since "perfect" is never possible, and because his fear of not being perfect enough was always eating away at him, no matter how much he did and how much success it brought him, Matt always felt that "I was never 'good enough.' My self-esteem was dependent on getting praise from others, especially at work, since I had no self-esteem. No amount of praise was enough, and I lived my life in this fog that I tried to lift by drinking."

  Because Matt needed to appear to be perfect, he exaggerated his accomplishments and minimized his failures in the hope of getting more approval. But in his heart, he knew he wasn't being authentic and truthful, which only further increased his desire to drink.

- Matt jumped to conclusions and personalized other people's actions. As a result, he was continually asking himself, *What did they mean by that comment? Why didn't they give me the acknowledgment and recognition I deserved? Are they jealous, or are they trying to imply that I'm not good enough?*
- Because he thought he was not good enough, Matt constantly felt that he should be doing more, and his self-talk contained a constant stream of "should" statements: *I should make more money. I should get promoted. I should be the hero on the team, rescuing my coworkers by taking on their responsibilities.* When he did rescue coworkers, and they didn't reciprocate, he ended up feeling angry and resentful.

As Matt changed his negative thinking traps, he dramatically curbed his desire to drink. Three years later, almost every aspect of Matt's life has markedly improved. He quit his old job and was inundated with more interesting opportunities. He changed his diet, started exercising regularly, and lost fifty-three pounds, which he has kept off. He also started spending more time with his wife and kids, something that had always come last, after his job and his drinking. As a result of all these positive changes, he decided that his life was much better when he completely abstained from alcohol, which was quickly validated after he briefly returned to drinking on two different occasions.

Matt's two returns to drinking were short-lived, lasting only a few days each time, and happened only at night. He said, "I knew I had a choice, but the few hours of semipleasure that drinking gave me was far outweighed by the self-contempt I felt afterward and the knowledge that drinking came at the ultimate cost of sacrificing my real happiness." Matt hasn't drunk any alcohol in over two years, enjoys attending AA meetings, and still revisits some of the 30-Day solutions in the program when he feels that he is getting off track.

How Do You "Fix" a Dark House?

*What you focus on expands, and when you focus on the good-
ness in your life, you create more of it. Opportunities, relationships, even money flowed my way when I learned to be grateful
no matter what happened in my life.*

—OPRAH WINFREY

Host and producer of the top-rated, award-
winning *The Oprah Winfrey Show*

In their program "The 11 Forgotten Laws," Bob Proctor and Mary
Morrissey ask, "What do you do when you walk into a dark house
and you can't see?" The answer, of course, is simple—you turn on a
light. You don't try to push away the darkness. You simply turn on
a light. And then another, and another. The solution is exactly the
same for overcoming negativity. Instead of trying to push away your
negative thoughts, you replace them by *choosing* to think of something more positive. As you fill your mental "house" with the light
of positive thoughts and expectations, there will be no room left for
the darkness of your negative thoughts.

Similarly, instead of focusing on quitting drinking, focus on
thriving in sobriety. Instead of focusing on resentment and anger
toward the people who have hurt you, focus on understanding and
forgiving them. Instead of focusing on your mistakes and your failures, focus on your lessons and your successes. Instead of focusing
on your limiting beliefs, focus on the positive beliefs you have written to replace them. Instead of focusing on images of what you *don't*
want, focus on images of what you *do* want. When you keep "turning on the lights," the rest will take care of itself!

Our clients tell us that when they finally "get this" and apply
it regularly in their lives, they wonder how and why they ever got
stuck in the mental trap of focusing on what they don't want. In ret-
rospect, the positive-focus approach seems so obvious, yet their un-

examined habitual thoughts and their drinking kept them from ever being able to see it clearly.

Negative Traps in Your Life

A pessimist sees the difficulty in every opportunity; an optimist sees the opportunity in every difficulty.

—WINSTON CHURCHILL (1874–1965)
Prime minister of Great Britain

In his book *The Power of Your Supermind*, bestselling author Vernon Howard explains the importance of identifying negativity in your life. He writes, "Honest self-observation dissolves pains and pressures that formerly did their dreadful work in the darkness of unawareness. This is so important I urge you to memorize and reflect upon the following summary: Detection of inner negativity is not a negative act, but a courageously positive act that makes you a new person."[8]

The **first action step** for today is to write down each of the negative thinking traps above in your journal and then write about how each one shows up in your life. Include specific examples, and be sure to add as many details as you can, such as when, where, and especially with whom. As you write about each, see if you can discern whose voice is speaking. Are there "should" statements coming from your father? Or negative labeling from your mother? Or your ex? Notice the tone of voice of these thoughts. Is it in your voice or someone else's? Is it accusatory, angry, or demanding? These are all clues to where the thoughts are coming from.

For example, we see many partners and spouses who try to read the other's mind—they try to discern how the other is feeling without asking. They may also struggle with deletion, where one will let a single negative comment completely delete other positive comments. Remember, even though you are looking at *internal* negative self-talk, negative comments can show up externally in a conversation or argument. For instance, you might use generalizations at times with your spouse or partner by internally getting annoyed with something he or she said and think to yourself, *You* always *do this*. Then you might eventually decide to say out loud, "You *always* do . . ." instead of, "It seems like at certain times you do . . ."

The next step is to write down how you can change each negative thinking trap. If you catch yourself thinking, *I can* never *quit drinking* (a generalization), then write down what is really true. When do you struggle the most not to drink? Weekends? Weekdays? When you are at a party, or when you are home alone? Also, is this really true? Do you know or have you read about people like yourself who have quit drinking and are happy? Last, what are the tone and voice of this generalization? Do you hear one of your parents' voices saying this in a condescending tone? Or an ex-spouse or former boss?

Another example might be a night where you almost always drink, but for whatever reason, you did not drink this time. What emotions did you experience? Did you feel frustrated, bored, or sad because you were not drinking? Did you feel that those emotions were permanent, like in the emotional reasoning trap, or were you able to recognize that they were temporary feelings and that you had the power to change them?

When you think about drinking and your past experiences of drinking, do you remember only how much fun you had (euphoric recall)? Do you delete the times you felt lonely and sad when drinking, or the mean and hurtful things you said while drinking, or how you felt the morning after a night of heavy drinking? Does your "drinking thinking" recall only the positive moments and delete all the negative ones?

This is a powerful process because you will start to recognize specific triggers, patterns, and places where you get caught up in negative thinking, which can lead you right back to drinking. Sometimes the awareness of these patterns in your life is all you need to make a lasting change.

For more examples of how these traps commonly show up for problem drinkers, you can visit today's companion website.

The Positive Thinking Trap

You have to see things as they really are but not worse than they are—that view of life only gives you the excuse not to do something.

—TONY ROBBINS[9]

Not all positive thinking is the same. As great as positive thinking is, it is possible for it to hold you back by basically tricking you into a state of complacency. Gabriele Oettingen, a professor of psychology at New York University, and her colleagues completed several studies of goal setting, and they discovered that by focusing only on positive thoughts, participants tricked themselves into believing they had already succeeded, which resulted in their having less drive to do the actual work required.[10]

They discovered that the optimal approach is to practice a technique called "mental contrasting," which includes positive thinking. First, spend several minutes thinking of your goal and imagining your achievement of that goal. Then, think about the obstacles that you will have to overcome and how you will do so. This is similar to the strategy we recommended on Day 3 in the Pendulum Solution and the one that hip and knee surgery patients used to recover almost twice as fast as others who didn't envision specific goals and recovery methods.

Our message here is this. Don't let a simplistic or overly positive attitude blind you to the actual challenges you will face and the work you will have to do to accomplish your goal. Have a positive expectation that you will succeed *and* think about how you will handle these inevitable challenges (cravings, uncomfortable feelings, office parties, and peer pressure). And, of course, keep doing the action steps and solutions in *The 30-Day Sobriety Solution.*

Day 17 Action Steps

One of the most powerful takeaways from The 30-Day Sobriety Solution, *outside of finally removing my desire to drink, was all the notes I wrote in my journal throughout the program. Now when I start to feel my "drinking thinking" kick back in, I just read my journal, and specifically some of my favorite entries, which almost immediately gets me excited about my future and inspires me to take positive action.*

—LENORE
30-Day Graduate from Dallas, Texas

Whether you call it positive self-talk, positive thinking, or simply optimism, the more you have in your life, the more you will thrive. Without a positive or optimistic outlook, the possibility of truly thriving in sobriety is almost nonexistent.

- **In a bad mood? STOP—and analyze your thoughts.** Ask yourself, *What am I thinking about? What is my negative self-talk? Whose voice is it? What is the tone of voice? What visual images am I focusing on?* Once you are aware of what is putting you in a bad mood, change your thoughts by using what you have learned today and in past solutions.

- **Write down your negative thinking traps.** Write down all the thinking traps in your journal and write about how each one shows up in your life. Include examples, such as when, where, and with whom, and be sure to include the euphoric recall trap if that is something you experience. Notice if those thoughts are in your voice or someone else's. For example, you may have started *The 30-Day Sobriety Solution* with the jumping-to-conclusions trap by saying or thinking, *Everything else I have tried to stop drinking has failed, so this program is going to fail, too.* Include examples in your life that show up in your conversations with friends and family.

- **Write down how to change each of your traps.** For example, if one of your traps is jumping to conclusions, ask yourself, *What is different about this attempt to quit from the other times I have tried, and what is different about this program compared with others I have tried?* If one of your traps is making "should" statements, ask yourself, *What statements could I use that would demonstrate my willing choice to participate instead of using guilt to motivate myself?* In a positive tone, ask, *What specifically is holding me back from what I want?* And if you find yourself making "should" statements to others about what they ought to do, change this by first asking them whether or not they would like any advice from you.

On the companion website, you will find a study that reveals the two most self-destructive words you can ever use, and the simple change you can make to eliminate them from your thinking and your speech. In addition, we explore a famous experiment with water that demonstrates how words and thoughts actually create a physiological change in your body. Be sure to visit http://Day17.Solutions.

The Affirmation Solution

The Power of Affirmations

I've always believed in magic. When I wasn't doing anything in this town, I'd go up every night, sit on Mulholland Drive, look out at the city, stretch out my arms, and say, "Everybody wants to work with me. I'm a really good actor. I have all kinds of great movie offers." I'd just repeat these things over and over, literally convincing myself that I had a couple of movies lined up. I'd drive down that hill, ready to take the world on, going, "Movie offers are out there for me, I just don't hear them yet." It was like total affirmations, antidotes to the stuff that stems from my family background.

—JIM CARREY[1]

One of the best ways to thrive in life and sobriety is to bombard your subconscious with inspiring thoughts, images, and affirmations. See yourself joyfully attending a party, drinking a sparkling mineral water; having a trim and healthy sober body; enjoying exciting work; interacting with interesting and supportive friends; being a role model to your children; and experiencing all your goals as already complete.

An affirmation is a statement that describes a goal in its already completed state, such as your 30-Day Vision Statement that you wrote on Day 2 as part of the Purpose Solution. Today we will teach you exactly how to write and use affirmations to accomplish your sobriety goals.

The Philosophy of Personal Achievement

Andrew Carnegie, the industrialist-turned-philanthropist, challenged a young and unknown journalist named Napoleon Hill to write a philosophy of personal achievement. Carnegie told Hill that if he committed to documenting and recording this philosophy of success over the next twenty years, he would introduce the journalist to the wealthiest, most successful men of the time. Hill immediately accepted the challenge.[2]

Over the next two decades, Napoleon Hill interviewed 504 people, including business titans Henry Ford, Charles M. Schwab, King Gillette, and John D. Rockefeller; inventors Thomas Edison and Alexander Graham Bell; and three US presidents. In 1937 he published his findings in a thirteen-step formula called *Think and Grow Rich: Teaching, for the First Time, the Famous Andrew Carnegie Formula for Money-Making, Based upon the Thirteen Proven Steps to Riches*, which sold more than thirty million copies.

Saying the book was ahead of its time is an understatement. Since Hill's book, countless books and studies have validated and expanded on his findings. *Think and Grow Rich* has influenced the field of personal development. Yet the word *rich* is somewhat misleading, because this book is not simply about accumulating monetary or material wealth but also about having an abundance of loving relationships, health, and joy.

One of the key tools for success in *Think and Grow Rich* is the power of affirmations.

Trust Us, Affirmations Actually Work!

Despite all the published research that affirmations work,[3] many people still doubt their effectiveness. Not only do affirmations work, but we consider the use of affirmations to be one of the top five techniques that ensure success, happiness, love, and sobriety.

We have both experienced firsthand how writing and practicing a new affirmation brings a goal to fruition. We both first used affirmations to create quantum leaps in our careers—Jack went from earning $8,000 a year to $100,000 and later to over $1 million a year. Dave went from being an unemployed college graduate to becoming the first employee of a promising start-up to earning double his previous salary. In both cases, our new incomes were nearly identical to amount we had written down and practiced daily in our affirmations. These successes taught us early on that the daily practice of affirmations is powerful. We have continued to find validation of their effect in our own lives and the lives of our clients, and we believe that affirmations need to be a core component of every recovery program.

The Magic of Affirmations

It's the repetition of affirmations that leads to belief. And once that belief becomes a deep conviction, things begin to happen.

—MUHAMMAD ALI

Napoleon Hill defines an affirmation as "repeated instructions to the subconscious mind, through the principle of auto-suggestion."[4] Affirmations are also called declarations or mantras, but the clearest explanation is that they are your goals written down in a completed state.

The conscious mind is rational. It distinguishes right from wrong and directs many of your thoughts. The subconscious mind records everything from your five senses (touch, smell, hearing, sight, and taste), stores this information, and replays it during your daily life to influence your thoughts and actions.[5] Affirmations can reprogram your subconscious to make sure that it helps you achieve your new goal.

By focusing your consciousness on affirmations, you remind yourself what you *want*. You engage in positive self-talk rather than negative self-talk. Repeating an affirmation numerous times a day improves its effectiveness, rewires your subconscious, and keeps you from getting sidetracked with negative self-talk. You maintain focus on your goals, and the repetition has a greater impact on your subconscious. All of this leads to a shift in beliefs, removes limitations, and drives your actions toward your goals.

In *The Magic of Believing: The Science of Setting Your Goal and Then Reaching It*, Claude M. Bristol writes, "Repetition of the same chant, the same incantations, the same affirmations leads to belief, and once that belief becomes a deep conviction, things begin to happen."[6] Once you shift your beliefs, the accomplishments you seek will soon follow as you start taking actions that move you toward your goal without even consciously thinking about it.

Eight Guidelines for Creating Effective Affirmations

To be effective, your affirmations should follow eight guidelines:

1. Start with the words "I am." The words "I am" are the two most powerful words in the English language. The subconscious takes any sentence that starts with the words "I am" and interprets it as a command—a directive to make it happen.

2. Use the present tense. Describe what you want as though you already have it and as though you've already accomplished it.

3. State it in the positive. Affirm what you want, not what you don't want.

4. Keep it brief. Make your affirmation short enough and clear enough that you can remember it easily.

5. Make it specific. Vague affirmations produce vague results.

6. Include an action word ending with *-ing.* The active verb adds power to the effect by evoking an image of doing it or experiencing it right now.

7. Include at least one dynamic emotion or feeling word. Include the emotional state you would feel if you had already achieved the goal. Some commonly used words are *enjoyment, joy, happiness, celebration, pride, calm, peace, delight, enthusiasm, love, security, serenity, thrill,* and *triumph.*

8. Make affirmations for yourself, not others. Your affirmations describe your behavior, not others' behavior. Instead of saying, "I am so happy my coworkers now accept and support my decision to live a sober lifestyle," you would say, "I am happily choosing to stand firm in my decision to live a sober lifestyle—even at company parties."

Here's an example of an affirmation that meets all eight criteria: "I am happily drinking sparkling mineral water at my daughter's wedding reception."

Your Total Sobriety Affirmation

By now you probably recognize many of these guidelines from other solutions. We used affirmations on Day 2 with your 30-Day Vision Statement and on Day 4 with your forgiveness affirmation.

Today your **first action step** is to write your Total Sobriety Affirmation. This is one paragraph composed of several affirmations that represent your completed sobriety goals and your personal transformation from being a problem drinker to being a person thriving in sobriety. To do this, you will build on three of the past solutions. And don't worry about having to make it "perfect." Just think of this as a first draft. As you repeat the affirmations over time, the changes you need to make will become obvious, so all that matters now is that you begin writing.

Start by revisiting the 30-Day Vision Statement you wrote on Day 2 and then revised on Day 10 with your core values. If your vision statement doesn't follow these guidelines, take a moment to update it. See the example below.

Day 2 Example. Every day I wake up feeling excited, vibrant, and passionate about living a meaningful and fulfilling sober life.

Updated Affirmation. I am enjoying waking up every day feeling excited, vibrant, and passionate about living my meaningful and fulfilling sober life.

We simply added "I am" to the beginning of the sentence and adjusted the rest accordingly.

The next step is to write an affirmation for each of the SMART goals you committed to on Day 6, as in the following example:

Day 6 Example. I will have an amazing group of friends who are supportive of my sobriety, and regularly find creative, healthy, and fun activities to do with me that make thriving in sobriety a reality in my life by January 31, [year], at 9:00 a.m.

Updated Affirmation. I enjoy playing with my amazing group of friends who totally support my sobriety by finding creative, healthy, and fun things we can do together.

The next step is to review the list of the five limiting beliefs you identified and rewrote on Day 11 in the Lie Detector Solution (which we hope you have been reviewing regularly). Rewrite each of these as positive affirmations. For example:

Day 11 Updated Belief. I can create a more successful career when I am sober because I am more awake, clearheaded, and focused.

Updated Affirmation. I am being recognized at work for consistently exceeding expectations, which has led to exciting opportunities for promotion and new friends.

Feel free to add any more affirmation statements that you would like. You might decide there is nothing else to add, but before you decide that, go back and reread the first two pages of the "Getting Started" chapter, where we asked you to determine if this book was a fit for you. If any of these questions apply to you, make sure you have an affirmation to deal with each of them. For example:

Getting Started Question. Are you concerned with the effects of your drinking on your finances, family relationships, health, weight, and/or career?

Updated Affirmation. I am leaving the doctor's office feeling happy and relieved after hearing that my weight, blood pressure, and resting heart rate are perfect for my age and body type, and that all my blood work results are positive.

———

By combining these affirmations, you will have a long paragraph that is now your personal Total Sobriety Affirmation. This affirmation is very powerful. Even though it might not have taken very long to put together, you have spent a significant amount of time over the course of this program building the pieces that you are now combining in this personalized new statement. And as you work with your Total Sobriety Affirmation, these statements will become a reality in your life. To see more examples of creating effective affirmations and some other completed Total Sobriety Affirmations, be sure to visit the companion website. This can be an especially valuable resource if you feel stuck or need help with completing this solution.

How to Use Your Affirmations

Written affirmations are ... very effective. But I have found that repeating a mantra aloud has a wonderful effect on my spirit. When I need to feel motivated, I might repeat, "I am inspired, disciplined, and energized" out loud two or three hundred times. To maintain the supreme sense of self-confidence I have culti- vated, I repeat, "I am strong, able, and calm." I even use mantras to keep me youthful and vital.

—ROBIN SHARMA

Author of *The Monk Who Sold His Ferrari: A Fable About Fulfilling Your Dreams and Reaching Your Destiny*[7]

Now that you are empowered with your personal Total Sobriety Af- firmation, you're probably wondering, *How do I use it?* The power comes from the repetition of reading it over and over until it be- comes locked into your subconscious. Therefore, we want you to re- view it a minimum of three times a day, 30 days in a row. The best times are when you first wake up in the morning, in the middle of the day to refocus yourself, and at bedtime. Repeating your affirma- tion right before you go to sleep gives your subconscious mind six to eight hours to focus on it.

Because affirmations are one our of favorite tools, when we are focused on manifesting something that is really important to us— such as a new career or health goal—we will write an affirmation statement and repeat it out loud fifty, one hundred, or even "two or three hundred times," as Robin Sharma recommends. After a while it becomes a mantra, which we repeat out loud while driving or work- ing out, or silently in a meeting or while waiting in line. *Find what works best for you, but remember, more repetition creates faster results!*

- **Read it out loud.** When appropriate, read your affirmations out loud in a firm, confident voice. This is not possible all the time, so it is just fine to read it silently to yourself when necessary. Both work. However, when you say your affirmation out loud, you can read it with more emotion.

- **Record it.** Record your affirmations and listen to them while you work, drive, exercise, or fall asleep. You can use your smartphone, an MP3 player, or an iPod or iPad.

- **Post it.** Write your affirmations on three-by-five-inch cards or sticky notes and carry them with you or post them where you will see them. You can also post them as the screen saver on your tablet or computer, as a note on your phone or tablet, or as a recurring meeting on your calendar. You can also use your phone to take a picture of your affirmations and store it in your photos. Make sure to protect your privacy where appropriate.

- **Adjust it.** Repeat your affirmations in the first person ("I am . . ."), second person ("You are . . ."), and third person ("He/she is . . ."). Or after you say "I," say your full name ("I, Jack Canfield, am . . .").

- **Use it.** When you catch yourself complaining, blaming, justifying bad behavior, or practicing any negative self-talk, replace that behavior by reviewing your affirmations.

- **Ask questions.** After reviewing each of your affirmations, ask a related question like you learned on Day 16 in the Quality Question Solution. For example, "How can I wake up every day excited and passionate about living a meaningful and fulfilling sober life?"

Supercharge Your Affirmations

Habits of thinking need not be forever. One of the most significant findings in psychology in the last twenty years is that individuals can choose the way they think.

—MARTIN SELIGMAN

Psychologist, educator, author of *Authentic Happiness: Using the New Positive Psychology to Realize Your Potential for Lasting Fulfillment*[8]

You can accelerate and deepen the impact of your affirmation using some or all of the following techniques.

- **Visualization.** After repeating the affirmation, close your eyes and visualize what you have just affirmed. See it as if you were looking out at the scene from inside of yourself. In other words, don't see yourself standing out there in the scene; see the scene as if you were looking through your own eyes while you experience what you are affirming.

- **Use your other senses.** Imagine what you would be feeling, tasting, smelling, and hearing when you successfully achieve what your affirmation describes—the sound of your voice as you casually decline the offer of an alcoholic beverage, the loving and nonjudgmental touch from your partner or family member, the taste of a delicious Starbucks Frappuccino, or the smell of your sober breath and the feeling of security you experience when you are pulled over at a sobriety checkpoint.

- **Include people acknowledging you.** Include the images and sounds of important people in your life congratulating you and telling you how pleased they are with your success at cutting back or quitting drinking for good.

- **Add emotion.** Feel the emotions that you will feel when you achieve that success. This is really important. The stronger the feelings, the more powerful the process.

- **Use tapping.** While saying your affirmation, tap on the eight acupressure points you learned on Day 13.

When you combine empowering affirmations with detailed visualizations and tapping, you have an unbeatable process to create massive change in a short amount of time.

"I Am an Alcoholic"

*Going to AA meetings actually made me want to drink . . . the
focus seemed to be that you should always be scared because
you were on the brink of drinking again. And I found it counter-
productive to be constantly calling myself an alcoholic and saying that I was helpless. Overall, I know it has helped millions of
people, and I respect that, but personally I found it to be negative in its approach and that the focus was always on "not drinking" instead of "thriving in sobriety."*

—JAMES
30-Day Graduate from Istanbul, Turkey

Between the two of us, we have attended hundreds of Alcoholics
Anonymous (AA) meetings. AA has helped Dave and three of Jack's
family members get and stay sober.

As much as we are grateful for the existence of AA and the millions of people it has helped worldwide, we feel that the recommendation to attend AA meetings should come with some advice.

One of the oldest rituals in AA meetings is to introduce yourself
at the start of the meeting by saying, "My name is Dave, and I'm
an alcoholic." You are also supposed to repeat this phrase anytime
before you speak at the meeting. And the reasoning behind this is
clear—denial is a major issue with alcoholics. If you can't first accept
that you have a problem, then overcoming it is impossible.

The problem, we believe, is that the phrase "I am an alcoholic" is
also an affirmation. The process of personally repeating this affirmation and hearing it repeated dozens and dozens of times in a single
meeting can be self-defeating—especially when you consider the impact of this constant repetition over the course of months and years
of attending meetings.

This phrase also regularly affects your self-image. A large part of
human behavior is influenced by how we see ourselves.[9] When you
have the self-image of an alcoholic, your subconscious will instinc-

tively work to create the reality that matches that image. Whatever identity you reinforce and hold on to is the one that will eventually win out. By repeating the phrase "I am an alcoholic" over and over again, you are ultimately reinforcing this self-image, consciously and subconsciously.

AA meetings can be a fantastic resource. They can help you overcome your guilt and shame and start to believe it's possible to get sober. However, if you decide to use AA as a resource, we recommend that you silently repeat your 30-Day Vision Statement from Day 2 every time you hear the phrase "I am an alcoholic." You can even choose to just introduce yourself without labeling yourself as an alcoholic, since this is not a requirement for attending.

Day 18 Action Steps

Napoleon Hill is widely credited with having influenced more people to create success than anyone in history. He concluded that affirmations were a critical part of the thirteen-step formula he published. That alone should convince you that if you are not using affirmations in your life, you need to start today.

- **Write your Total Sobriety Affirmation.** Using the eight guidelines for writing affirmations, update your 30-Day Vision Statement from Day 2 (if necessary). Also, rewrite your SMART goals from Day 6 as affirmations, rewrite your new beliefs from Day 11 as affirmations, and review the questions from the "Getting Started" chapter and write any additional affirmations for anything you feel is missing. This is your own personalized and incredibly powerful Total Sobriety Affirmation.

- **Use your Total Sobriety Affirmation daily.** Repeat your Total Sobriety Affirmation at least three times a day. And use the tips and supercharging recommendations that are provided in the Affirmation Solution.

- **Listen to the thriving-in-sobriety guided affirmations.** On the companion website, we have created some guided affirmations to help you reinforce, both consciously and subconsciously, what is most important to *you* over the long run. After listening to this recording of our favorite affirmations, you will feel more confident, inspired, and empowered.

On the companion website, we have posted additional Total Sobriety Affirmations, which are a great resource to help you write yours. We also include a list of some of our favorite affirmations that you might wish to add to your list. Visit the website at http://Day18.Solutions.

Day **19**

The Attraction Solution

Using the Law of Attraction to Accelerate Your Success

Every thought vibrates, every thought radiates a signal, and every thought attracts a matching signal back. We call that process the law of attraction. The law of attraction says: That which is like unto itself is drawn. And so, you might see the powerful law of attraction as a sort of Universal Manager that sees to it that all thoughts that match one another line up.

—ESTHER and JERRY HICKS[1]

The law of attraction is known as the "universal law." Like attracts like. The core teachings of the law of attraction are found everywhere—from ancient texts, religious and spiritual teachings to modern-day philosophy, psychology, and self-help books.[2] Whether you intentionally "use" the law or not, just like the law of gravity, it is always affecting you. It is critical that you learn how to leverage this incredibly powerful force in a positive way. In today's solution, we will teach you exactly how.

All of the principles and techniques covered in solutions 11 through 20 are related to harnessing and directing this powerful force. Visualization, affirmation, positive thinking, focusing on what you *do* want rather than what you *don't* want, releasing your limiting beliefs and emotional wounds through tapping, and practicing gratitude are all tools that will raise your level of vibration and activate this force to attract what you want into your life.

Today we will dive even deeper into how to make sure you are on the right side of this law as you create your sober and happy life.

Ask, Believe, Receive

And whatever you ask in prayer, you will receive, if you have faith.

—MATTHEW 21:22

Ask. Believe. Receive. These are the three steps to manifesting what you want using the law of attraction. Let's look at this simple formula.

1. Ask for what you want. The first step is to get really clear about what you want. What does your ideal life thriving in sobriety look like? Think of it as if you are filling out a purchase order to the universe. You can have everything you want. All you have to do is add it to your online shopping cart. Take time to design your ideal life—including your inner experience, like how you want to feel, your attitude, your beliefs, and your physical sensations (relaxed, calm, pleasure), as well as the outer physical world. Write it all down. Also remember that every thought you think, every desire you have, every preference you have is sending out an "ask" to the universe. The old adage that "what you think about comes about" is true.

2. Believe it. Have unwavering faith that you *will* receive what you are asking for. The power of belief has been proven. The more you believe that you will get it, the more you will manifest it. Remember the placebo effect, which has been proven to cause resolution of symptoms (and real physiological change) in up to 80 percent of the patients in clinical trials who are treated with nothing more than sugar pills, saline injections, or fake surgeries.[3]

3. Receive it. Act as if it is already yours. This means thinking like, talking like, dressing like, acting like, and feeling the feelings you would feel like the person who has already achieved your sobriety goal. This is called "being a vibrational match" for what you want. This includes keeping yourself in a state of love, joy, and appreciation. Think about this in regard to thriving in sobriety. Imagine you are an actor who has been cast in the role of being the sober you that you dream of. Start acting the part now. How would you act? What would your self-talk be? How would you show up at a social function? Think and feel the part now.

We're going to add a fourth step to this formula—what you do when you achieve or receive what you want—the practice of gratitude.

4. Be grateful for it. Be thankful for getting what you want. As we'll explore more fully in Day 20, gratitude is the healthiest of all human emotions, so whenever you receive or achieve what you want, take time and pause to experience your appreciation and gratitude—to God, the universe, and any people who helped contribute to your success.

If you repeat this process—ask, believe, receive, and be grateful—continually, you will find that health, wealth, fulfilling relationships, and lasting sobriety will come to you quickly and easily.

A Lawyer's "Secret" to Sobriety

The solutions I learned from The 30-Day Sobriety Solution *have been extremely effective in maintaining sobriety and thriving in it; they are the foundation upon which my sobriety is based.*

—DAN

30-Day Graduate from Jackson, Wyoming

Dan's childhood had looked great from the outside. His dad was a successful doctor, his mother loving and supportive. His siblings were fun, smart, and frustrating in a "normal" kind of way. His family was full of high achievers, and even though Dan felt he had to work harder than many of his peers, he was more than willing to put in the time to live up to his parents' and his own expectations. His hard work paid off—he graduated from law school, passed the bar exam, and eventually started his own successful law firm. He fell in love, got married, and became a father to two beautiful, healthy children. It seemed like Dan had it all.

But all of these successes took a toll on Dan. Deep down he was always afraid of failing, of letting his parents down, of not being a great father, and of not being able to financially support his family. Over the years he found escape from these fears by drinking.

His drinking started socially, but by the time he was in his late twenties, it had become a problem and was getting worse. As his law firm became more successful, he drank alone more often. At first he mostly drank in the evening, but then began drinking over lunch, and eventually through the afternoon and evening. Dan tried quitting a dozen times over the years, but nothing worked. He told us:

> I was a highly educated, practicing attorney with nearly eight years of running my own law firm, yet everything was on the brink of collapse. I could no longer work a normal workday. My lovely wife was on the verge of asking me to leave the house and separating me from my two young kids. My friends were wondering why I was acting so terrible and erratic. My binge drinking had finally spiraled completely out of control.

One day in his early forties, Dan found *The 30-Day Sobriety Solution.* Even though he was skeptical about his ability to get sober, let alone be happy sober, he was encouraged. As he worked through the program, he was excited to recognize the techniques from other books he had read, although he had not been able to "translate" them effectively into helping him to quit drinking until now. Dan had practiced the law of attraction and "ask, believe, and receive," but until *The 30-Day Sobriety Solution,* he had not known how to apply it to sobriety. Over the course of the program, Dan felt like he actually discovered *the real secret*—the secret of sobriety.

Today Dan has over three years of sobriety, something he had always hoped for but previously doubted would ever happen. Better yet, he is actually happy. He saved his marriage, is the father he always dreamed of being, and is flourishing in his career. Dan recently shared, "I continue to use the solutions I learned in *The 30-Day Sobriety Solution* to improve my connection to the person I want to be and know I can be. I move closer to that person every day."

For Dan, attending Alcoholics Anonymous meetings is a valuable ongoing support for his sobriety. When he sees new people attend meetings right after they hit rock bottom, their puffy faces, dejected attitude, and overwhelming feelings of fear and desperation continually remind Dan of the pain drinking once caused him. He enjoys being able to offer hope and inspiration to others that lasting change *is* possible.

The "Daydreamer's Dilemma"

Financial success, or any other kind of success, does not require hard work or action, but it does require alignment of thought. You simply cannot offer negative thought about things that you desire and then make up for it with action or hard work.

—ESTHER and JERRY HICKS[4]

Do you like to daydream? We do. It can be a fun escape. Maybe you put on some great music and let your imagination run wild. Sometimes the daydreams are just fun and really aren't important to you, but other times these daydreams are about goals that you believe hold the key to your ultimate happiness and fulfillment. And guess what? You are right.

Have you ever paid close attention to what happens *after* you seriously start thinking about achieving those goals? Usually some form of doubt sets in, which we call the "Daydreamer's Dilemma." For example, have you noticed that, when you dream about being sober, how proud everyone will be, and all the great changes you will make in your personal and professional life, almost immediately, the "what-ifs" start to kick in. *What if I tell everyone and I fail again? What if I decide I don't want to change? What if I am not happy when I'm sober? What if this is just meant to be my life? What if I simply can't do it?*

Do you do this in other areas of your life, too? You start thinking about a dream or goal, but then your thinking immediately shifts to how disappointed you, or others, will be when you fail? Unfortunately, this is an all too common phenomenon. *Most people are great at wanting "more," but lousy at believing they can have it, or receive it.* They are more accustomed to and comfortable with *not* getting what they want. And by "want," we don't mean getting the newest iPhone. We are talking about the life-changing "wants"—finding the love of your life, landing your dream job, having total financial freedom, and absolutely loving your new sober life.

However, getting what you really want often makes you uncomfortable because you are not used to it. You may have gotten used to following up your big "wants" with the expectation that you will not get them. Because of the law of attraction, this negative expectation virtually guarantees the opposite outcome of what you really want. In their book *Money, and the Law of Attraction: Learning to Attract Wealth, Health, and Happiness*, Esther and Jerry Hicks talk about this in relation to money:

> Most of you are much closer to a financial fortune than you are even allowing yourself to purely desire, because, in the thought that it might come, you right away begin thinking of how disappointed you will be if it does not come in. And so, in your lackful thought, you do not allow yourself to desire or to expect anything magnificent in terms of money;

and that is the reason why, for the most part, you are living rather mediocre financial experiences.[5]

Your **first action step** for today is to pay attention to what thoughts and feelings come up the next time you are thinking— or daydreaming—about what you really want. If you catch yourself doubting your success, expecting failure, or thinking about why you can't accomplish your goal, acknowledge the thoughts and then go through the steps of the "ask, believe, receive" process with your goal.

Input Equals Output

Psychologists have shown that the more television you watch, the lower are your levels of energy and self-esteem. At an unconscious level, you don't like or respect yourself as much if you sit there hour after hour watching television. People who watch too much television also gain weight and become physically unfit from sitting around too much.

—BRIAN TRACY[6]

Dave's wife is a child therapist who knows that, in order to have a lasting positive impact on younger children, she has to work with their parents. One of the most basic concepts she teaches parents is that input equals output, or as it is often stated, "Garbage in, garbage out." In other words, don't expose young children to violent movies, books, video games, and TV shows, especially most nightly news programs, which primarily report murder, suicide, rape, deadly diseases, fires, and car accidents. Repeated exposure to these stories and images negatively affects children's personality, behavior, and how they interact with other kids. Some parents are surprised at how quickly their children's behavior changes for the better when they eliminate most exposure to these influences.

But the negative influence of negative news does not stop when you become an adult. If you are in the habit of watching the news before you go to bed, you are filling your head with negative, disturbing images and thoughts, which your subconscious focuses on all night. In his book *100 Ways to Motivate Yourself*, Steve Chandler writes:

> The news is not the news. It is the bad news. It is deliberate shock. The more you accept it as the news, the more you believe that "that's the way it is," and the more fearful and cynical you will become.
>
> If we realized exactly how much vulgar, pessimistic, and manipulative negativity was deliberately packed into every daily newspaper and most television shows and Hollywood movies, we would resist the temptation to flood our brains with their garbage. Most of us are more particular about what we put in our automobile's gas tank than we are about what we put in our own brain every night. We passively feed ourselves with stories about serial killers and violent crime without any conscious awareness of the choice we are making.[7]

However, the good news is that you can easily change this, and we have five key recommendations to help you with your **second action step** for today.

First, stop watching the news—at least the typical news programs that focus primarily on negative news. This doesn't mean you have to ignore all news—simply use news resources that allow you to pick and choose what you want to read. With all the online news aggregators available, you have virtually unlimited options. And if you want local news, visit your local affiliate's website, or see if they have an app for your phone. When you visit any of these websites, simply ignore the "bad news" unless you feel strongly that it is relevant.

Second, take a hard look at the TV shows and movies you watch, the books you read, and the video games you play. Be deliberate about your choices. We are not saying you should avoid *all* scary, violent, or negative content that makes you afraid and worried, but we are saying you should consciously limit it and actively choose other content that puts you in an inspired, positive, and uplifted state of mind. And if you do choose to watch TV before bed, pick something funny, inspiring, or educational.

Third, pay attention to your feelings. Ask yourself, *Does this TV show, book, game, or movie add any real value to my life?* If not, stop it.

Fourth, pay attention to any "inputs" that have a negative impact on you—not just broadcast media, but people, websites, social media sites, smartphone applications, specific locations, or even certain topics of discussion.

Last, revisit the Forgiveness Solution. Because you attract energy that matches the vibration of your feelings, being negative, angry, and unforgiving ensures that you'll attract more people and situations about which you'll be negative, angry, and unforgiving. If you feel that you haven't been able to fully embrace forgiveness, for others *and* for yourself, we encourage you to take yourself through the Total Truth Process again.

Drunk-a-Log

One of the favorite questions to ask that I learned in The 30-Day Sobriety Solution *is, "Am I moving closer to or farther away from my next drink?" It is a simple way for me to have awareness about my current state of mind, and make adjustments in my life when necessary.*

—SUSAN

30-Day Graduate from Philadelphia, Pennsylvania

Yesterday we talked about the value of attending Alcoholics Anonymous meetings, and shared some advice on how to deal with the "I'm an alcoholic" affirmation. And today we shared Dan's story and the ongoing support that AA has given him. Because AA can be a great resource, and because you can find meetings almost anywhere, we want to touch on one other important component in AA meetings—the "drunk-a-log."

When people in recovery share their life stories, a lot of it focuses on their drinking escapades or their drunk-a-log. At an AA speaker meeting with an experienced speaker, it can be effective in connecting you to the pain associated with drinking, as you recall from Day 3 and the Pendulum Solution. But in meetings where one person after another stands up to share their drunken experiences, the law of attraction means that you get more of what you focus on. When you spend time sharing and listening to one drinking story after another, you are constantly focused on drinking, which is what you *don't* want—and not focused on sobriety, which is what you *do* want.

Our recommendation comes down to one of our common themes—awareness. Stay aware of how you feel after attending a meeting. Do you feel depressed and agitated or uplifted and inspired? When Dave attended AA meetings that were dominated by drunk-a-logs, he usually felt worse afterward. However, after Dave attended meetings where someone new to AA would share painful stories of alcohol abuse, he would relive his own pain all over again, feel grateful for his own sobriety, and leave with a renewed sense of purpose.

So, if you do decide to attend AA meetings (which we don't believe you need to do unless you feel they are helpful), pay close attention to how you feel. After attending a meeting, ask yourself, *Am I moving closer to or farther away from my next drink?* Also pay attention to who attends the meetings. AA meetings differ dramatically from one to the next, and each meeting tends to have its own "regulars," which will tell you a lot about the type of meeting and the people it attracts. Do attendees look healthy and have a positive attitude? Is there anyone whom you could look to as a role model? Or does the meeting seem to be full of unhealthy, negative people? Dave attended ten different AA meetings before he found one that felt like a fit—and to this day he still occasionally attends this same meeting because many of the people who attend are thriving in sobriety. If you choose to attend AA meetings, shop around until you find a meeting that is right for you.

Your *New* Story

I had a thinking problem, not a drinking problem!

—CRAIG FERGUSON[8]

It's important to create a new story for yourself and to leave your old story behind. One of the reasons this is true is because we keep repeating the same story—the story that is full of blaming, complaining, rationalizing, and justifying. Maybe you blame your parents for your drinking, or the lousy economy or your manager at work. Maybe you rationalize that you *deserve* to drink excessively on the weekends because of how hard your job is, or you justify your condition by thinking that everyone has health issues so your drinking is no big deal. You keep telling the same story, and you keep getting the same results, which leads to your **third action step.**

It is time for you to tell a *new* story. The story of the "new you"—the vibrant, passionate, sober you who is no longer held captive by the desire to drink. The "new you" has transformed—emotionally, physically, spiritually, and financially. Esther and Jerry Hicks say, "You have to begin to tell the story of your life as you now want it to be and discontinue the tales of how it has been or of how it is."[9] When you spend more time focusing on, thinking about, and talking about how you want your new life to be, and less time thinking about and talking about how your old life was and current life is, your life will radically change for the better. Here are some important guidelines to follow as you write your new story. As you write it, don't worry about crafting the perfect story with perfect grammar. You are not writing a paper to be graded. The value is in the clarity you get from the process of writing it out.

- **Start one year in the future.** Write your new story as if it is one year from today, but write it in the present. For example, start by writing, "Today is September 3, [year], and I am . . ." Then describe what you are experiencing as if you were writing a letter to someone about your current experience and the journey that got you there.

- **From the one-year-in-the-future frame of mind, reflect back.** Briefly share some details about your life before you started *The 30-Day Sobriety Solution* (capturing whatever feels important to you as if you were looking back at this time from a year in the future), and then continue forward, working through the program and beyond—up to one year in the future. For example, after the sentence above, you might continue by writing: "When I purchased *The 30-Day Sobriety Solution*, I was struggling. My drinking had reached a point where it was affecting my health and relationships. I no longer felt like not drinking was a realistic option, and I knew there had to be more to life." Then your story might continue with your experience with the program to date—your challenges, your successes, and your breakthroughs.
- **Write about what you want.** Write about what you want your future life to look like as if you were already experiencing it. This is the fun part, and you can really embrace your creativity. Do not judge what you want. This is your chance to capture your dreams in writing, so take your time and enjoy it! What does your drinking look like? Do you abstain completely, or are you able to have a "take it or leave it" approach, having a drink or two when you want, but never feeling like you need to drink to be happy or relaxed? Then move into the really interesting part of the story—all the personal and professional changes you have experienced. Some resources you can use are the "new you" that you wrote on Day 2, your core values from Day 10, and the new beliefs you wrote on Day 11—and any other solutions you have done so far that have helped you get more clarity on what thriving in sobriety means to you. Consider including the following areas in this part of the story: your health, your job and career, what you are doing for fun and recreation, how you are growing personally and spiritually, what is happening with family and friends, your love life, what your physical environment looks

like, your finances, and how you are contributing and giving back to others.

Although we encourage you to dream as big as you want, remember this is just one year from today, so go for what you want, but keep it believable. For example, it might not be likely for you to more than double your existing income or to move into a house worth four times your existing house's value in one year. But it is very possible to fall madly in love, get into the best shape of your life, find a new job or start your own business, pay off a substantial amount of debt, make new friends, start and excel at a new hobby, and find rewarding ways to give back to your community.

Day 19 Action Steps

The positivity and enthusiasm of The 30-Day Sobriety Solution *is infectious, and even though I am naturally a little cynical, the program effectively cut through that.*

—THOMAS
30-Day Graduate from London, England

Like attracts like—it really is that simple. Whatever you have more of in your life today, you will naturally continue to attract: people (problem drinkers or role models), money (wealth or poverty), and happiness (fun or boredom). If you want to change it, then understanding how to leverage the law of attraction is one of the most powerful tools at your disposal. These action steps will help you do that.

- **Use the "ask, believe, receive" process.** Now that you have clarity about what you want, practice asking for it, believing it, receiving it, and appreciating it. Use this process when you catch yourself in the "Daydreamer's Dilemma," and use it with your new story.

The real value comes from making the "new you" as real as possible, and the best way to accomplish this is through practice and repetition.

- **Change your inputs.** Stop watching the nightly news, or any news that primarily reports negative, fear-inducing, or manipulative stories, images, and videos. Use an online news aggregator instead, such as Google News, or search for one in your app store. Ask yourself if the TV and movies you watch, the books you read, and the video games you play leave you in a positive or negative frame of mind. Reduce your exposure to negative influences, especially right before bed. Let go of any resentments, anger, or thoughts of revenge that you may be holding on to—including those directed toward yourself—as these strong feelings will only attract more of that energy into your life.

- **Write your new story.** Write your new story of what you really want in the present tense as if it is one year from today. Get clear on what you want to accomplish over this next year, including what your drinking looks like, what has changed, and what is now happening in your health, career, finances, fun and recreation, personal growth, friends and family, romance, physical environment, and contribution/giving back. Keep this where you can read it at least once a week, and update it as you get more clarity.

On the companion website, we discuss the two "faces" of envy and how to really use it to your advantage. We also share an example of a completed new story, to help guide you in writing yours. Visit the companion website at http://Day19.Solutions.

The Gratitude Solution

Awakening the Power of Gratitude and Appreciation

Of all the "attitudes" we can acquire, surely the attitude of gratitude is the most important and by far the most life changing.

—ZIG ZIGLAR

By choosing to focus on what you have rather than what you don't have, you can reach a state of appreciation and gratitude. And as you learned yesterday in the Attraction Solution, you attract more of what you focus on. So when you focus on appreciating all that you have, you attract more to appreciate.

Cultivating the practice of gratitude in your daily life is one of the most transformative tools you can use to achieve a life of sobriety. Today the Gratitude Solution will teach you exactly how to easily integrate this life-changing attitude.

Gratitude: The Secret of Sobriety

Develop an attitude of gratitude, and give thanks for everything that happens to you, knowing that every step forward is a step toward achieving something bigger and better than your current situation.

—BRIAN TRACY

What if you could be 25 percent happier, and it would take you only a few minutes a day to accomplish this? Robert Emmons, one of the world's leading experts on the science of gratitude and author of *Thanks! How the New Science of Gratitude Can Make You Happier*, proved exactly how to do this. His research discovered that participants who kept a daily journal and described five things for which they were grateful were 25 percent happier than other groups who did not keep a journal. The journaling group members felt better about their lives as a whole and were more optimistic about the future.[1]

In many ways, when we think of "happy" we think of a state or emotion that can't really be measured. However, in the last decade, research on happiness[2] shows that it actually can be measured and increased. Dr. Sonja Lyubomirsky writes in *The How of Happiness: A Scientific Approach to Getting the Life You Want*:

> In becoming happier, we not only boost experiences of joy, contentment, love, pride, and awe but also improve other aspects of our lives: our energy levels, our immune systems, our engagement with work and with other people, and our physical and mental health. In becoming happier, we bolster as well our feelings of self-confidence and self-esteem; we come to believe that we are worthy human beings, deserving of respect. A final and perhaps least appreciated plus is that if we become happier, we benefit not only ourselves but also our partners, families, communities, and even society at large.[3]

So practicing gratitude boosts your happiness. And when you are happier, you have more energy, better health, more confidence, and improved relationships with your family and friends. As we have discussed before, one of the most common myths that problem drinkers believe is that they cannot be happy and sober at the same time. Therefore, any solution that is proven to boost happiness by 25 percent that can be done without drinking is one you must use. The

Gratitude Solution really is, in many ways, the secret to thriving in sobriety. When Dave started practicing gratitude in the early stage of his sobriety, he found that it had one of the most dramatic impacts of anything he did, and it took him only a few minutes to do before getting out of bed.

An Attitude of Gratitude

When you are grateful, fear disappears and abundance appears.

—TONY ROBBINS

Consider this—the more grateful people are for the gifts you give them, the more inclined you are to give them gifts. Right? The appreciation and gratitude they express reinforces your giving. This same principle holds true on a universal and spiritual level. Like attracts like, so your gratitude will attract even more things into your life to be grateful for.

However, when you focus on what you don't have and haven't achieved, you will only attract more scarcity into your life. When you focus on the negative (what you don't have or don't want) and are overly judgmental of yourself (focusing on what you did wrong), then overcoming a challenge like cutting back or quitting drinking becomes much more difficult. If you focus on the times you "failed" when you tried to cut back or quit drinking, the shame and embarrassment you feel will only move you closer to your next drink.

The Gratitude Solution is best captured by a phrase you have probably heard in the 12-step and self-help worlds countless times— have an "attitude of gratitude." No matter what you have in your life today—even if your drinking has taken away a lot—you need to be grateful for it. Be grateful for your friends and family, for living in a country full of opportunity, for having a home, a car, a job, and anything else you can think of—including having found this book.

It may help to remember that almost half the world's population—more than three billion people—lives on less than $2.50 a day.[4]

An attitude of gratitude is not as much about "feeling" as it is about "being." It is easy to feel grateful when things are going your way—it is the natural response. But should you feel grateful if you lose your job or a loved one passes away? Catholic Benedictine monk Brother David Steindl-Rast, one of the world's leading teachers of gratitude and the founder of Gratefulness.org, writes: "Times that challenge us physically, emotionally, and spiritually may make it almost impossible for us to feel grateful. Yet, we can decide to live gratefully, courageously open to life in all its fullness. By living the gratefulness we don't feel, we begin to feel the gratefulness we live."[5] The secret to gratitude is that it is a choice—a conscious, deliberate choice.

Being grateful makes you happier and healthier, attracts more fulfilling relationships and positive role models, and moves you more quickly down the path to thriving in sobriety, all without even realizing you are doing it. And, as your life improves, you find less need or desire to escape your reality through drinking.

The Opposite of Gratitude

Today I am thrilled about how much my life has improved and how grateful I am that there is no temptation to drink whatsoever. And what is so exciting is that I get to focus on achieving my other goals in life, now that alcohol is no longer part of it.

—JAMES

30-Day Graduate from Istanbul, Turkey

Negativity is the opposite of gratitude. In our society it is so easy to get caught up in negative thoughts and emotions rather than gratitude. We commute to work in bad traffic or crowded mass transit. We hear daily news stories about terrorism, corruption, and a struggling economy. And by the age of twenty-one the average adult will have seen a million commercials—the core intention of which is to play on our fears that we are not enough and we need "more" to be happy.[6] This results in an overall feeling of lack rather than a feeling of gratitude for who we are and what we already have.

Susan's Attitude of Gratitude

The longer I am relieved of my symptom, the more I experience feelings of gratitude for my recovery. More frequently, the feelings arise from an overall sense of joy that I feel in my newfound life in sobriety. These feelings are enhanced by the certainty of the course my life would have taken had it not been for the saving grace of my Higher Power and discovering the life-altering techniques and solutions of The 30-Day Sobriety Solution.

—DESIREE

30-Day Graduate from Harare, Zimbabwe

Susan and her husband were eating dinner at a charming little pub they had frequented hundreds of times. Susan was drinking wine, as she did almost every night of the week, while socializing with her husband, the waitstaff, and other friends. But on this evening, Susan saw the rest of her life flash in front of her. She saw herself having the same meaningless conversations over and over again, watching the same meaningless TV shows, and the only thing that made it bearable was the wine. That night, she knew her life had to change—forever.

During the day Susan was a successful owner of two small businesses, a well-respected and liked member of the community, a great mother to four mostly grown-up children, and a loving and supportive wife. Because of these successes, Susan felt that at the end of the day she deserved to wind down by drinking wine. Sometimes she drank three "big glasses," and other times more, but rarely was it none.

What Susan found most hypocritical about her drinking was her love and passion for personal growth and physical health. Over the years she had gone to various personal development workshops, from Tony Robbins to a wide variety of spiritual retreats, and she even regularly practiced yoga and meditation. Yet, here she was, in her midforties, and still drinking almost every night.

As Susan shared, "I felt like a fake. Inside I felt horrible and sorry for myself, while everyone around me thought I was so happy and had it all together. I would attend all of these spiritual trainings, and spread words of encouragement to others to help them change and be happy, but I was failing at doing it in my own life."

When Susan found *The 30-Day Sobriety Solution,* she said, "I felt like I had discovered the missing numbers to my combination lock." Because of all the personal work she had done, she was familiar with a lot of the solutions and had used some of them to create successful businesses and relationships, but until she found *The 30-Day Sobriety Solution,* she hadn't thought to apply them to stopping her drinking.

Upon starting the program, she quickly realized, "My problem is not drinking; my problem is thinking I can solve or fill an emptiness within myself by drinking." As Susan started getting clear on what she really wanted in life, she was able to let go of her guilt and shame, and was finally able to imagine and believe she could thrive in sobriety.

The Gratitude Solution was one of Susan's favorites because, as she practiced daily gratitude, her decision to stay sober became easier and easier.

After three months of abstinence, in the midst of the holiday season, Susan decided to "test" drinking again and drank one or two glasses of wine on three different nights. Although she was encouraged by her newfound control, she realized that drinking no longer brought her any happiness, peace, or freedom. Today she has been sober for almost two years, is working to open a spiritual retreat center, and recently accomplished one of her lifelong goals of writing a book on meditation.

Goals and Gratitude

I once heard a sober alcoholic say that drinking never made him happy, but it made him feel like he was going to be happy in about fifteen minutes. That was exactly it, and I couldn't understand why the happiness never came, couldn't see the flaw in my thinking, couldn't see that alcohol kept me trapped in a world of illusion, procrastination, paralysis. I lived always in the future, never in the present. Next time, next time! Next time I drank it would be different, next time it would make me feel good again. And all my efforts were doomed, because already drinking hadn't made me feel good in years.

—HEATHER KING
Author of *Parched: A Memoir*[7]

People in general are obsessed with more—more money, more power, more recognition, and more alcohol. But this "more" that we are lusting for comes with the biggest price tag of all—it destroys our enjoyment of the present.

In the Outcome Solution, we explored how to create an outcome-focused, purpose-driven goal-setting strategy to make thriving in sobriety a reality in your life. Having dreams, setting goals, and desiring specific outcomes are key to thriving in sobriety, but focusing too intently on your *future* goals can make you feel incomplete or inadequate in the *present*.

You want to avoid creating more stress in your life by thinking that you are somehow not okay because you are not "there" yet. The everyday challenges of life are stressful enough without judging yourself as not okay because you haven't achieved one or all of your goals yet. You don't want to become so obsessed with getting to where you want to go that you are unable to enjoy the present. You must learn that all you have is the present moment—the here and the now—and to create the future of your dreams you must embrace and appreciate the present.

As Eckhart Tolle reminds us, "Are you stressed? Are you so busy getting to the future that the present is reduced to a means of getting there? Stress is caused by being 'here' but wanting to be 'there,' or being in the present but wanting to be in the future."[8]

The secret to all success, as well as the secret to sobriety, is to appreciate everything you have and all that you are experiencing in the present while still actively pursuing the creation of what you want to have and what you want to experience in the future. When you choose to have an attitude of gratitude, you avoid falling into the state of "not enoughness." The key is to make the choice—and it is a choice—to fully enjoy everything you have today while you are working to create your ideal tomorrow.

There is one more thing we'd like to mention about the pursuit of goals. The achievement of your goals is *not* the most important thing. It's *who you become* in the process of achieving those goals that is most important. In order to achieve any worthwhile goal, you may need to learn new information, develop new skills, build new teams, forge new alliances, and develop or deepen important personal qualities and attributes like courage, commitment, patience, and perseverance. And the growth you experience—what you learn and who you become—is much more valuable than all the money, possessions, power, and prestige that you'll ever acquire.

Day 20 Action Steps

After I completed the Gratitude Solution, I wrote letters of gratitude to four of my family members. Although it was a challenging and emotional process, the instant I put the letters in the mail I realized how uplifting and inspiring it was to express appreciation to others. At that moment, the power of gratitude was unquestionable and was only further reinforced when I talked to the recipients of the letters.

—BYRON

30-Day Graduate from Phoenix, Arizona

The Gratitude Solution is all about cultivating gratitude to increase happiness, which leads to more energy and confidence, better health, and improved relationships. We like to call the action steps for today the "Magic Three of Gratitude." When you do these three things, you will transform your life.

- **In your journal, list twenty-five or more things you are grateful for.** The main purpose is to start building your "gratitude muscle." It might surprise you that this is difficult at first. There are no rules about what to include—the list can range from gratitude for your family, friends, and pets to gratitude for refrigeration and indoor plumbing. The more challenging you find it is to make this list, the more important it is to implement this solution in your life. Here's one of Jack's recent gratitude lists.

  I am so happy and grateful for:
  1. How the sunlight comes into our bedroom in the morning
  2. Inga, my wife, especially for how she makes me laugh
  3. All my friends, especially everyone at TLC (Transformational Leadership Council)
  4. My children and my grandson

5. Living in California—the weather, the ocean, the diversity
6. Joey, who is the cutest dog in the world, and my cats
7. Patty, my wonderful friend and incredible business partner
8. *Chicken Soup for the Soul*
9. All my Facebook fans
10. Television (especially *The Voice* and *Dancing with the Stars*)
11. Movies
12. Music, Pandora, SiriusXM radio, and Sonos
13. The internet, Amazon.com, Google, and Wikipedia
14. *Monday Night Football*
15. Comedians (especially Louis C. K., Chris Rock, Sebastian Maniscalco, Jim Gaffigan, Ron White, Paula Poundstone, Paul Rodriguez, and Russell Peters)
16. Steve Jobs, my Apple computer, iPhone, iPad, and all my apps
17. My health
18. My hair
19. My house
20. My car
21. My blender
22. My hair dryer
23. Erica's and Kristen's massages
24. Whole Foods
25. Veronica, my assistant, and all the rest of my staff
26. Having such good food in the refrigerator
27. All my Train the Trainer students and graduates

- **When you wake up in the morning, think about five or more things that you are truly grateful for.** The key to this action step is to not only think about what you are grateful for, but to close your eyes and spend a few minutes actually *feeling* grateful. Do this first thing in the morning—we find the best time is before you even get out of bed, but during your morning meditation or in the shower works fine, too. You can deepen the experience if you take the time to *visualize* an image of each thing as you think of it (or write it down in your journal) and *feel* the emotions of appreciation or gratitude in your body. We know we are really into feeling grateful when we feel our chest expand, a smile forming on our face, or tears welling up in our eyes. The more deeply you feel your feelings, the more powerful the impact will be. Let yourself really feel the love you have for your spouse or lover, the joy you experience when you play with your children, the excitement you feel about your work, the peace you feel when you are playing your guitar, or the freedom you experience when you are riding your motorcycle.

You can focus on the same five every morning, or focus on new ones every day. We like to see which ones spontaneously jump into our consciousness when we start the exercise.

The practice of beginning each day with this gratitude exercise will eventually lead you to naturally waking up happy and excited to start your day. This is because over time you are anchoring the experience of waking up to the positive experience of feeling deep gratitude. This simple practice can totally transform your life. On the companion website, you'll find a guided recording that will lead you through this morning gratitude process.

- **Tell Someone how much you appreciate him or her, either face-to-face, with a phone call, in an email, or by writing a letter.** This can have a huge impact on your relationships. After learning this simple technique, Dave wrote cards to both his young daughters and his wife, letting them know how grateful he was to have them in his life. Years later, his daughters shared with him how meaningful it was to actually have in writing how much their father appreciated them.

  It's all too easy to forget the emotional wall that drinking can create between you and your loved ones, and this simple action step can start to reestablish critical connections. Writing only three letters of gratitude over a three-week period leads to increased happiness and life satisfaction, while also reducing symptoms of depression.[9]

As always, be sure to visit the companion website for some additional information and material on today's solution, including a guided recording that will lead you through the morning gratitude process. Visit the companion website at http://Day20.Solutions.

The Review Day and Bonus Solution

Using the Secrets of Advertising to Create an
Unshakable Belief in Yourself and Your Dreams

The thing is, if I don't have sobriety, I don't have anything.

—MATTHEW PERRY

Actor and addiction-awareness activist in recovery[1]

Now that you have finished Phase III, "Creating an Unshakable Belief in Yourself and Your Dreams," you have learned some of the
same techniques advertisers use to get you to buy their products, but
instead you are using them to counteract that influence.[2] In 2013,
US advertisers spent more than $2 billion on advertising alcohol.[3]
When you think of taking a tropical vacation, is the first image that
comes to your mind a bottle of Corona beer, glistening with water
droplets, sitting on a small table on the sand next to your beach
chair? And when you hear, "Great Taste, Less Filling," what do you
see?

There is a reason why we have you constantly repeat and review
the solutions that you learn, so you think of them as habitually
as you think of an advertising jingle or slogan—repetition works!
That's why you are repeating your affirmations over and over, and
that's why you are visualizing every day. When you create and con-

sistently focus on the mental images of the outcomes you want in your life and link them to a strong emotion, you are using the exact same technique as the makers of that Corona commercial. But instead of linking the feelings of relaxation, joy, and pleasure you experience when you are on vacation to a bottle of beer, you are linking the feelings of relaxation, joy, and pleasure to your experience of being sober.

Through constant repetition over time, these advertising jingles become embedded in your subconscious, leading you to make choices without your conscious awareness, just like the wine buyers whose purchases were influenced by the nationality of the music being played in the store that we mentioned in Day 12. And what about all the alcohol commercials linking socializing, laughing, and having fun with friends to always having a beer, a glass of wine, or a cocktail in your hand? The bottom line is that you are now empowered to use the same techniques that advertisers have spent billions on and thoroughly tested through their advertising campaigns to help you achieve your goal of thriving in sobriety.

In Phase III, you learned how the law of attraction affects your daily life, the importance of practicing gratitude and appreciation every day, and how the questions you ask can shape your future. And perhaps, most importantly, you now have a deeper understanding of your negative thinking patterns and how to release and replace them. On the companion website we review each of these key concepts further, and also share another special video from us.

You will also find this week's bonus solution, the Frequently Asked Sobriety Questions Solution, which includes answers to the most frequently asked questions we get from our sobriety coaching clients. You'll find answers to questions you did not even realize you wanted to ask, and without having to pay the thousands of dollars our coaching clients had to pay for these same answers. Make sure to visit the companion website at http://Day21.Solutions to get started right now with the Phase III review.

Cultivating Courage and Positive Relationships to Thrive in Mind, Body, and Spirit

---

Every significant vital sign—body temperature, heart rate, oxygen consumption, hormone level, brain activity, and so on—alters the moment you decide to do anything ... decisions are signals telling your body, mind, and environment to move in a certain direction.

—DEEPAK CHOPRA[1]

Congratulations and welcome to Phase IV, "Cultivating Courage and Positive Relationships to Thrive in Mind, Body, and Spirit." This phase is often completed during the fourth week of *The 30-Day Sobriety Solution*, unless you have chosen the 60- or 90-day option. The end is in sight, and you are likely experiencing a wide range of emotions. Maybe you feel excited and empowered. Or possibly you feel scared and unsure. Or maybe you miss some of the secrecy and excitement you used to get from hiding alcohol or sneaking drinks. Or perhaps you are planning for Day 31—for what, how much, where, and with whom you are going to drink again. In fact, you might have started planning and thinking about that moment when you first decided to abstain for 30 days.

If so, that is okay—you are not alone. But we have to caution you that the more time you spend living in the future and planning the next time you will drink, the less time you have in the present to make positive lasting changes in your life. If you find yourself thinking about the next time you can drink, simply acknowledge that you feel this way and then review and choose to do one of the past solutions to change your thinking—such as asking yourself empowering questions, practicing visualization, reciting your affirmations, analyzing and changing your negative thinking, practicing gratitude, or using the "ask, believe, receive" process. Any one of these techniques can easily shift your focus, and these are *only the tools you learned last week*. Imagine what you can accomplish when you are able to leverage all of the tools and techniques in *The 30-Day Sobriety Solution*.

In Phase IV, you are going to add some new transformational tools to this toolkit. Today we are going to tackle one of the most important topics of all—fear. Let's get started.

The Courage Solution

Successfully Confronting Your Fears

> *Courage is resistance to fear, mastery*
> *of fear, not absence of fear.*
>
> —MARK TWAIN

As you move forward on your journey to thriving in sobriety, you are going to have to continue confronting fears that arise. Fear is natural. Whenever you start a new project, take on a new venture, or put yourself out there, as you have done with *The 30-Day Sobriety Solution*, fear is a normal reaction.

Unfortunately, many people let fear stop them from taking the necessary steps to achieve their dreams. Successful people, on the other hand, feel the fear along with the rest of us, but don't let it keep them from doing what they want to do—or have to do. They understand that fear is something to be acknowledged, experienced, and taken along for the ride. Today we'll cover how to let go of fear, so that living a courageous life thriving in sobriety comes naturally.

The Courage Solution

You have to face your fear. And do the same with anger, do the same with jealousy, do the same with hatred. And a signifi-

cant point to remember is: if you witness anything—fear, anger, hate—if you simply watch them as they arise, without any judgment or condemnation, they will disappear, leaving a tremendous amount of energy that you can use for creativity.

—OSHO

Author of *The Book of Understanding: Creating Your Own Path to Freedom*[1]

You experience fear for many reasons. You fear that you are either not "enough"—pretty enough, smart enough, talented enough, or creative enough—or at some level you are afraid of what might happen if you become the person of your dreams. You may fear that if you do "shine" it will be at the expense of the people you love, and you might lose their love. You may be afraid of the unknown and afraid of change. And, of course, you are afraid to fail. However, your deepest fear may be of your own brilliance and power. Bestselling author and spiritual teacher Marianne Williamson captured this best when she wrote:

Our deepest fear is not that we are inadequate. Our deepest fear is that we are powerful beyond measure. It is our light, not our darkness, that most frightens us. We ask ourselves, who am I to be brilliant, gorgeous, talented and fabulous? Actually, who are you not to be? You are a child of God. Your playing small doesn't serve the world. There's nothing enlightened about shrinking so that other people won't feel insecure around you. We are all meant to shine, as children do. We are born to manifest the glory of God that is within us. It's not just in some of us, it's in everyone. And as we let our own light shine, we unconsciously give other people permission to do the same. As we are liberated from our own fear, our presence automatically liberates others.[2]

Fear of your own brilliance and power leads you to complacency and comfort. So you trick yourself into believing that taking the "comfortable" approach serves you. On Day 2 you learned that change comes at the edge of your comfort zone. You may drink excessively because on some level you are afraid of letting your own light shine. But when you have the courage to face your fears, which you have demonstrated by making it this far in *The 30-Day Sobriety Solution*, not only is achieving your own dreams possible, but you give hope, inspiration, and permission to those around you to also reach for their dreams.

Two Types of Fear

Fear is a chameleon that can be a wise guide in one moment and a terrible tyrant the next. Respect fear, but never let it be your master. If physical danger is involved, listen well; if psychological danger challenges you, then do what you most fear—live as a peaceful warrior.

—DAN MILLMAN

Author of *Way of the Peaceful Warrior*[3]

There are two types of fear. There is the rational fear of mortal danger, where something threatens your survival, such as stumbling upon a rattlesnake in your path or seeing a car heading toward you weaving in and out of its lane. Recognizing these dangers puts you on alert so that you can protect yourself.

The other type of fear is psychological or irrational fear, which you experience more often, such as the fear of public speaking, the fear of asking out someone you like, or the fears that come up when you think of never drinking a drop of alcohol again. This type of fear is self-created and self-sabotaging. It creates stress, anger, resentment, and other negative emotions.[4] Today is about facing your irrational fears—the ones that are really holding you back from getting what you want.

Fear or Fantasy?

I personally believe this: We have only today; yesterday's gone and tomorrow is uncertain. That's why they call it the present. And sobriety really is a gift . . . for those who are willing to receive it.

—ACE FREHLEY
Guitarist, founding member of the rock band Kiss, and in recovery[5]

Hopefully by today, your fears related to drinking have reduced in frequency and intensity. But recovery is an ongoing process, and fears can come and go like the tide. So what is fear? Fear is often explained as the anticipation of pain. We like to explain FEAR as the acronym for Fantasized Experiences Appearing Real. What this means is that you are the one who is creating your own experience of fear by imagining something negative in the future . . . you are the one creating the movie in your mind. And because your brain cannot tell the difference between a real event and a vividly imagined event, you actually experience the fear as real in your body.[6] You want to remember that *you* are 100% responsible for creating the fear by imagining the negative future event. As Eckhart Tolle reminds us in his book *The Power of Now*, "Unease, anxiety, tension, stress, worry—all forms of fear—are caused by too much future, and not enough presence."

You are using the power of your creative imagination to scare yourself. But this fear is not real because you have no real way of knowing what the future will bring.

This type of fear is *not* rational. For years Dave was convinced that getting sober would negatively affect his career, his happiness, his friendships, and his social life. This irrational fear immobilized him from taking any serious steps to get sober. Even when he did take action, he really only had "one foot in" because deep down he was afraid of the pain he believed he would experience if he was sober. When he finally did get sober, he realized how misguided and irrational his fears had been. Today Dave's career and his social life are flourishing, and the real love he experiences in his relationships with his wife, children, family, friends, and clients was unimaginable during his drinking years. But think about this—if he had visualized sobriety as powerful and happy (as you learned to do on Day 15), he would have been using his mental power of visualization to motivate himself instead of to scare himself.

When you understand that almost all of your fears are self-created, then *you* have the power to change them. You can visualize a positive outcome by imagining a picture of what you *do* want rather than what you *don't* want. You can also stop and look at the actual facts, which show your fear is irrational. And you can simply bring yourself back to the present moment where you are safe and fine.

Fear of Failing, Yet Again . . .

There's no such thing as failure. Mistakes happen in your life to bring into focus more clearly who you really are.

—OPRAH WINFREY

Failure is an emotionally charged word, loaded with negative connotations. This is especially true with problem drinkers. Most likely this isn't the first time you have tried to change or stop your drinking, and in the past you may not have succeeded or, as most would say, you "failed." And each of these failures probably led to more fear around your drinking, lower self-esteem, and reinforcement of the limiting belief that you couldn't stop.

You might remember that Dave was a high performer at work, yet for almost a decade his attempts to quit drinking all ended in failure. Even though he had many accomplishments in other areas of his life, Dave *felt like a failure*. He didn't understand why he couldn't stop drinking when he no longer even liked it. Dave reached the point where he was afraid to let anyone know he was going to try to quit drinking "yet again," because he fully expected to fail. However, when Dave finally redefined failure as feedback, everything changed.

Failing Forward

I didn't fail, I found more than ten thousand ways that won't work. Every wrong attempt discarded was another step forward.

—THOMAS EDISON (1847–1931)
America's most successful inventor, on inventing the lightbulb

Many people fail to take action because they're afraid to fail. Yet, failure is an important part of the learning process. Failure is just a way we learn by trial and error. Success is the result of good judgment, and good judgment is the result of experience. And experience is frequently the result of bad judgment, which leads to failing. *Therefore, failure is necessary to succeed.*

In her highly acclaimed book *Mindset: The New Psychology of Success,* Dr. Carol Dweck breaks down the myth that we are either born with "natural" talent or not. She argues that a huge part of success is determined by how we have defined failure in our life. Those who have a "growth mindset" realize that failure is necessary to succeed. She writes:

> Do you know that Darwin and Tolstoy were considered ordinary children? That Ben Hogan, one of the greatest golfers of all time, was completely uncoordinated and graceless as a child? That the photographer Cindy Sherman, who has been on virtually every list of the most important artists of the twentieth century, failed her first photography course? That Geraldine Page, one of our greatest actresses, was advised to give it up for lack of talent?[7]

Another inspiring example of redefining failure is Esther Earl,[8] the girl who died at the age of sixteen from thyroid cancer and inspired the book *The Fault in Our Stars* by John Green. Not only did this book become a bestseller, it also went on to be a hit movie, grossing more than $300 million.[9] At the age of fourteen, two years after she had been diagnosed with cancer, Esther wrote a letter to her seventeen-year-old self and instructed her parents to read the letter if she died before she was able to open it. In the letter she wrote, "If you haven't done something amazing, don't forget to try. The worst that can happen is you fail, and then you can try again until you succeed."[10] If a fourteen-year-old terminally ill child can redefine failure, you can, too.

You only really fail if you perceive or interpret your results as a failure. But when you redefine failure as just feedback, you "fail forward." When your past attempts to cut back or quit drinking didn't end with the results you wanted, that wasn't failing, it was just feedback. Rather than feeling embarrassed, guilty, or disappointed about "failing" again, and losing the opportunity to learn from it, instead acknowledge and recognize what worked and what didn't work.

There is only one way you can truly fail, and that is to give up.

Today's **first action step** is to redefine failure by writing in your journal about any past attempts you made to either cut back or quit drinking. Write down specifically what you did and what you learned each time. Maybe your only lesson was that your last approach didn't work; however, maybe you learned which times and in which situations you struggle the most to stay sober. Perhaps your past attempts came down to trying to use willpower alone because you never did any personal growth work. Or perhaps you discovered something that actually worked for a while.

For example, Dave tried to quit drinking by using what is commonly referred to as the "marijuana maintenance" program, which consisted of replacing alcohol with pot, which didn't work. He also used his strong willpower to quit for weeks, and even once for months, but throughout those times he would constantly be thinking about and planning when he could drink again. In each of these examples, Dave learned that unless he dealt with the root cause of his drinking, he would always come back to drinking or other addictive behaviors. He also learned that his willpower was a great asset he could use in early sobriety, but the key to thriving in sobriety was to do the personal growth work that dealt with the root cause.

After completing this action step, take a second to acknowledge what you learned and congratulate yourself for taking action and getting feedback.

How Hannah Failed Forward

I don't like my sober life, I love it. Even though I have an occasional drink, The 30-Day Sobriety Solution *has taught me how to never let alcohol be the negative and dominant force it was in my life for decades.*

—HANNAH

30-Day Graduate from Sydney, Australia

When she was twelve years old, Hannah's parents divorced, and Hannah responded like most adolescents do—by becoming more independent. This included drinking alcohol for the first time, and from that moment on she loved alcohol and getting drunk. Hannah got drunk whenever she could throughout her teenage years, and one night while drinking she met her future husband. From a drinking perspective, they were a perfect match and started living together soon after graduating from high school. But by the time Hannah was thirty, she was a single mother of three young children and had a nightly drinking habit that almost always ended with her being drunk.

For the first time in her life, she was ready to face her drinking problem, so she attended Alcoholics Anonymous and managed to string together three months of sobriety. Even though she learned many valuable lessons over those three months, she struggled with the concept of "always focusing on not being drunk." Eventually she returned to drinking—slowly at first, but within months she was back to nightly drinking.

For the next several years, almost every month Hannah tried a new way to stop or cut back her drinking. In her midforties, even though she had created a good life in many ways, she just couldn't stop drinking. She owned a successful hairdressing salon; she had become a certified neurolinguistic programming practitioner (an alternative type of therapy to understand and change human behavior) and ran a small life-coaching business; and she had an open and honest relationship with her children, acknowledging her drinking problem with them and sharing her desire and attempts to change. But every night she returned home with one thing on her mind—alcohol. And almost every night she would drink either two bottles of wine or half a liter of vodka. Then one day she came across *The 30-Day Sobriety Solution*. Hannah recalls:

> I felt like *The 30-Day Sobriety Solution* was breathing life back into me. Every day I learned new tools and techniques that actually worked. I was finally able to imagine a happy life without alcohol, something that had always escaped me. And one of the surprising results was that for the first time in my life, I felt like I was not alone, even though I was doing the program alone at home.

Hannah believed she had found the solution to her lifelong drinking problem, but she still found herself struggling with the two "people" battling it out inside of her—the person who depended on alcohol to live and cope with life, and the new person who was sober and happy but had never been given a chance to really exist since she was twelve. Hannah said, "I was scared about who I was without alcohol, and now that I really saw sobriety as a possibility, it became even more scary. And so I let that fear lead me back to where I felt safe—drinking."

The first two times Hannah began *The 30-Day Sobriety Solution*, she let her fear take over and gave up before she finished. But Hannah knew that she had to be persistent. She was not the same person she had been before she started the program, and so when she started *The 30-Day Sobriety Solution* once again, she discovered that the saying "third time's a charm" was true for her.

> The third time through the program was amazing. This time I was able to finish it, and on the other side I found the happiness I had been searching for my whole life. My new story is exciting and full of unlimited potential. I have rediscovered my passion for music, dancing, and laughing, and I finally know what it feels like to be truly in love. I met a wonderful, supportive, and loving man, one that alcohol would never have let into my life, and we recently became engaged.

After far surpassing her longest time sober as an adult, today Hannah has found she can occasionally have a drink without the risk of returning back to her previous levels. She knows the part of her that was addicted to excessive drinking is long gone, and the part that now replaced her is stronger, healthier, and happier, and, most importantly, will never rely on alcohol again.

Thriving

Inaction breeds doubt and fear. Action breeds confidence and courage. If you want to conquer fear, do not sit home and think about it. Go out and get busy.

—DALE CARNEGIE (1888–1955)
Author of *How to Win Friends and Influence People*

Think back to one of your greatest accomplishments. Most likely you had to push yourself in some way to overcome some fear. In fact, right before you have done most of the amazing things in your life, you likely felt scared.

Our goal with *The 30-Day Sobriety Solution* is for you to *thrive*. And yes, that means thriving in sobriety, but it goes way beyond just cutting back or quitting drinking. The key to thriving in sobriety is thriving in life—living to the highest potential both personally and professionally. To thrive, you must grow. And not just for these 30 days. Growth is a lifelong process if you want to be happy and fulfilled. And what is necessary to keep growing? Action—but not just any action. When you act to confront your biggest fears, you grow the most. The presence of fear is a signal that you have an opportunity to grow.

To sum this up: *Thriving* requires *growth*. *To grow* requires *action*. And this *action* must be directed toward *overcoming your fears*. Or, in short:

Thriving = Overcoming Your Fears

Facing irrational fears can be challenging, but the reality is that you must overcome them in order to thrive. In *The Magic of Thinking Big*, David J. Schwartz writes, "Action cures fear. Indecision, postponement, on the other hand, fertilize fear. . . . When we face tough problems, we stay mired in the mud until we take action."[11] Many people fear that taking action will be more painful than not taking action, so they procrastinate. And this procrastination feeds the fear. The solution is to just get going. Take action. Even the smallest step can break this cycle.

Let's look at this equation in relation to problem drinking. Every problem drinker fears cutting back or quitting drinking for one reason or another. Overcoming this fear is one of the greatest demonstrations of courage. When you have successfully dealt with many of the driving factors that led you to drinking in the first place, as *The 30-Day Sobriety Solution* helps you do, you will no longer be holding yourself back from all your other goals. The time you spent drinking, recovering from your drinking, or planning your next time drinking will be restored to you, as well as your confidence, self-worth, and pride, which will accelerate your success in other areas.

Fear Is Your Compass

A compass is "something that helps a person make choices about what is right, effective, etc."[12] To us, fear also serves as a compass, telling us if we're on or off course. Tony Robbins says, "If you can't, you must, and if you must, you can."[13] We agree. Those very things you are most afraid of will actually provide you with the greatest insights and growth when you do something about them. You have started with what may be one of your greatest fears—cutting back or quitting drinking. The question to ask yourself now is, *What's next?*

The **second action step** for today is to write a list of the fears you have not addressed due to your drinking. Then write down the "benefit" you experience from letting this fear hold you back—yes, there is always some benefit you believe you are getting from letting this fear stop you. Last, write down how you will specifically be able to overcome these fears during the rest of, or after, the program. Use the following set of questions to guide you.

What would I do if I wasn't afraid? (Start with the words "Up until now.")

- **Fear.** *Up until now, I have been afraid to explore new career opportunities.*

What benefit have I been getting from letting this fear stop me?

- **Benefit.** *The benefit of letting this fear control me is that I don't have to update my resume or risk being rejected for a new position.*

What would I do if I had no fear?

- **Overcoming.** *I am excited to explore new career opportunities because now that I am sober, I have more time and more energy, and I am performing at a higher level. I also have a deeper understanding of my strengths and what I really want in life, and I can now use some powerful techniques I'm learning to help me succeed in an interview and in a new career.*

What would I feel and experience if I took that action?

- **Feelings.** *Exploring different career opportunities makes me feel happy, successful, excited, and alive.*

Remember, your problem drinking has probably held you back more than you realize. Dave always knew deep down he was meant to help motivate and inspire others, but the idea of it scared him, not only because his existing job felt so safe, but because he also knew he couldn't do it while drinking. Dave also had always wanted to be fit and healthy, but again his fear of having to stop drinking stopped him from committing to it. He also wanted to be more active in his children's lives and coach their sports teams, but he was afraid the time commitment would interfere with his drinking.

But once Dave removed drinking from his life, and addressed the underlying causes of his drinking, he was able to accomplish all of these goals and many others that he had "buried" beneath his drinking. Within a year he lost sixty-six pounds, ran seventy-five miles in one weekend—including two marathons—and completed the challenging P90X program. Within months he was coaching his oldest daughter's basketball team, and he started taking the necessary steps to build a new career, including developing the program that became this book.

Your fears signal your opportunities, and when you conquer your fear of significantly cutting back or quitting drinking, you will discover how easily and quickly you can overcome other fears that have held you back.

Just Say Yes!

Without fear there cannot be courage.

—CHRISTOPHER PAOLINI
Author of *Eragon*

Before you can face your fears, you first have to be aware of them. You may have accommodated a fear for so long that you just assume the way you are acting is natural and not recognize it as fear. For example, if you have a fear of rejection, you may automatically avoid social situations where you know you won't be able to drink to lessen your anxiety. Perhaps you rationalize this as a personality trait, saying you are "introverted." But if you were to honestly explore this, you might discover that you have just become so accustomed to letting your fear run the show that you don't even notice that you are on autopilot when making decisions that keep you from experiencing and facing your fears.

You probably have friends or family members who are so firmly rooted in their ways that anytime you ask them to do something new or different, they promptly turn you down. They would never acknowledge any fear and there is no option of convincing them otherwise. You can look at this as a subconscious response in reaction to the idea of doing something outside their normal behavior. This is because they have become "stuck" in their comfort zone. And the longer they stay "stuck," the harder it is to break free and be aware that it is occurring.

You can probably relate to being like this at times. Problem drinkers are masters at getting "stuck" in drinking rituals and building their lives around being able to drink the way they want to. And underneath all of this, feeding this continued behavior, is fear. The challenge is breaking free from it.

In the movie *Yes Man*, the lead character, played by Jim Carrey, is "stuck" until he attends a personal growth seminar and agrees to say "yes" to anything he is asked. His life improves dramatically with this simple change. He gets a promotion at work, falls in love, and improves his relationships with his friends and coworkers. Yes, we know this is just a movie, but it conveys a deep message about the power of saying *yes*. Having the courage to say yes to things you usually say no to—assuming they are not dangerous—and breaking out of your comfort zone and your routine behaviors are essential to creating a fulfilling life.

Your **third action step** for today is to write in your journal about the times you have turned down opportunities or invitations to try something new and how this has affected you. This can include pursuing a new career, developing new friendships, going dancing, traveling to a new destination, attending a family reunion, personal growth training, meditation, couples counseling, joining a health club, going to an AA meeting, going back to school, hiring a coach, taking piano lessons, or simply accepting an invitation to go out to lunch.

Many times, turning down these opportunities will be related to your drinking, but some may not be. Regardless, your responses to new opportunities are likely to be so automatic that you don't even realize you're saying no or when fear is guiding you. So we encourage you to be courageous and ask your friends and your family members when they have seen you turn down invitations and opportunities in order to stay in your comfort zone.

Most importantly, just pay attention. Make a conscious decision right now that you are going to stop and listen when someone asks you do to something. This declaration will shift your awareness enough to notice it in the future. Then say yes! If it really scares you, it might be exactly what you need to do to have a breakthrough. One of the mantras we teach our students and coaching clients when we are discussing overcoming your fears is "Oh, what the heck, go for it anyway!"

However, when you are stretching into saying *yes* more often, remember to use common sense. Saying yes to a weekend bachelor party in Las Vegas or a wine-tasting tour in Napa Valley with your own private limousine service when you have just decided to not drink would not be a good idea.

One more thing. If you are still struggling to say yes to a new opportunity, silently ask yourself, *What if I said yes to this offer?* Then pay attention to the feelings that come up—sometimes just asking this question is enough for you to recognize fear and not let it take over.

Your Personal Barometer for Measuring Fear

The danger lies in refusing to face the fear, in not daring to come to grips with it. If you fail anywhere along the line, it will take away your confidence. You must make yourself succeed every time. You must do the thing you think you cannot do.

—ELEANOR ROOSEVELT (1884–1962)
US First Lady and humanitarian[14]

Do you remember the first time you drove a car? What about your first date or first kiss? Or when you first took the stage in a play, or stepped onto the court or field for your first playoff game? You probably felt at least some fear in each of these experiences, which included a physical response. Your body physically reacts by pumping adrenaline into your muscles. Your breathing and heart rate increase, pumping more blood throughout your body.

For example, if you think about a future speaking engagement where you have to get up in front of thousands of people, you may experience fear. Psychologically, you'll have negative "what-if" thoughts. *What if I completely freeze on the stage? What if the presentation doesn't work? What if I mess up and my manager wants to fire me?* Physically, you'll have "fear spots." You might feel a sunken pit in the bottom of your stomach, or tension in your jaw, shoulders, arms, feet, neck, or even your mouth and lips. You might fidget, bounce your leg up and down, or rub your fingers against the palms of your hands. You might sweat, even profusely, or your mouth might dry up so that it is hard to speak.

In order to acknowledge and respond to your fears, you must be aware of them. Your body is a barometer for emotions, and as you get better at "reading" your barometer, you will get better at responding to fear.[15]

The **fourth action step** for today is to take some "measurements." First, think about anything that scares you about your drinking, such as its effect on your health, relationships, career, and finances. Take a minute to feel that fear. For example, imagine getting a call from your doctor asking you to come in for more testing on your liver. Notice how and where your fears show up physically. Repeat this process for other fears, making note each time of your physical reaction. We are aware that imagining what you *don't* want to happen goes against our past advice, especially at this stage of the program, but the value you will get from becoming aware of the physical sensations you experience when you are afraid will far outweigh any negative impact.

Now, think of other fears you might have, such as public speaking, flying, talking to your boss about a promotion, your spouse glumly asking you, "Can we talk?" or whatever else comes to mind. Some fears will elicit different physical responses and different levels of intensity. Make note of how each fear manifests itself physically.

The goal with this exercise is to simply identify how your body reacts to fear. When you know what physical symptoms to watch out for, the presence of fear becomes far easier to identify. You will most likely discover that fear shows up at surprising times and places.

Day 22 Action Steps

We're miserable because we think that we are mere individuals, alone with our fears and flaws and resentment and mortality.

—ELIZABETH GILBERT
Author of *Eat, Pray, Love*[16]

You are not alone. The experience of fear is universal. But how you respond to fear is individual. When you face your fears and use the tools we have been teaching you, you develop courage and confidence, and thriving in sobriety will become your reality. Be sure to review the text above for additional details on these action steps.

- **Write down your past attempts to cut back or quit drinking.** Brainstorm, in writing, as many of your past attempts to change your drinking as you can recall. What did you do and what did you learn? How did you fail forward?

- **Write down your "drinking" fears, how you will overcome them, and how that will feel.** Write down each fear you have related to your drinking that you have yet to overcome. Then write down the benefits you have experienced by letting that fear run you. For instance, if you are afraid that you won't be able to deal with stress without drinking, the benefit you have by letting this fear run you is that you probably *do* give yourself permission to temporarily forget the stress in your life when drinking. Last, write down how you will overcome those fears now and how it will feel when you do that. Be sure to refer back to the text for the questions to ask yourself.

- **Say *yes*.** Think back to the times you have turned down offers, invitations, and opportunities related to your career, health, family, or friends. Were they related to drinking or automatic responses to avoid change? Consider new opportunities that come up and ask yourself, *What if I said yes to this?* Notice how that feels, and see if irrational fear is driving your decisions.

- **Recognize, acknowledge, and embrace the presence of fear.** Write down how your body reacts to fear, including fears specific to your drinking and other general fears. Remember, fear is your compass, so follow it. When you feel fear, acknowledge it, be thankful for it showing up, and then ask yourself, *What would I do if I wasn't afraid?* And do exactly that. To help neutralize fears, shift your focus every fifteen seconds between the physical sensations you are feeling and the feelings you want to feel instead (courage, confidence, peace).

On the companion website, you'll find a famous and entertaining video on the fear of failure. Be sure to visit it at http://Day22.Solutions.

The Emotional Sobriety Solution

Successfully Handling Your Emotions

Even though The 30-Day Sobriety Solution *is about quitting or cutting back on alcohol, so many of the techniques are easily applied to other areas of life. My life has changed in amazing ways after only seventy-five days of sobriety. I am sleeping better. I am eating better. I even go running, which is the first regular exercise I have done in over ten years. And one of the most significant changes has been in the emotional realm. My newfound awareness of my thoughts and feelings, and my ability to be more emotionally present with others, has changed my life.*

—THOMAS

30-Day Graduate from London, England

One of the keys to thriving in sobriety, and life, is learning to maximize your positive emotions and minimize the negative. When you started drinking, it was most likely to minimize your negative experiences, have more fun and laughter, feel the joy of connecting with others, and heighten the celebration of special occasions. But over time, your drinking most likely changed into a behavior for dealing with stress, anger, disappointment, and sadness. Over many years, drinking became your automatic response to any intense and uncomfortable emotion. Whether you were bored, coping with feelings of social awkwardness or unexpressed feelings in your relationship, or avoiding fears about money, your solution became alcohol.

But as you know, alcohol isn't a solution. It can numb out your feelings temporarily, but in the long run it only makes everything worse, until your solution has now become your problem.

Emotional Sobriety

If you want to improve your life, you have to learn how to consciously manage your emotions. This is called emotional intelligence,[1] or as psychologists and addiction specialists refer to it, "emotional sobriety."[2] Today's solution will teach you how to achieve emotional sobriety so that the stress of negative emotions will not lead you back to drinking.

According to psychologists like Tian Dayton, author of *Emotional Sobriety: From Relationship Trauma to Resilience and Balance*, emotional sobriety means being able to experience and regulate strong emotions rather than repress or run away from them. It means that you have the skills to live in the present rather than being caught in the past or being obsessed with the future. When you're emotionally sober, you can tolerate and express strong emotions, and you are able to create deep and intimate connections with other people. Your mind-set allows you to be resilient in the face of unexpected difficulties.

Many problem drinkers (96 percent, according to many experts) grew up in a dysfunctional family,[3,4,5] meaning that the odds are overwhelmingly high that you didn't learn the skills of emotional sobriety. Had your parents not also been "emotionally ignorant," you would have learned how to always bring yourself back into emotional balance when you were frightened or hurt. You would have learned how to soothe yourself. But because you didn't learn the tools for doing that, you turned to alcohol to calm yourself.

Today is about learning two more effective tools for dealing with your negative emotions so that you can achieve a greater state of emotional sobriety.

Emotion or Feeling?

Emotions that spontaneously occur all day long, such as those you experience when someone cuts you off in traffic, when you learn that the dog jumped up on the table and ate your dinner, or when someone puts you down in front of others at work. Emotions also seem to come up out of nowhere—like when you wake up in a bad mood or are suddenly overcome by a feeling you can't explain.

The truth is that we actually create most of our emotions that seem to occur spontaneously and seemingly out of our control, by how we think about people and events, by the meaning we ascribe to them, and by the stories we tell ourselves.

Simply put, *all events are meaningless until we assign some meaning to them.* What is just is, until we interpret it as good, bad, or neutral. For example, if you are sitting in a movie theater and a man steps on your foot while attempting to get into his seat, your immediate reaction might be one of irritation or anger. However, if you look up and see he is carrying a white cane and realize he is blind, you may feel understanding, compassion, or concern. The event was the same, but the thought that it was not intentional changes your experience. *Changing your thought changes your experience.*

The words *emotion* and *feeling* are usually used interchangeably, but psychologists make an important distinction between them. Emotions are instinctual responses to your outer environment that you feel as physical sensations. They are usually intense, brief, and accompanied by a physical reaction. For example, in the case of the blind man stepping on your foot, you might quickly feel irritation or anger as well as a physical contracting of muscles in your face, chest, stomach, and arms.

In other situations, you might feel a positive emotional reaction as a sense of expansion or a wave of relaxation in your body. Emotions such as joy, fear, and sadness occur all day long, mostly without your conscious control and often outside your awareness. So your emotions are the result of outside stimuli and they give you information that *something* is going on.

On the other hand, feelings are the result of your conscious reaction to an emotion. These are usually less intense, but last longer and are affected by your beliefs, attitude, and views on "right" and "wrong." For example, when a driver runs a red light and narrowly misses hitting your car, your initial *emotional* reaction might be one of fear or anger, but after a second, you might suddenly *feel* grateful that you were not hit. Or you might begin to wonder why the person was in such a hurry and think maybe they were rushing to the hospital. Your thoughts after you experience an emotion determine your longer-term feelings, for example, how you feel the rest of the day (in a bad mood because "everyone's driving is crazy" or in a state of constant anxiety because you dwell on the thought that you might die in an automobile accident). The quality of your feelings depends on the quality of your thoughts and beliefs after you experience a burst of emotion, whether you are consciously aware of them or not.

So why does this matter? Emotions, or more specifically your initial emotional reactions, are your natural, temporary, intense, and instinctual reactions to a situation. *However, how you respond to those initial emotions determines the quality of your happiness. And how you respond can be changed over time by the techniques you are learning in this program.*

In order to experience an emotionally balanced life, you first need to be aware of your emotions. Many people who struggle with alcohol have lost touch with their emotions, for fear of not being able to handle the consequences of feeling or expressing them. In your effort to escape feeling or expressing those emotions, you shut down. The first step in healing is to have the courage to feel emotions with the confidence that you *can* handle them.

Your Emotional Sobriety Filter

Consider your emotional reaction to the following scenarios: (1) You are hiking in the woods, and a bear comes crashing out from the trees ahead of you; (2) You are at a zoo, and you walk up to a glass wall, and suddenly a bear runs out from behind some trees in the enclosed cage and charges at you. You would probably feel an immediate automatic response of fear in both situations because a bear was running toward you; but your fear would be more intense in the woods than at the zoo, where your conscious mind would kick in and remind you that the glass wall will protect you from being attacked. This is just one more example that illustrates that you *can* change your emotional reaction to an event by expanding your awareness (*there* is *a glass wall*) and changing how you think about it (*this wall will protect me from the bear*). This is why the work of examining and changing your limiting beliefs that we explored in Day 11 is so important.

Now consider this with regard to your drinking. You walk into a bar (not a bear!) and see your favorite bartender making your favorite drink, or you hear that subtle pop as the cork is removed from a bottle of wine, or you feel a light spray envelop your face when a can of beer is opened. Today one of these situations might instantly create an intense desire to drink with a very real physical reaction before you are able to stop it—such as your mouth watering, a tingling anticipation in your stomach, or the automatic clasping of your hand as if you were picking up a cold bottle of beer. And that reaction could lead you to drink.

However, you can learn to consciously and intentionally override these *automatic* emotional and physical reactions. The key is learning how to skillfully manage the process that occurs as an emotion becomes a feeling. Your ability to do this will influence how happy or unhappy you'll be.

This brings us to the "Mental Makeover" process, which will help you trace a triggering emotion back to its source so you can resolve and release it. The "Mental Makeover" consists of four stages: awareness, acceptance, analyzing, and assigning.

Awareness

In order to work with an emotion, you have to first become aware that you are experiencing it, so you want to notice the physical sensation that accompanies it in your body. For instance, you might notice a tightness around your eyes, a clenching of your jaw, a tension in your neck and across the back of your shoulders, a slight pain in your stomach and lower back, a cramping in your buttocks, or tightening in your thighs.

For example, several years ago, when Dave was driving by a school, he noticed a school zone speed limit sign, which reminded him of the time his wife got a speeding ticket there. He then remembered that his wife had attended a party a year later where she met the same police officer who had given her the speeding ticket. He then remembered that the party had been hosted by a mutual friend we'll call Mary, who had once asked Dave for some very specific information, which he had then spent hours compiling and providing to her. Although it had been over a year since he had helped her out with the information, she had never acknowledged or thanked him for it, even though Dave had heard from his wife that she had received it. That whole train of thought took place in a matter of seconds, without Dave's conscious awareness of it, and it triggered an emotional response that resulted in a feeling of tension throughout his entire body. And here's the point of all of this—*in a matter of seconds Dave's mood had significantly changed for the worse.*

But because Dave was consciously practicing the stages of the

"Mental Makeover" at the time, he quickly noticed the sensation of his body tensing up. Without this "awareness" he could have never moved on to the second stage of the "Mental Makeover"—acceptance.

Acceptance

"Acceptance" is allowing yourself to fully accept and experience whatever emotion is happening. One of the ways you can get stuck is by trying to push away sensations and emotions that you don't want to feel (loneliness, sadness, hurt, pain, and fear). You may ignore them (distracting yourself by staying busy or having the radio on all the time), repress them by tightening up against the feeling (resulting in neck and lower back pain, a spastic colon, and other diseases), or cover them up with drugs and alcohol.

In order to heal yourself and feel alive again, you need to allow yourself to simply experience and accept the emotion, knowing that whatever you fully experience will subside as it passes on through. It is just energy in motion, e in motion, or e-motion. When you don't resist the emotion, it will resolve itself. Many teachers of meditation, which we will discuss in more depth tomorrow, would say that these first two stages alone are enough for healing and transformation to occur. However, we think there are two other stages that can be extremely useful.

Analyzing

Once you have allowed yourself to experience the emotion, you "Analyze" it. What stimulated the emotion in the first place? Where did it come from?

Sometimes figuring out what triggered your emotional reaction is easy; other times it can be extremely challenging, like trying to remember a dream. If you focus on it quickly enough, you might figure out the trigger, but sometimes it can take a little longer to emerge from your subconscious so that you can figure it out.

Let's look at Dave's story again. When he drove by that stop sign, he noticed his body tense, which led him to the awareness that something had just triggered a negative emotional reaction. By accepting this awareness instead of ignoring or fighting it, he was able to trace it back to its source. Because he was able to quickly analyze what happened, he could follow his train of associations back to the trigger: speed limit sign —> wife getting a speeding ticket —> party his wife went to that the police officer was at —> party was thrown by a friend —> that friend had asked for help, which Dave provided, and she had never thanked him.

This had bothered Dave for some time, so this memory could have been triggered in countless ways. Even though your first reaction might be *How will I ever be able to analyze it effectively enough to determine the source?* the reality is your brain will keep taking you back to your unresolved emotions in one way or another.

To help you think about what triggers your emotional reactions, here are some common emotional triggers that problem drinkers experience. Take a minute to review this list and note in your journal if any of these affect you.

- **Early sobriety triggers.** You are grumpy or short-tempered at certain times of the day or on specific days. This often relates to the time of day when you used to start drinking, or when you started to look forward to or started to plan your drinking. When you remove drinking as a coping mechanism, you will have an adjustment phase while you discover and implement new ways to cope.
- **People triggers and drinking triggers.** Certain people trigger negative reactions in you. Be careful not to immediately assume it is directly related to them. The way they look, the way they talk, their tone of voice, or even their body language may be the same as someone in the past who has hurt you in some way, which may trigger an unconscious emotional response. When

you are no longer drinking, you may now feel much more intensely anything that used to trigger your drinking, because you are not numbing out those feelings with alcohol.

- **Pet peeves.** These might include foot tappers, obnoxious laughers, overly disorganized or overly organized people, people talking too fast or too slow, constant interrupters, sloppy dressers, people sharing too much or too little, or people texting or talking on their cell phones while driving or on the bus or train.

Sometimes, no matter how hard you look, you won't be able to immediately analyze and determine what stimulated the emotion. That is okay. It will keep coming up in one form or another until you eventually recognize and deal with the emotion. As you work with this process, you will eventually figure out the source. That said, give yourself permission to experience the emotion rather than resist it.

Assigning

The last stage of the "Mental Makeover," "Assigning" is where the real magic can happen. You specifically assign a new meaning to the thought, belief, or rule that is creating the negative feeling you wish to release. By embracing the power of questions, you can actually change a feeling and replace it with one that leaves you feeling better—which some people refer to as a "better-feeling thought."

For example, imagine that you get in your car and head off to work tomorrow. There is a bit more traffic than usual and you start to get agitated. When another driver cuts you off, coming dangerously close to hitting you, you immediately yell and bang your hands on the steering wheel. However, this time instead of letting that emotion shift into an overall feeling of lasting frustration that sticks with you all morning, you change your frame of reference by asking yourself some questions.

You ask yourself, *How would I react if that was my grandmother driving the other car?* Or, *What would my reaction be if I knew that person had just found out their child was being rushed to the emergency room?* Or, *Are these opportunities I'm being given to develop and test my awareness, like some kind of freeway samurai training?* Suddenly you notice that your feelings shift. You realize that your initial anger quickly dissipates, and you feel back in control of your feelings.

What would happen if every time you are cut off in traffic you choose to think a better-feeling thought? With continued practice over time, your automatic emotional reaction will shift from one of instant anger to something more positive.

Inevitably, life is going to hand you situations that you don't have any control over—bad drivers, the weather, airline delays, power outages, computer crashes, the economy, and deaths of people you care about. You also don't have any control over coworkers who obsessively look at their phones, laugh obnoxiously, slurp their coffee, chew with their mouths open, or wear too much makeup. But you ultimately do have complete control over how you let these experiences make you feel—only you can decide that.

Consider Dave's example again, and his awareness of his unresolved resentment. Because Dave was able to identify the source of this trigger, he had a breakthrough. Dave started by asking himself this empowering question: *How am I responsible for the feeling I created?* He understood that if he did help create it, he could avoid creating it again in the future. As he explored this question, Dave realized this was a recurring theme in his life. Someone would ask for his help, and he would then provide far more than they even asked for and then expect them to be overly appreciative of his extra effort. When they were not, he would feel resentful.

As Dave asked himself how else this showed up in his life, he realized that at times he wanted to help someone so much that he would offer unsolicited feedback and advice. Some of these people then felt obligated to accept his offer, but because they hadn't asked for it in the first place, they wouldn't act on it or later express any appreciation for it, and Dave would feel unappreciated and resentful once again. However, after this one simple insight, Dave realized he had no right to resent Mary. He also forgave himself for wanting to feel needed and useful, and, most importantly, he decided he needed to change his standards, which we will talk more about in the next section.

As you analyze the source of your emotional reactions, you might discover that your negative emotional response is the result of your actions being incongruent with your core values. For example, you might notice that the morning after you drink you tend to wake up in a negative emotional state. You may just write this off as part of a hangover, but it is also likely that you intuitively realize your decision to drink heavily was out of alignment with your core values. If love and family are two of your core values, and you choose to go out and drink instead of spending time with your spouse and your kids, when you sober up in the morning it is normal to experience a negative emotional reaction. So when you explore the source of your negative emotions, always be sure to ask yourself if your actions are aligned or out of alignment with your core values.

Let's go over some questions that can help you in this stage, which are related to some of the examples we gave in the first stage, "Awareness."

- **Someone slurping coffee.** *What affirmation can I silently repeat and visualize when I hear this sound to create a positive association? Is it possible that I have some annoying bad habits that I might not notice? Does my coworker have a physical limitation that he or she is unable to change that causes this?*
- **Positive/successful/fit/rich/sober people.** *Am I jealous? How would my perception of them change if I stopped looking for their faults and focused on their positive qualities? If I appreciated their positive qualities, would that help attract more positive qualities into my life? Is it possible I am unfairly judging them based on past experiences with other people I have met?*

- **Negative/mean/unfriendly/overweight people.** *If I knew all the "bad stuff" that happened to them in their life, is it possible I would understand their perspective? What are they like with their family and friends? Is there something I am doing that keeps attracting this type of response from them? Do I feel this way simply because they are different from people I usually spend time with? Does something about them remind me of something I don't like about myself?*

- **Afraid/sad/angry/bitter about not drinking or missing a drinking event.** *What am I missing? What "price" will I pay if I did drink? How will drinking affect my dreams, my health, my family, and my finances? Is it time to try a new approach to life, knowing I can always go back to my old life if I choose to? How will I feel in the morning if I decide to drink? Do I know or have I read about someone who is thriving in sobriety? What can I learn from them?*

- **Drinking triggers.** *What does the smell of beer, wine, or liquor really mean to me? Does it mean that I am letting a poison control my life? That I am not free to make healthy decisions? Does it mean long-term failure? What does the look, feel, and sight of my favorite alcoholic beverage represent? Being unhealthy? Wasting money? That I'm ruining my relationships?*

These are just a few of the questions you can ask yourself. The key is to focus on questions that change the perception or the meaning of the event that triggers the negative emotion.

You also might notice another recurring theme emerging here—practicing forgiveness for yourself and for others. You can't change what happened in the past, but you can change the meaning you ascribe to the past. Many people tend to revisit past mistakes, regrets, and resentments. If you find that you keep getting drawn back to negative past events, go back and use the action steps on Day 4 in the Forgiveness Solution to finally let them go.

Change Your Standards of Success

Asking the right questions can often lead to a breakthrough, but examining "standards" or "rules" that you judge yourself by is also important to completing this "Mental Makeover." Your standards might include your physical (or intellectual) weight, how much alcohol you drink every week, your level of income, how hard you work, or how much time you devote to helping others.

Going back to Dave's story, when he realized that he was responsible for creating many of his own past resentments, he consciously created a new standard for helping others. Before, his standard included helping everybody, sometimes even including those who didn't ask for it. He was still committed to making a difference by helping others, but he decided that his new standard would be to help someone once they proved they really "wanted" his help. He decided to test their commitment by having them read a specific book or complete a detailed questionnaire. If they followed through in a timely manner, he would then gladly invest more time with them.

Dave was shocked by the overall impact this made in his life. He found that most people loved to ask for help, but when it required work and follow-through to get it, they no longer wanted it. Instead of initially spending hours with these people, he spent only minutes, and if they didn't follow through, he didn't feel any resentment. Dave now had plenty of time to help the people who did follow through, and he found that he was actually excited about working with them. It was clear these people were action-oriented, which he knew would lead to their success. Dave loved the rewarding feeling that came from helping someone create new success, and over time many of these people became trusted friends and colleagues.

When Dave explored the source of an unexpected mood change, he experienced a major shift from an underlying, long-standing feeling of disappointment and lack of appreciation into an experience of fulfillment and joy. This simple awareness led him to create a new standard, saved him countless hours of unhappiness, and removed a self-destructive behavior.

One more thing to be aware of is to not set your standards so high that they are impossible to live up to. For example, when some people decide to quit drinking, they also decide they are going to quit smoking, start working out five days a week, and completely change their diet. We entirely understand and appreciate this enthusiasm, but we also know that most people who set their standards of success too high end up having a major setback that leads back to drinking.

Having standards that motivate you to create more personal and professional success is great, but if you set too many standards at too high a level, you set yourself up for failure. Cutting back or quitting drinking sets a major new standard for your life, so initially focus all your efforts on that one change so that you succeed in it.

Ask yourself what unconscious rules or unrealistic standards of success you are holding to that you might need to change in order to eliminate some negative emotions and make yourself happier and make your goals easier to achieve. We are not saying to give up goal setting or to stop confronting and addressing any fears that might be blocking your success. We are saying that there are most likely standards that you are holding yourself to that you can never live up to, so you are in a constant state of letting yourself down.

Before reading any further, take time to write down in your journal any self-imposed or unconsciously adopted standards that might be holding you back right now, and then rewrite them so it is easier for yourself to "win," like in the examples below.

Old Standard. If I don't accomplish my goals as I have written them, I have failed.
New Standard. The only way I can fail is by not learning from the experience and no longer continuing to try.

Old Standard. Everything I do has to be perfect.
New Standard. I do everything well enough to meet the needs

of the task, leaving myself enough time to lead a balanced and healthy life with my friends and my family.

We know that this "Mental Makeover" process can initially seem a little intimidating, but you might be surprised at how easy and intuitive it really is once you try it. When you have the initial "Awareness" of an uncomfortable or negative feeling or mood, simply "Accept" it. Then, ask questions to "Analyze," and "Assign" new meanings to it. When necessary, change any unrealistic standards or rules you have related to it.

Now we want to teach you another incredibly powerful process that is a perfect complement to the one you just learned.

The Work

I discovered that when I believed my thoughts, I suffered, but that when I didn't believe them, I didn't suffer, and that this is true for every human being. Freedom is as simple as that. I found that suffering is optional. I found a joy within me that has never disappeared, not for a single moment. That joy is in everyone, always.

—BYRON KATIE

Author of *Loving What Is: Four Questions That Can Change Your Life*[6]

Let's look at one other simple and effective inquiry process that you can use to facilitate your emotional sobriety. This method, called The Work,[7] was developed by Byron Katie and helps you question the thoughts that create your emotional suffering.

This simple five-step process can help you live with less anxiety and fear; create deeper connection and intimacy with your partner, parents, and children; understand what makes you angry and resentful; become less reactive less often and with less intensity; and feel a new sense of ongoing vigor and well-being.

In its most basic form, The Work consists of four questions and three turnaround statements. You start by choosing a behavior or event that is triggering your negative feeling, usually something that you think *shouldn't be that way*. It might be that your spouse doesn't listen to you, your boss doesn't respect you, rush hour traffic is too congested, your parents should have loved you more, your brother shouldn't have made fun of you at the wedding, the people on Wall Street should act more responsibly, and so on.

Then ask yourself, *What is the underlying thought or belief I have about that person or situation?* The answer is the statement you will use for the exercise. For example, your statement could be as simple as "My mother should pay more attention to me." The next step is to take that statement and put it up against the four questions and turnarounds of The Work as follows.

The 4 Questions

1. Is it true? (Yes or no. If no, move to 3.) Can you absolutely know that what you are thinking is true? Be still and wait for your heart's response.

2. Can you absolutely know that it's true? (Yes or no.) Ultimately, can you really know what anyone else should or shouldn't do? Can you absolutely know what is in their best interest to do or not do? Or what they should think or not think?

3. How do you react (what happens) when you believe that thought? Do you experience anger, hurt, stress, or frustration? How do you treat the other person? Do you punish them in some way? Do you try to change them in any way? How do these reactions feel? How do you treat yourself? Does that thought bring stress or peace into your life? Be still as you listen.

4. Who would you be without that thought? Close your eyes. Picture yourself in the presence of this situation. Now imagine being there without the thought. What do you see? What would your life look like without that thought?

Then turn the thought around. Find at least three specific, genuine examples of how each turnaround is true for you in this situation. Here's our statement again: "My mother should pay more attention to me."

1. **Turn the thought around first to yourself.** (*I* should pay more attention to me.)
2. Next, **turn the thought around to the other.** (*I* should pay more attention to my mother.)
3. Third, **turn the thought around to the opposite.** (My mother *does* pay attention to me, or I *don't* need my mother to pay attention to me.)[8]

The turnaround sentences get you to focus your attention back on what you can change in yourself, which is the real source of your liberation—not trying to change the other person or the world, which is the source of your pain and suffering.

Let's take Dave's experience of being upset with Mary, who had not expressed appreciation for all the work he did to help her out.

Using the four questions, Dave will investigate his statement *Mary should have taken the time to personally appreciate me for helping her.*

1. Is it true? Is it true that she should have appreciated you? Be still, and wait for your heart to respond.

I'm not sure.

2. Can you absolutely know that it's true? Ultimately, can you really know what Mary should or shouldn't do? Can you absolutely know what is in her best interest to do or not do? Can you absolutely know for sure?

No. I can't know for sure what anyone should do. I don't know what else was going on in her life.

3. How do you react (what happens) when you believe that thought? What happens when you believe "Mary should have appreciated me," and she didn't? Do you experience anger, hurt, stress, or frustration? How do you treat Mary? Do you avoid her at a party? Do you try to change her in any way? How do these reactions feel? How do you treat yourself? Does that thought bring stress or peace into your life? Be still as you listen.

Angry, hurt, unappreciated. And cut off from connecting to Mary. Then I feel isolated and shut down.

4. Who would you be without that thought? Close your eyes. Picture yourself in the presence of Mary in this situation. Now imagine looking at Mary, just for a moment, without the thought *I want her to express her appreciation to me.* What do you see? What would your life look like without that thought?

I'd be relaxed, calm, and at peace. I wouldn't need anything from her. I would just be present with her. I could just experience the joy of me being myself without needing anything from her.

The Turnarounds. Find at least three specific, genuine examples of how each turnaround is true for you in this situation. For example:

1. To yourself. (I *don't appreciate* myself *enough.*)
2. To the other. (I *don't appreciate Mary.*)
3. To the opposite. (*Mary* does *appreciate my help,* or I don't *need Mary's appreciation.*)

Finally, stop and notice how you feel after you take yourself through this process.

———

Once you have learned the four questions and turnaround statement format, you can take yourself through it in your journal—and eventually just in your mind—whenever you are upset, or at night as a way to simply clear out any negativity that you may have built up over the course of the day. The Work will leave you in a state of natural peace and joy, where the desire for alcohol doesn't exist.

You can also learn how to use this process by watching a few short videos of Byron Katie actually guiding someone through the four questions and the turnarounds, which you'll find on today's companion website.

Day 23 Action Steps

Not only does the Emotional Sobriety Solution allow you to recognize and change the negative emotions you experience daily, it also teaches you emotional resilience. Just as regular workouts result in a quicker recovery from intense exercise, today's solution teaches you how to quickly recognize and break free from your negative emotional states.

- **Practice the "Mental Makeover" when you experience negative emotions.** You can do this process in your head, although we highly recommend that you do it in writing when you can. Make sure to record any breakthroughs or insights you have during the process in your journal. You can find a detailed example on the companion website. The steps below are a brief review:

  - **Awareness.** Notice when and where negative emotions show up, as well as some of the most common negative emotional triggers and track down the source of these emotions.
  - **Acceptance.** Allow yourself to experience the emotion—it is there for a reason, and fighting it will only guarantee that it will keep coming back.
  - **Analyzing.** Determine what triggered or stimulated the emotion in the first place by reviewing the list of common problem

drinker triggers, and make note in your journal of which ones are currently holding you back.

- **Assigning.** Ask questions in order to free yourself from being triggered again by this particular emotion. Write down in your journal any self-imposed or unconsciously adopted standards that might be holding you back, and rewrite them to allow yourself to succeed. Refer to examples in today's solution.

- **Practice The Work.** Pick a behavior or a situation that upsets you, and take yourself through the process of The Work described above. Write down your insights in your journal.

The companion website includes a detailed example of the "Mental Makeover" process, some links to several videos of Byron Katie demonstrating The Work, and an introduction to The Sedona Method—another simple and powerful technique to help you effectively let go of painful and unwanted feelings. Be sure to visit the companion website at: http://Day23.Solutions.

The Meditation Solution

Meditate to Release Stress and Develop Inner Peace

*Whatever our past, whatever our present, all of us have the ca-
pacity to change ourselves completely through the practice of
meditation.*

—EKNATH EASWARAN (1910–1999)
Meditation teacher and author[1]

Would you like to have a healthier heart, a stronger immune system, and be less susceptible to bouts of depression and anger? What
about reducing stress while increasing your productivity and creativity? Hundreds of studies have proven that these are just some of the
benefits you can expect from the practice of meditation.[2]

Meditation is not new. It has stood the test of time, dating back
over five thousand years.[3] By adding the practice of meditation to
your new life of thriving in sobriety, you dramatically improve every
aspect of your life. Whether you want better health, more financial
freedom, or just to be happier without feeling the desire to drink,
today will show you how to accomplish this.

The Benefits of Meditation

Have you ever felt winded after climbing a short flight of stairs? If
you have, it is probably the result of not exercising regularly. Have

you ever felt short-tempered, easily distracted, or just unhappy? Although it is human nature to occasionally experience these feelings, those who don't meditate regularly feel them more often. Meditation is to the mind what exercise is to the body.

The National Institutes of Health (NIH) reviewed 813 scientific studies of subjects who meditated for at least two weeks.[4] In his book *Transformation*, bestselling author Bill Phillips explains that the people in these studies "often experienced lower blood pressure, a healthier heart rate, strengthened immune systems and improved sleep (reduced insomnia). People also reported a reduction in muscle tension, backaches and pain, improved memory, and better cognitive performance."[5]

That alone is reason enough to practice meditation, but the benefits are even greater for problem drinkers. Meditation has been found to be an effective technique to prevent relapse in recovery from addictive behaviors, such as alcoholism.[6] Phillips recounts: "In longer-term scientific studies, a significant reduction in relapse rates among those in recovery from addictive habits has also been documented."[7]

The Myths of Meditation

Meditation suffers from a towering PR problem, largely because its most prominent proponents talk as if they have a perpetual pan flute accompaniment. If you can get past the cultural baggage, though, what you'll find is that meditation is simply exercise for your brain.

—DAN HARRIS

Author of *10% Happier: How I Tamed the Voice in My Head, Reduced Stress Without Losing My Edge, and Found Self-Help That Actually Works—A True Story*[8]

Meditation sometimes gets a bad rap. That it is only for new agers or hippies. That it is a spiritual or religious practice. That it is difficult, or takes years of dedicated practice to benefit from it. Or that it is only for saints and holy men. These are all meditation myths! If you don't believe us—just ask the United States Marines or the Super Bowl XLVIII champions.

The Seattle Seahawks used meditation in their training to help them become one of the best teams in football. Russell Okung, a sixth-overall NFL draft pick who signed a $48 million contract, said to ESPN, "Meditation is as important as lifting weights and being out here on the field for practice. It's about quieting your mind and getting into certain states where everything outside of you doesn't matter in that moment. There are so many things telling you that you can't do something, but you take those thoughts captive, take power over them, and change them."[9]

Psychologist Amishi Jha, director of the University of Miami's Contemplative Neuroscience, Mindfulness Research and Practice Initiative, teaches US Marines meditation to achieve mental resilience in a war zone. Jha says, "We found that getting as little as twelve minutes of meditation practice a day helped the Marines to keep their attention and working memory."[10]

What Is Meditation?

Meditation is a technique for quieting the mind and achieving a clear, relaxed, and peaceful state of consciousness. You are fully awake and alert, but not focused on your thoughts or feelings. Meditation is an opportunity to slow down—to create an inner state of connectedness and peacefulness that allows you to get in touch with your higher self and whatever gives your life purpose and meaning. The ideal state when meditating is one of focused awareness, where you are no longer distracted by your thoughts; however, if and when thoughts arise, you simply notice them, without judgment, and let them pass by as if they were a ship passing in the distant horizon.

In his TED Talk (a talk designed to spread powerful ideas, usually in eighteen minutes or less), "All It Takes Is 10 Mindful Minutes," Andy Puddicombe, who is considered a leader in the modern mindfulness movement, said, "Most people assume that meditation is all about stopping thoughts, getting rid of emotions, somehow controlling the mind, but actually it's much different than that. It's more about stepping back, seeing the thought clearly—witnessing it coming and going—without judgment, but with a relaxed, focused mind."[11]

Meditation, Mindfulness, and Bad Habits

Yesterday we looked at how negative emotions can unconsciously control how you feel and what you do. The first step in changing this is making the unconscious conscious, which starts with being conscious of the present moment, including your thoughts, feelings, and physical sensations. And one of the best ways to cultivate mindfulness is through meditation.

The practice of meditation develops your ability to observe your thoughts and feelings without judgment. With continued practice, you can bring this mindfulness into your daily life. As David Sheff writes in his book *Clean*, "Research has shown that mindfulness meditation, as one version of therapy is called, effectively interrupts cues. Addicts are taught to recognize and sit with their feelings—to experience them with curiosity and acceptance rather than react impulsively to them. This makes them better able to defuse their triggers."[12]

As we have discussed, problem drinkers love to fulfill their short-term desires. They tend to be more impulse driven and believe that drinking is an effective solution for dealing with stress, frustration, anger, fear, disappointment, and grief. They also often believe that they *need* to drink to experience pleasure and happiness. And most of these beliefs are unconsciously driven.

When you meditate, you can stop reacting to the constant mental chatter of your thoughts and beliefs, and simply observe and accept them instead. Problem drinkers often report that meditating is like being an impartial observer, seeing their true self for the first time and finally understanding the root cause(s) of their desire to drink. Meditation also allows you to observe and eventually silence the inner "voice" that might be constantly judging or critiquing you. Over time it allows you to experience inner peace and a true sense of freedom—feelings most problem drinkers once believed only came from drinking.

Cleaning Up Your Mental Clutter

Think about all the things that cause you stress—a looming deadline at work, a disturbing call from your doctor, having an argument, getting stuck in traffic, preparing for a presentation, losing a sale, an unexpected auto repair bill, or losing your cell phone. All of these can create stress, and in many ways the quality of your life is determined by the amount of stress you do or don't experience.[13]

Stress is the underlying cause of more than 60 percent of all human illness and disease.[14] In a *New York Times* article, Sandra Blakeslee writes, "Chronic stress sets into motion a cascade of biological events involving scores of chemicals in the body—serotonin, cortisol, cytokines, interleukins, tumor necrosis factor and so on. Such stress lowers resistance to disease and alters gene expression. When people are under stress, wounds tend to heal more slowly, latent viruses like herpes erupt and brain cells involved in memory formation die off. The precise molecular steps underlying all of these changes have been mapped out."[15]

When you experience stress your body releases cortisol, which is often referred to as the "stress hormone."[16] In *The Biology of Belief,* Bruce Lipton notes that this hormone is given to patients who are receiving organ transplants. Why? Because cortisol is so effective at weakening the body's immune system that it cannot fight the newly transplanted organ as effectively.[17]

Stress also causes "cortical inhibition,"[18] which means the smart part of your brain can't function as well, often resulting in poor decision making, lack of focus, and even the inability to make decisions. Simply put, stress makes you dumber.

Enoch Gordis, MD, the former director of the National Institute on Alcohol Abuse and Alcoholism, writes, "Drinking alcohol produces physiological stress, that is, some of the body's responses to alcohol are similar to its responses to other stressors. Yet, individuals also drink to relieve stress. Why people should engage in an activity that produces effects similar to those they are trying to relieve is a paradox that we do not yet understand."[19] So not only does problem drinking often lead to negative consequences, and therefore stress, but also the actual consumption of alcohol creates physiological stress.

Another reason problem drinkers frequently experience more stress than others is because excessive drinking often creates added strain on finances, career, health, and family. In addition, when problem drinkers are finally able to quit or cut back drinking, they lose their primary coping mechanism for stress—alcohol. So the ultimate irony for a problem drinker is that drinking often leads to increased stress, but in the beginning *not* drinking can also cause stress and increase the odds of relapse.

No other technique in this program is more effective or more proven to relieve stress than meditation. When your mind is "cluttered" with stressful thoughts and feelings, fear and anxiety, shame and guilt, you become physically and mentally impaired. Meditation can help you overcome this. Just as cleaning your home or office can help you feel less stress, meditation helps you to "declutter" your mind—eventually freeing you from negative patterns of thinking and emotions and unconscious self-defeating behaviors. However, the benefits of meditation for problem drinkers don't stop there—meditation provides another ssignificant benefit.

Meditating Your Way to Happiness

On Day 7, we first introduced you to the importance of serotonin and dopamine. Serotonin helps regulate your mood, prevents depression, and makes you feel happy. Dopamine also affects your mood and your, ability to focus and feel pleasure.[20] Alcohol naturally stimulates the release of these neurotransmitters, which is one of the reasons it is addictive, and when you stop drinking it takes time before your brain will start producing these again at normal levels. Besides the food and supplements we recommended that naturally stimulate the brain's production of serotonin and dopamine, meditation also increases the production of serotonin and dopamine.[21]

Breathing Away Cravings and Anxiety

The single most effective relaxation technique
I know is conscious regulation of breath.

—ANDREW WEIL, MD

Author of *8 Weeks to Optimum Health: A Proven Program for*
Taking Full Advantage of Your Body's Natural Healing Power[22]

Take ten seconds now to notice your breathing—do not try to change it. Now take thirty seconds and breathe deeply—intentionally breathing in slowly, feeling the air fill and extend your stomach, holding it in for a few seconds, then slowly exhaling completely. What changes did you notice? Most likely you experienced a physical response, such as your shoulders dropping or your heart rate slowing, as well as an emotional response, such as feeling calmer or more centered.

Proper breathing is critical to effective meditation and to your health and wellness, yet it is one of the most overlooked practices taught to achieve optimum health. Breathing serves two primary purposes. It supplies your body with oxygen and rids your body of waste and toxins. When you practice breathing exercises, not only do you more effectively oxygenate your body and free it from toxins, you also reduce stress, calm your mood, and feel more energized.

There are many different breathing exercises you can learn, but we especially like the 4-7-8 Relaxing Breath Exercise taught by Dr. Andrew Weil. It consists of five simple steps you can do anywhere and anytime. Place the tip of your tongue against the ridge of tissue just behind your upper front teeth, and keep it there throughout the entire exercise. You're going to be exhaling through your mouth and inhaling through your nose.

1. Exhale completely through your mouth, making a "whoosh" sound.
2. Close your mouth and inhale quietly through your nose to a mental count of four.

3. Hold your breath for a count of seven.
4. Exhale completely through your mouth, making a "whoosh" sound while mentally counting to eight.
5. This counts as one breath. Now repeat steps 2 through 4 three more times—for a total of four breaths.

You can watch a video of Dr. Weil demonstrating this technique at www.drweil.com. (Once you get there, type "The 4-7-8 Breath" into the search window.) Dr. Weil says, "You *must* do this at least two times a day," but he also says that you can do it as many times as you wish. However, in the first month, you should not do more than four consecutive breaths each time. Dr. Weil says it is a very useful tool to fight any craving and "the most powerful antianxiety measure" he has ever found.[23] Your **first action step** today is to practice this method and then continue to do it at least twice a day. The best time to do it is right before you meditate.

How to Practice Meditation

The ultimate reason for meditating is to transform ourselves in order to be better able to transform the world. To put it another way, we transform ourselves so that we can become better human beings and serve others in a wiser and more effective way. Meditation thus gives our life the noblest possible meaning.

—MATTHIEU RICARD

Author of *Why Meditate: Working with Thoughts and Emotions*[24]

Meditation is often described as "simple but not easy." It is simple because the steps are not complex. But it can take practice to actually silence your mind and effectively let go of all the nonstop chatter and thoughts that barrage your mind.

There are many effective ways to practice meditation. We have outlined the key steps to meditating common to most practices, but we encourage you to explore other techniques after completing this program. The **second action step** for today is to listen to the guided meditation on the companion website that leads you through the steps below.

- **Start with ten minutes, but build a habit.** When you are not using the guided meditation, we recommend starting with ten minutes of meditation a day. Studies say this is the best way to get the most value. However, you can leverage the power of creating "tiny habits," as we covered on Day 9 in the Action Solution, and begin with as little as two minutes and build from there.

- **Pick a comfortable, quiet place.** Ideally, find a time and location free from noise and potential interruptions. Pay attention to your posture. In his book *Wherever You Go, There You Are*, Jon Kabat-Zinn captures this best by saying, "Sit in a way that embodies dignity."[25]

- **Deep breathing.** Focusing on your breathing, let go of everything else. Breathe in through your nose, down to your stomach, and back out through your mouth. Find a relaxing rhythm, such as breathing in for four seconds, holding for two, and breathing out for six. Or use the 4-7-8 method described above. Do either one of these for four repetitions. You do not need to focus on your breathing throughout the meditation, but bringing your focus back to breathing helps to silence your mind. You can keep your eyes open, gazing at a space on the floor in front of you with a soft focus, or you can close your eyes, as most people generally prefer to do.

- **Release all tension.** Imagine a ball of soft golden light, roughly the size of a tennis ball, radiating healing energy. Scan your body for any areas that might be holding tension and imagine this ball moving to those areas. Picture the healing energy from the ball dissolving the tension, and as you breathe out, the tension is released from your body.

- **Meditate.** The ideal state is to ultimately silence all of your internal thoughts and dialogue. Here are two effective techniques.

One is to simply focus on your breathing and direct your attention to the sensation of air passing through the tip of your nose as you inhale and exhale or the expansion and contraction of your belly. When you notice any thoughts coming up, just accept them and let them go, and come back to concentrating on the sensation of your breathing. Another technique is to use a mantra. One that we like is to repeat "I Am" over and over again. Say "I" as you slowly breathe in, and "Am" as you slowly breathe out. If and when thoughts come up, you can picture the thought in a bubble and just let it float away, without judgment or contemplation. With either technique, when a thought comes up (and in the beginning you'll have lots of them) and you find yourself caught up in the thought, once again just let it go and return your attention back to your breath or the mantra.

As you meditate, the best approach is one of overall acceptance—accept your breath, accept your active mind, accept your rhythm, accept all parts of yourself, accept any thoughts and feelings, and accept the flow of the meditation. Don't get discouraged or beat yourself up if you find it challenging to silence your mind—even people who have practiced meditation for years still experience this challenge. This is why meditation is called a practice. Even if you feel like you are struggling, you are still benefiting from the practice.

Another way to help focus your attention is to count while breathing. Start with "one" on your first exhale, and then count "two" silently to yourself on the next exhale, and then "three" on the next exhale, all the way to "ten." When you reach ten, just start over again at one. It is perfectly normal to become distracted by a thought and lose count. Just accept it and gently bring your attention back to the breath, and start again at one.

You can vary your practice—by adding music, meditating in nature, and using different mantras and breathing techniques. We have provided a list of some of our favorite meditation music on the companion website.

Powerful Meditation Variations

At the root of addiction is a natural impulse to satisfy our human needs for security, comfort, self-esteem, sensory gratification, and power. But at a deeper level, we know that that our addictions cannot fill the emptiness inside ourselves and will not lead to lasting peace and inner satisfaction. Identifying the void you have been trying to fill and replacing life-damaging beliefs and behaviors with those that are life-supporting—including meditation and other practices for higher consciousness—will serve you immeasurably on your journey to healing and transformation.

—DAVID SIMON

Coauthor of *Freedom from Addiction: The Chopra Center Method for Overcoming Destructive Habits*[26]

Once you begin to see the power of meditation in your life, you may want to expand on the techniques we've given. Here are three variations using other solutions you've learned that can complement your meditation practice. When you have time, we recommend that you integrate these into your daily routine.

- **The 4-Minute-Mile Solution.** After you have released the tension in your body with the golden ball of light and completed your deep breathing exercise, but before you drop into meditation, is also a great time to practice your visualizations from Day 15 in the 4-Minute-Mile Solution. Meditation quiets the mind and powerfully connects you to the universal source, from which all things manifest. Attach positive emotions and feelings to your detailed images in order to make them more powerful. You can also visualize at the end of your meditation, when your relaxed state will deepen the impact of your visualizations.
- **The Quality Question Solution.** When you meditate you are essentially tapping into a deeper and higher part of your own subconscious mind and into a higher energy outside of yourself,

which can be referred to as Source, God, Higher Power, Universal Intelligence, or the Quantum Field. Whatever you choose to call it is unimportant. However, meditating is incredibly powerful in revealing answers to your questions that align with your life purpose. Diana Robinson says, "Prayer is when you talk to God; meditation is when you listen to God."[27] The practice of meditation allows you to accept and quiet all the incessant thoughts and chatter in your mind so you can actually "listen" to the answer. We often find that when we come out of a meditation, we are reconnected with what is really important to us. This enables us to let go of the worries, regrets, fears, and resentments that were holding us back.

After you have released the tension from your body, simply ask the question you want answered, being sure to use the format you learned on Day 16 in the Quality Question Solution. Then let it go and begin meditating. During, or after your meditation, you might find you have connected with the answer, or it might come to you in future meditations.

When Jack was searching for a title to his collection of inspirational stories, he asked for a title in meditation. Eventually he saw a picture of a hand come out and write the words *Chicken Soup* on a green chalkboard. Within minutes, it evolved into *Chicken Soup for the Soul*, which became a bestselling book and book series and evolved into a multimillion-dollar brand recognized around the world.

- **The Gratitude Solution.** A perfect time to practice gratitude is when you are coming out of your meditation, when you have heightened clarity about what is truly important. So take a minute and silently give thanks for some of the things you are most grateful for.

A guided meditation for each of these variations is on the companion website.

Day 24 Action Steps

I can't tell you how much I'm enjoying being back in school, having the chance to work on my writing, including my second novel, with some big-name authors; it's life changing. Also, I am still happily sober. I go to the gym regularly, I moved in with my girlfriend, and I meditate every day—all things I never would've imagined myself doing before.

—THOMAS
30-Day Graduate from London, England

The practice of meditation is truly transformational. It will help you become happier, healthier, more relaxed, and more creative.

- **Practice breathing.** Inhale through your nose to a count of four, hold your breath to a count of seven, and exhale to a count of eight out your mouth. Repeat four times. Complete this two or more times a day.

- **Listen to the guided meditation and start meditating ten minutes or more a day.** Use the following guidelines; however, feel free to add meditation music. We list some good options on the companion website. You can also use different mantras or experiment with different meditation practices.

  - **Location.** Find a comfortable and quiet location and sit upright "in a way that embodies dignity."
  - **Breathing.** Focus on deep breathing, in through your nose, down to your stomach, and back out through your mouth. Your eyes can be open, gazing at a space on the floor in front of you, or as most people prefer, closed.
  - **Tension.** Imagine a ball of soft golden light radiating healing energy and move it toward any areas of tension in your body. As you exhale, picture the ball dissolving the tension.
  - **Meditate.** Silence your thoughts and internal dialogue. You

can repeat a mantra, like "I Am," as you breathe in and out, or focus on the sensation of your breathing. If you find it challenging to silence the thoughts that come up, simply notice them without judgment and gently repeat your mantra or focus on your breathing.

- **Integrate the meditation variations.** Over the next few weeks, practice each one of these variations, either on your own or using the guided meditations on the companion website.

  - **The 4-Minute-Mile Solution.** Right before or after you meditate, practice your visualizations. As best you can, be sure to experience the feelings of achieving your goal.
  - **The Quality Question Solution.** Release your tension with the golden ball of light, ask a question that you want answered, and then meditate, allowing for the answer to emerge.
  - **The Gratitude Solution.** Finish your meditation by focusing on five or more things you are grateful for, remembering to really work at *feeling* the gratitude, not just thinking about it.

All the guided meditations are on the companion website, as is information on the topic of drinking and stress, and some additional resources and techniques on breathing. Be sure to visit the companion website at http://Day24.Solutions.

The Mind and Body Solution

Thriving in Your Mind and Body Through Nutrition

> *When health is absent, wisdom cannot reveal itself, art cannot become manifest, strength cannot be exerted, wealth is useless, and reason is powerless.*
>
> —HEROPHILUS (335–280 BC)
> Greek physician

Imagine yourself one year from today. You are thriving in sobriety. You are in love, have great relationships with friends and family, and work with passion. You have discovered your life purpose and are living it every day. You have found balance in your life, and have time for work, friends, family, and hobbies. You are financially free, and maybe you are even regularly volunteering at a local nonprofit organization. You have found a deep sense of peace and spirituality in life, fueled by personal-growth work you love doing.

This probably sounds fantastic, if you make one assumption—you are physically healthy. Your quality of life starts with your body, and to thrive in sobriety, you want to be physically healthy. The Mind and Body Solution will start you down the path to thriving physically, so you can have the health, energy, and vitality you need to create success throughout your life.

The Mind-Body Connection

Seventy percent of all patients who come to physicians could cure themselves if they got rid of their fears and worries.

—O. F. GOBER, MD

Chief physician of the Gulf, Colorado and Santa Fe
Hospital Association in the 1940s

Each of the last three days touched on a common theme for Week 4—your body. Your strong emotions—fear, sadness, excitement, and joy—elicit a physical response. When you meditate, you balance your body's systems, bringing your breath, posture, heart rate, and brain into a relaxed and aligned state. Today we continue with this theme.

Your mind, your thoughts and beliefs, directly affect your body by influencing what, when, and how much you choose to eat. The reverse is also true. The food you put in your body affects what you think and believe and how you feel. The Mind and Body Solution is about what to feed your body for lasting recovery, energy, and health, and it is about the importance of the mind-body connection and how to successfully approach changing your diet.

Plato wrote, "The greatest mistake physicians make is that they attempt to cure the body without attempting to cure the mind; yet the mind and the body are one and should not be treated separately!"[1] Even though many of the solutions up until this week have focused on your mind, much of what you have done also applies directly to successfully changing your body.

Graduates of *The 30-Day Sobriety Solution* often say that changing their diet was easy compared with cutting back or quitting drinking. In part, because the work they did in this program, such as visualizing themselves thriving in sobriety, healthy and fit, helped them eat and exercise better. And once they learned how to recognize and change their limiting beliefs related to drinking, it was much easier to recognize other limiting beliefs that were holding them back from thriving physically.

Most problem drinkers also find that their poor eating habits, such as eating late at night, eating greasy and unhealthy food, or consuming too many calories, are directly related to their drinking. Once you remove alcohol, eating healthy becomes much easier, and you instantly eliminate a huge source of empty calories. You feel emotionally healthy, happier, and more stable than when you were drinking. So now, even when you have a bad day, or just get down, you know how to cope and change that state, whereas in the past you might have dealt with stress, fear, worry, anxiety, or self-esteem issues by drinking beer, wine, or cocktails, and eating pizza, candy bars, or nachos.

New Standards for Your New Body

One of the most exciting things we get to see, literally, are the physical changes our clients go through when they get sober. Sometimes these changes are obvious, such as weight loss, less puffiness in the face, a healthy skin color and glow, and clearer, more alive eyes. Many of these changes happen even if your eating is still somewhat unhealthy while you are getting sober. However, in the long run, it is critical that you embrace an overall healthy diet to thrive physically.

As we mentioned on Day 1 in the 100% Solution, there is a reason why we have waited to include this topic, which is that if you try to accomplish too many big goals at once, you may fail at all of them. Remember, not only do you have a dependency on alcohol, you also have a dependency on sugar because alcohol is essentially fermented sugar. So, for most people, quitting drinking while also changing your diet and dramatically cutting back on sugar is a recipe for failure. You may find by today that your cravings have already reduced dramatically, but some changes in your diet may curb your alcohol cravings further.

Nutrition and exercise are crucial in recovery. We have attended plenty of Alcoholics Anonymous meetings where we were overwhelmed by cigarette smoke, donuts, junk food, coffee, and empty sugar packets spread around the room. Too many attendees were overweight and unhappy. This is not what we consider thriving in sobriety. Not all AA meetings are like this, but these types of meetings remind us of the importance of not trading your dependency on alcohol for one on cigarettes, sweets, or overeating.

When your mind and body are healthy, there is no limit to what you can achieve. The first step toward this is to establish a new rule, or standard, for nutrition and exercise. Any progress, no matter how small, in your diet and exercise is positive—even if you just read a good article on nutrition, do one push-up, or eat one less serving at dinner.

We want you to be flexible when you make any nutritional changes or take on any intense new workout regimens. If a strict all-or-nothing approach has worked for you in the past, go ahead and try it; however, not until *after* you have finished the program. And better yet, after at least three months of sobriety.

The challenge of starting a strict diet now is that, if you slip, it can lead to feelings of guilt, frustration, and failure. Your self-esteem may take a hit because anytime you make an agreement with yourself and break it, you tend to feel worse about yourself. So approach today's solution as a learning opportunity—one where you can embrace small changes in your diet. As you continue to practice and apply these solutions, thriving physically will come naturally.

Reclaiming Your Body from Alcohol

Freeing your body and mind from being a "prisoner" of alcohol can be one of the most rewarding experiences of your life. Dave always dreamed of getting fit and healthy, but couldn't do it while drinking. Here is his journey to thriving physically:

In 2004 I was drinking almost nightly. I rarely exercised and I certainly didn't pay attention to what I was eating. I weighed an all-time high of 252 pounds. My drinking, weight, and lack of exercise were having a profoundly negative impact on my overall health.

I had two visits to the emergency room, one for alcohol poisoning and one for a heart attack scare. My doctor discovered that I had an enlarged heart. Another doctor was concerned because my liver appeared enlarged and I might need a biopsy. I had incredibly high counts in my blood work, including cholesterol, triglycerides, and the tests related to my liver. I also was frequently sick and even experienced strange, unidentifiable discomfort and pain in various areas of my body at random times.

Finally, in 2007, I got sober, and even though I still wasn't thriving in sobriety, I had managed to put together ten consecutive sober months for the first time in my adult life. As I contemplated my life in sobriety and my friend Bryan taking his life, I knew things had to change. Fortunately, my recent blood work revealed improvements in every area, but a recent photo of me and my daughter told me otherwise. I felt lousy—overweight, unhappy, and unhealthy.

Over the next year, I became dedicated to my health, and it ended up being a year that changed my life—especially my body and mind. I did programs like P90X, Bill Phillips's *Body for Life* and *Transformation,* and I incorporated ideas from one of my favorite health/fitness/nutrition books by trainer-bodybuilder Tom Venuto called *The Body Fat Solution: Five Principles for Burning Fat, Building Lean Muscles, Ending Emotional Eating, and Maintaining Your Perfect Weight.* I also read at least forty books on fitness, nutrition, strength training, and running.

Roughly one year after I looked at that photo, I ran seventy-five miles in a weekend, completing two marathons, a half marathon, and a nine-mile run. This was a way of challenging myself and celebrating the transformation I was able to make. My weight reached an all-time low of 169 pounds (83 pounds less than my heaviest weight), and I was stronger than I had ever been in my life. Since I regularly get requests to see some before and after photos, we have included some on the companion website.

Most exciting, and ironic, was that these improvements weren't that hard. But when I was drinking, they seemed impossible—I had started countless diets and workout programs over a ten-year span, but all of them ended with very little results because the drinking was always there. Going from drinking almost every night to being sober, and practicing the solutions we teach in this program, not only freed up an abundance of time and hangover-free energy but also led to a thriving-in-sobriety mind-set. As a result, adding in exercise and sticking to a healthy diet were easy.

You, too, will find that starting new healthy habits comes much more easily now, because you are not the same person who started this program.

The Real "Cost" of Alcohol and Your Health

Which intoxicating substance is associated with the most lethal violence? The correct answer, by far, is alcohol. It's involved in more homicides than pretty much every other substance combined. Alcohol's relative importance has grown over the last fifteen years, as aging populations of cocaine users account for a declining proportion of violent crime.

—HAROLD POLLACK

University of Chicago professor and frequent
contributor to the *Washington Post* blogs[2]

One of the most common fears we hear from our clients is that their drinking has caused irreversible health issues. Although these fears are justified, remember that your body has amazing restorative capabilities. And when you start integrating healthy nutrition and exercise into your life, you can completely change your body's overall health and reverse decades of drinking abuse.

As common as it is to have concerns about your health because of your drinking, it is also common to rationalize away the various issues with your health and say that they are unrelated to your drinking. But let's be absolutely clear here—alcohol is a poison. And when you continuously put poison in your body, every system in your body can be negatively affected. Where in your body these issues show up will vary depending on your hereditary and environmental conditions, as well as your age, diet, and exercise habits. Health issues that you quickly disregard as unrelated to your drinking might not be as unrelated as you think.

Problem drinkers tend to live in denial, and even when they accept that they have to cut back or quit their drinking, they don't always fully acknowledge the potential consequences of continued drinking. Here are the health problems that heavy drinking, and in some cases even moderate drinking, can cause:

- Liver disease[3] and/or cirrhosis of the liver[4]
- Brain damage[5] or dementia[6]
- High blood pressure[7] and irregular heartbeat[8]
- Stomach ulcers, esophageal ulcers, and gastritis[9]
- Cancer of the breast, head and neck, colon, and liver[10]
- Slower healing/recovery from illness or injury[11]
- Damage to retrospective memory (learning, retention, and retrieval)[12]
- Higher risk of more than two hundred diseases, including tuberculosis and pneumonia[13]

Not only does heavy drinking directly affect the health of your body, it can also lead to other very serious consequences. Alcohol is a factor in:

- 40 to 50 percent of traffic fatalities
- 40 percent of suicides and fatal falls
- 50 percent of sexual assaults and trauma injuries
- 60 percent of all fatal fires, drownings, and homicides
- 48 percent of hypothermia and frostbite cases[14]

The negative consequences of drinking on the female body can be even more severe. One study showed that women who had two to four drinks a day increased their breast cancer risk by 41 percent; another study showed that women who drank three or more drinks a day on average had a 69 percent higher risk of getting breast cancer. Women are also at a 40 percent higher risk than men of developing high blood pressure from excessive drinking.[15]

Last, and to us the most shocking, is a recent report from the World Health Organization that disclosed that *every ten seconds* someone dies from problems related to alcohol use.[16] Although we don't want you to dwell on the potential negative health consequences from excessive drinking, it is crucial that you are not in denial about what drinking alcohol can "cost" you.

Remember, it doesn't have to be this way, just as one 30-Day Graduate shared:

> *The 30-Day Sobriety Solution* has given me back time. I no longer have a daily time constraint at night to start drinking. My goals are no longer determined by the massive amount of time my drinking took from me. The overall freedom I experience today is incredible. Every morning I look in the mirror and see a clear-eyed and healthy reflection and I get to live a happy and fulfilling life that is free from the constant worries and fears that my drinking might tragically take my life and leave my children without a mother.

Your Body's Incredible Restorative Powers

The best way to detoxify is to stop putting toxic things into the body and depend upon its own mechanisms.

—ANDREW WEIL, MD

Your body has a remarkable ability to heal itself. When you stop drinking and start eating right, your body can begin healing and reverse years or even decades of abuse.[17]

For example, in a common living-donor transplant, a donor gives roughly 50 percent of his liver to a recipient. Not only is this enough to cure the recipient, but the donor's liver grows back to its original size in six to eight weeks.[18,19] Your whole body is constantly regenerating, eliminating old cell matter and processing vitamins, minerals, and protein to create new cell matter:

- Every 120 days—new red blood cells
- Every 90 days—new skeleton
- Every 60 days—new brain cells, tissue
- Every 49 days—new bladder
- Every 45 days—new liver and new DNA cell material
- Every 30 days—new hair and new skin
- Every 5 days—new stomach lining[20]

Roughly six billion cells are turned over every day by your body.[21] Once you remove alcohol from your body, this regenerative process really starts to benefit you. As you provide your body with the proper nutrition, the healing is even more rapid.

It Was Just One Pound . . .

Primary food is more than what is on your plate. Healthy relationships, regular physical activity, a fulfilling career and a spiritual practice can fill your soul and satisfy your hunger for life.

When primary food is balanced and satiating, your life feeds you, making what you eat secondary.

—JOSHUA ROSENTHAL

Founder and president of the Institute for Integrative Nutrition[22]

Our goal for today is to provide you with some basic nutritional advice from several nutritional experts we consulted to make sure the information we are providing is accurate and appropriate for the problem drinker.[23] As a reminder, on Day 7 we addressed some of the specific nutritional issues excessive drinking can lead to, such as serotonin and dopamine deficiencies and sugar addiction. We are not going to repeat most of that information today, so we recommend you take a few minutes to review it.

Not only is the topic of nutrition complex, in recent years it also has become much more specific to each individual. What might work great for one person might not for another, in part because of food sensitivities, intolerances, and allergies.[24] Therefore, on the companion website we have included some of our favorite books, experts, and resources regarding diet and nutrition; but we recommend you explore these in greater depth only after you complete *The 30-Day Sobriety Solution*.

The effects of a healthy diet that is right for your body can be life changing. You will lose weight, have more energy, experience less stress, feel happier, get sick less frequently, and your cravings for foods high in fat, salt, and sugar will diminish greatly. And if you combine this with a healthy exercise routine, you will get stronger faster.

We have used the word *diet* a lot today, so we want to be clear. Diet essentially just means the food you put in your body, not a weight-loss regimen. So when we say *diet*, we mean what you choose to eat and drink as part of your normal routine or lifestyle. The best diet is one you can sustain for the rest of your life.

Weight is usually gained and lost slowly. If you are overweight, most likely it came from putting on one pound a month. Gaining one pound a month reflects a surplus of roughly 100 calories a day, so if you give up a few candy bars, sugary sodas, or bags of chips each week, you could lose one pound a month or twelve pounds in a year. Just as we have said in the other solutions, a *long-term strategy* for your nutrition is far more effective than a *short-term* extreme diet.

Key Nutrients for a Healthy Body

To eat healthy, you should try to get the right balance of water, protein, carbohydrates, essential fats, vitamins, minerals, and phytonutrients into your diet.[25] On the companion website we provide more information about each of these, but there is one that is so critical, and so relevant to you as a problem drinker, it is essential we address it first—*water*.

Water is an essential nutrient, and the basis for all life, including your body. Your muscles are 75 percent water, your blood is 82 percent water, your lungs are 90 percent water, your bones are 25 percent water, and your brain is 76 percent water.[26]

Most of us go through life dehydrated. In *Your Body's Many Cries for Water,* Dr. F. Batmanghelidj writes, "We have forgotten how to respond to our numerous thirst signals. But if, instead of taking painkillers and medication, we just drank lots of ordinary tap water, we would probably find that not only the pain but also the condition would go away forever."[27]

This is even more relevant to heavy drinkers than to other people, because drinkers often live in a dehydrated state. Don't wait to drink water until you are thirsty or you are already dehydrated. The general rule of thumb is to drink one ounce of water for every two pounds of body weight every day (one-third liter of water for every 10 kilograms). So, if you weigh 200 pounds, you should drink one hundred ounces of water each day. That's roughly twelve 8-ounce glasses of water a day (or if you weigh 90 kilograms that would be just under three liters of water a day). If you're 140 pounds, that's roughly nine 8-ounce glasses of water every day. Also, you need to add another six to eight ounces of water for every fifteen minutes you work out. And please note that caffeinated drinks, sodas, and alcoholic beverages do not count as water.

For most people it takes some time to get used to drinking this much water, but we find one effective method is to start the day with two large glasses of water, especially since your body becomes dehydrated throughout the night. Another rule of thumb that's even easier to follow is always drink eight ounces of water for every two waking hours. Even if you weigh over 150 pounds, this will end up being a little below what is recommended, but it is very likely a significant improvement to what you are doing now.

Your **first action step** for today—assuming you don't drink this much water already—is to start doing so right now. One expert we consulted with also recommends that you drink alkaline water, which can be purchased at various health food stores, or start your day by drinking a warm cup of water with freshly squeezed lemon juice—both of which can help you flush out accumulated toxins.

Hardwired for Fats, Sugars, and Salts

Just as it is important to know what nutrients your body needs to be healthy, it is equally important to know what foods you should avoid. In general these include processed foods containing fat, sugar, and salt. It can be challenging at first to limit these, because not only does consuming them trigger a release of opioids and dopamine (two chemicals in the brain that produce pleasure), humans are also genetically wired to prefer calorie-dense foods. And the most calorie-dense food you can find is fat, which has significantly more calories per gram than any other food.[28] In addition, many food manufacturers produce and market foods high in sugar, fat, and salt (in part because they know how addictive they are), which has helped result in the World Health Organization estimating that more than 1.4 billion people in the world are overweight.[29]

However, not all fat, sugar, and salt are bad. You need salt and essential fats, but not at the level that most industrialized countries consume. If you can eliminate other forms of sugar from your diet, such as candy, sweets, refined sugar found in white pasta, and anything with high-fructose corn syrup, you will dramatically curb other food cravings and also curb alcohol cravings. As we recommended in Day 7, you can get your sugar "fix" instead from eating fruit or drinking fruit smoothies.

Strategies for Healthy Eating

Within two months of starting The 30-Day Sobriety Solution, *I was closer to my family, performing better at work, coping with stress much more easily, had lost thirty pounds, was training for a marathon, and my social life actually improved.*

—ROBERT
30-Day Graduate from Vienna, Austria

There are several strategies that have worked well for us and our clients and allow you to still be healthy while occasionally enjoying some "bad" food. For example, Bill Phillips's bestselling programs recommend you eat healthy six days a week, and eat whatever you want one day a week. This works well because each week you can plan out which day fits your schedule best. So if you have a party or work event on a particular day, you can make that your free day and eat whatever you want. What you often find is that the free day is enjoyable and allows you to eat some of your favorite unhealthy foods, but by the end of the day you don't feel all that great and are ready to return to eating healthy the following morning.

Tom Venuto recommends another approach we like, which is to eat healthy 90 percent of the time. The other 10 percent, you can eat whatever you want. This approach works well when you know you have several things going on that week and want to have some freedom at those events. However, when you use either of these two approaches, it is difficult to turn off the cravings. When you eat the fatty, sugary, and salty foods, you reactivate your cravings for more. If you take a "free" meal or eat whatever you want at lunch, it can be very challenging to go back to eating healthy again for dinner. So if you do use this approach, we find it works best if you plan most of your free meals for the end of your day.

Ultimately, it may be better to cut out processed sugar completely. Research shows that for most people, after a week of no sugar the desire for it basically disappears.[30] Jack discovered that when he cut all processed sugar out of his diet, after a week he could watch others eating ice cream and chocolate cake, with no desire for it at all. If he ever does order dessert at a restaurant, he just orders a bowl of fresh seasonal berries. But if you feel this is too challenging, at least now, just start one of these two options so that you still limit the amount of sugar you consume.

With either the free day or 90 percent plan, you want to free yourself from any guilt around these meals or days. The idea behind a free day or meal is that you grant yourself permission to eat what you want. If you end up regretting or feeling guilty about it, you defeat the purpose.

Another successful strategy is replacing meals or snacks with a healthy smoothie. As we mentioned in Day 7, you should not skip meals (eat at least three a day), always eat breakfast, eat at least every five hours, and ideally get your vitamins and nutrients from food and your sugar "fix" from fruit. A smoothie, often referred to as a protein drink, can accomplish all of this. Remember to check out the alcohol detox smoothie recipe we posted on the companion website for Day 7.

You can buy different smoothie/protein mixes and powders, and mix in fresh or frozen fruits or vegetables. One expert we consulted recommended using whole fruit (not fruit juice—which contains too high a concentration of sugar) or adding chia seeds, as both of these increase the amount of fiber in the smoothie, which reduces sugar shock (large fluctuations of blood sugar levels in a short amount of time) and therefore also reduces the likelihood of alcohol cravings.

What Works for One Might Not for Another . . .

According to a study by the US Centers for Disease Control and Prevention (CDC), food allergies among children increased approximately 50 percent between 1997 and 2011. Food allergies now affect fifteen million Americans,[31] and all indications point to this trend continuing. Food allergies, sensitivities, and intolerances force you to change how you approach your diet, so it is absolutely critical you learn what works best for *you*. Dave's daughters, for instance, have had significant food allergies. When they were eight and five, they already had a long list of health issues. They would get sick constantly and were on antibiotics almost monthly. They took prescription medication for severe reflux, and had to increase the dosage many times. Finally, a new food intolerance blood test became available, which revealed that both daughters had a severe gluten intolerance, and one also had a severe soy intolerance. By removing these foods from their diet, their health issues disappeared.[32] They were off medication within a couple of weeks and have been healthy ever since.

After seeing the profound impact of changing their children's diets, Dave and his wife, Anya, also took the blood test and discovered that they, too, were regularly eating foods to which they had moderate to severe intolerances. Anya was having severe migraines regularly and Dave was occasionally experiencing stomach pain and digestion issues. Once they removed these foods from their diet their health dramatically improved.

In these cases, the health implications of food sensitivities and intolerances are obvious, but since the body can build up some resistance to foods you eat regularly, other types of allergies might not be as apparent. The continued exposure to foods that cause allergies, sensitivities, or intolerances can worsen as you get older, and result in a wide variety of health issues, some that might not seem food-related at all. And one of the most aggravating consequences can be an inability to lose weight despite following a healthy nutrition plan and exercise routine.

Lyn-Genet Recitas's bestselling book *The Plan: Eliminate the Surprising "Healthy" Foods That Are Making You Fat—and Lose Weight Fast* has brought mainstream attention to this problem. The core premise of the book is this: "Foods that are revered by traditional weight loss programs, such as turkey, eggs, cauliflower, beans, and tomatoes, may be healthy in a vacuum, but when combined with each person's unique chemistry, they can cause a toxic reaction that triggers weight gain, premature aging, inflammation, and a host of health problems including constipation, migraines, joint pain, and depression."[33]

Because this topic is so important to your individual health, we couldn't overlook it; however, there is a lot of confusion and misinformation in the world regarding food allergies, sensitivities, and intolerances, including what the best approach is for diagnosing them, and determining their overall impact on your health. Therefore, we highly recommend you talk to a qualified doctor, nutritionist, or health care professional if you believe this is something affecting you.

Day 25 Action Steps

I think, at a certain point, it's better for women not to have any alcohol, because it can make your face, breasts, and midsection get very bloated.

—SHARON STONE
Actor

By cutting back or quitting drinking you have taken the most important step to reclaiming your health, and today's focus is all about how to accelerate that process.

If you feel overwhelmed by this topic, please feel free to come back to it at a later date. The main goal of today was to introduce you to some basic nutritional concepts, share facts that remind you of the ultimate "cost" to your health if you return to excessive drinking, and provide you with resources here and on the companion website, to which you can refer when ready.

- **Drink lots of water.** Drink one ounce of water for every two pounds of weight, and more if you exercise. Or drink at least eight ounces of water every two hours you are awake. This change alone can have a profound impact on your health and energy.

- **Keep a food journal.** Write down everything you eat and drink over a twenty-four-hour period (you can even make a photo collage or use a smartphone app to track it). This can be done after you finish the program, and your goal is simple—awareness. Many eating habits are unconscious, and until you consciously decide to record what you eat and drink, what and how much you *think* you eat and drink often differs from the truth.

- **Make small changes to your diet**. Every week add a new positive change to your diet. The first one can be to drink the proper amount of water. In another week add a new one—such as cutting back on a specific sugary or fatty treat you enjoy, not taking second servings at dinner, or eating fast food one less time a week. *To make sure you remember to do this, stop now and put reminders on your calendar.*

On today's companion website, you will find the list of the top recovery foods, the key nutrients your body needs to thrive physically, a list of foods that promote good moods, and a list of foods that promote bad moods. You'll also find a list of some of our favorite books, experts, and resources on diet, nutrition, food allergies, and detoxes and cleanses. Be sure to visit http://Day25.Solutions.

Day **26**

The Positive Addiction Solution

Adding Fun, Healthy, and Confidence-Building Activities to Your Life

> *It is the spinning-free, mentally relaxed Positive Addiction state that provides an extremely optimal condition for our brains to grow.*
>
> —WILLIAM GLASSER, MD (1925–2013)[1]

If you had ten to twenty extra hours a week, what would you do with that time? To thrive in sobriety, not only do you need to answer this question, but also how you answer it will directly impact the quality of your life, and likely determine whether or not you return to your previous level of drinking.

Cutting back or quitting drinking will give you extra time, even if you previously drank while multitasking—taking care of your kids, watching TV, paying bills, cleaning your house, or networking with peers. The reality is that your drinking affected your decision making, and as you change your drinking, your energy level, interests, and daily decisions will also change.

The Positive Addiction Solution prepares you for your new life of thriving in sobriety, and tells you how to avoid a major sobriety killer—boredom. By learning the "what and why" of exercise, you will discover how you can get more fit and actually enjoy it. You will also learn how an apparent "weakness" can actually lead you to being stronger and happier, as well as help you discover and embrace new fun activities in your new life.

The Top Five Factors Affecting Your Health

The way you think, the way you behave, the way you eat, can influence your life by thirty to fifty years.

—DEEPAK CHOPRA[2]

Dr. Deepak Chopra has stated that the top five influencing factors for health are "food, water, breathing, exercise, and sleep." In yesterday's solution, we discussed the importance of feeding your body the right foods at the right times, and in the right quantities, as well as how critical drinking enough water is to maintaining your optimum health. Two days ago, we discussed the importance of proper breathing, and you learned to breathe as an effective technique for ridding your body of toxins, reducing stress, and feeling more energized. And today we will address exercise and sleep.

Imagine how much your overall energy, self-confidence, and physical health will be transformed by embracing the top five influencing factors for your health. Even if you only start with small changes in each of these areas and combine that with cutting back or quitting drinking, you will be able to experience remarkable positive results in a relatively short amount of time.

The Magic Pill

What if there was a pill that would keep you fit and lean as you aged, while protecting your heart and bones? What if it was as good for your brain as for your body, if it made you stronger, more confident, and less susceptible to depression? What if it improved your sleep, mood, and memory and reduced your risk of cancer, all while adding life to your years and years to your life? A great number of studies have found that exercise can provide all these benefits and more, even for people who begin late in life. We are learning that much of the physical decline that older people suffer stems not from age but from simple disuse.

—JOHN ROBBINS

Author of *Diet for a New America: How Your Food Choices Affect Your Health, Your Happiness, and the Future of Life on Earth*[3]

If you want to change how you feel, get moving. This is true for everyone, but it is even more so for problem drinkers. Not only do you get all the benefits that John Robbins mentions, but you are also less likely to drink again. The Research Society on Alcoholism[4] recently published a study that found that "alcohol consumption and loss of control over drinking are greater among individuals who do not exercise regularly."[5]

We see this as common sense. After exercising, do you usually want to drink alcohol or eat fatty or sugary foods? As long as the exercise is fairly strenuous, the answer is most likely no. If you were feeling "down" before you exercised, you usually find that your mood has improved. If you get your body excited, your mind will follow. We encourage you to test this the next time you are feeling unhappy—get up and do some jumping jacks or push-ups, take a short jog, power walk around your neighborhood, or do some deep breathing exercises combined with yoga poses. Then notice how you feel afterward.

The Science of Exercise

A strong body makes the mind strong.

—THOMAS JEFFERSON (1743–1826)
Third president of the United States

Shawn Achor spent over a decade at Harvard University researching and lecturing on what makes people happy, and he published his findings in *The Happiness Advantage: The Seven Principles of Positive Psychology That Fuel Success and Performance at Work*. His research included a study of three groups of patients who treated their depression with medication, exercise, or a combination of the two. Over the course of six months, 38 percent of those who only used medication slipped back into depression and 31 percent who used a combination of medication and exercise relapsed. However, the relapse rate of the test group that only exercised was a scant 9 percent, once again confirming that exercise really is the "magic pill."[6]

Like meditation, exercise has also been proven to increase the production of serotonin, addressing an important deficit many people in early sobriety experience. Furthermore, exercise stimulates the release of endorphins within thirty minutes from the start of activity, which results in minimizing pain and discomfort and creating feelings of euphoria.[7] When you consider this along with some of the other obvious benefits, such as helping you relax and sleep[8]— and improving your body image and self-confidence—exercise is a perfect example of a positive addiction.

Dave's New Habits

Dave realized that embracing new fun and healthy activities was a critical component to thriving in sobriety:

Growing up, I was extremely active, always learning and playing a wide range of sports; however, once I discovered drinking in college, I found myself watching more sports, and participating less and less. When I got sober I realized two important things: My apparent "love" for watching sports was much more about using it as an excuse to drink. And I mostly avoided playing sports, and learning new ones, because they often conflicted with my desire to drink.

Once I was free from alcohol, embracing new physical activities gave me a lot of enjoyment. The first thing I did was start coaching my oldest daughter's basketball team, which not only helped me become more engaged in my children's lives but also helped me become more active.

Soon after, I started playing racquetball at lunch. Our company had two racquetball courts, but finding other players at my skill level was challenging. I ended up starting a racquetball ladder, and more than fifty-five people signed up. Over the next year and a half, I met lots of new coworkers through the ladder and advanced my game. I also played in leagues at a local recreation center, took lessons, and played in a variety of tournaments. One simple idea dramatically improved my physical fitness and created more positive relationships at work and in my personal life.

Although racquetball was enjoyable, I realized that I love variety, and since I was now coaching both of my daughters' basketball teams, I also wanted to play. However, I had never played organized basketball and was not very good, despite having learned a lot about technique and drills from coaching. I checked with the local recreation center and found out that I could start a team in the league, so I reached out to some coworkers. A few were interested, but I still needed four more players. I also belonged to 24 Hour Fitness, and decided to play in the pickup games to see if I could find anyone there. In order to do this, I had to overcome some fear because I wasn't nearly as skilled as everyone else on the court. Even though I wasn't very good, I ended up meeting some great people (and some really good players) who were interested in joining my team because I was organizing the league. That filled the last two spots, and helped to make our team somewhat competitive.

This experience taught me some critical lessons: First, if you are willing to organize, people will follow (even if they have a lot more experience and skill than you). Second, the lessons I learned in the league helped me become a far better coach for my daughters. And last, my family came to watch some of my games, just as they'd watched some of the racquetball tournaments, and this taught my daughters that sports activities can be great at any age or skill level.

I have continued to exercise in a variety of ways, practicing yoga, taking martial arts classes, skiing (and teaching my daughters), joining five different boot camp programs over a three-year period, hiking, completing obstacle races (like the Tough Mudder, a ten-to-twelve-mile obstacle course designed to test physical strength), and bicycling with my wife and kids.

The reason I share this with you is because I had always wanted to do these things, but I had unconsciously made my drinking a higher priority. However, once I began all these physical activities, my health and energy improved dramatically. It also increased my self-confidence, strengthened my relationship with my wife and kids, and helped me create new healthy relationships.

Exercising Is Easy

The market is inundated with bestselling books, blogs, and programs on fitness and exercise that all claim to have the answer you have been searching for—whether you want to lose weight, get six-pack abs, drop two dress sizes, or just have more energy. As great as many of them are, they can sometimes lead you to believe that implementing an exercise program must be complicated or difficult. And with so many options, it can be overwhelming, resulting in no action being taken at all.

The truth is that exercising is easy, and all that matters is that you start. We both have done numerous different workouts and fitness programs and have read hundreds of books and articles, and most of them have the exact same common goals: increase your breathing and heart rate (endurance), build muscle, increase flexibility, and improve your balance and core strength.

This doesn't mean you shouldn't try different approaches. We certainly have—and not because we are searching for "the answer," but because we appreciate variety and also because our fitness goals change over time. But some of the healthiest, strongest, most vigorous people we know have been doing the exact same exercises for decades. They know what works, have an established routine, and find peace of mind by not mixing it up. Others, like us, get bored with the same routine and need to try new things to stay engaged. Either approach can be equally effective.

If you have always embraced a healthy exercise routine and feel you are knowledgeable on the topic, feel free to skim through the next few sections.

Getting Started

Physical fitness is not only one of the most important keys to a healthy body, it is the basis of dynamic and creative intellectual activity.

—JOHN F. KENNEDY (1917–1963)
Thirty-fifth president of the United States

Here are a few simple recommendations to help you get started. First, if you haven't been working out, get approval from your doctor or health care professional. Going from a sedentary lifestyle to exercising can be dangerous if you have certain existing health conditions, especially heart disease.

Second, if you are just beginning, start small. This advice should be familiar by now. If you push yourself too hard right away, the initial soreness you will likely experience in the first week or two may deter you from continuing. However, if you do experience intense soreness, which can be very common when doing new exercises that are engaging new muscles, it only lasts one to two weeks at the most.

Third, you don't need a lot of time to dramatically improve your fitness. A lot of research has been done in the last few years on high-intensity interval training (HIIT) and high-intensity circuit training (HICT). This research has proven that as little as a seven-minute workout using just your body weight is enough to provide many of the fitness benefits that prolonged endurance training provides, as well as build muscle.[9] One of these workouts was published recently in the *New York Times Magazine*,[10] which we provide a link to on the companion website.

Last, don't be afraid to start by taking brisk walks outside. Not only is this good exercise, according to Richard Ryan, professor of psychology, psychiatry, and education at the University of Rochester, but research demonstrates that "being outside in nature for just twenty minutes in a day was enough to significantly boost vitality levels."[11] By exercising outdoors in nature, you can noticeably shift your state of mind.

There are two core components of a balanced fitness plan that will provide you the greatest health benefits: aerobic training and strength training. Although flexibility and balance can be extremely beneficial to your overall health, aerobic and strength training often incorporate exercises that improve flexibility and balance as well.[12]

Aerobic Training

Ninety percent of the stimulation and nutrition to the brain is generated by the movement of the spine.

—DR. ROGER SPERRY (1913–1994)
Nobel Prize–winning brain scientist[13]

Aerobic exercise is simply getting your heart rate up and maintaining it, but at a level of intensity where your breathing is still relatively comfortable. The benefits of aerobic exercise include strengthening your heart and lungs, reducing stress, burning calories, gaining energy, and improving your thinking. This can include just about any type of exercise, whether it is running, power walking, weight lifting, or even yoga, as long as you are exercising at a pace that keeps your heart rate elevated. However, if your workout becomes too intense— meaning when you talk out loud you can't finish a sentence without gasping for air—you are exercising anaerobically. In this state you often become uncomfortable. You might want to consider purchasing a heart rate monitor when starting a new exercise plan, as it will help you to know your limits so you can "train, not strain" your heart. Plus, you can use it to measure your progress. Just visit your local sporting goods store or Amazon.com.

Although there is nothing wrong with anaerobic exercise, and inevitably you will transition between both modes at times during your exercising, anaerobic exercise is generally only important for those who compete. If you are only concerned with the health benefits of exercise, then you should focus on exercising aerobically, which is great news because this is much easier. The main reason you might want to exercise anaerobically, or simply be forced to, is if you are doing activities or sports such as basketball, football, soccer, tennis, or swimming that require intense bursts of energy.[14]

Strength Training

After the age of thirty-five, you lose roughly a half pound of muscle each year.[15] That means if you don't do any strength training, every year you will lose muscle and gain weight in the form of fat unless you consume fewer calories. In addition, even if you maintain your weight, you will basically be replacing muscle with fat. And as this happens, you will look bigger. Over the course of a year, the impact is minimal; however, the cumulative impact over years or decades can be enormous, which is why strength training should be an integral part of your exercise routine.

There are countless ways to build muscle, so we will only touch on a few key concepts. However, there are additional resources on the companion website, including some of our favorite strength training programs. Strength training is not just for men. Women also greatly benefit from integrating this into their exercise routine because muscle is 18 percent more dense than fat and burns more calories at a resting rate than fat.[16] There is little risk of women becoming overly muscular—this typically only happens if you are specifically training for that goal.

Even if you do strength training just once a week, you can still see results. One of the most common ways to build muscle is to work with weights. One key to working with weights is to pay attention to when you reach "failure." This is the point where your arms or legs start to shake and you can barely bring the weight back up. Reaching failure is a significant way to accelerate muscle growth. Just be careful that you don't switch to poor form as you do your last few repetitions, as that is how injuries happen. Working with a trainer and having a spotter are highly recommended for when you first begin in order to learn correct form.

Although using weights is a very common method to build muscle, there is a growing trend that uses just your body weight for resistance. These workouts often include variations of push-ups, pull-ups, lunges, squats, and various abdominal exercises to build core strength. The great thing about these types of workouts is that they don't require special equipment and are usually done at a pace that gives you an aerobic workout as well.

Last, we have primarily focused on exercise outside of specific sports and activities. By integrating various active sports and activities in your life you can easily, and often more enjoyably, leverage the benefits of exercise. Depending on the sport, likely results include building specific muscle groups, improving balance and flexibility, and getting a mixture of aerobic and anaerobic exercise.

Ten Tips to Start Exercising and Never Stop

For me, the temptation to drink often surfaces with boredom, long business trips, and when working on really large projects, so now I know when and how to prepare.

—JAMES

30-Day Graduate from Istanbul, Turkey

When is the last time you worked out and regretted it? What is wonderful about exercise is that it is one of the few things you can do in life that you won't regret. The only possible exception to this is if you injure yourself by pushing too hard. Here are some tips to help make integrating exercise in your life easy:

- **Work out in the morning.** Your willpower diminishes as the day goes on, so it is best to start your day with the things you are most likely to skip. Also, working out in the morning carries over to the rest of your day. You more often feel naturally motivated to get important tasks done, and your desire to eat poorly is lessened.

- **Reward yourself.** Treat yourself to something special for working out that day, such as fifteen minutes of watching funny videos on YouTube, or give yourself a bigger reward for working out a certain number of days in the month, such as scheduling a massage or buying yourself a new piece of clothing.

- **Use accountability.** Find a workout partner. Or use one of the many free apps available for your iPhone or Android that tracks and shares your workout with friends. To increase your accountability, make an agreement that if you don't follow through with your workout, you will pay your workout partner some amount of money (enough that it will bother you), or some other consequence that you prefer to avoid.

- **Stop setting goals.** This might sound counterintuitive, but it can be easy to get discouraged if you have a lot of weight goals and other benchmarks with which you measure your success. If you do set a goal, make it easy to accomplish, such as just exercising for twenty minutes four times a week. Feel great about showing up, and focus on effort, not results.[17]

- **Join a team or group.** Find a sport or activity that requires exercise and join a team or group, or if necessary, start your own team.

- **Combine exercise with errands or commuting.** If you can, walk or ride your bike when you run errands, commute to work, or go to lunch. Find ways to exercise as you go about your day, like taking the stairs instead of the elevator, or parking in the furthest spot in the parking lot. Jack has a rule that he always walks up two flights of stairs or down three instead of taking the elevator.

- **Enter a race or other athletic competition.** You are more likely to follow through when you know you have an event to prepare for.

- **Make a playlist of your favorite music and listen to it while working out.** Not only does music release endorphins that increase tolerance for pain,[18] it can also evoke a positive emotional response, making your workout more enjoyable. Jack has several playlists of upbeat music on his iPod, including a set of tracks of Marine Corps cadence tapes from drill instructors at Parris Island that he uses to keep him motivated and on a steady pace when he is running.[19]

- **Don't take more than one day off.** Better yet, don't take any days off from exercise. The more you integrate exercise into your daily life, the easier it is to continue.

- **Put your gym bag or workout clothes on the floor near your bedroom door, in your car, or somewhere else where you can't miss them.** When you see your bag or clothes, or better yet have to step over them in the morning, it will remind you to work out.

But I Need a Drink to Get a Good Night's Sleep

If food, water, breathing, exercise, and sleep are the five most important things for your health as Dr. Deepak Chopra claims, then imagine how much more important these are to the problem drinker. Excessive drinking poisons your body, increases your cravings for unhealthy foods, dehydrates you, can reduce your capacity to absorb nutrients, is detrimental to exercise, and, based on a review of twenty-seven studies, is disruptive to your sleep.[20]

According to the director of the Edinburgh Sleep Centre, "Alcohol on the whole is not useful for improving a whole night's sleep. Sleep may be deeper to start with, but then becomes disrupted. Additionally, that deeper sleep will probably promote snoring and poorer breathing. So, one shouldn't expect better sleep with alcohol."[21] Researchers also found that alcohol decreases sleep duration and increases wakefulness, especially for women.[22]

We all need regular sleep. Even though everyone is a bit different, the average person needs between 6.5 to 7.5 hours. (It is estimated that only about 3 to 5 percent of the population needs less than 6.5 hours of sleep to function normally.[23]) In an interview, Daniel Kripke, an acclaimed researcher on sleep, explains, "People who sleep between six and a half hours and seven and a half hours a night live the longest, are happier, and most productive."[24] Sleeping either less or more than this range strongly correlates to a significant decline in your productivity and ability to focus, in addition to being more irritable and having impaired judgment—all of which can negatively affect your overall happiness.

Studies have also validated that exercise can significantly improve sleep, including sleep duration and sleep quality, even in those that have struggled with insomnia. Sleep is also critical for rejuvenation and body repair from intense exercise. However, exercise does not necessarily result in sleep improvement right away. Rather, it can take up to two months before this benefit is experienced. Although exercise improves sleep, you should not exercise within a few hours of your bedtime.[25]

Along with exercise, there are a few other things you can do to improve your sleep. First, take naps between twenty and forty minutes—anything over forty minutes may cause you to go into REM sleep, which will make you more tired when you wake.[26] John D. Rockefeller, Winston Churchill, and Albert Einstein are just three examples of well-known people who were known to take short naps.[27]

Second, disengage from your day the last twenty minutes of the night, either by reading (or listening to) fiction, meditating, or even practicing gratitude. If you are still having issues with sleep, try to maintain a regular schedule for going to bed and waking, keep your bedroom at a cool temperature, stay away from caffeine in the evening, and use the bed only for sleeping, sex, and possibly reading.

Drinking alcohol negatively affects at least four of the five healthiest things you can do for your body: food, water, exercise, and sleep. So just removing alcohol from your life can dramatically improve your health. Now imagine if you start making other small changes in these areas, such as eating a little healthier, drinking more water, exercising for five minutes a day, focusing on your breathing, and sleeping at least six and a half hours a night. Your body's capacity to heal itself, as well as the added benefits to your overall happiness, productivity, and vitality that come with improvements in these areas, will make thriving in sobriety a reality.

Your **first action step** for today is to start exercising (if you are not already). This can be as simple as taking a brisk seven-minute walk or a five-minute jog.[28] The key is to get started right away by building your exercise "muscle." Seriously, you might even want to put this book down and go for a seven-minute walk right now.

The Positive Addict

On Day 3 in the Pendulum Solution, we introduced you to the idea of positive addiction: If you become positively addicted to things that have a beneficial effect on your mind or body, such as meditating or running, you will live a longer, happier, and more fulfilling life.

If you have struggled with addiction in the past, you have more options and more advantages than your nonaddictive counterparts, as long as you are able to channel that all-or-nothing behavior toward positive addictions instead of negative addictions, like drinking. And this advantage, when your energy is properly focused, will actually make you stronger and happier than others who haven't had the same challenges with addiction.[29] We are not saying that you should simply replace your drinking with another activity that you become compulsive and obsessed with, rather that you leverage the inherent positive traits that addictive personalities have to excel at a healthy activity, while still embracing variety and balance.

When you become positively addicted in sobriety, you often experience exciting and surprising success, which, in turn, is very fulfilling both personally and professionally. This phenomenon feeds into the "Why is your drinking your greatest gift?" concept from Day 3. When you remove the negative addiction and replace it with its opposite, positive addiction, you are able to finally experience great success and pleasure in your life.

Laughing Your Way to Sobriety

Laughter is the tonic, the relief, the surcease for pain.

—CHARLIE CHAPLIN (1889–1977)

Comic actor-director

Did you know that children laugh up to three hundred times in a single day, but adults laugh only roughly fifteen times a day?[30] A new exercise routine, which set out to rectify this discrepancy, is gaining worldwide recognition and acceptance and is now in seventy-two countries and in more than six thousand clubs. Deemed a "complete well-being workout," Laughter Yoga combines unconditional laughter with yogic breathing, and the driving reason behind its success is simple—laughing is loaded with positive benefits.[31]

It is estimated that 60 to 90 percent of all doctor visits are stress-related.[32] Numerous studies have demonstrated that laughter has physical benefits on the body, such as lowering blood pressure, improving blood circulation, and helping boost the immune system.[33] And one of laughter's biggest benefits is stress reduction. In a study on heart disease, cardiologist Michael Miller, director of the Center for Preventive Cardiology at the University of Maryland Medical Center, says, "The old saying that 'laughter is the best medicine' definitely appears to be true when it comes to protecting your heart health."[34]

And the emotional benefits are just as significant. Have you ever been in a heated argument, and then someone says something funny (usually accidentally), or something happens, like one of you farts, and instantly you both start laughing? What happened to the negative emotions that you were experiencing? Most likely they vanished or significantly diminished. In fact, it is often hard to return to that same level of emotional intensity. Laughter releases "feel-good" hormones like dopamine and endorphins, which relieve physical tension and emotional stress, and help to rejuvenate your body and mind. And there is nothing quite like connecting a group of people through sharing a good laugh together, as long as the source of the humor does not belittle or hurt another person or group.

As you explore new activities, look for some that make you laugh. For example, we have both taken improvisation workshops. Not only did we laugh a lot during the workshops, but they also helped us bring more humor and lightheartedness to our personal and professional lives. Jack also listens only to the comedy channels on SiriusXM radio when he is driving.

Adding Variety to Your Sobriety

The 30-Day Sobriety Solution attracts a lot of high-functioning problem drinkers—people who have had successful careers, and from the outside, you would not expect that they have a drinking problem. When anyone gets sober, but especially when high-functioning problem drinkers do, they tend to replace the time they spent drinking with work, essentially replacing one compulsive behavior with another one. This might work in the short term, but it doesn't in the long term. Eventually an out-of-balance life leads back to drinking.

Lasting sobriety, and thriving in sobriety, can only be attained and sustained by balancing your life with some fun activities and enjoyable hobbies—maybe things from the past that you stopped doing, or new things you have always wanted to do. We know you might be thinking, *I don't have time*, and our response is always the same: if you don't have time, then how did you have time to drink?

Contrary to what you might think, engaging in activities that are fun not only make you a better spouse, friend, and parent, as well as healthier and happier, they also make you a better and more productive person at work.

Your **second action step** for today is to go through the list of "101 New Activities for Your New Life of Thriving in Sobriety" and see what interests you. You will notice that some of these are things you might do just once, or once in a while, where others might become daily or weekly activities. As you read the list, trust your intuition. Don't worry about the "how" right now, just your desire or interest in doing them. Also, it is very likely you already have a good idea of the activities you have enjoyed in the past and stopped doing, and the "one of these days" or "someday, I'll" activities you have always wanted to start. Write all of these down, either in your journal or somewhere else you can easily review. If there are activities you think of that are not on the 101 New Activities list, write those down as well.

Once you have completed your list, pick one of the activities to do. Ideally, pick one that's easy to do, since starting small and building momentum is the most important thing; however, if there is another one you are really excited about, you can pick that one as well. If you are having a hard time deciding which activity to start with, consider the topics we discussed today. If it is an aerobic exercise, strength training, or it will make you laugh, then you will likely get doubly high value from doing that activity. You can even combine today's first action step of starting to exercise with this one. For example, if you have always wanted to learn a martial art, sign up for classes. Just remember, your goal is balance and variety. We wouldn't recommend you pick an activity, such as "learning the guitar," and become compulsive about practicing, playing, and studying.

Once you have picked your activity, do something *right now* to move it forward. Register for a class, call a friend for advice, do internet research, schedule times on your calendar, or actually begin the activity right now, if you can. The sooner you get started, the more likely you will follow through.

When Jack was participating in a twelve-week teleseminar called the "Happy, Healthy, Wealthy Game," he was asked what his major goal for the seminar was. Jack responded, "To really get in shape." At that point, the trainer said, "Great! Put down the phone and do ten push-ups right now." Jack said, "No, you don't understand. I mean, like I need to join a gym or get a personal trainer to work out with." The trainer responded, "No, I mean *right now*! Ten push-ups." This dialogue went back and forth about five times until Jack finally put down the phone and did ten push-ups, which resulted in him then setting and reaching his goal of eighty push-ups in a row. This is an illustration of what we mean by "Start now!"

The last part of this action step is to make sure you don't forget the rest of the activities on your list. We recommend that you create a recurring appointment in your online calendar for the first Saturday of every month, and in the details of that appointment include your list of activities. If you use a physical calendar, write down a monthly appointment to review your list. Then every month you will be reminded to look over your list of activities and see if there are any you want to start during the next month. Sometimes you might want to do a certain activity during a certain time of the year, like skiing or surfing, in which case you would make a separate calendar entry to remind you to do those activities. Regardless, creating and using a personal reminder system is key to your success, just like it is at your job. If you don't schedule the activities, the force of your old habits can take over. Adding new activities into your life takes conscious intention and effort.

The **third action step** for today is a powerful guided process called Rediscovering Your Joy, which you will find on the companion website, that takes you back through your life to explore and discover what brings you true happiness and fulfillment without alcohol. If you are having any challenges choosing activities, this process will help you get more clarity.

One 30-Day Graduate shared the value of:

> One of the most powerful solutions while doing *The 30-Day Sobriety Solution* was the breakthrough experience I had with one of the guided meditations. This one in particular took me back to a time in my life where I could actually see the younger version of myself that was happy without drinking. This was a wake-up call—I remembered and saw that I had been sober and happy before in my life, so there was no reason I couldn't do it again. I even realized, and believed, that my sober future was full of new adventures and "highs," which finally got me excited about not drinking.

So get started now picking new activities!

101 New Activities for Your New Life of Thriving in Sobriety

After I got back to LA, I tried to keep all these things in mind. But what really helped me get back on track was starting to pursue a new dream. I had wanted to be a pilot all my life, and I decided to start taking flying lessons.

—PATRICK SWAYZE[35]

1. Go for a brisk walk.
2. Listen to audiobooks or self-help content while driving.
3. Make a playlist of your favorite music and listen to it while exercising.
4. Practice smiling—yes, this is actually proven to make you feel better.
5. Learn to play a new instrument or practice the instrument you already know.
6. Read books, especially memoirs of people in recovery.
7. Take a dancing class (ballroom, hip-hop, swing, jazz, two-step, or salsa).
8. Take a day off from work and use it just for you. (Call in "well.")
9. Go for a hike and take a picnic.
10. Research cities and countries you want to travel to, and even plan your trip—whether you are serious about going or not.
11. Sign up for local-deal emails (such as Groupon and LivingSocial), and when you see an activity you have wanted to try, buy it.
12. Watch funny YouTube videos (such as funny animal videos or stand-up comics).
13. Take a class at a local college, recreation center, YMCA, and so on.
14. Get into nature, or even a local park, for twenty minutes a day.
15. Join a men's group or a women's group.

16. Take a yoga or Pilates class.
17. Spend more time with inspiring and positive family members and friends.
18. Go camping.
19. Reorganize a room in your house.
20. Visit the Meetup website (www.meetup.com) to find a group or get-together that interests you.
21. Paint a room or a wall.
22. Give a back rub or a massage.
23. Do a random act of kindness and don't wait for or expect a thank-you or any kind of recognition.
24. Start a home improvement project.
25. Join a creative writing group.
26. Cuddle your spouse or partner.
27. Take an improv or comedy workshop, or join an improv group.
28. Create a family website, online photo, or video album.
29. Join a local boot camp, CrossFit gym, or other specialized local gym.
30. Go to a play, a musical, an opera, or a concert.
31. Attend a sporting event.
32. Play a board game or card game, especially with loved ones and friends. (Amazon.com reviews can be a perfect resource to find the right game.)
33. Join a book club.
34. Reach out to a friend from your past with whom you want to reconnect.
35. Become a coach for your children's teams, or volunteer as a coach for any team.
36. Find and attend free speaking events in your area.
37. Join a local public speaking group (such as Toastmasters International).
38. Take singing lessons.
39. Have a party or get-together.
40. Go to AA meetings or other recovery program meetings such as

Rational Recovery (RR), SMART Recovery, Women for Sobriety (WFS), or Harm Reduction Abstinence and Moderation Support (HAMS).

41. Join a cooking class or try cooking new recipes.
42. Make a vision board or vision book.
43. Write down all of your goals for every area of your life.
44. Start or join a mastermind group, a group of like-minded people who meet regularly to brainstorm ideas and tackle challenges together.
45. Watch funny TV shows or search the internet for the funniest or most inspiring movies and watch one per week.
46. Go to a comedy club or an improv club.
47. Do something artistic such as drawing, sculpting, or painting.
48. Pamper yourself at a spa, or simply schedule a massage.
49. Randomly stop what you are doing and do ten push-ups, jumping jacks, sit-ups, squats, or pull-ups.
50. Start a blog on a topic you are passionate about.
51. Start or join a team in a local recreation league.
52. Play fantasy sports or start a fantasy sports league.
53. Get involved with a nonprofit organization, whether it is through donating, volunteering, or even starting your own.
54. Give yourself permission to be silly sometimes.
55. Sign up for a seminar or a conference.
56. Go on a road trip.
57. Do something fun with your children, or just engage them by asking them interesting questions. (Search online for "great questions to engage your children in conversation.")
58. Take up sewing, knitting, or needlework.
59. Start martial arts training.
60. Research getting a pet, and get one if you are ready for the commitment.
61. Write a bucket list (everything you want to do before you die).
62. Go to church or engage in religious or spiritual events in your community.

63. Sell some of your stuff and use the money to start a new hobby.
64. Write down all your important dates, such as anniversaries and birthdays, and set up a system so that you never forget them.
65. Create a document with all of your favorite quotes and continue to update it.
66. Organize your life, office area, kitchen, basement, or garage.
67. Take up a new activity with your spouse, girlfriend/boyfriend, or friend.
68. Learn how to type.
69. Hire a life coach.
70. Try a new aerobic exercise class or do one at home.
71. Do a yard project, like planting flowers, making a rock garden, or building a patio.
72. Take up photography or videography.
73. Make jewelry.
74. Learn how to use a new software program on your computer.
75. Get a new degree or certification.
76. Visit a museum, art gallery, zoo, or botanical garden.
77. Donate blood.
78. Let someone go ahead of you in line who appears to be in a rush.
79. Take a friend out to lunch, dinner, or coffee.
80. Brainstorm rewards you can give yourself for sobriety milestones (30 days, 60 days, and so on).
81. Sign up for a 10K, marathon, triathlon, or some other physically challenging event.
82. Collect something, like baseball cards, basketball cards, coins, stuffed animals, records, or theater posters.
83. Go mountain biking or cycling.
84. Take a chance on a new hairstyle.
85. Clean and organize your car.
86. Teach someone something that you have learned.
87. Become a Boy Scout or Girl Scout leader or a Big Brother/Big Sister.

88. Write a thank-you letter or email to someone who has had a positive impact on your life, whether it is a family member, a friend, or even a teacher from high school.
89. Buy yourself a new wardrobe and/or workout clothes.
90. Plan a surprise night for a loved one.
91. Make a special meal for your family or friends.
92. Take up woodworking, cabinetmaking, or metalworking.
93. Learn a new language. (Check out Rosetta Stone or a Berlitz class.)
94. Find an inspiring place outside your house to read, meditate, study, or do work, such as a library, park, or nice coffee shop.
95. Write down what you would tell a tourist to see or do when visiting your city or state, and then do these things yourself.
96. Do *The 30-Day Sobriety Solution* again, or redo your favorite days and exercises.
97. Learn to play chess, bridge, Go, Scrabble, or backgammon.
98. Play an interactive video game where you actually exercise while playing, such as Wii Sports, which includes tennis, baseball, golf, bowling, and boxing.
99. Try out different restaurants around town.
100. Go to the beach, lake, or river.
101. Perform karaoke.

"Boy, I'm going to pay for this tomorrow at yoga class."

*We act as though comfort and luxury were the chief require-
ments of life, when all that we need to make us happy is something to be enthusiastic about.*

—ALBERT EINSTEIN

The "Permission Slip" for Fun!

*I had my first vacation without drinking, and it was thrilling. On
occasion I found myself romanticizing drinking, but what surprised me was that the people who were drinking to excess, like
I always did on vacation, seemed to be having fun, but often
were annoying many of the people around them.*

—SUSAN

30-Day Graduate from Philadelphia, Pennsylvania

Would you consider yourself a high-functioning alcoholic? Do you
lead what appears to be a successful life, at least from the outside,
but know that drinking is still an issue in your life? If you can relate to this, then we have one last suggestion for you today. And it's
important!

Dave and our many graduates share how alcohol was the one,
and often only, way they could let themselves "turn off" for the day.
They would work hard all day or all week, and then drink to relax.
This behavior became so ingrained over time that they didn't give
themselves permission to stop "doing" until they started drinking.
Drinking was essentially the trigger, or the "off switch," that allowed
them to relax. This created a major challenge when they chose to become sober. They felt like they had to be productively working every
waking hour because they had forgotten how to give themselves permission to stop and have fun without drinking.

If this sounds like you, it's critical that you consciously give
yourself permission to start a new hobby or practice an existing

one, join an activity like a book club or a cooking class, or just relax. To give yourself conscious permission, set a goal before the activity. For example, when Dave goes to a movie with friends, on a date with his wife, or does something fun with his kids, but feels a little stressed about his work or home responsibilities, he asks himself one simple question, *What is the outcome I most want from this activity? What is my goal?* and then answers it with a goal statement: *My goal is to have a fun time with my friends*, or *My goal on this date is to be a supportive and loving husband, really listen to my wife, and have fun.*

If you find that it's hard to relax without alcohol, this process can be very powerful. Once Dave integrated this into his life, he was finally able to let go of all his responsibilities and actually have fun and be present for the fun and relaxing activities—all because that was his *goal*. And Dave loves to accomplish his goals. Your **fourth action step** is to start asking yourself the question, "What is the outcome I want from this activity?" right before you do anything to relax and have fun.

Day 26 Action Steps

Up until I found The 30-Day Sobriety Solution, *it always seemed like to conquer alcohol I needed to have a boring and somewhat painful life that would not involve much with social activities. And that I probably would be committing myself to a life with not much fun. But* The 30-Day Sobriety Solution *got me excited about being sober.*

—ANN
30-Day Graduate from New York City

Your state of mind is shaped by your habits. If you go through life doing the same things over and over again, you will continue to get the same results over and over. Today is about discovering and adding new positive habits or activities to your new life.

- **Start exercising.** If you are not already exercising, start today. It can be as simple as taking a brisk walk. Use the "Ten Tips to Start Exercising and Never Stop" to make certain this new habit sticks.

- **Review the 101 new activities list.** Write down all the activities that interest you, and add any others you can think of. Pick one and do something right now to get started. Take the rest of the list and set a monthly recurring appointment so you are consistently reminded to add new activities to your life. You may want to type up and print this list, or your edited version of it, and put it on your refrigerator or your wall.

- **Listen to "Rediscovering Your Joy," the guided meditation on today's companion website.** After reviewing the activities, listen to this guided process and write down any observations and breakthroughs you have right after completing it.

- **Set relaxation and entertainment goals.** Start consciously setting goals (in your mind) and ask yourself, "What is the outcome I want from this activity?" before doing any activity. Whether the goal is to have fun, let go of any stress, socialize, or just learn a new activity without judging yourself, this simple internal "permission slip" process works!

The companion website at http://Day26.Solutions includes some of our favorite exercise books and programs and the "Rediscovering Your Joy" guided process.

Day 27

The Love and Relationship Solution

Surrounding Yourself with Positive and Supportive Relationships

Personal relationships are the fertile soil from which all advancement, all success, all achievement in real life grows.

—BEN STEIN
Writer and actor

Relationships are a requirement for everything in life because you cannot achieve anything without them. Think about all the relationships you have (including relatives, friends, clients, associates, coworkers, staff, retailers, customers, students, teachers, fans, colleagues, audience members, coaches, bosses, board members, or mentors) and how each of those relationships somehow helped you accomplish something in your life. The irony is that in the twilight years of your life, all those *things* you thought you always "wanted" won't matter very much. What will matter are the relationships themselves—especially with your family and closest friends.

To cut back or quit drinking, and to thrive in sobriety, you need to develop and maintain relationships with your friends and family that are positive and nurturing, or you will eventually return to drinking. The Love and Relationship Solution will show you how to heal any damaged relationships from the past, how to avoid another sobriety killer—loneliness—and finally, how to free yourself from what is potentially the most damaging relationship in your life—your relationship with alcohol.

What Will Your Greatest Regrets Be?

We are happy when we have family, we are happy when we have friends, and almost all the other things we think make us happy are actually just ways of getting more family and friends.

—DANIEL GILBERT

Psychologist and author of *Stumbling on Happiness*

Bronnie Ware, a palliative care nurse, spent years caring for patients in the last twelve weeks of their lives and recorded their dying epiphanies. She recognized that there were five regrets that burdened most of her patients, two of which were directly related to relationships: not spending enough time with family, and letting important friendships fade away. "It all comes down to love and relationships in the end,"[1] she concluded.

Most of us can relate to these regrets. The "We really should get together" comments that never get followed up on, or the "I have a big work deadline" that keeps you from attending your kid's sporting event or family get-together. Think back to some of the most fulfilling, meaningful, and happy memories of your life. Were you alone? If not, who were you with? Most likely the memories that stand out include being with your family or your friends.

So what are friends? The best definition we've heard is that friends are the family you have chosen for yourself. And to thrive in sobriety, you must look carefully at the family you have chosen—the people you spend time with, and maybe more importantly, the people you decide *not* to spend time with.

Drinking Is Just a Substitute for Love

If you have love in your life, it can make up for a great many things that you lack. If you don't have it, no matter what else is there, it isn't enough.

—ANN LANDERS (1918–2002)
Author of a syndicated advice column

For most people, problem drinking doesn't happen overnight. It starts off innocently enough with parties, hanging out with some close friends, and celebrating special events. Over time it consumes a little more of your free time, and without even realizing it, drinking becomes a central aspect of your decision making. It affects the activities you do and the places you go, but most importantly it affects the people you spend time with. What starts out as a social habit eventually leads to something you prefer to do in isolation—where drinking alone becomes a normal part of life. Some of you reading this may have reached this stage before starting *The 30-Day Sobriety Solution*, and some of you may not have.

But regardless of what stage you are at, one thing is true for all problem drinkers—excessive drinking, and all addiction, is at some level a substitute for love. As Deepak Chopra and David Simon explain, "Addictive behaviors and substances are poor substitutions for the love that flows in nourishing relationships. Learning to heal our core relationships and cultivate skills in conscious communication can provide the inner peace that eliminates the need for self-medication."[2] Your excessive drinking is trying to fill a void in your life, and a big part of that void is love. And without love, you can become addicted to your guilt, shame, and suffering.

Not only is your drinking a substitute for love, it also acts as a substitute for any authentic and meaningful connection. The ultimate irony is that the family and friends who can help you the most, end up being the exact people you push away the most. And like we discussed on Day 4 in the Forgiveness Solution, you also end up not loving or even liking yourself, and in the end, alcohol becomes your best and only "friend."

Deep down we all want to be loved, and yet our deepest fear is that we won't be. Tony Robbins says that *all* our fears, regardless of our age, gender, culture, or country, can be reduced down to two primary fears: the fear of not being enough, and the fear of not being loved.[3] And it is the feeling of not being enough and the pain of not being loved that ultimately leads many people to drink. But sadly, the effects of excessive drinking usually just make you even less capable and less lovable.

To avoid this downward spiral and create the sober life you want, it's critical that you learn how to heal, rebuild your broken relationships, and also create new healthy relationships.

Your **first action step** for today is to write in your journal about how drinking has negatively affected your relationships and/or led to isolation and loneliness. Have you pushed away family or friends because they don't drink or are critical of your drinking? Have you had outbursts of self-pity or anger that have pushed people out of your life, or maybe even cost you your job? Have you made or kept friends, or spent more time with certain family members, in part because they drink or were supportive of your drinking? Have you spent money on alcohol that required sacrifices elsewhere in the family budget? Have you done things when you were drunk, like getting caught having inappropriate sex with someone, that cost you an important relationship? Do your peers see you as a leader, someone deserving of a promotion, or as the "fun guy or gal" that is always willing to go out and party? Would they want you representing them at an important business meeting over dinner and drinks? Would you rather drink alone? When you drink, do you sometimes feel all alone, even when you are with others?

Merging the Two Yous

It was to the point where I felt it was negatively affecting my relationships and getting in the way of things I wanted to accomplish in life. So I quit [drinking].

—TIM MCGRAW
Country music recording artist in recovery[4]

There are essentially two people living inside of you. Think of it like a split personality, although these two identities are aware of each other, and each of them desperately wants to be expressed.

Who are these two identities? They are the "sober you," who knows alcohol is holding you back and wants more from life, and the "problem-drinker you," who is fully committed to your destructive relationship with alcohol. These two identities are at odds with each other, resulting in an internal struggle for control of your thoughts, beliefs, emotions, feelings, and actions. And because the rules and beliefs of each are so different, they are continuously sabotaging each other's efforts.

Before starting *The 30-Day Sobriety Solution*, the "sober you" was losing this battle most of the time, but was able to take control long enough to start the program. And since Day 1, you have been strengthening and empowering this part of yourself—learning and applying powerful tools and techniques for it to thrive—with the goal of eventually resolving this internal conflict, and consequently removing your overwhelming desire to drink. The challenge is that the "problem drinker you" will not go away quietly. It has been in control for a long time, and it's now scared. It can see things are changing, and eventually it will become desperate to regain control.

Let's revisit Hannah's story from Day 22. Hannah found herself struggling with two "people" battling inside of her: the person who depended on alcohol to live and cope, and the new person who was sober and happy. Hannah said, "I was scared about who I was without alcohol, and now that I really saw sobriety as a possibility, it became even more scary. I let that fear lead me back to where I felt safe—drinking."

As you finally get close to letting go of the "problem drinker you" for good, it is very common for that part of you to make one last stand. And it is in this moment that you will face what perhaps will be your greatest challenge, or your greatest desire to give in to your urge to drink. You can concede control back to the "problem drinker you" like Hannah did for almost a year and return to your old drinking habits, or you can essentially recruit the "problem drinker you" to the "sober you" team.

What do we mean by this? The key to resolving this once and for all is to acknowledge that this "problem drinker you" actually had a positive intention at first. It wasn't out to turn you into an alcoholic or lead you down the path of being an unhealthy problem drinker, it just wanted to feel good. And maybe it even wanted to help protect you from pain you were feeling over a past trauma. Regardless, this desire to feel good initially had an honorable intention, even though it didn't serve you in the long term. The goal is to retrain this part of you, or to essentially make you whole again. Your **second action step** for today is to listen to a guided meditation called the Merge Meditation, which will release you from this internal conflict by merging your two identities, finally freeing the "sober you" to forge ahead unburdened.

Cleaning Up Your Messes

At the time, Lisa [his wife] wasn't sure how to deal with what was happening to me, and to us. She was trying to change my behavior, without realizing that the only person who could change it was me. Negotiating and arguing and threatening don't work, though those are natural responses. But her actions had only been making things worse for both of us, to her frustration.

—PATRICK SWAYZE[5]

Being human means making mistakes. And some of your greatest lessons come from some of your biggest mistakes. These mistakes often involve other people whom you care about and end up hurting. It might be related to your drinking, and it might not. But what it definitely relates to is your ability to thrive.

Leading up to today, you have learned an incredible amount—the importance of optimism and gratitude, your beliefs about emotional sobriety, and the power of your subconscious. Not only do all of these affect your life and the choices you make, but they are also directly affected by the "messes" in your past, especially the ones you haven't cleaned up. If you have hurt others or made mistakes and still feel guilty and ashamed about it, this affects your level of optimism, how you see yourself, your beliefs, your emotional sobriety, your feelings of gratitude, and ultimately your decision to drink or not.

Cleaning up your messes, or making amends, is critical to your happiness. Making amends has been popularized by Alcoholics Anonymous, but it is a practice that everyone who is happy and fulfilled in life embraces. You might notice this is very similar to something we asked you to do in Day 4; however, today we are asking you to explore *all* of your relationships and how they have been impacted by your drinking, which may lead to some new realizations.

The **third action step** for today is to look at your list from the first action step of relationships that drinking negatively affected and make note of any that need to be addressed. Who are the people you care about that you have hurt and whom you need to apologize to? And what do you feel embarrassed, guilty, or ashamed about that you need to forgive yourself for? You need to both clean up your relationship messes with others and forgive yourself for your past actions in order to get totally free.

It is important for you to put this list in a location that you can easily refer back to, and set a target date to clean it up by. It is not usually practical or wise to try to clear all of these up right away. You might be ready to address some now, and you might not be ready to address others for quite some time. Regardless, you want to be consciously aware of this list so if an unexpected opportunity presents itself, you can address it instead of bury it. On the companion website we provide you with a framework to help you complete your list, as well as some valuable conversation guidelines you can follow to help ensure the conversations go smoothly.

Because we know how difficult making amends can be, we highly recommend you pick the easiest relationship first and make a plan to clean it up now. Many of our clients have put this off again and again, until they finally do it and then realize that not only was it easier than they thought, but it turned out to be one of the most meaningful, fulfilling, and freeing experiences in their life.

The Myth Behind Your Messes

My first reaction to it [a diagnosis of Parkinson's disease] was to start drinking heavily. I used to drink to party, but now I was drinking alone and . . . every day. Once I did that, it was then about a year of like a knife fight in a closet, where I just didn't have my tools to deal with it.

MICHAEL J. FOX

Actor and author of *Lucky Man: A Memoir*[6]

One thing more than anything else holds people back from effectively cleaning up their messes—the fear of being vulnerable. We live in a world that celebrates strength, perseverance, knowledge, leadership, individualism, and competitiveness. But when it comes to being vulnerable, most people consider this a sign of weakness. This couldn't be more false.

Being open and vulnerable is one of the most effective ways to connect with another person. The irony is that your fear of being vulnerable is often due to a fear of being judged and not accepted, but the exact opposite is what usually happens. When you openly share your true feelings and concerns—whether it is your challenges with drinking, concerns about inadequacy, or social anxiety—these feelings create an honest, authentic, and compassionate connection. In an article in *Forbes* magazine, Lawton Ursrey writes, "Vulnerability is where we all can: find great strength, realize substantial and meaningful growth through the lens of hindsight reflection, and generate deeper human connections with ourselves and others."[7]

Sharing your story, your faults, and your challenges is what makes you normal, and because we all feel vulnerable at times, you will discover that as you clean up your messes you create a level of intimacy and honesty with the other person that perhaps you have never experienced before.

Keep Your Agreements

Your life works to the degree you keep your agreements.

—WERNER ERHARD

Founder of *est* (Erhard Seminars Training) and The Landmark Forum[8]

Many of your messes might exist because of broken agreements. Agreements are an integral part of any relationship. You are constantly making agreements with your coworkers, spouse, children, roommates, family, friends, and neighbors, and how you handle those agreements impacts the quality of your relationships. Unfortunately, many people go through life not realizing how often they make and break their agreements, especially in their personal lives. In work, we understand that if we commit to do something by a certain time and we don't do it, there is usually a consequence. We lose the trust of our managers and our peers. We might end up being micromanaged on future projects or it might cost us a promotion or a raise. However, once you move into the personal realm, most people tend not to take their agreements as seriously.

You might make agreements to help a friend move, bring cookies for the PTA meeting, mow the lawn, clean the garage, spend more time with the kids, do the dishes, pick up the laundry, feed the cats, walk the dog, keep your house or apartment clean, return the book you borrowed, not mess up the living room, put away the tools, and the list goes on. Most times we agree to things without thinking if we really have the time for them; we don't write our agreements down, and if we do, we fail to read our lists.

As you read this you may be thinking to yourself, *I am not one of those people.* But be aware that most of us are oblivious to all of the agreements that we make and never follow through on.

The **fourth action step** for today is to write down how not keeping agreements shows up in your life. Think about how many times in the past you have told others you were cutting back or quitting drinking and did not. Write down all the broken agreements you think you have and everyone you can think of that you might have a broken agreement with. Consider the agreements you may have made at home with your family and also ones with your friends. Did you agree to save money, help a friend on a special project, or schedule a lunch or some other get-together? Did you tell your spouse or your child that you would attend a specific event, help them with a project or homework, or work fewer hours? How often did you not follow through with your agreements? Or maybe you eventually followed through, but a lot later than you promised.

When you are able to honestly notice and review the agreements you make, you will be surprised at how many you have broken, or completed much later than you agreed to. Stop for a minute and think about all the times someone made an agreement with you and didn't follow through. How did it make *you* feel? Have you ever been stood up by a friend? Or when you were a child, did a parent or loved one not keep a promise that was important to you? If so, you might find just thinking about it brings back a little of that pain.

The truth is that broken agreements dramatically affect your life. They cause you to lose the trust of others, damage relationships, lower your self-confidence and self-esteem, and even negatively affect your energy level. But when you keep your agreements, you gain trust, build self-confidence and self-esteem, and have greater clarity, focus, and energy. In fact, your self-confidence rises or falls in direct proportion to how diligently you keep your agreements.

Contrary to what many think, there is no such thing as unimportant broken agreements. Some broken agreements might have a greater external consequence, but each has a price. For example, if you agree to not drink and drive, but decide to drive after having only "a few drinks" and get in an accident, the consequence could be life changing. If you agree you will start coming home from work on time and don't, it might not seem like much of a consequence, but the truth is that you are slowly eroding the other person's trust in you. And over time, if you add one "small" broken agreement on top of another, the end result is the same—a damaged relationship. In fact, many divorces are the result of years of small broken agreements that add up to a total loss of trust.

As significant as broken agreements are to your relationships, there is one relationship they affect more than any other.

Every Agreement Is with Yourself

Every agreement has one thing in common—you are also making an agreement with yourself. When you tell someone else you will do something, your brain also registers this as a commitment to yourself. And if you don't follow through, *you* are also learning not to trust yourself.

Think about all the personal agreements you only make with yourself, whether they are related to your drinking, what time you are going to get up in the morning, or when you are going to work out. Unfortunately, the agreements you break the most are the ones you make exclusively with yourself. Why? If you have only agreed with yourself to do something, you might feel like it is no big deal if you don't follow through. But it *is* a big deal! When you don't do what you say you will, you create a state of self-doubt and confusion in your mind that ultimately undermines your ability to take action.

So stop reading now and add to your list all the agreements that you make and break with yourself and then write down how this impacts your life.

Whom Do You Spend Time With?

As I worked through The 30-Day Sobriety Solution, *I occasionally found myself surprised at how obvious some of the solutions were, but my drinking was blinding me from seeing them. For example, in the Love and Relationship Solution, when "ranking" the people I surrounded myself with, it was clear how two specific friendships were continuing to hold me back. And because of how much I had already changed at this stage in the program, I found that not only was it relatively easy to let go of these relationships, but it was a critical step to freeing myself from drinking.*

—BRIAN

30-Day Graduate from Trenton, New York

We all know there are people that hold you back. Maybe they are always complaining and blaming, or getting drunk and acting like an idiot, or doubting and making fun of you, or putting others down. People like this are toxic. And if they also drink excessively, they will make it impossible for you to thrive in sobriety if you actively keep them in your life.

One of the easiest ways to change who you are is to change whom you spend time with. It really is that simple. And once you have cleaned up your messes, this becomes easier to change because it is very possible that the best role models in your life are the people that you have avoided or hurt the most because of your drinking.

And if you are going to be successful, you have to start hanging out with successful people. And by "successful," we do not mean someone who necessarily makes a lot of money—the world is full of wealthy people who are unhappy. Being really successful means having healthy relationships with your family and friends, working in a career that you enjoy (or at least grants you the freedom to do the other things you love), being physically and emotionally healthy, and contributing to others in a positive way.

The **fifth action step** for today is to write down a list of everyone you spend any time with—whether they are coworkers, neighbors, family, or people at the bar. Also write down anyone that you would *like* to spend time with, but due to your drinking maybe you have avoided, such as a positive role model in your family. Then next to each name write a number from 1 to 5 in relation to how much they drink. The more they drink, the *lower* the number. For example, a 1 is someone who drinks excessively, and a 5 is someone who doesn't drink much, or at all. If you are not sure, then make an educated guess or rate that person a 3.

Next, write down a second number related to the person's overall influence in your life. If she is an extremely positive influence, she is a 5, and if she is exceedingly negative, she is a 1. Whether or not the person drinks will also affect this rating. For example, you might have a friend who seems happy and successful—he has a great job, is physically fit, and is in a happy marriage—but you know that he drinks excessively. That person would not be a 5, but possibly a 3 or a 4.

Then add these two numbers together. You will notice that this "ranking system" is heavily weighted against drinkers—if they drink a lot, the odds of them getting an overall 5 or better is unlikely. As much as possible, you should avoid spending time with anyone who has a total score of 6 or less, because he or she will eventually pull you down.

An old fisherman's technique says that if you put a crab in a bucket, you have to put a lid on it, or the crab will climb out. But if you put a bunch of crabs in a bucket, you don't need a lid. Why? Because if one crab tries to escape, the other crabs end up grabbing the legs of the escaping crab and pull it back down. This is exactly what a 6 or less does to you—the person pulls you right back down to his or her level no matter how hard you try or how much you want to change.

On the other hand, anyone on your list with an 8, 9, or 10, you would want to spend more time with. When you identify those that are a great influence in your life, make an effort to be with them. And when you are with them, be curious. Ask them about their philosophy of life and what some of their "secrets of success" are, and then try some of them out for yourself. These new "success secrets" might include reading what they read, attending a specific workshop they have attended, or trying out a new morning or evening ritual that has been successful for them.

You might even discover they are great role models in helping you accomplish a specific goal, such as running a marathon, exploring your spirituality, or having a healthier relationship with your spouse. Or he or she may even be a role model for life—someone who embodies the values and character traits you most want in your life, and exemplifies real success to you.

I'm Not Being Fair!

Free of alcohol, I learn that while I do love people, I hate small talk, am bored by the idle banter, and am wildly uncomfortable in big rooms with people I don't know. I want a real connection, not a surface one, and in its absence, I will medicate my discomfort and boredom.

—ROB LOWE[9]

You might be asking yourself, *Isn't it hypocritical for me to avoid others who act exactly like I used to?* No, it isn't. You can let them know that you are making some changes in your life that require you to allocate your free time differently. You are not helping them, yourself, or the people you do want to spend time with by letting the people who are ranked a 6 or less play an active role in your life. The best thing you can do is make positive changes and hope that it will inspire them to do the same.

Another question might be *What if that person is my coworker or my mother?* If it is someone you don't live with, the answer is simple—you must do everything you can to minimize the time and impact they have in your life. If it is a coworker and you socialize with them, stop it. And when you are at work, make sure the time you spend with them is only work related. Don't go on breaks or out to lunch with them. If you sit nearby, find creative solutions, such as wearing noise-reduction headphones if they are allowed.

If it is a close family member, like your mother who lives nearby, you still have to prioritize what is best for you. That might mean hiring someone to help take care of her, or just telling your mother that you are working on a personal or professional project that requires most of your free time right now. Remember, it is critical to put yourself first.

I'm Married to a Bad Influence!

*You are the average of the five people
you spend the most time with.*

—JIM ROHN

One of the most challenging situations is having a spouse or partner who is currently struggling with drinking or is just very toxic and negative. The best thing you can do is to work on yourself, love the person as best you can, and lead by example, showing the possibilities of change. Over time partners will often follow in your footsteps, especially when it's clear you have changed for good. Not only do they want what you now have in your life, they also know that if they don't change they will probably lose you.

On the other hand, if you are living with someone who is violent and abusive, you may need to consider getting totally out of the relationship. As you progress in your sobriety, your willingness to put up with abusive behavior will lessen. And when you escape an abusive relationship and build nurturing relationships in your life, your need to numb out your pain will also diminish.

Regardless of your current situation, whether you are with someone who is just constantly negative and cynical or someone who is intentionally emotionally or physically abusive, we recommend that you set certain boundaries for yourself. The most important boundary is to make and communicate the decision to *not* spend time with your spouse or partner when they are drunk. Ultimately if they don't change, they are going to want you to drink again, so spending time with them while they are intoxicated can be very risky. Without coming across as judgmental or resentful of their drinking or attitude, explain that you love them, but you need to make this change because you are concerned for your own well-being.

The second boundary you can set for yourself is to ask them to see a counselor, work with a therapist, or attend a personal growth workshop—either with you or without you. On the companion website for Day 30 we have listed some of our favorite personal growth workshops. This can be particularly useful if their challenge has more to do with being overly negative than with drinking. Just because you have decided to make this change in your life, your spouse or partner might need some time to accept that he or she may have to change as well. It is important you give them the space to reach this realization on their own.

I'm Being Selfish!

My family and my friends have helped. I don't like yes-people. I don't want yes-people around me; I think they're extremely dangerous. I like people who are honest with me and tell me the truth. I can take it. I have much more respect for someone who tells me the truth. My real friends tell it to me like it is; I don't need "enablers." I need people who tell me what's what.

—NAOMI CAMPBELL[10]

When you make changes like those we recommend, you may feel as if you are being selfish—selfish for not spending time with certain people, selfish for focusing on your own needs and personal growth, and selfish because you know how those changes will affect your family and friends.

Yet the exact opposite is true! It's less selfish! One of the most courageous and *unselfish* things you can do is to cut back or quit an addictive behavior, like drinking.

When you successfully cut back or quit drinking and are thriving in life, you are actually able to finally live a more unselfish life. Not only will your newfound health and happiness naturally inspire others, you'll also have more time and money to volunteer in service of others, whether it is volunteering for a nonprofit group, helping out at your kids' school, or just teaching someone in the neighborhood how to play the guitar, bake a pie, or fix their car. And over time you'll find that you are mostly surrounded by loving, supportive, and positive friends and family.

Day 27 Action Steps

After completing The 30-Day Sobriety Solution *and finally quitting drinking, one of the eye-opening experiences was how many of my drinking "friends" were no longer interested in spending time with me. At first I felt a little hurt, but I quickly realized they did me a favor. They were standing in my way, preventing me from becoming the person I really desired to be.*

—NATHALIE
30-Day Graduate from Winnipeg, Canada

The Love and Relationship Solution can be summarized best by one of Tony Robbins's well-known quotes—"The quality of your life is in direct proportion to the quality of your relationships."[11]

- **Write down all the negative impacts drinking has had on your relationships.** Use the questions in the text (and additional ones on the companion website) and write in your journal about how drinking has hurt your relationships.

- **Listen to the Merge Meditation.** Listen to the guided meditation on the companion website to finally merge the identities of "problem drinker you" and "sober you" so you can release any internal conflict that might lead you back to drinking.

- **Create a list of relationships you need to clean up.** Using your notes about how drinking has negatively affected relationships in your life, make a list of any relationships that you feel need to be cleaned up—whether this means you need to forgive yourself, apologize to a friend or family member, or both. Use the framework on today's companion website to help you complete this list and review the conversation guidelines to help you create a positive outcome from your discussion.

- **Write down your broken agreements.** Most likely many of the relationships you listed in the previous step are messes in part because of broken agreements. Write down all the broken agreements you have made to others—big or small. Be sure to add all the agreements you make and break with yourself and the overall impact on your life.

- **Make a list of everyone you spend time with, and then "rank" those relationships in your life.** Your list should include personal and professional relationships, as well as people you might not spend much time with currently, but would like to. For example, maybe you have a family member that you consider a positive influence, but because you drink you avoid them. After creating this list use the ranking system we discussed above and assign them a final "ranking." As a guide, avoid spending time with anyone with a final ranking of 6 or below.

You'll find some new ideas that will help you build stronger relationships in your life on today's companion website, including tips on how to be a better listener, some advice regarding *what* you say verses *how* you say it, and, of course, the Merge Meditation. Go to http://Day27.Solutions.

The Review Day and Bonus Solution

Nurturing Your Body, Mind, and Spirit

> *Energy of the body has to be kept in balance through the use of other energies that come in the form of breath, food, water, sunshine, exercise, and sleep.*
>
> —DEEPAK CHOPRA[1]

Wow, can you believe you only have two days left after today? As we mentioned at the beginning of Phase IV, you might be surprised to realize you have mixed feelings. You might feel excited and proud of your dedication and achievement, or you might feel, as one of our recent graduates shared, "sad to say good-bye to my companion." Remember, even though you are about to become a 30-Day Graduate, you can still revisit your favorite solutions, continue to expand your knowledge by reviewing all the content on the companion website, work through *The 30-Day Sobriety Solution* again, or perhaps most importantly, support others who are trying to overcome their problem drinking.

Phase IV, "Cultivating Courage and Positive Relationships to Thrive in Mind, Body, and Spirit," introduced you to several ways you can maintain balance in your life. In the last six days you learned a simple but powerful breathing technique that can reduce stress, regulate your mood, create more energy, and release toxins from your body. You discovered the real "cost" of alcohol to your body and why drinking enough water is essential to your health and wellness. You also explored how exercise can improve your body image and confidence, help you sleep better, reduce your risk of cancer, and add years to your life. Finally, you learned that alcohol actually deprives you of sleep, and that getting the right amount of sleep will not only increase your productivity and ability to focus, but will help you live longer and be happier.

In addition, you uncovered the many benefits of meditation, which makes you happier, healthier, less stressed, and more creative. You learned how to identify and overcome fear, and how to live a life that is not controlled by your negative emotions. And yesterday, in the last solution of Phase IV, you explored how to heal your damaged relationships and make your family and friends the most satisfying part of your life.

Visit today's companion website for a review of all of this week's key concepts in addition to your fourth and final bonus solution, the Sobernomics Solution, which teaches you the basics of sobernomics and outlines a path for creating financial wealth and security with your newfound sobriety. Go to http://Day28.Solutions to get started now.

Also, check out the last special video from us and be sure to complete the Phase IV review.

Creating Your Personalized Plan to Thrive in Life

The most effective way I know to begin with the end in mind is to develop a personal mission statement or philosophy or creed. It focuses on what you want to be (character) and to do (contributions and achievements) and on the values or principles upon which being and doing are based.

—STEPHEN COVEY (1932–2012)
Author of *The 7 Habits of Highly Effective People*[1]

You finally made it—Phase V, the last phase of *The 30-Day Sobriety Solution*. We are excited to close out your journey with two powerful solutions, specifically designed to empower you with a purpose and plan to move beyond these 30 days. However, before we get started we want to take a minute and review the ongoing action steps we asked you to do during the last two weeks, or Phases III and IV of the program. Now don't get us wrong, this does not mean you are off the hook for the ongoing action steps from the first two weeks, or Phases I and II. We recommend you also go back and review those, which you can find at the beginning of week 3, or Phase III.

Once again, we know how much we are asking of you during the course of this program. But we also know that if you complete all the solutions in 30 days, as well as all the "required" action steps, it would still take less time than your drinking would have taken from your life in 30 days. One night a week of drinking is about the same amount of time this program takes every week, especially if you sleep in or are less productive during the mornings after you drink.

So let's take a look at these ongoing action steps that will help you thrive in sobriety and thrive in life.

The Top Fourteen Ongoing Action Steps
(in Order of Importance)

1. Journaling. No, this isn't new, but it bears repeating given its importance (Day 1).

2. Meditate daily. Yes, we consider meditation powerful enough to rank it higher than the following action steps (Day 24).

3. Visualize daily the images and short movies that focus on what you want (Day 15).

4. Practice gratitude every morning by thinking about five things you appreciate (making sure to feel the emotion of it as well). Pick one or more people a day to actively appreciate by telling them in person, by phone, or in a letter or email (Day 20).

5. Clean up any past relationships and spend time with people who are good role models. Surrounding yourself with people who are positive role models and who embody the kind of person you want to be is one of the easiest ways to sustain change in your life (Day 27 and Day 4).

6. Review your Total Sobriety Affirmation (Day 18) and ask your 30-Day Vision question (Day 16).

7. Exercise and add some new activities to your life (Day 26).

8. Use the "ask, believe, receive" process and change your negative inputs, such as watching nightly news (Day 19).

9. Feel your fear and take action anyway (Day 22).

10. Take control of your emotions, change your self-talk, and discover the source of your negative emotions and change them (Day 17 and Day 23).

11. Drink enough water and make small healthy changes in your diet (Day 25).

12. Say "yes" more often, and be sure your answer isn't guided by fear (Day 22).

13. Practice the 4-7-8 breathing exercise twice a day (Day 24).

14. Create a vision board, which we asked you to complete within a month, and spend a few minutes looking at it every day (Day 15).

Okay, are you feeling overwhelmed after reading this? Don't be! Many of these won't take more than an extra minute or two and can be done as you go about your normal day. And you can remind yourself by printing and posting your own prioritized list or setting up a daily recurring calendar entry. For example, thinking about five things you are grateful for when you wake up in the morning can be done while you are in the shower or while you are brushing your teeth, and visualizing can be done almost anywhere and anytime. And many of these just take a little bit of extra awareness as you go through your day, such as recognizing and overcoming your fear, discovering the source of your negative emotions, changing your self-talk, and using the "ask, believe, receive" process. And while drinking more water means that you might have to go to the bathroom a little more often, you could review your affirmation statement and ask your 30-day Vision question at the same time.

We don't expect you to do everything on this list every day; however, it is most beneficial for you to do most of them as often as possible if you want to continue to thrive in sobriety after you finish this program.

So, let's get started on the Vision Solution.

The Vision Solution

Discovering Your Life Purpose and Vision

When I chased after money, I never had enough. When I got my life on purpose and focused on giving of myself and everything that arrived into my life, then I was prosperous.

—WAYNE DYER

We believe that each of us is born with a life purpose. Identifying, acknowledging, and honoring this purpose is perhaps the most important action you will take after completing *The 30-Day Sobriety Solution*.

When you take the time to understand what you are here to do—and then pursue it with passion and enthusiasm—you will find that cutting back or quitting drinking will come more easily. The Vision Solution will show you how to finally discover what you are meant to do with your life, and how to create a vision that is perfectly suited to your unique gifts.

What Were You Put on This Earth to Do?

If you don't build your dream, someone else will hire you to help them build theirs.

—DHIRUBHAI AMBANI (1932–2002)
Indian business leader[1]

451

If you are like most people, the idea of finding your life purpose is scary. What if you think you know what your life purpose is, but are wrong? What if you can't figure it out? What if you discover that what you are "supposed" to be doing is completely different from what you are doing today?

We want to start by dispelling a few misconceptions about a life purpose. You do not have to know your life purpose to be successful. You do not have to know your life purpose to be happy. And your "day job" does not have to focus on your life purpose in order for you to be fulfilled. Wherever you are today and whatever you have come through to get here—regardless of your income, age, or status—are perfect. We believe there is a reason and a purpose for your past and a purpose for everything that has brought you to this point in your life. We all have different lessons to learn and paths we have to take.

For example, Jack discovered what he was put on this earth to do early in life. He determined his true purpose and discovered how to inject passion and determination into most of his activities. And he learned how knowing his purpose allowed him to bring an aspect of fun and fulfillment to virtually everything he does.

On the other hand, Dave struggled to discover his life purpose early on. While he always felt a strong connection to helping others and believed he was meant to inspire and teach, his drinking was always a major distraction. It wasn't until he got sober, and started thriving in sobriety, that he could finally clearly see and start to believe in his purpose.

However, Dave realized later that his years of struggling with drinking were a necessary part of his path, and even though he felt like he had wasted almost eighteen years of his life drinking, this was the journey he had to take in order to do the fulfilling work that he now does. He eventually came to understand that what he used to consider his "mess" was actually the foundation of his message. And now he can help people with getting sober *because* of his past, not in spite of it. You might recall from the Lie Detector Solution that sometimes all you need to do to empower yourself in the present and future is to assign a new meaning to something in your past.

Now let's begin to uncover your life purpose!

Discovering Your Life Purpose

Your work is to find out what your work should be. Clearly discover your work and attend to it with all your heart.

—THE BUDDHA[2]

When you don't have purpose, you can lose focus on what you are supposed to be doing and become sidetracked. When you are aware of your purpose and consciously align your activities with it, things seem to take shape and easily fall into place. You naturally attract the resources, people, and opportunities you need.

When you know your life purpose, it becomes a compass that guides you and helps you coordinate and organize all of your actions and activities. To live with purpose means that everything you do is an expression of that purpose. If not, your action plan and goals may not be fulfilling. As Stephen Covey aptly states in *The 7 Habits of Highly Effective People*, if you don't figure out your purpose, you might find you're "climbing the ladder of success only to realize, when you get to the top, you're on the *wrong building*."[3]

Or as another 30-Day Graduate shared, "It [*The 30-Day Sobriety Solution*] allowed me to live a life that was congruent with my values and my desire to lead by example. Today I finally get to fulfill my life purpose, instead of always knowing my drinking would deny me of it." There are countless examples of what can happen when you get clarity and focus on your purpose. There are many ways to define your life purpose; however, we are going to introduce you to a simple four-step process that we have found to be incredibly effective. As you work through the next few sections, have fun. There are no right or wrong answers. The goal is to begin to identify and acknowledge what really ignites your passion and makes you come alive.

The Life Purpose Exercise

The positive format of The 30-Day Sobriety Solution, *combined with all of the life-changing tools and techniques, has done what years of therapy and AA meetings never could—it helped me discover my life purpose, which finally made achieving sobriety a reality in my life for the first time since my husband passed away eight years ago.*

—MISSY

30-Day Graduate from Grand Rapids, Michigan

Up until today it is possible that your life purpose was based on misguided beliefs and experiences. Maybe your parents always told you what you should do when you grew up, or maybe someone convinced you that you were not smart enough or talented enough to do what you wanted to do. Or maybe you let your habit of drinking act as the guiding force instead of your purpose.

The **first action step** for today is to complete a four-step process we call the Life Purpose Exercise. The questions are simple, but the answers won't always come easily. As you do this exercise, accept whatever answers come to mind. Don't judge what comes up, and don't worry about how you would accomplish it, or even if it is possible. And don't think about how anyone else might react. Just answer the questions in writing as honestly as you can. If you would like to be guided through this process, visit the companion website and listen to the Life Purpose Exercise audio.

1. Your Passion

- What excites you? What are you passionate about?
- Think about some of your happiest memories, from childhood to your most recent. What was it about those experiences that made you feel the most alive? What emotions did you experience? Did you feel joy, happiness, fulfillment, freedom, love, or an authentic connection? Who was there?
- What are you doing when you lose all sense of time?
- If money wasn't an issue, what would you do?
- What are your biggest accomplishments, and what made them significant? Was it how the accomplishment made you feel, the difference you made, or the challenges you had to overcome?
- Have you had to overcome specific challenges, like drinking, dyslexia, depression, racism, abuse, or divorce, and through that process realized you can help others do the same?

As you read through your responses, look for any common threads such as emotions, people, or experiences. For example, maybe you remember a variety of events where you felt important, helpful, and energized, and in each of them you were connecting and helping people in a specific way. Maybe you helped a friend handle something he or she was struggling with, or listened compassionately to a loved one share a problem with you, or simply did a favor for a stranger. You may have a passion for helping others, and as you compare those moments you might realize that you felt the most joy when working with a specific group of people, whether it was kids, young adults, elders, or a group of people struggling with addictive behaviors.

Or maybe you felt most alive when you expressed your creativity in specific ways such as painting, creating a website, or writing. Or maybe you felt most alive when you were using your body teaching yoga, building a house, or working in the garden. Whatever you realize ignites your passion and brings you joy, write it down. There are probably many things that make you feel alive, so write them all down.

2. Your Talents and Strengths

- What are you good at?
- What do you think others would say you are good at? Better yet, over the next few weeks, actually ask coworkers, friends, and loved ones what they think you are good at. Sometimes it is hard to be objective about what your unique talents are; however, your friends and family can often see them more clearly than you.
- How do your strengths and talents relate to your passions?
- Do you believe you have a specific talent or strength that you haven't taken the time to develop yet? For example, you might recall the story of "The Alcoholic King" from Day 2, the Purpose Solution, which illustrates how you might have been dreaming about all the great stuff you were going to do in your life while you drank.
- Think about your happiest moments again—what strengths or talents were you using to create them?

Be sure to write down at least three or more of your top strengths and talents before moving forward.

3. Your Legacy

- What lasting difference or contribution would you like to make in your life? Let the answer come from your heart.
- What, if anything, are you doing to create that today?
- Are you making a difference in your current job? In any other way?
- If so, is there a way you can do more of that?

Don't worry about thinking you need to make a *big* impact. You do not have to affect thousands of lives to make a difference, in fact, one of the most meaningful ways to give back is to start with your loved ones, especially if your drinking has previously affected your ability to spend quality time with them. Write down whatever comes to mind.

4. Your Life Purpose

When you combine your passions and your unique strengths and abilities, and use these to consistently make a difference in the world, it is life changing. You will no longer look to external things (like material possessions) to feel happy or impress your family and friends. Instead, you will wake up in the morning feeling the inner sense of peace and joy that in the past you tried to create by drinking.

As you start to write out your life purpose, remember it is only a first draft—nobody gets it perfect the first time. Ideally you want your life purpose statement to be no more than two sentences that describe using some of your passions and strengths in a way that contributes to others in some way.

If you are fortunate enough to already have a career that allows you to express your purpose, that is fantastic. However, this may not be the case. As you become clearer about your true purpose, you may decide that you want to change your career to one in which you can more fully express your purpose, but you might also find that the income generated by your current job gives you the freedom to express your life purpose *outside* of your work. However, if you can find or create a job that is aligned with your purpose, it makes thriving in sobriety a lot easier.

Your life purpose is about giving, not getting. True happiness and lasting fulfillment come from making a difference in the world. But "making a difference" means something different for everyone. For some, that might mean being an honest and talented auto mechanic or the best barista at the local coffee shop. And for others that might mean starting a nonprofit organization. The key here is to remember that whatever makes you come alive will automatically be of service to others. That's part of how we are all wired.

Here are the life purpose statements we created for ourselves using this process. Even though they are both brief, notice how they give insight into our passions, our talents, and the contribution we want to make.

- **Jack's Life Purpose:** Using my unique abilities to speak and write, I inspire and empower people in a context of love and joy to live their highest vision in harmony with the highest good of all concerned.
- **Dave's Life Purpose:** Using my passion and my sense of humor, I inspire and teach people how to thrive in sobriety by applying the principles and techniques taught in *The 30-Day Sobriety Solution*.

This exercise is not about writing the "perfect" life purpose statement. Rather, it's about creating awareness about what your unique abilities are, what really makes you come alive, and how you want to express that in a way that contributes to others. As your awareness expands and you proactively choose activities that better express your unique qualities and desires, you will feel happier and more fulfilled, making thriving in sobriety your everyday experience.

How Thomas Found His Life Purpose

Sobriety has become second nature. I can't really explain it, other than soon after completing The 30-Day Sobriety Solution *I just stopped thinking about drinking, even though I still go to the pub with friends.*

—THOMAS

30-Day Graduate from London, England

Thomas was in his midthirties when he realized his life had not turned out like his childhood dreams. Not that this surprised him, as he had always been a little cynical. Thomas grew up in England, which is known for its strong drinking culture, and like most of his friends he had his first drink at the age of fourteen.

When Thomas started college, drinking was not a big part of his life, but in college he drank a lot, and even though he was surrounded by heavy drinkers, he realized that his drinking was different. He was never satisfied drinking just on the weekends, and the rare nights he didn't drink he would spend thinking about his next chance to drink. By the time he left college, drinking had become an essential part of his life.

Thomas found a variety of jobs out of college, none of which he was passionate about, but all of which funded his drinking habit. But now that he wasn't immersed in college life, he couldn't hide from the reality of how bad his drinking had actually become. He drank almost every night, usually staying out later than his friends and colleagues, and almost always drinking more than they did. Bad hangovers were now a normal part of his life.

Eventually he got a job teaching English, which wasn't his dream job, but it did reignite his passion for literature. Regardless, Thomas continued drinking excessively and rarely was sober for two consecutive days. He could see forty on the horizon. He tried a variety of online programs and self-help books, and even attended a live quit-drinking seminar, but nothing worked until he came across *The 30-Day Sobriety Solution*.

Today Thomas has over two and a half years of sobriety, and he realized that cutting back was not an option for him. Like many graduates, he found that *The 30-Day Sobriety Solution* and his continued sobriety helped him get in touch with his life purpose. He realized that his love for literature was not just limited to reading—his real passion and calling was to write. Ironically, this led him back to the same place where his heavy drinking had begun—college. Thomas shared recently, "I can't tell you how much I'm enjoying being back in school, having the chance to work on my writing, including my second novel, with some big-name authors; it's life changing. Also, I am still happily sober. I go to the gym regularly, I moved in with my girlfriend, and I meditate every day—all things I never would've imagined myself doing."

The Corporate Vision/Mission

Most successful companies, whether they are small businesses or the largest corporations, have clear vision and mission statements.

Having a clear vision and mission statement helps ensure that the company does not stray from its core values and objectives. They keep the company in check and on track, and when someone says, "Let's create this product or service," the company can refer to the vision and mission statements and say, "Wait, this new product or service does not help our end mission; therefore, we need to either rethink our vision and mission or not go this route."

Numerous companies have failed because they strayed from their core mission. Your vision and mission statements will keep you from letting anything—including alcohol—pull you away from fulfilling your life purpose.

Even though having a vision and mission is so critical for your success in life, most of us only have a general idea of what we want to have, do, and be in our life, and almost no one has a written vision statement for their life. Without a vision for your ideal life, you don't know what you are aiming for, and you don't have a way of knowing if you are moving closer to or farther away from the life that will bring you the happiness, meaning, and fulfillment that you want.

Clarify Your Vision of Your Ideal Life

We know that one of the keys to thriving in sobriety is to have a clear and compelling vision of your ideal life. That vision directly affects the actions you take today. As you become clearer about what your ideal life looks like, your daily decisions naturally support that ideal.

In the first two days of this program you started to uncover what the "new you" might look like when you finally removed the destructive force of alcohol from your life. Since that time you have been adding to that awareness by rediscovering your core values, by writing goals, and by completing today's Life Purpose Exercise. Now it's time to use all of this new knowledge to write your vision.

Your vision will describe in detail what your ideal life looks and feels like. To create a balanced and successful life, your vision needs to include the following seven areas: work and career, finances, free time and recreation, health and fitness, relationships, personal goals including sobriety, and contribution to the larger community. In the diagram of the Vision Compass, which appears below, notice what sits in the middle of all these areas—your life purpose. If you keep

The Vision Compass

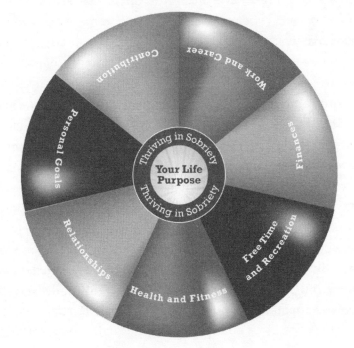

your life purpose in mind as you write your ideal vision, thriving in sobriety will be a natural by-product of successfully accomplishing your goals in the seven main areas of your life.

When you honestly examine your life, you may realize that as a problem drinker, your obsession with alcohol replaced your life purpose. Alcohol can become such a central and often overbearing part of your life that—over time—it simply "drowns" any hope of living a life of purpose and meaning because each of the seven critical areas of life is negatively impacted by your drinking.

The Vision Compass

Yes, gymnastics had been my dream—and it stung like hell to know I'd missed my chance to achieve it. But I somehow knew instinctively that when one dream dies, you have to move on to a new one. The unhappiest people in this world are those who can't recover from losing a dream—whose lives cease to have meaning. I wasn't going to let that happen to me. It was a revelation that would later save my life.

—PATRICK SWAYZE[4]

The **second action step** today is designed to help you clarify your vision. Start by putting on some relaxing music and sit quietly in a comfortable environment where you won't be disturbed. Then close your eyes and ask your subconscious mind to give you images of what your ideal life would look like if you could have it exactly the way you want it. (If you would rather be guided through this process, listen to the Vision Compass Creator on the companion website.)

Remember, at this stage in the journey, it is not necessary to know exactly how you are going to get there. All that is important is that you figure out where *there* is. If you get clear on the *what*, the *how* will become apparent over time.

- **First, visualize your ideal job or career.** Where are you working? What are you doing? With whom are you working? What kind of clients, customers, or job do you have? What does your ideal day at work look like? Is it your own business? Are you able to use your unique abilities and your passions? How does your career make you feel—alive and passionate, grateful and successful, fulfilled and creative?[5] How have your productivity, attitude, and energy improved at work now that you are clearheaded?

- **Now focus on the financial area of your life.** What is your annual income? How much money do you have in savings and investments? What is your total net worth? How much money have you saved from cutting back or quitting drinking and your drinking related activities? Next: What does your ideal home look like? Where is it located? Walk through your perfect house, filling in all of the details. Now picture any other important possessions your finances have provided, such as your ideal car, jewelry, art, clothes, musical instruments, electronics, tools, boats, and so on.

- **Now focus on your free time and recreation.** What are you doing with your family and friends in the free time you've created for yourself? Are you pursuing new hobbies, perhaps implementing ideas from the 101 New Activities list you created? What kinds of vacations are you taking? What do you do for fun? Are you totally abstaining from alcohol or only having a drink or two on occasion?

- **Next, what is your ideal vision of your body and your physical health?** Are you open, relaxed, and feeling happy all day long? Are you full of vitality? Are you physically thriving? Are you flexible as well as strong? Do you exercise, eat good food, and drink lots of water? Have you reached an ideal, healthy weight? Is your blood work healthier? Are you disease free with all of your organs functioning at their optimum level?

- **Now move on to your ideal vision of your relationships.** What is your relationship with your family like? Who are your friends?

What is the quality of your relationships with your friends and family, and how have those relationships changed? Are they loving, supportive, empowering? What kinds of things do you do together? Are you the role model to your children that you always dreamed of being, or are you a new parent? Have you rekindled the passion in your marriage, or met and fallen in love with your soul mate? Or are you enjoying the freedom of being single?

- **Now focus on your personal goals.** Do you see yourself going back to school, getting more training, attending workshops, working with a coach, seeking therapy for a past hurt, or growing spiritually? Do you meditate, go on spiritual retreats with your church or synagogue, or belong to a support group? Are you learning to play an instrument or writing your autobiography? Are you running a marathon, learning to surf, or taking an art class? Are you continuing to use the tools and techniques you learned in *The 30-Day Sobriety Solution*? Are you easily accomplishing personal goals that eluded you during your drinking days?

- **Finally, focus on the community you live in and the community of people with whom you spend the most time.** What does your ideal community look like? How do people interact with each other? Are they friendly, peaceful, supportive, interesting, and fun? What kinds of community activities do you participate in? What about your charitable or volunteer work? What do you do to help others and make a difference? How often do you participate in these activities? Who are you helping? How do you feel?

You can write down your answers as you go, or you can do the whole visualization exercise first and then open your eyes and write down your answers. In either case, make sure you capture everything in writing before you move on to the final step.

Aligning Your Vision Compass

Substance-abusing writers are just substance abusers—common garden-variety drunks and druggies, in other words. Any claims that the drugs and alcohol are necessary to dull a finer sensibility are just the usual self-serving bullshit.

—STEPHEN KING[6]

Now that you have directed your Vision Compass toward what you want in each area of your life, it's time for your **third action step**— to write out a powerful vision statement that is in alignment with your values, purpose, strengths, talents, and passions. Although you might now have a lot of details written down for each area, start by capturing the essence of your vision for each area in only one or two sentences. As you write them, follow these three guidelines.

1. Write them as an affirmation. Use the same guidelines for writing an affirmation that you learned on Day 18 in the Affirmation Solution. Start with the words "I am . . ." Use the present tense. State it in the positive. Be brief. Be specific. Include an *-ing* action word. Include emotion/feeling words. Describe *your own* behavior, not others'.

2. Include your core values. Include some of your core values that you identified on Day 10 in your vision.

3. Include your unique abilities, strengths, talents, and passions. Where applicable, include your purpose, and add all your strengths, talents, and passions to each area.

To help you get started with this process, we have included examples from Dave's vision statement. When you read these, Dave's values, passions, strengths, and life purpose should all become clear.

- **Work and career.** I am drawing on my passion, love of learning, and sense of humor to courageously inspire and teach people how to overcome their addictive behaviors by implementing the techniques taught in *The 30-Day Sobriety Solution*.

- **Finances.** I am thrilled and proud that every year my wife and I have a positive net income across our businesses and are able to save 20 percent of our annual gross income for traveling, retirement, and emergencies.
- **Free time and recreation.** I am passionate, excited, and full of love from spending high-quality time with my family and friends, including participating in fun activities, playing sports, going on dates with my wife, playing with our animals, going to movies, watching funny TV shows, and taking wonderful family vacations.
- **Health and fitness.** I am full of energy, vitality, and strength from fueling my body with nutritious whole foods 90 percent of the time, drinking ninety ounces of water every day, and vigorously exercising for at least twenty minutes five days a week.
- **Relationships.** I am thoroughly enjoying a strong sense of connectedness, love, and support through my relationships and different roles in life as a parent, spouse, coach, friend, peer, nonprofit board member, speaker, author, CEO, and leader.
- **Personal goals.** I am feeling confident, focused, and at peace from daily practicing meditation and visualization and regularly attending personal-growth-related seminars and workshops.
- **Contribution to the larger community.** I am experiencing a deep sense of purpose, fulfillment, and happiness from dedicating at least two hours a week to give back to recovery organizations and individuals who need help overcoming their addictive behaviors.

When you complete this exercise, you will have an incredibly powerful vision that will actually get you excited to get out of bed in the morning. If not, it simply means that you haven't yet dared to write down what you truly want. Keep at it until you do. We'll remind you again not to let not knowing how to go about creating it stop you from writing it down. As we stated before, the *how* will show up once you commit to what you want. There is unbelievable power in having clarity about what you want in life! As you complete the first draft of your vision statement, acknowledge yourself for the significance of this accomplishment. Only a very small percentage of people ever take the time to create a clear and compelling vision for what they want in life.

We recommend you read your vision statement every day—perhaps first thing in the morning. It will take you only one or two minutes at the most. And as you review your statement, you will get additional clarity about what is authentic in your statement and what isn't. When you have these insights, just make a note of them. Over time your small updates will result in an amazingly accurate vision statement that you will love reviewing.

Using Your Vision Compass to Thrive in Sobriety

I got into trouble when I didn't have baseball. It was the catch-22 of my problem: without baseball, I had little reason to stop using; while I was using, I would never be allowed to return to baseball.

—JOSH HAMILTON[7]

Once you have identified what you want in the seven main areas of your life and integrated your core values and life purpose to create a compelling and inspiring vision statement, it's time to bring this vision to life. To help you manifest all the different aspects of your vision, here are our top nine tips to avoid getting "lost" along your journey to thriving in sobriety and life.

1. Review your vision daily. When you review your vision statement, you keep your conscious and subconscious minds focused on what you want. For example, Dave keeps his posted on his medicine cabinet mirror and reads it out loud every morning. Jack keeps his on his iPad and reads it every morning and visualizes each part of it as if it were already accomplished.

2. Share your vision for maximum impact. You'll find that when you share your vision with people who are positive and supportive, not only do they often want many of the same things, they often will offer advice, contacts, time, and resources to help you achieve it. You'll also find that each time you share your vision, it will feel more real and attainable to you. And most importantly, sharing it strengthens your own subconscious belief that you can achieve it.

3. Follow your heart. Whenever you feel discouraged, come back to your life purpose and what really makes you feel good, regardless of the potential reward. Jim Loehr and Tony Schwartz, authors of the *New York Times* bestseller *The Power of Full Engagement: Managing Energy, Not Time, Is the Key to High Performance and Personal Renewal*, write: "Purpose also becomes a more powerful source of energy when it moves from being externally to internally motivated. Extrinsic motivation reflects the desire to get more of something that we don't feel we have enough of: money, approval, social standing, power or even love. 'Intrinsic' motivation grows out of the desire to engage in an activity because we value it for the inherent satisfaction it provides."[8] So focus on doing what brings you the greatest satisfaction.

4. Write out your goals. Go back to Day 6, the Outcome Solution, and use the SMART guidelines to write specific, measurable, attainable, realistic, and time-bound goals for each of the seven areas of your new vision statement. Put your list of goals where you'll see it every day.

5. Embrace high intention . . . and low attachment. Do what you can to create your desired outcomes, and then let it go. Sometimes you will get the intended result by the date you want and other times you won't. Whatever happens, just keep moving in the direction of your vision and your goals. It's also important to remember that sometimes the universe has other plans for you that are better than the ones you had in mind. Remember, it's not the destination that matters nearly as much as the personal transformation you experience along the journey to that destination.

6. Your joy is your inner guidance system. Smartphones and cars now have GPS technology that helps you find your destination and gives you feedback when you get off course. What you may not know is that you also have an internal guidance system that you were born with, and that gives you feedback about whether or not you are on course. And that feedback is simply the amount of joy you are experiencing. When you are experiencing joy, whatever you are doing is aligned with your purpose. It's a feedback system that you've always had, but many of us were taught to ignore or not trust it. From now on, pay attention to your experience of joy. Follow your heart and do what makes you feel most alive.

7. Be patient and practice persistence. Think about the saying, "It takes ten years to become an overnight success." Overnight successes are an exception and actually come from years of work, being incredibly resilient in the face of setbacks, and persisting when many would be inclined to give up. Then a sudden major breakthrough changes everything. Maybe it was being cast in the right role in a hit movie, having a blog post or YouTube video go viral, or gaining the attention of one of the leaders in your industry. Whatever the success, it came from years of work—developing one's craft while being turned down for countless roles, writing a thousand blog posts before one took off, or working in an industry for a decade before gaining attention and recognition. So keep following your purpose and doing what you love, knowing that your success will eventually come.

8. Take action. Keep taking steps, no matter how small, toward the achievement of your vision. When you encounter the inevitable roadblocks and setbacks along the way, the momentum you have created will carry you through.

9. Surround yourself with supportive people. Whether you spend time with role models that have accomplished parts of your vision, learn from leading experts in your field, work with a coach, or belong to a support group, remember that the people you spend time with will dramatically shape the results you experience. So choose wisely.

If your progress in transforming your vision into reality doesn't match your expectations, come back to these tips. Schedule a time in your calendar to review them once a month, and evaluate whether or not you are applying them in your life. The bottom line—you have to use these principles and techniques to manifest your vision.

Always Come Back to Your "Why"

I knew very well right then that this [going to rehab] is actually going to be the best, strongest road to get me back to the two things I love, which are my home life and my career, and finding the balance in those two. I need them both. I've got to play [music], and I need to be a husband. I love it.

—KEITH URBAN
Singer-songwriter[9]

Dave had to overcome countless hurdles to bring *The 30-Day Sobriety Solution* into reality. On many occasions, he seriously considered giving up on his dream, but he always came back to one thing—his "why."

Dave felt he needlessly wasted years of his life suffering with problem drinking, so early in his sobriety he realized that his "why" was to help reduce the amount of time others needlessly suffered. When he felt like quitting, he reminded himself that there might be other people just like him who needed help. And if he could reach them sooner than he was able to be reached, then maybe he could help them save years of their life, their relationships, their health, or their career.

When you discover your life purpose and remind yourself that your unique talents, strengths, and passions make you the only person in the world that can fulfill that purpose, then you will discover that nothing can hold you back. Your "why" will make sure you push through and persevere no matter what setbacks you experience. So your **fourth action step** for today is write down your "why" statement—the deep-down drive that motivates you to keep going. Most likely this is very similar to your life purpose statement, like Dave's is, but is just coming at it from a slightly different perspective.

Day 29 Action Steps

Over the years I have become a fan of self-help, but it wasn't until I did The 30-Day Sobriety Solution *that I was able to really apply self-help material in my life to facilitate a major breakthrough. One of the most important discoveries came from the Vision Solution, which allowed me to finally get clarity around my purpose and vision.*

—LENORE
30-Day Graduate from Dallas, Texas

When you discover and commit to living your life purpose, and you create a vision for the key areas of your life around this purpose, you'll find that your life will actually unfold much more effortlessly than you ever imagined possible. The most important thing now is to stop and do the exercises we have just outlined. Be sure to review the detailed instructions in this chapter, or use the guided recordings on the companion website to complete today's action steps.

- **Write a life purpose statement.** Use the four-step Life Purpose Exercise to (1) identify your passions, (2) recognize your talents and strengths, (3) discover the legacy/contribution you want to make in your life, and (4) integrate these three steps to write your one- to two-sentence life purpose statement.

- **The Vision Compass.** Get clear about what you want by visualizing what your ideal life looks like in these seven areas: work and career, finances, free time and recreation, health and fitness, relationships, personal goals, and contribution to the larger community. We recommend that you listen to the Vision Compass Creator audio on the companion website to guide you through this essential process.

- **Write your vision statement.** Sum up each of the seven areas by writing one or two sentences in the form of an affirmation. Integrate your core values, unique abilities, strengths, talents, and passions where possible. Review your vision statement daily.

- **Write down your "why."** What is your "why"? Write a paragraph about what deep in your soul motivates and drives you to keep going in life in spite of obstacles and setbacks.

On the companion website at http://Day29.Solutions, you can access the guided recordings for the Life Purpose Exercise and the Vision Compass Creator. We also include some additional methods for discovering your life purpose, more examples of people's life purpose and vision statements, more information on how to turn your vision and life purpose into actionable goals, and some inspirational stories.

The Sobriety for Life Solution

Wrapping Up The 30-Day Sobriety Solution

> *As you transcend your own limitations and tendencies, you will naturally show loving-kindness to others. As your own light shines more brightly, you illuminate the world.*

—DAN MILLMAN

Author of *Everyday Enlightenment*[1]

Day 30! Congratulations! We know the level of commitment it takes to complete *The 30-Day Sobriety Solution*, and we applaud your dedication. More importantly, we applaud your willingness to get out of your comfort zone: abstaining from alcohol, working through emotionally challenging exercises, and getting through all the various solutions and resources. As you worked through these challenges, it is likely you found yourself in unfamiliar territory at times. In those moments you had two choices—resorting to your familiar coping mechanism by drinking, or embracing your discomfort knowing it is living on the edge of your comfort zone that facilitates the greatest growth and progress toward thriving in sobriety and thriving in life.

Before starting *The 30-Day Sobriety Solution*, you had unknowingly put in place numerous self-imposed limits, specifically limits on your ability to successfully cut back or quit drinking and thrive in sobriety. Today it is likely you have freed yourself from those limits. You have broken your past conditioning and opened up a whole new world of opportunity. How much success, happiness, and fulfillment you experience beyond this program is up to you. You can choose to slowly let your old conditioning take back over, or you can choose to continue down the path of personal development beyond these 30 days by applying what you have learned.

The Sobriety for Life Solution will show you how to make sure your self-imposed limits are gone forever, so that thriving in sobriety is a lasting reality for you.

Can You Become a "Normal" Drinker?

We believe that *anything is possible*, at least within reason. There is no question that some people can go from being an alcoholic to having the coveted "take it or leave it" attitude of a "normal drinker." And there are numerous studies[2] that validate this fact, but that doesn't mean we recommend it. And in fact, for most of you, we don't.

The obvious reason that you want to be a "normal drinker" is that the opposite of normal is "abnormal." And who wants to be abnormal? "Normal drinker" is one of those phrases used commonly by our clients, which is why we reference it. However, the first thing you need to drop is this label from your vocabulary. The act of using it, or thinking about being a "normal drinker," actually holds you back. It creates a belief that abstinence is not normal—and by now you have enough information to know that isn't true.

In Day 1, the first guideline was to abstain for at least 30 days (the 30-Day Reboot), but we also said you could wait until Day 8. So if your goal is to cut back, the requirement to abstain for 30 days still stands. We also mentioned that this program reaches those of you who are "all along the continuum of problem drinking, which means that no cookie-cutter, one-size-fits-all solution exists." So to answer the question "Can I have a healthy relationship with alcohol—where I only drink on occasion and rarely more than one or two drinks?" we need to explore some additional topics, and then return to it. Even if you already know that complete abstinence is your path, read these next four sections carefully, as they will still be of great value.

Last, we want to remind you that we are using this definition of sobriety: "moderation in or abstinence from consumption of alcoholic liquor or use of drugs."[3] So when we say "sobriety," we do not necessarily mean abstinence only.

Are You Depriving Yourself?

I now set off on a path of attempting controlled social drinking in the way I saw other people do it. I studied them, and for a while my life consisted of going up to the Windmill for lunch and having one or two lagers, and then in the evening maybe a glass of wine with dinner or a scotch after eating. The reality was, as much as I may have been trying to establish some kind of normal day like other people, what it really amounted to was these two drinking sessions with me desperately trying to kill the time in between them, often by sleeping all through the afternoon. This schedule was purely alcoholic in its development and focus, and our life just crumbled as a result.

—ERIC CLAPTON[4]

Honestly ask yourself the following questions: *What do you really want when you think about drinking? What are the first thoughts that enter your mind? Do you still think about getting drunk? Who comes to mind when you think about drinking? Do they have issues with alcohol? What future events do you think about when you consider drinking again? Are these occasions where you would usually drink a lot?*

One of the greatest challenges of transitioning from being a problem drinker to someone who has a healthy relationship with alcohol is that your history with drinking is dominated by memories and experiences of drinking to excess. The idea of having only one or two drinks is a foreign concept, and in the past you would have thought you were depriving yourself.

Many of our clients share how annoying it is when they could only have a couple of drinks the entire night. In fact, most considered it *such* an annoyance they wouldn't even bother drinking at all. *Does drinking one or two drinks make you feel like you are making a sacrifice?* If the answer is yes, then we can virtually guarantee you will *not* be successful cutting back.

A true "take it or leave it" attitude means it simply doesn't matter to you. For example, can you imagine walking into a casino and not gambling at all? Or gambling for just a few minutes? Assuming you do not have a gambling addiction, the answer is probably yes. You are able to play a few hands of blackjack, get a call from a friend who needs help, and leave the table without thinking twice. This is exactly how you should feel about drinking. If not, it is likely you have not done the work you need to do in order to return to a healthy relationship with alcohol.

If you find that the questions above still trigger thoughts and desires of excessive drinking, then it is likely that beginning to drink again will eventually lead you back to where you started. You might be able to successfully "control" your drinking in the beginning, but if you don't have a true "take it or leave it" attitude, you will become obsessed with planning and managing it. And this is not healthy or sustainable.

"Testing the Water"

In AA, people feel that if they slip and have a drink they're lost entirely, back to day one. That attitude in itself can sometimes be enough to turn a slip into a full relapse, since it can lead to the attitude that if you've had one drink, you're off the wagon, so you may as well keep drinking.

—DR. HOWARD J. SHAFFER

Psychologist at the Center of Addiction
Studies at Harvard Medical School[5]

At some point, you might decide that you are going to drink again. But rather than this being deliberate and planned, it might be a spontaneous decision. You may find yourself at a party or have a lousy day, and decide to drink. This is okay, and more common than you think; however, what you do after this can change everything.

In part, this is related to an abstinence-only approach. There tends to be a collective belief around this topic that can be highly destructive. Alcoholics Anonymous has popularized the concept of counting days since your last drink as a way of celebrating your success. Although we love the idea of celebrating your successes, this approach sometimes has an unintended side effect.

It feeds into the all-or-nothing attitude that many problem drinkers have, and when you have one drink, you experience a major letdown. Instead of chalking it up as valuable feedback, you feel like you've lost all of your previous "days" or "years" of continuous abstinence and have to start all over. Now you are back to Day 1. And if you attend AA, this letdown can be even more pronounced.

For example, many AA meeting formats include a question such as, "Is there anyone present who is at his first AA meeting, or is in his first 30 days of sobriety?" If you have to answer yes to this question after all the work and progress you have made, then you can end up feeling like a failure. And this can lead to an attitude of "Oh, well, I am starting over, so I might as well go party for a few more days and get it out of my system." Before you know it, one weekend turns into one week, and then one month, and it could be years before you can turn things around again.

Some of our graduates had over a year of sobriety, and then decided to "test" drinking again, sometimes with just two or three drinks. After this experience, they realized that drinking wasn't a positive influence and returned to abstinence. If they were to follow standard AA guidelines, they would have to start over counting days, but we believe this isn't a fair representation of the changes they have made in their lives. It is critical that you don't judge your "testing the water" as an all-or-nothing event that somehow redefines the work you have done in the past as no longer applicable. If these 30-Day Graduates had treated their return to drinking as a complete failure requiring them to start all over, who knows if and when they would have become sober again.

Sometimes the information you get from "going back out there" can be invaluable. We are not saying you should drink again just to get that information, but if you decide to, then make sure you learn from the experience. As long as you practice some basic self-awareness and are honest with your feelings around the experience, it will be obvious whether or not you can maintain a healthy relationship with alcohol.

Thriving in Sobriety Through Abstinence

For most of you, abstinence is going to be the path that best serves you. And you are not alone.[6] Conservative estimates show that at least 23.5 million American adults are living in recovery from alcohol or drug abuse,[7] and this doesn't include all the teetotalers who just choose to not drink or use drugs in the first place.

Sometimes the real magic of thriving in sobriety comes when you actually decide you are done with drinking for good. When you know that door will never be opened again, you start to really understand your relationship to alcohol. The back and forth can be emotionally exhausting, and can take you away from doing the work you need to do. It goes back to the 100% Solution from Day 1—when you are not 100% committed to abstaining, you let the ongoing debate continue in your head.

However, when you decide you are never going back, the real

you shows up. You cannot hide behind the hope that you will drink again, which frees you to deal with the emotions and fears that often accompany the plan to never drink again. And once you have overcome those, you truly are free to live a thriving life in sobriety.

Thriving in Sobriety Through Cutting Back

In 1995 Audrey Kishline knew her drinking was a problem, and even though she had practiced abstinence at times, her goal was to cut back. After doing a lot of research, not only did she believe she could successfully do this, she founded Moderation Management, a group dedicated to helping teach others how to manage their drinking. Although the program grew quickly, she failed to apply the principles to her own life and drank more than she was "allowed." Eventually she drove while intoxicated and took the lives of Danny Davis and his twelve-year-old daughter.[8]

Yes, you can successfully cut back your drinking for the rest of your life, but if that is your goal, we have some recommendations so your story doesn't end up mirroring that of Audrey, who went to prison, continued drinking (often heavily) throughout the rest of her life, and committed suicide in December 2014. First, *you need to journal*—specifically and honestly—about your experience with drinking. The nature of addiction is to trick you into thinking you are under control when you are not, which is why moderation doesn't work for so many people. If you decide to drink again, then take an analytical approach. Write down your experience—when you drink, how much you drink, and with whom. As long as you are honest, it will be clear whether you can successfully maintain a cutting-back approach.

Second, *never drink alone*. No exceptions. This is not healthy. And ideally don't drink at home either. Keep your home environment healthy and completely free from alcohol, if possible. When you limit your drinking to social situations outside of the home, it dramatically improves your ability to be successful in cutting back.

Third, *pay attention to the quantity and alcohol content of what you drink*, especially in relation to your new tolerance. Remember, when you stopped drinking for a while, you changed your tolerance. If you decide to drink the same amount of alcohol you did in the past, it can be very dangerous. Two drinks today, after a period of abstinence, might make you feel buzzed or even drunk. Pay special attention to serving sizes or measurements, because a bar might serve you a glass of wine that is between five and six ounces, but if you go to a party, you might be served a glass with ten to twelve ounces.

Fourth, *avoid binge drinking situations* and drinking practices that often accompany binge drinking. Don't do shots or put yourself with groups of people where most are going to be drinking excessively. It isn't fun, and you might even discover how dumb people are (and you were) when drinking excessively. It can easily trigger you to excessively drink. If you find yourself in these situations, don't drink at all—that way it is far less likely that you will "give in" and decide to go from two drinks to too many.

If you choose to drink, drink slowly. Take your time, and don't be afraid to not even finish your drink. If you are drinking something at room temperature such as red wine, sip it instead of going through drinks quickly like you did in the past. Your new approach should be very different from your old approach, and *the best way to make sure you don't fall back to your old habits is to replace them with new healthy habits*.

Last, notice if you seem to be craving alcohol. Cravings give you fantastic feedback because they let you know that you do not have a healthy relationship with alcohol. *If you have cravings, it is time to abstain*—you can always revisit cutting back as an option later on.

When you are really ready to have a healthy relationship with alcohol, the ultimate irony is that you won't care. The "take it or leave it" attitude will be fully entrenched, and it simply won't matter. Dave always felt very confident that he could have a drink on occasion and be completely fine, but he realized that he just doesn't care. However, he knows the people who love him care and would understandably be concerned, so he chooses to not drink. This choice is made even easier because alcohol no longer holds any power over his life.

Deciding Your Approach

I continue to use the solutions I learned in The 30-Day Sobriety Solution *to improve my connection to the person I want to be and know I can be. I move closer to that person every day.*

—DAN

30-Day Graduate from Jackson, Wyoming

Think back to a serious past relationship that ended in a breakup, possibly after a lot of tough conversations and struggling back and forth. Maybe you were even engaged or living together at the time. After you broke up, how often did you see each other? Was it easier if you didn't see the other person at all, at least for a while? You would probably agree that seeing someone after a breakup isn't ideal.

The process of cutting back or quitting drinking is much like ending a serious relationship. In fact, it is sometimes much harder, as you try to integrate two identities that have been "battling" each other—the "sober you" and the "problem drinker you." Just like when ending a human relationship, if you keep feeding alcohol and hope to the "problem drinker you," you make moving on very hard.

However, if you don't see the other person again until years later, it is often much easier. Similarly, for cutting back to really be a successful option, you need a lot more than 30 days of abstinence. *We recommend a minimum of six months*. And most of our cutting-back success stories came after a year or more of no drinking. The best approach is to not worry about it. If you know you are not ready today, then decide now that you will revisit this question in one month, six months, or whatever amount of time feels right to you. But whatever time frame you decide on, stick to it.

So, your **first action step** after reading today's solution is to make this decision: Are you going to move forward with abstinence (at least for the near term) and revisit the question later? Are you going to move forward with abstinence as your long-term approach? Or are you going to see if cutting back is a long-term option for you— making sure to follow our recommendations?

The Gift of Giving Back

This is the only perfection there is, the perfection of helping others. This is the only thing we can do that has any lasting value or meaning. This is why we are here. To make each other feel safe.

—ANDRE AGASSI[9]

One of the most surefire ways to ensure your success and happiness in sobriety is to find a way to give back—especially to those who are struggling with some of the same challenges you have overcome, as well as to any of the many other worthy causes and individuals in need of support.

The Corporation for National and Community Service (CNCS) released a report indicating that "volunteering provides individual health benefits in addition to social benefits. This research has established a strong relationship between volunteering and health: those who volunteer have lower mortality rates, greater functional ability, and lower rates of depression later in life than those who do not volunteer."[10]

When you offer to help others with no expectation for them to reciprocate, it has an incredibly powerful and positive impact in your life. All human beings—including you—have a core need to connect with others, and a great way to connect is by lending an unselfish hand. Dan Millman writes, "Find a form of service that calls to you, that suits your abilities, aptitudes, qualities, and interests, that makes time fly, that draws forth your best, that tells you you've arrived home and found yourself."[11]

Your **second action step** for today is to decide how and where you want to give back. Use your list from the Positive Addiction Solution on Day 26 to see if any of the activities you have chosen involve giving back, or if you can choose to do them in a way that gives back. Take a minute and write down some things you would like to do over the next six months to contribute to the lives of others.

Giving back and being of service to others addresses another important need we have discussed—your serotonin deficiency in early sobriety. In *The Power of Intention,* Wayne Dyer writes, "Research has shown that a simple act of kindness directed toward another improves the functioning of the immune system and stimulates the production of serotonin in both the recipient of the kindness and the person extending the kindness. Even more amazing is that persons observing the act of kindness have similar beneficial results. Imagine this! Kindness extended, received, or observed beneficially impacts the physical health and feelings of everyone involved!"[12]

Remember, you make a difference whether you want to or not. It just depends on whether you are going to make a positive or negative difference.

Are You Moving Closer to or Farther from Your Next Drink?

It's easy to make things more complicated than you need to, when in fact the answer is right there. In the Attraction Solution on Day 19, we introduced you to the question "Am I moving closer to or farther from my next drink?" We recommend that you ask yourself this question at least once a week. When you consciously pay attention to where you are, especially in regard to the direction you are headed, it becomes surprisingly easy to catch yourself before it's too late. You might want to post this question on your bathroom mirror so you are sure to see it every day—especially when you are shaving or putting on your makeup before going out to a social event.

You can also ask yourself variations of this question in relation to each of your goals, relationships, and any other area of your life where you want to ensure that you are making progress. *Am I moving closer to or farther from having the relationship I desire with my spouse/ partner/child/parent?* When your answers continue to show that you are moving away from your desired goal, you need to adjust your behavior.

If you are unsure, ask yourself this follow-up question: *On a scale of 1 to 10, with 10 being high, how convinced am I that I will stay sober?* To get even more clarity you can add a time frame to the end of the question, such as *for the next day, the next week,* or *the next month.* If your answer is less than an 8, there is reason for concern; however, not all 8s are created equal. For some of you an 8 might mean "very convinced," and for some of you anything below a 10 is a risk— so once again make sure you tailor this to your own unique rating system.

Do You Miss Happy Hour?

My new drug is golf. It's my drug of choice. I also think that if I go back to using, all of this will go away. I'd rather have my big trailer.

—SAMUEL L. JACKSON[13]

Some of the most successful and happy people we know allocate an hour of their day to themselves. Motivational speaker Tony Robbins refers to this as the "Hour of Power," where you integrate some of the most beneficial personal growth practices to help you gain clarity, appreciate the present moment, become more physically fit and vibrant, and get mentally prepared to take on your greatest challenges.

Now that you are almost done with *The 30-Day Sobriety Solution,* we highly recommend you implement a new kind of "Happy Hour" for your new life thriving in sobriety. And you can even start this hour at the same time you used to start drinking; however, many people also find doing this in the first hour of the day sets them up for success the whole day. We recommend you test both approaches and see what works best for you.

This hour can include a variety of different solutions you have done, or are already doing daily. For example, you may start with an integrated meditation practice for fifteen minutes, which includes meditation, visualization, gratitude, and sometimes asking yourself an important question. Then exercise for fifteen minutes, combining aerobic and strength training, while occasionally repeating one of your favorite empowering affirmations. And finish off the hour by making a simple and healthy breakfast, and—instead of watching the news, which is mostly negative—reading an inspiring book during or after eating.

Your **third action step** for today is to take a few minutes and design your new "Happy Hour." However, if this seems like a big-time commitment, start small. You can even start with just five minutes, five days a week, and then increase your time by five minutes every week. For example, the first week you might do a five-minute meditation, then the second week you add five minutes of exercise after your meditation, and the third week you add an additional five minutes to exercising. There is no right or wrong way; just get started.[14]

The Defining Characteristic of Thriving People

One defining characteristic of successful people is that they never stop growing and learning. They are continuously looking for ways to improve themselves both personally and professionally. In many ways the opposite of growth is stagnation and boredom, and when boredom lasts for too long, you are likely to seek out unhealthy ways to break free from it such as drinking, using drugs, overeating, gambling, inappropriate sex, and high-risk behavior like driving too fast. Successful people are rarely bored because they are constantly developing themselves physically, emotionally, and spiritually by reading, exercising, playing sports, playing an instrument, spending time in nature (which is rarely boring), traveling, attending workshops, and constantly working on the fulfillment of their most meaningful and heartfelt dreams. Most importantly for you, in relation to *The 30-Day Sobriety Solution*, we recommend you keep revisiting and working the solutions on a regular basis.

This doesn't mean that you have to engage with the same level of time and effort you have for these last 30 days, but it does mean that continual personal growth has to be part of your life moving forward. The great news is that there are countless fun ways to continue to bring personal growth into your life. Here are some suggestions.

- **Repeat *The 30-Day Sobriety Solution.*** We regularly hear comments like this one, "The third time through the program was amazing." Doing the program again will help you better integrate the tools and techniques into your life, overcome other addictive behaviors (smoking, overeating, gambling, prescription medications, and so forth), and more importantly, result in additional breakthroughs. We know some people who have done the complete program four times, and others who have repeated the same day ten times. Repetition adds value!

- **Read memoirs of people in recovery.** Many of the high-profile quotes in this book come from memoirs. When you read other stories of recovery and success, you will have insight into your own story. To make best use of these books, take notes, and spend some time journaling about a particular person's story and what really affected you and why. We have included a list of our favorites on today's companion website.

- **Read self-help books and books about the lives of people you admire.** We have referenced a lot of our favorite books throughout this program that can add incredible value to your life. You can also read autobiographies of the people you most admire and respect. Take notes, and apply at least some of what you learn. There is also a list of our recommended self-help books on the companion website.

- **Attend conferences, workshops, retreats, and seminars.** A live training facilitated by experienced instructors can be one of the best investments you ever make. When you are able to learn and apply great content in a group setting, it can lead to incredible growth, inspiration, and also new friends for life. Some of our best friends today are people we met in training seminars we attended. A list of our favorite conferences, workshops, retreats, and seminars is included on today's companion website.

- **Remain teachable and open.** In life, you will sometimes be a teacher, but you always need to be a student. If you are not willing to learn from others and to look at things from a different perspective, you will stop growing. On the companion website we have included a list of other ways you can continue to grow.

- **Make your car your college.** If you spend more than ten minutes commuting a day, use some of this time to listen to inspirational and educational CDs, podcasts, or audiobooks. Some of our favorites are listed on today's companion website.

- **Don't let the top two "sobriety killers" creep into your life.** Although we have mentioned various "sobriety killers" throughout the program, there are two that we regularly see lead people back to excessive drinking—boredom and loneliness (or isolation). Revisit the 101 New Activities list and pick something new to do every day or week. And we have some information on how to join or start up your own mastermind group on the companion website.

Day 30 Action Steps

Before success comes in any man's life, he is sure to meet with much temporary defeat, and, perhaps, some failure. When defeat overtakes a man, the easiest and most logical thing to do is to quit. That is exactly what the majority of men do. More than five hundred of the most successful men this country has ever known told the author their greatest success came just one step beyond the point at which defeat had overtaken them.

—NAPOLEON HILL[15]

- **Decide on your plan.** Write down what your strategy is for the next 30 days regarding drinking—specifically stating whether you are going to cut back or abstain. If you have decided to abstain for the short term (instead of the long term), how long will you "test" this approach out before revisiting? If you decide cutting back is your plan, make sure you review and use the guidelines we covered for this approach.

- **Write down how and where you want to give back.** Pay attention to what type of activities fit your strengths, qualities, passions, and interests, and pick one or more ways that you would like to contribute and give back over the next six months.

- **Design your new "Happy Hour."** Start a daily ritual dedicated to your overall health, wellness, and vitality that includes the solutions we have covered in this book—such as meditation, visualization, exercise, practicing gratitude, and eating healthy. This is best done at the start of the day. Begin with just five minutes a day, five days a week, and add additional time each week until you have built up to a full hour. Consider starting this new routine the same time you used to start drinking.

- **Review your "before you" and your before photo, and keep journaling.** Take a minute and acknowledge how far you have come since you started the program. It is human nature to focus on the gap between your ideal vision and your actual results and overlook what you have accomplished and how far you have actually come, so go back in your journal and read the "before you" exercise that you did on Day 2. Also look at the photo you took of yourself from Day 1, and consider taking a picture of yourself today and see if you notice any positive differences (less bloating, clearer eyes, healthy skin). Last, but not least, we want to remind you to keep journaling, at least every few days. It doesn't have to be a lot, but a life worth living is a life worth recording. Journaling provides constant insights and is a way for you to see who you are today and how far you've come on your journey of thriving in sobriety.

As you finish the final sections for today be sure to celebrate your successful completion—it takes an extraordinary amount of dedication and perseverance to work through all the content and action steps, and you should be incredibly proud. So right now take a moment, shut your eyes, take a deep breath, and really acknowledge and appreciate yourself for all that you have accomplished over the course of this program. As always, you can find the companion website for today at http://Day30.Solutions, where we list some of our favorite books, CDs, and trainings. In addition, we have included our favorite solutions, tools, and resources from *The 30-Day Sobriety Solution* that you can use to easily continue moving forward.

WRAPPING UP *THE 30-DAY SOBRIETY SOLUTION—NOW WHAT?*

The 30-Day Sobriety Solution helped me accomplish so many goals and "firsts" in my life, such as my first sober birthday as an adult. This success helped me believe that I don't need alcohol to celebrate special occasions, even New Year's Eve and the Fourth of July—two holidays I was certain I needed to drink to enjoy.

—BYRON

30-Day Graduate from Phoenix, Arizona

You are about to embark on an amazing year, one that will surely include some memorable and exciting moments, as well as some challenging and tough ones. And mixed within these moments will be a year full of firsts. This might include your first birthday as an adult without drinking, or the first Christmas, Fourth of July, Thanksgiving, or wedding anniversary where you are not drunk. Each first brings you one step closer to becoming the person you want to be and are meant to be. Each first brings you closer to the life you always knew, deep down, you could live.

By today, you know how far you have come; you, and others around you, can see the transformation you have made in just 30 days. Or perhaps you may not be so sure. You might feel a little different and notice you are thinking somewhat differently, but you are not sure if you have really changed that much. Our experience is that the transformation does happen—almost without fail—as long as you do the work we have outlined. However, for some people it works more quickly, maybe because they have already done a lot of personal growth work or have a less challenging history to deal with. And for others, it just takes a little longer to get the level of honest self-awareness necessary to really break through and overcome some of the limiting patterns that have been in place for decades.

One day in the near future, you will look back and surprise yourself. You will think back to the person you were in the past, and you won't recognize that person. You will realize that all your work and faith paid off, and that each little change you made added up over time to completely transform who you are for the better.

The only thing that can hold you back from experiencing this transformation is giving up. Remember, our greatest triumphs often come after our darkest and most challenging moments—as if the universe is saying, "I am going to give them one last huge test to make sure they are really serious." And when you pass that test, all of a sudden you go from feeling like a fish out of water to swimming with the current.

You find that a sense of natural congruency exists—starting with your core values and continuing through your thoughts, beliefs, feelings, and actions—that leads to the outcomes you want and expect. You discover that you can actually listen to and trust your intuition, and you no longer struggle with erratic emotions, negative thinking, and the overwhelming bouts of sadness and disappointment you experienced when drinking.

Instead you are able to quickly notice and identify when you have a setback, what the root cause is, appreciate it for the lesson it teaches you, and then overcome it. You find that so many of the tools and techniques you learned have not only helped you to thrive in sobriety, but have led to better relationships with your loved ones, better finances, more career opportunities, new friendships, and on top of that, you are the healthiest you have been in many years.

As you move forward beyond today, know that your future will take care of itself as long as you take care of the present. Achieving success and thriving in sobriety is an exciting journey—enjoy every moment of it! It has been an honor and a privilege to be your guides up to this point, and we eagerly look forward to the day where our paths cross and we have the opportunity to get to know one another. Here's to your new life thriving in sobriety!

Jack Canfield and Dave Andrews

THE 30-DAY GRADUATES

Share Your Story

Once you have successfully completed *The 30-Day Sobriety Solution*, we would love to hear from you—not only your stories of success, but also your challenges and anything that was difficult for you. Let us know how you are doing, what solutions were the most valuable for you and why, what was the most difficult for you and why, as well as anything else you would like us to know.

Nothing is more powerful than a true story—*your story*—to inspire others. When people read about others like themselves who have successfully faced and overcome the same challenges and obstacles they are faced with, they become inspired and they start to believe— not only that it *is possible* to change, but that they *can* change. But this can only happen if people like you share their stories, just like the courageous people whose stories we included in this book. In fact, you might have even decided to buy this book because you read one of the testimonials we included in the front of the book or one of the stories in the book itself.

Whatever "your" story is, it might be exactly what someone else needs to hear in order to inspire him or her to take that first step.

To share your story of hope, courage, and recovery—please go to the companion website at http://30DaySuccessStories.com or simply email your story to SuccessStories@The30DaySolution.com. Please be assured that by sharing your story you are not giving us permission to publish it. Our staff will review it and, if we are interested in publishing it, we will contact you for approval, including the option to share your story anonymously.

Website: http://30DaySuccessStories.com
Email: SuccessStories@The30DaySolution.com

ACKNOWLEDGMENTS

Our Mutual Acknowledgments

Stephen Hanselman, our literary agent at LevelFiveMedia, who believed in this book when many others didn't. Steve has been described as "the agent every writer dreams of having." We agree. Your friendship, faith, expertise, and guidance are so appreciated.

Julia Serebrinsky, who helped edit the original book proposal.

Judith Curr, president and publisher of Atria Books, who immediately caught the vision of what we were doing and championed the book.

Leslie Meredith, our editor at Atria, for your honest and thoughtful feedback and your commitment to delivering excellence. Your contribution and insight were indispensable.

Jennifer Phelps, for your incredible dedication and commitment to this project. You did it all: editing, fact-checking, rewrites, and even helping us maintain the woman's perspective throughout. Your excellent writing ability and being willing to go the extra mile no matter what are what kept us sane, especially during the last couple of weeks of the editing process.

Tehsin Gul, from Pakistan, who designed the original cover concept for the book, and all the other great designers who submitted their cover designs on 99designs.com.

Steve Harrison, co-owner of Bradley Communications, for introducing us to each other.

Anoop, Anya, Brad, Brian, Cheryl, Christina, Christopher, Forrest, Jerry, Karla, Lenore, Liz, Meg, Nathalie, Pat, Sheira, Tamara, and Teresa—the wonderful group of eighteen people who read the first draft of the book, completed all the exercises, validated that the program worked in the form of a book, and gave us valuable feedback for improving it. Thank you all for your time, your courage, and your commitment.

Ann, Byron, Chris, Dan, Desiree, Diane, Hannah, James, Jessica, John, Matthew, Mike, Robert, Susan, and Thomas—for so courageously sharing your stories of success in quitting and cutting back drinking with us. Even though your names have been changed, you know who you are. Your willingness to openly and honestly share your experience with *The 30-Day Sobriety Solution* has been invaluable in assisting us to reach and help others, and we are forever grateful for you agreeing to be part of this book.

Jack Canfield's Acknowledgments

Dave Andrews, for originally creating "The 30-Day Sobriety Solution" online coaching program, on which this book is based. Your decision to integrate the best ideas and techniques from the human potential movement with the best from the recovery movement was a needed breakthrough whose time had come. I have enjoyed the process of writing this book with you—all of it, from the late night conversations to the silly humor that kept us sane. You have been great to work with.

My wife, Inga, who bravely put up with the long hours and several lost weekends, especially between Thanksgiving and Christmas, when the final push was on to finish the book. I appreciate how you not only didn't complain (too much!), but you also went out of your way to lovingly support me by scheduling massages, doing all the shopping, and doing more than your fair share of cooking and cleaning up.

Patty Aubery, my partner and co-CEO of the Canfield Training Group, for running the company virtually by herself for the months I was completing the book, and for always being there to encourage me to keep going when I feel tired or overwhelmed. Thanks for always believing in me and demanding my best even when I can't yet see it.

Veronica Romero, my personal assistant and office manager for the Canfield Training Group, who took care of virtually everything else for months, in addition to helping with typing, photocopying, scanning, faxing, and emailing chapters back and forth between Dave and me, and who oversaw getting all the permissions for the cartoons that appear in the book.

Lisa Williams, our director of marketing, and Lexi Wagner, who are responsible for all the marketing, PR, and social media (Facebook, Twitter, Pinterest, and YouTube) as well as publishing our biweekly *Success Strategies* ezine, which keeps everyone informed and excited about all our projects, including this book.

Russ Kamalski, our COO, who worked tirelessly with Patty to create our Train the Trainer Home Study Program while I was writing this book. Your ability to pull this off with minimal input from me during the video editing process is what allowed me to focus on this book.

Jesse Ianniello, Donna Bailey, Teresa Collett, Alice Doughty Refauvelet, Andrea Haefele, Kajsa Garrett, Jody Schwartz, and Dwain Jeworski—the rest of my staff, who kept the ship running while I was buried in this project.

Janet Switzer, for doing a great deal of the final editing and proofreading of the Tenth Anniversary Revised Edition of *The Success Principles: How to Get from Where You Are to Where You Want to Be,* which allowed me to finish writing this book.

Kathleen Seeley, our senior associate trainer, whose commitment and creativity in helping Patty Aubery redesign our live Train the Trainer Program and helping with the online Train the Trainer Program allowed me to focus on *The 30-Day Sobriety Solution.*

Kim Kirberger, my sister and the coauthor of most of the *Chicken Soup for the Teenage Soul* books, who read a lot of the manuscript and provided valuable feedback.

Oran, Christopher, and Riley, who have all had to deal with their own battles with drugs and alcohol, and have emerged victorious. I have learned a lot about courage, commitment, and perseverance from you. I appreciate having shared parts of the journey with you.

Dave Andrews's Acknowledgments

In the summer of 2008, as I was listening to Tony Robbins's *Personal Power II* while driving to a class for my master's degree, I asked myself a question that changed my life—*Why don't they teach this to people in recovery?* With the recent passing of a friend of mine who took his life while in recovery, I knew there had to be a better answer. At that moment I decided to create the program that came to be called "The 30-Day Sobriety Solution," and ultimately this book. I called my wife, Anya, and shared the idea with her, and she *loved* it. I want to thank the following:

Anya, who believed in me when I no longer believed in myself. You stood by me when most would not. Without you not only would this program not exist, but I am not even sure I would be alive. Thank you for being able to see the "real me" hiding behind my addiction. You are my best friend and my soul mate, and I am the luckiest person in the world to get to spend the rest of my life loving you.

Briana and Ella, my two amazing daughters, who have brought more joy, pride, and love to my life than I ever dreamed possible. You have taught me more than I can ever teach you, and I am in awe that I get to be your father. Briana, your courage and intuitiveness at the young age of five to tell me you thought I was going to die finally woke me up to the ultimate cost of my drinking. Ella, your spirit and energy remind me of myself as a child, and your enthusiasm, talent, and generosity are an inspiration to me every day.

Bryan Duke, who is one of the most charismatic people I have ever met. Without you I would never have had the insight and dedication to search for answers like the ones included in this program. Your memory will never be forgotten, and I only hope your family, and your two children, can find some peace that your passing helped inspire *The 30-Day Sobriety Solution.*

Jack Canfield, who courageously agreed to partner with a first-time author because he believed in me and my vision. Wow, working with you has been a dream come true. Your passion and commitment to making a difference in this world are unmatched. The last few weeks of this project were awe inspiring, as I watched you work "magic" on the final edits, all while putting in sixteen-plus-hour days. Even though the final push was exhausting and intense, it was incredibly rewarding, and your sense of humor helped keep us sane.

Chris, who was the first person to complete "The 30-Day Sobriety Solution." You were my "light" when I lost my way. Every time I doubted myself, or the program, you were always there reminding me of the impact it had in your life. I will always be grateful for you finding my website that one day many years ago, and forever changing both of our lives.

All the people whom I have coached, everyone who has worked their way through "The 30-Day Sobriety Solution," and everyone who has listened to my interviews, read my blog posts, and watched my videos. Your transformational stories, many of which are in this book, have been my sustaining inspiration. You have all played a role in this book being published, and your invaluable feedback has allowed me to make this program much more effective and even better than I thought possible.

Advocates for Recovery (AFR) and executive director Tonya Wheeler, whom I consider it an honor to know and serve on the AFR Board with, as well as the great team, including Heidi Williams and Suquana Charley. And to the rest of the AFR Board, who are my friends and role models: Merlyn Karst, Sarah Roisman, Juli Edwards, Bert Singleton, and Megan Marx. You all are such a positive force in the world of recovery.

Young People in Recovery (YPR) and president and CEO Justin Luke Riley, whose commitment and leadership skills are an inspiration. It has been an honor and privilege to get to know you and serve on the Board of YPR. You are truly the voice of your generation's recovery movement. And to Doug Rudolph and AJ Senerchia at YPR, who are leading the way by changing the youth recovery landscape.

Tony Robbins, whom I started listening to in my late teenage years. Your passion and life-changing content breathed life into the idea to create this program, and ultimately this book. I am forever indebted to you, and to so many other amazing teachers we quote from and mention in *The 30-Day Sobriety Solution*, for providing me the information, tools, and techniques I needed to not just change my life, but to help facilitate change in others.

Alcoholics Anonymous (AA), which helped me finally overcome the incredible guilt and shame I felt about my drinking and started me down the path to actually believing I could be happy sober. You have ensured that anyone who is suffering from alcoholism can find free support in almost any decent-sized city around the world. Thank you.

Art and Mike, my first two sponsors in AA, who helped me embrace the power of journaling and are amazing sober role models, and Jim for helping me find my way to them. And every other sponsor in AA who so unselfishly gives their time, compassion, shared personal experience, and wisdom to help others find a way to the other side of addiction.

Oran Canfield, who encouraged me one last time to reach out to Jack regarding this book, after I had all but moved on from the possibility.

Judy, my mom, who has always been there for me no matter what. Your lifelong commitment to helping others has always served as a positive example for me to follow. My childhood is full of wonderful, loving memories with you, and you instilled in me a lifelong desire to grow and learn that eventually helped carry me to the other side of my alcoholism. Your encouragement and support have never faded, and your detailed feedback on virtually every solution in *The 30-Day Sobriety Solution* is something I will never forget. And to your husband, Norm, my stepdad, who always taught me to do what is right, regardless of what others around me are doing.

Peter, my dad, who taught me one of my most important life lessons. When I was a young child, you came out in a society that discriminates and modeled to me what real courage is. You taught me how important it is to never be afraid to be true to who you are. And to Ron, for being such a loving life partner to my dad. It has truly been a gift to watch your love and commitment to each other grow deeper every year.

Mike, my brother, who has been a positive role model to me my whole life. You, more than anyone, have taught me how to live a life in alignment with my core values. Your passion for fighting for just and equal rights is a gift to this world. I am incredibly lucky to have you and your amazing life partner, Carol, as family. You both serve as moral and ethical compasses in my life.

Anne, my aunt, who I know is watching over our family. I will always remember your infectious laugh and your smile that could light up a room.

Ernie, Ruth, Leo, Lorraine, and Jan, my grandparents, who each helped make this book a possibility in one way or another. In particular, at Ernie's funeral service, I had the important realization and clarity that no matter what challenges I faced, I had to publish "The 30-Day Sobriety Solution" as a book so that I could reach more people who were searching for alternative answers for a way to thrive in sobriety.

Al and Donna, my in-laws, who embraced me as their daughter's boyfriend right from the start. You introduced me to so many of the amazing authors, such as Og Mandino, that we included in this book. And you have always been so supportive and loving. Thank you. I could never have asked for better in-laws.

Ryan, my brother-in-law, who is the younger brother I never had. It amazes me that I have known you since before you were even in high school. You are an amazing man and I feel lucky to have you in my life!

Jillian and Ana Lucia, my two nieces, who inspire me with their love for life. I love you both and only hope that your generation struggles less from addiction than mine.

My wonderful dogs and cats, past and present. I especially have to thank my dogs, because every time I had writer's block, had too much pent-up energy, or just needed to let off some steam, my dogs were always there for me, even if they were sometimes annoyed by the attention.

Starz, which created a wonderful culture and work environment, with so many great people. You provided a positive time and place where I was able to finally turn my life around. Leaving Starz to follow my passion with the work I do full-time today was one of the hardest decisions I have ever had to make.

Jon Seashore, Chris Yonker, Denise Winston, Adam Carroll, Tracy Cook, James Ross, Chris Winters, Josh Kauffman, Dan Markel, Gabriel Dicristofaro, Sean Marshall, Nancy McCaughey, Brian Gretz, Michael Casey, Ryan Judd, and Jeff Hill, who are some of my mastermind group members, past and present. You made sure that I could imagine persevering past another obstacle when I couldn't imagine doing so. And so many others, including the wonderful PSI community in Colorado that Dan Gibbons helped create and foster for decades. Your role in the publishing of this book will never be forgotten.

30-DAY RESOURCES

We know that cutting back or quitting drinking can be a challenging, lonely, and scary process. The following resources are available to help you succeed. To get the most up-to-date information on current 30-Day Resources, visit http://30DayResources.com or call us toll free at 1-844-My30Day (1-844-693-0329).

Private Coaching

When it comes to successfully cutting back or quitting drinking, and creating the results you desire in every area of your life, having your own personal coach will help you produce extraordinary results far more quickly than doing it on your own. That's why we developed an exclusive coaching program centered on *The 30-Day Sobriety Solution*, specifically designed to help you overcome sobriety-related challenges, and lead you to a life thriving in sobriety—one where you can finally achieve breakthrough success in accomplishing all your dreams, including attaining greater financial wealth, greater health and fitness, greater passion and joy in your relationships, or overall greater happiness and fulfillment.

To learn more, see: http://30DayResources.com/Coaching or call us toll free at 1-844-My30Day (1-844-693-0329).

Live Trainings and Workshops

If you could wave a wand and magically transform one thing in your life, what would it be? Would you remove the desire to drink? Wake up excited for the day ahead and full of gratitude for the joy and abundance in your life? Lead a life of service, helping others overcome some of the same challenges you have faced, while still making enough money to support your dreams? Enjoy more loving and intimate relationships with your spouse, family, and friends—that don't include drinking?

All of these things are possible, and much more. However, there is no magic wand. To create your ideal life requires time, effort, and energy. The good news is, there's a simple way for you to dramatically accelerate your journey and get big results fast. It is a live training called Breakthrough to Sobriety.

By delivering the most effective and life-changing teachings and techniques from *The 30-Day Sobriety Solution* in a positive, inspiring, and private environment with other enthusiastic, growth-focused individuals, the Breakthrough to Sobriety training will help you finally achieve the lasting results you desire.

To learn more, see: http://30DayResources.com/Training or call us toll free at 1-844-My30Day (1-844-693-0329).

Online Training

Are you looking for additional support, resources, and accountability to help you learn and apply the 30-Day sobriety solutions in your life? Do you want to take your sobriety, and your success, to the next level? By leveraging the flexibility, privacy, and power of the internet, we have created several online trainings that perfectly complement *The 30-Day Sobriety Solution* and your goal to cut back or quit drinking, or to get reinspired in recovery.

To learn more about these online trainings, see: http://30Day Resources.com/OnlineTraining or call us toll free at 1-844-My30Day (1-844-693-0329).

Hire Jack or Dave to Speak

Whether you are looking for an inspiring, fun, and thought-provoking keynote speaker for your conference or organization, or you are seeking a more interactive experience, with customized exercises and activities that meet your needs, Jack and Dave are both able to deliver this to your audience.

To learn more about the presentation formats, including keynote, training, and group facilitation options, see:

http://the30daysolution.com/speaking

or

www.JackCanfield.com/book-jack

Employee Assistance Programs

The cost of excessive alcohol consumption in the United States has reached a staggering $223.5 billion, which largely comes from losses in workplace productivity (approximately $160 billion) and health care expenses for problems caused by excessive drinking (approximately $24 billion). With numbers like these, it is critical that employers offer a variety of solutions to employees to help them overcome problem drinking, especially cost-effective solutions like *The 30-Day Sobriety Solution*.

To learn more about The 30-Day Sobriety Solution Employee Assistance Program, and how you can bring it to your company, see: http://30DayResources.com/eap or call us toll free at 1-844-My30Day (1-844-693-0329).

PERMISSIONS

NOTES

Getting Started

1. From an interview on the *Today* show, September 2010.
2. Marissa B. Esser et al., "Prevalence of Alcohol Dependence Among US Adult Drinkers, 2009–2011," *Preventing Chronic Disease* 11, no. E206 (November 11, 2014): 1–11, doi:http://dx.doi.org/10.5888/pcd11.140329.
3. Dotson Rader, "He Found His Voice," *Parade*, January 9, 2005.
4. For a list of various books, studies, articles, and other programs that advocate cutting back on drinking, see http://the30daysolution.com/cuttingbackfootnote.
5. Demi Lovato, "Sober Is Sexy!" *Seventeen*, August 6, 2011, www.seventeen.com/health/tips/demi-lovato-sober-is-sexy.

PHASE I: MASTERING THE ABSOLUTE BASICS TO GET FROM WHERE YOU ARE TO WHERE YOU WANT TO BE

Day 1: The 100% Solution

1. Manning Marable, Leith Mullings, et al., *Let Nobody Turn Us Around: Voices on Resistance, Reform, and Renewal: An African American Anthology* (Lanham: Rowman & Littlefield Publishers, 1999) or also see www.goodreads.com/quotes/199214-take-the-first-step-in-faith-you-don't-have-to.
2. Jack Canfield and Mark Victor Hansen, *Chicken Soup for the Soul* (Deerfield Beach, FL: Health Communications, 1993).
3. Stephen King, *On Writing* (New York: Scribner, 2000).
4. See Dr. Gail Matthews's research on the factors that accelerate goal setting achievement at www.dominican.edu/academics/ahss/undergraduate-programs-1/psych/faculty/fulltime/gailmatthews/researchsummary2.pdf.

5. See www.glamourmagazine.co.uk/celebrity/celebrity-galleries/2011/01/teetotal-celebrities#!image-number=8.

6. For a list of various books, studies, articles, and other programs that advocate cutting back on drinking, see http://the30daysolution.com/cuttingbackfootnote.

7. For the full definition, see www.thefreedictionary.com, s.v. "sobriety."

8. John Assaraf and Murray Smith, *The Answer: Your Guide to Achieving Financial Freedom and Living an Extraordinary Life* (New York: Simon & Schuster, 2008).

9. Jack Canfield and Janet Switzer, *The Success Principles* (New York: Harper-Collins, 2015).

10. Josh Hamilton, *Beyond Belief: Finding the Strength to Come Back* (New York: Faith Words, 2008).

11. Patrick Swayze and Lisa Niemi, *The Time of My Life* (New York: Atria Books, 2009).

12. David Hinckley, "Average American Watches 5 Hours of TV per Day, Report Shows," *New York Daily News*, March 5, 2014, www.nydailynews.com/life-style/average-american-watches-5-hours-tv-day-article-1.1711954.

13. You can easily access the companion website for *The 30-Day Sobriety Solution* for any day by following the easy-to-remember format: http://Day##.Solutions. For example, today is http://Day1.Solutions and tomorrow is http://Day2.Solutions. These are not case sensitive, so uppercase or lowercase is fine. The companion website is a great way to access the most up-to-date resources, exercises, and audio recordings to help you thrive in sobriety.

Day 2: The Purpose Solution

1. Tony Robbins, *Money: Master the Game—7 Simple Steps to Financial Freedom* (New York: Simon & Schuster, 2014).

2. Ayn Rand, *The Fountainhead* (New York: Penguin Books, 1943).

3. For more information on how the subconscious mind works, see Irene Colville, "Does the Unconscious Mind Hear Negatives?" Center for Counseling and Hypnosis, www.hypnocenter.com/articles/does-the-unconscious-mind-hear-negatives-.

4. See www.goodreads.com/author/quotes/38285.C_G_Jung.

5. T. Harv Eker, *Secrets of the Millionaire Mind: Mastering the Inner Game of Wealth* (New York: HarperCollins, 2005).

6. Paulo Cohelo, *The Alchemist* (New York: HarperCollins, 1993).

7. To read more about Naomi Campbell, see www.bangshowbiz.com/products/showbiz/index.html?id=2010244175518187104&ch=Showbiz.

Day 3: The Pendulum Solution

1. Lao Tzu, *Tao Te Ching*, translated by Jonathan Star (New York: Penguin, 2001).
2. See www.imdb.com/title/tt0416449/news?year=2012.
3. Andre Agassi, *Open* (New York: Random House, 2009).
4. Brené Brown, *I Thought It Was Just Me* (New York: Penguin Group, 2007).
5. See http://thinkexist.com/quotation/character_cannot_be_developed_in_ease_and_quiet/13579.html.
6. See www.goodreads.com/author/quotes/399.Napoleon_Hill.
7. Sigmund Freud, *Beyond the Pleasure Principle* translated by James Strachey (Seattle: Pacific Publishing Studio, 2010).
8. William Glasser, MD, *Positive Addiction* (New York: Harper & Row, 1976).
9. See www.goodreads.com/author/quotes/33117.Drew_Barrymore.
10. E. Tory Higgins, "Beyond Pleasure and Pain," *American Psychologist*, December 2007.
11. Charles Duhigg, *The Power of Habit: Why We Do What We Do in Life and Business* (New York: Random House, 2012).
12. Eric Clapton, *Clapton: The Autobiography* (New York: Broadway Books, 2007).

Day 4: The Forgiveness Solution

1. Lewis B. Smedes, *The Art of Forgiving: When You Need to Forgive and Don't Know How* (Nashville: Moorings, 1996).
2. Stephanie Sarkis, "30 Quotes on Making Mistakes," *Psychology Today*, September 30, 2011, www.psychologytoday.com/blog/here-there-and-everywhere/201109/30-quotes-making-mistakes.
3. To read more about how guilt and shame lead to relapse, see Maia Szalavitz, "Being Ashamed of Drinking Prompts Relapse, Not Recovery," Time.com, last modified February 7, 2013, http://healthland.time.com/2013/02/07/being-ashamed-of-drinking-prompts-relapse-not-recovery.
4. Thanks to John Gray and Barbara DeAngelis, who first taught us this process.
5. Stephen M. Silverman, "Ewan McGregor Reveals Battle with Alcohol," *People*, July 5, 2005, www.people.com/people/article/0,,1079768,00.html.

6. See Stephanie Sarkis, "30 Quotes on Forgiveness: Ponder These Words of Wisdom," *Psychology Today*, February 1, 2011, www.psychologytoday .com/blog/here-there-and-everywhere/201102/30-quotes-forgiveness.

7. John Green, *The Fault in Our Stars* (New York: Dutton Books, 2012).

8. See http://thedailylove.com/todays-quotes-forgive-them-and-let-it-go.

9. Tony Robbins, "Stop Your Limiting Beliefs: 10 Empowering Beliefs That Will Change Your Life," *The Anthony Robbins Blog*, August 1, 2013, http:// training.tonyrobbins.com/stop-your-limiting-beliefs-10-empowering-beliefs-that-will-change-your-life/.

10. Kristen Johnston, "Guest Post," Veronicavalli.com, February 5, 2014, http://veronicavalli.com/2014/02/guest-post-by-kristen-johnston/.

11. See http://thedailylove.com/are-you-trying-to-change-someone-2/.

12. Kamal Ravikant, *Love Yourself Like Your Life Depends on It* (CreateSpace Independent Publishing Platform, 2012).

13. *The Anonymous People* is a film by director Greg Williams about the 23.5 million Americans living in long-term recovery from addiction to alcohol and drugs. You can also rent it and watch it online at Amazon .com, Netflix, iTunes, and Vudu.

Day 5: The Believe-in-Yourself Solution

1. See www.goodreads.com/author/quotes/69188.Frank_Lloyd_Wright.

2. To read more about expectancy theory, see https://wikispaces.psu.edu/ display/PSYCH484/4.+Expectancy+Theory.

3. Brooke Hauser, "Blake Lively: Her Allure Photo Shoot," *Allure*, October 2012, http://www.allure.com/celebrity-trends/cover-shoot/2012/blake-lively.

4. See "Powerful Placebos," *The Wellness Chronicle* 2, no. 2 (December 15, 1998), http://medicine.creighton.edu/wellness/V2N2/V2N2.htm.

5. See Sandra Blakeslee, "Placebos Prove So Powerful Even Experts Are Surprised: New Studies Explore the Brain's Triumph over Reality," *New York Times*, October 13, 1998, www.nytimes.com/1998/10/13/science /placebos-prove-so-powerful-even-experts-are-surprised-new-studies-explore-brain.html.

6. See J. Bruce Mosely et al., "A Controlled Trial of Arthroscopic Surgery for Osteoarthritis of the Knee," *New England Journal of Medicine* 347 (July 11, 2002): 81–88, www.nejm.org/doi/full/10.1056/NEJMoa013259#t= article.

7. Steven Locke and Douglas Colligan, *The Healer Within: The New Medicine of Mind and Body* (New York: Plume, 1997).

8. King, *On Writing.*

9. Aly Weisman, "14 People Who Failed Before Becoming Famous," *Business Insider*, February 20, 2014, www.businessinsider.com/people-who-failed-before-becoming-famous-2014-2?op=1.

Day 6: The Outcome Solution

1. Canfield and Janet Switzer, *Success Principles*.
2. To read more about Kristin Davis, see Barbara Ellen, "Charlotte's Web," *Observer*, February 10, 2002, www.theguardian.com/theobserver/2002/feb/10/features.magazine27.
3. Mihaly Csikszentmihalyi, *Flow: The Psychology of Optimal Experience* (New York: Harper & Row, 1990).
4. Brian Tracy, *Eat That Frog!: 21 Great Ways to Stop Procrastinating and Get More Done in Less Time* (San Francisco: Berrett-Koehler Publishers, 2007).
5. For more general information on the positive effects of goal setting, see Daniel Wong, "Reflections of a Compulsive Goal-setter," *The Duke Chronicle*, April 5, 2011, www.dukechronicle.com/articles/2011/04/06/reflections-compulsive-goal-setter.
6. See www.notable-quotes.com/z/ziglar_zig.html.
7. To learn more about SMART criteria, see http://en.wikipedia.org/wiki/SMART_criteria#cite_note-Doran-1981-2.
8. To learn more about structural tension, see Robert Fritz, *The Path of Least Resistance: Learning to Be the Creative Force in Your Own Life* (New York: Random House, 1984).

Day 7: The Review Day and Bonus Solution

1. See www.glamourmagazine.co.uk/celebrity/celebrity-galleries/2011/01/teetotal-celebrities#!image-number=14.
2. To read more about hormones that can make you happy, see M. Farouk Radwan, "Hormones That Make You Happy," www.2knowmyself.com/Hormones_that_make_you_happy.
3. To read the entire article, see "Alcohol Use Disorder," *New York Times Health Guide*, March 8, 2013, www.nytimes.com/health/guides/disease/alcoholism/causes.html.
4. To learn more about this 90-day period, see Tony O'Neill, "The 100-Day Hangover," *The Fix*, April 19, 2011, www.thefix.com/content/one-big-pain-brain.
5. We wish to thank Dr. Tony O'Donnell and Michael McCarthy for their guidance on nutrition and quitting drinking. We'll have more from them on Day 25's companion website.

PHASE II: REMOVING THE MENTAL AND EMOTIONAL BLOCKS THAT PREVENT YOU FROM THRIVING IN SOBRIETY

1. For more on the drunk dream and overcoming addiction, see "Elton John Opens Up About Overcoming Addiction in New Memoir," *Huffpost Celebrity*, July 17, 2012, www.huffingtonpost.com/2012/07/17/elton-john-talks-overcoming-addiction-memoir_n_1680055.html.

Day 8: The "Why Can't You Just Quit?" Solution

1. For more thoughts on willpower, see Rick Warren, "Healing Choices: A Mind for Repentance," *Daily Hope with Rick Warren*, May 21, 2014, http://rickwarren.org/devotional/english/healing-choices-a-mind-for-repentance.
2. For the full definition, see www.merriam-webster.com, s.v. "willpower."
3. John Ortberg, *The Life You've Always Wanted* (Grand Rapids, MI: Zondervan, 1997).
4. To read more about willpower, see Kirsten Weir, "What You Need to Know About Willpower: The Psychological Science of Self-Control," American Psychological Association's *Mind/Body Health Campaign Report*, 2012, www.apa.org/helpcenter/willpower.aspx.
5. Rick Warren, *The Purpose Driven Life: What on Earth Am I Here For?* (Grand Rapids, MI: Zondervan, 2012).
6. To find out more about decision making and willpower, see Drake Baer, "14 Surprising Things That Affect Your Willpower and Decision Making," *Business Insider*, April 15, 2014, www.businessinsider.com/surprising-things-that-affect-your-willpower-and-decision-making-2014-4.
7. For more on decision fatigue, see John Tierney, "Do You Suffer From Decision Fatigue?" *New York Times Magazine*, August 17, 2011, www.nytimes.com/2011/08/21/magazine/do-you-suffer-from-decision-fatigue.html?pagewanted=1&%2334&sq&st=cse&%2359;&scp=1&%2359;decision%20making%20fatigue.
8. David Sheff, *Clean: Overcoming Addiction and Ending America's Greatest Tragedy* (New York: Houghton Mifflin Harcourt, 2013).
9. See www.goodreads.com/author/quotes/102037.James_Gordon.

Day 9: The Action Solution

1. Caroline Knapp, *Drinking: A Love Story* (New York: Random House, 1996).
2. From an interview on *The Conversation* with Amanda de Cadenet, May 2012.

3. Brian Tracy, *No Excuses!: The Power of Self-Discipline* (New York: Vanguard Press, 2010).

4. See Diane M. Tice and Roy F. Baumeister, "Longitudinal Study of Procrastination, Performance, Stress, and Health: The Costs and Benefits of Dawdling," *Psychological Science* 8 (1997): 454–58.

5. For more information about procrastination, see Eric Jaffe, "Why Wait? The Science Behind Procrastination," *Observer* 26, no. 4 (April 2013): www.psychologicalscience.org/index.php/publications/observer/2013/april-13/why-wait-the-science-behind-procrastination.html.

6. Steve Chandler, *100 Ways to Motivate Yourself: Change Your Life Forever* (Franklin Lakes, NJ: Career Press, 2004).

7. David K. Reynolds, *Constructive Living* (Honolulu: University of Hawaii Press, 1984).

8. This concept is based on Canfield and Switzer, *Success Principles*.

9. Stephen M. Silverman, "Ewan McGregor Reveals Battle with Alcohol," *People*, July 5, 2005, www.people.com/people/article/0,,1079768,00.html.

10. William Harris, "How Newton's Laws of Motion Work," HowStuffWorks .com. July 29, 2008, http://science.howstuffworks.com/innovation/scientific-experiments/newton-law-of-motion.htm.

11. Maxwell Maltz, *Psycho-Cybernetics: A New Way to Get More Living out of Life* (New York: Prentice-Hall, 1960).

12. To read more about why things catch on, see Kare Anderson, "The Secret Behind Why Things Catch On," *Forbes*, February 18, 2013, www.forbes .com/sites/kareanderson/2013/02/18/the-secret-behind-why-things-catch-on.

13. Jennifer Chang, "Tiny Habits: Behavior Scientist BJ Fogg Explains a Painless Strategy to Personal Growth," *Success*, October 8, 2013, www .success.com/article/tiny-habits.

14. Steve Chandler, *Time Warrior: How to Defeat Procrastination, People-Pleasing, Self-Doubt, Overcommitment, Broken Promises and Chaos* (Anna Maria, FL: Maurice Bassett, 2011).

Day 10: The Core Values Solution

1. Henry Kimsey-House et al., *Co-Active Coaching: Changing Business, Transforming Lives,* 3rd ed. (Boston: Nicholas Brealey Publishing, 2011).

2. Dotson Rader, "Interview with Robert Downey Jr.," *Parade*, February 4, 2008.

3. See www.brainyquote.com/quotes/quotes/m/martinluth135188.html.

4. See www.goodreads.com/author/quotes/50316.Zig_Ziglar.

5. Stephen R. Covey, *The 7 Habits of Highly Effective People: Powerful Lessons in Personal Change* (New York: Free Press, 1989).

Day 11: The Lie Detector Solution

1. See www.brainyquote.com/quotes/authors/d/deepak_chopra.html.

2. Maltz, *Psycho-Cybernetics*.

3. To read more about how alcohol can affect your sex life, see Chris Iliades, "Why Boozing Can Be Bad for Your Sex Life," Everydayhealth .com, last modified January 4, 2012, www.everydayhealth.com/erectile-dysfunction/why-boozing-can-be-bad-for-your-sex-life.aspx.

4. Esser at al., "Prevalence of Alcohol Dependence Among US Adult Drinkers."

5. See http://en.wikipedia.org/wiki/Harvard_Law_School.

6. Melissa Healy, "Resveratrol in the Diet Is No Help at All, Study Says," *Los Angeles Times*, May 12, 2014. Also, see www.medpagetoday.com/ Endocrinology/GeneralEndocrinology/45738.

7. For the full definition, see www.merriam-webster.com, s.v. "intoxicate."

8. Stanton Peele and Archie Brodsky with Mary Arnold, *The Truth About Addiction and Recovery* (New York: Simon & Schuster, 1992). To read a chapter online, see http://lifeprocessprogram.com/the-truth-about-addiction-and-recovery-are-people-born-alcoholics.

9. For the most current list of the top-grossing actors of all time, see www .boxofficemojo.com/people/?view=Actor&sort=sumgross&p=.htm.

10. For a complete list of teetotalers, see http://en.wikipedia.org/wiki/List_of _teetotalers.

11. King, *On Writing*.

12. Alan H. Cohen, *Why Your Life Sucks . . . and What You Can Do About It* (New York: Bantam, 2005).

13. To read Christina Ricci's full interview with *BlackBook*, see "Drive, She Said," bbook.com, April 21, 2008, www.bbook.com/drive-she-said/.

Day 12: The Subconscious Mind Solution

1. To read Bruce Lipton's interview "Mind, Growth, and Matter" from *Succeed Magazine*, June 7, 2012, see www.brucelipton.com/resource/ interview/mind-growth-and-matter.

2. For the full definition, see www.merriam-webster.com, s.v. "subconscious."

3. Joseph Murphy, *The Power of Your Subconscious Mind* (Englewood Cliffs, NJ: Prentice-Hall, 1963).

4. To read more about how the subconscious mind records life events, see

Dietrich Klinghardt, "Applied Psycho-Neurobiology," mercola.com, www
.mercola.com/article/applied_psycho_neurobiology/apn.htm.

5. John A. Bargh and Ezequiel Morsella, "The Unconscious Mind,"
Perspectives on Psychological Science 3, no. 1 (January 2008): 73–79. To read
the full paper, see www.ncbi.nlm.nih.gov/pmc/articles/PMC2440575.

6. Bruce H. Lipton, *The Biology of Belief: Unleashing the Power of Consciousness,
Matter & Miracles* (Carlsbad, CA: Hay House, 2008).

7. Steven Kotler, "Learning to Learn Faster Part II: How to Read Faster and
Solve Problems Like MacGyver," *Forbes*, July 3, 2013, www.forbes.com/
sites/stevenkotler/2013/07/03/learning-to-learn-faster-part-ii/2.

8. Dr. Drew Pinsky, "Keynote Address by Dr. Drew Pinsky" (presented at the
Fifth Annual Luncheon for the Arapahoe House, Denver, September 18,
2014).

9. To read more about the lottery and bankruptcy study, see Amy Wolf,
"Lotteries: From Big Bucks to Bankruptcy," *Research News at Vanderbilt*, July
7, 2009, http://news.vanderbilt.edu/2009/07/lotteries-from-big-bucks-to-
bankruptcy-83864.

10. Leonard Mlodinow, *Subliminal: How Your Unconscious Mind Rules Your
Behavior* (New York: Vintage Books, 2012).

11. Debra Ollivier, "Leonard Mlodinow on Subliminal: How Your
Unconscious Mind Rules Your Behavior," Huffingtonpost.com, last
modified August 7, 2012, www.huffingtonpost.com/debra-ollivier/
leonard-mlodinow-on-subliminal-how-your-unconscious-mind-rules-
your-behavior_b_1575795.html.

12. Bill Wilson, "The Next Frontier: Emotional Sobriety," *Grapevine*, January
1958.

13. For more studies on the development of the personality in early
childhood, see Linda Carroll, "Personality May Be Set by Preschool,"
Msnbc.com, last modified January 15, 2008, http://www.nbcnews.com
/id/22554554/ns/health-childrens_health/t/personality-may-be-set-
preschool/#.VQdRxI7F-Sq.

14. For more information on how the brain develops in early childhood,
see Judith Graham, "Children and Brain Development: What We Know
About How Children Learn," Bulletin #4356, *Cooperative Extension
Publications*, The University of Maine, http://umaine.edu/publications
/4356e.

15. For studies on thought suppression, see Jeremy Dean, "Why Thought
Suppression Is Counter-Productive," *PsyBlog*, May 22, 2009, www.spring
.org.uk/2009/05/why-thought-suppression-is-counter-productive.php.

16. For more about the subconscious mind and negatives, see Abdallah Nacereddine, "How the Subconscious Mind Functions," Unspecial.org, www.unspecial.org/2011/12/how-the-subconscious-mind-functions.

Day 13: The Tapping Solution

1. Roger Callahan, PhD, *The Five Minute Phobia Cure: Dr. Callahan's Treatment for Fears, Phobias and Self-Sabotage* (Wilmington, DE: Enterprise Publishing, 1985).

2. You can get a quick overview of the technique at www.EFTuniverse.com and in Nick Ortner, *The Tapping Solution* (Carlsbad, CA: Hay House, 2013). Also see Dawson Church, *The EFT Manual* (Fulton, CA: Energy Psychology Press, 2014), which is a new and completely revised edition of the original EFT manual written by Gary Craig. Both of these books are eminently practical and easy to read and apply. Also see Jack Canfield and Pamela Bruner, *Tapping into Ultimate Success: How to Overcome Any Obstacle and Skyrocket Your Success* (Carlsbad, CA: Hay House, 2012). This book also contains a ninety-minute DVD that teaches and demonstrates the various EFT tapping protocols. You can also watch free videos on YouTube that demonstrate the basic EFT tapping procedure. Finally, if you would like further help in applying tapping to your recovery, you can locate a local practitioner by going to http://Practitioners.EFTuniverse.com.

3. Kari Reed, "Battling a Giant with Really Small, Surprisingly Effective Rocks," in *The EFT Manual*, by Dawson Church (Fulton, CA: Energy Psychology Press, 2014), 31–32.

4. Mair Llewellyn-Edwards, "Using EFT for a Headache Leads to Recovery in Alcohol Addiction," Eftuniverse.com, www.eftuniverse.com/addictions/using-eft-for-a-headache-leads-to-recovery-in-alcohol-addiction.

5. Church and Brooks also performed a randomized, controlled trial demonstrating that cortisol levels drop quickly after a brief EFT treatment, in tandem with reductions in psychological stress. See D. Church, G. Yount, and A. J. Brooks, "The Effect of Emotional Freedom Techniques (EFT) on Stress Biochemistry: A Randomized Controlled Trial," *Journal of Nervous and Mental Disease* 200, no. 10 (2012): 891–96, doi:10.1097/NMD.0b013e 31826b9fc1.

6. Gloria Arenson, *EFT for Procrastination* (Santa Rosa, CA: Energy Psychology Press, 2009).

7. Dawson Church and Audrey J. Brooks, "The Effect of a Brief EFT (Emotional Freedom Techniques) Self-Intervention on Anxiety, Depression, Pain and Cravings in Healthcare Workers," *Integrative Medicine: A Clinician's Journal* (October/November 2010): 40–44.

8. We wish to acknowledge Robert Elias Najemy, the founder and director of the Center for Harmonious Living in Athens, Greece, for his work on tapping and addiction, from which we have drawn upon extensively for this solution.

9. We want to remind you again that if you have developed a strong dependency on alcohol, or if you have detoxed from alcohol several times in the past, you run the risk of more serious side effects such as tremors, seizures, DTs, and visual, auditory, and tactile hallucinations—even death. So once again we advise you to work with a doctor to determine if you need medication and monitoring.

10. Javier Gomez, "EFT Tapping for Unresolved Grief Curbs Beer Craving," Eftuniverse.com, www.eftuniverse.com/addictions/using-eft-for-unresolved-grief-aids-an-alcohol-problem-as-a-side-benefit.

PHASE III: CREATING AN UNSHAKABLE BELIEF IN YOURSELF AND YOUR DREAMS

1. Eckhart Tolle, *The Power of Now: A Guide to Spiritual Enlightenment* (Novato, CA: New World Library, 1999).

Day 15: The 4-Minute-Mile Solution

1. Charles A. Garfield, *Peak Performance: Mental Training Techniques of the World's Greatest Athletes* (New York: Warner Books, 1989).

2. For studies on how visualization is just as powerful as doing, see Frank C. Bakker et al., "Changes in Muscular Activity While Imagining Weight Lifting Using Stimulus or Response Propositions," *Journal of Sport & Exercise Psychology* (1996), http://journals.humankinetics.com/AcuCustom/Sitename/Documents/DocumentItem/8962.pdf.

3. Maltz, *Psycho-Cybernetics*.

4. To read about Roger Bannister's historic moment, see "On This Date 1950–2005," BBC.com, http://news.bbc.co.uk/onthisday/hi/dates/stories/may/6/newsid_2511000/2511575.stm.

5. See Bruce Lowitt, "Bannister Stuns World with 4-Minute Mile," *St. Petersburg Times*, December 17, 1999, www.sptimes.com/News/121799/Sports/Bannister_stuns_world.shtml.

6. From an interview on the *Oprah Winfrey Show*, 1997.

7. For the full definition, see www.thefreedictionary.com, s.v. "reticular activating system."

8. For more information about the brain's processing speed, see Steven Kotler, "Learning to Learn Faster Part II: How to Read Faster and Solve Problems

Like MacGyver." *Forbes*, July 3, 2013, www.forbes.com/sites/stevenkotler /2013/07/03/learning-to-learn-faster-part-ii/2. This source references a study that found Lipton's figures conservative, calculating that the subconscious is as much as two million times faster than the conscious.

9. For more information on goal setting and the RAS, see Ruben Gonzalez, "The Neuroscience of Success," *Ruben Gonzalez the Luge Man Blog*, www .thelugeman.com/motivational_speaker_the_neuroscience_of_success. htm.

10. For more information about the brain's RAS filter, see Sheila Kloefkorn, "How to Train Your Brain for Success," *Phoenix Business Journal*, May 23, 2014, www.bizjournals.com/phoenix/blog/business/2014/05/how-to-train-your-brain-for-success.html?page=all.

11. See Angie LeVan, "Seeing Is Believing: The Power of Visualization," *Psychology Today*, December 2, 2009, www.psychologytoday.com/blog/ flourish/200912/seeing-is-believing-the-power-visualization.

12. See www.goodreads.com/author/quotes/8435.Norman_Vincent_Peale.

13. To learn more about adding all the senses to your visualization practice, see JoAnn Dahlkoetter, "Sochi Olympics and Sports Psychology for Athletes," Huffingtonpost.com, last modified April 12, 2014, www .huffingtonpost.com/dr-joann-dahlkoetter/sochi-olympics_b_4582950 .html.

14. See Mary C. Lamia, "Emotional Memories: When People and Events Remain with You," *Psychology Today*, March 5, 2012, www.psychologytoday .com/blog/intense-emotions-and-strong-feelings/201203/emotional-memories-when-people-and-events-remain.

15. Greg Miller, "How Our Brains Make Memories: Surprising New Research About the Act of Remembering May Help People with Post-traumatic Stress Disorder," *Smithsonian Magazine*, May 2010, www.smithsonianmag.com/science-nature/how-our-brains-make-memories-14466850/?no-ist.

16. See Mike Bundrant, "Success or Stress: The Impact of Your Subconscious Self-Questioning," *Living Green Magazine*, December 11, 2013, http:// livinggreenmag.com/2013/12/11/people-solutions/success-stress-impact-subconscious-self-questioning.

Day 16: The Quality Question Solution

1. Brian Tracy, "How to Trigger Great Ideas," *Brian Tracy's Blog*, www .briantracy.com/blog/business-success/how-to-trigger-great-ideas.

2. See www.pbs.org/wgbh/nova/einstein/wisd-nf.html.

3. For more tips on working with the subconscious mind, see "How to

Reprogram Your Subconscious Mind," Hubpages.com, March 20, 2013, http://thegoalsettingg.hubpages.com/hub/subconscious_mind.

4. Michael J. Gelb, *How to Think Like Leonardo da Vinci: Seven Steps to Genius Every Day* (New York: Dell Publishing, 2000).

5. Niurka, *Supreme Influence: Change Your Life with the Power of the Language You Use* (New York: Harmony Books, 2013).

6. See www.woopidoo.com/business_quotes/authors/amory-lovins/index.htm.

7. Dotson Rader, "Interview with Robert Downey Jr.," *Parade*, February 4, 2008.

8. Gelb, *How to Think Like Leonardo da Vinci*.

Day 17: The Eternal Optimist Solution

1. Norman Vincent Peale, *The Power of Positive Thinking* (New York: Prentice-Hall, 1952).

2. For more information about how our thoughts can determine our emotional states, see Ben Martin, "Stress and Personality," *Psych Central,* 2006, http://psychcentral.com/lib/stress-and-personality/000106.

3. Tolle, *The Power of Now*.

4. For more stories about how small choices saved lives on 9/11, see Madison Park, "Small Choices, Saved Lives: Near Misses of 9/11," CNN.com, September 5, 2011, www.cnn.com/2011/US/09/03/near.death.decisions.

5. See www.goodreads.com/author/quotes/7275.Helen_Keller.

6. Fred R. Shapiro, ed., *The Yale Book of Quotations* (New Haven, CT: Yale University Press, 2006).

7. Esther and Jerry Hicks, *Ask and It Is Given: Learning to Manifest Your Desires* (Carlsbad, CA: Hay House, 2004).

8. Vernon Howard, *The Power of Your Supermind* (Pine, AZ: New Life, 2011).

9. Robbins, *Money: Master the Game*.

10. Erik Sherman, "This Easy 'Mental Contrasting' Technique Can Help You Achieve Your Goals," *Business Insider*, October 29, 2014, www .businessinsider.com/this-easy-mental-contrasting-technique-can-help-you-achieve-your-goals-2014-10?nr_email_referer=1&utm_source= Sailthru&utm_medium=email&utm_term=Business Insider Select&utm _campaign=BI Select %28Wednesday Friday%29 2014-10-29&utm_ content=BISelect.

Day 18: The Affirmation Solution

1. From an interview in *Movieline*, July 1994.

2. See JM Emmert, "Rich Man, Poor Man: The Success of Napoleon Hill," *Success*, January 5, 2009, www.success.com/article/rich-man-poor-man.

3. Hans Villarica, "How the Power of Positive Thinking Won Scientific

Credibility," *The Atlantic*, April 23, 2012, www.theatlantic.com/health /archive/2012/04/how-the-power-of-positive-thinking-won-scientific-credibility/256223, and http://exploringthemind.com/the-mind/the-truth-about-affirmations.

4. Napoleon Hill, *Think and Grow Rich: The Original 1937 Unedited Edition*, reprint. (Wise, VA: Napoleon Hill Foundation, 2012).

5. For more information about the differences between the conscious mind and the subconscious mind, see Michael Carroll, "Understanding Your Mind; Conscious and Unconscious Processing: How to Utilise the Recourses of Your Unconscious Mind," Nlpacademy.co.uk, July 2008, www.nlpacademy.co.uk/articles/view/understanding_your_mind_ conscious_and_unconscious_processing.

6. Claude M. Bristol, *The Magic of Believing: The Science of Setting Your Goal and Then Reaching It* (New York: Fireside, 1985).

7. Robin S. Sharma, *The Monk Who Sold His Ferrari: A Fable About Fulfilling Your Dreams and Reaching Your Destiny* (New York: HarperCollins, 1997).

8. Martin E. P. Seligman, *Learned Optimism: How to Change Your Mind and Your Life* (New York: Random House, 1991).

9. Paul J. Brouwer, "The Power to See Ourselves," *Harvard Business Review*, November 1964, https://hbr.org/1964/11/the-power-to-see-ourselves.

Day 19: The Attraction Solution

1. Hicks, *Ask and It Is Given*.

2. For more about how the law of attraction actually works, see Srinivasan Pillay, "Is There Scientific Evidence for the 'Law of Attraction'?" Huffingtonpost.com, last modified November 17, 2011, www .huffingtonpost.com/srinivasan-pillay/is-there-scientific-evide_b _175189.html.

3. To read an interview with Dr. Lissa Rankin, author of *Mind over Medicine: Scientific Proof That You Can Heal Yourself*, see www.drfranklipman.com/ interview-with-dr-lissa-rankin.

4. Esther and Jerry Hicks, *Money, and the Law of Attraction: Learning to Attract Wealth, Health, and Happiness* (Carlsbad, CA: Hay House, 2008).

5. Ibid.

6. Brian Tracy, *No Excuses! The Power of Self-Discipline* (Boston: Da Capo Press, 2010).

7. Chandler, *100 Ways to Motivate Yourself*.

8. "Craig Ferguson Speaks from the Heart." See www.youtube.com/watch ?v=7ZVWIELHQQY.

9. Esther and Jerry Hicks, *Money, and the Law of Attraction*.

Day 20: The Gratitude Solution

1. Robert A. Emmons, *Thanks! How the New Science of Gratitude Can Make You Happier* (New York: Houghton Mifflin Company, 2007). Also, to read more about the power of gratitude, and see what some critics of Emmons's study are saying, see http://greatergood.berkeley.edu/article/ item/gratitude_research_why_bother.

2. Sara Rimer and Madeline Drexler, "Happiness and Health," *Harvard Public Health*, Winter 2011, www.hsph.harvard.edu/news/magazine/happiness-stress-heart-disease.

3. Sonja Lyubomirsky, *The How of Happiness: A Scientific Approach to Getting the Life You Want* (New York: Penguin Press, 2008).

4. Anup Shah, "Poverty Facts and Stats," Globalissues.org, last modified January 7, 2013, www.globalissues.org/article/26/poverty-facts-and-stats.

5. For more about Brother David Steindl-Rast and to read more about his ideas on gratitude, see www.gratefulness.org/qbox/item.cfm?qbox_id= 32.

6. Emmons, *Thanks!*

7. Heather King, *Parched: A Memoir* (New York: Chamberlain Bros., 2005).

8. Tolle, *The Power of Now*.

9. Steven M. Toepher, Kelly Cichy, and Patti Peters, "Letters of Gratitude: Further Evidence for Author Benefits," *Journal of Happiness Studies* 13, no. 1 (January 2012): 187–201, doi:10.1007/s10902-011-9257-7.

Day 21: The Review Day and Bonus Solution

1. From an interview on *Larry King Live*, August 2002. To read the full interview with Matthew Perry, see http://transcripts.cnn.com/ TRANSCRIPTS/0208/22/lkl.00.html.

2. WikiHow contributors, "How to Identify Persuasive Techniques in Advertising," WikiHow, *The Free How-to Guide*, www.wikihow.com/ Identify-Persuasive-Techniques-in-Advertising (accessed December 16, 2014).

3. See www.statista.com/statistics/245318/advertising-spending-of-the-alcohol-industry-in-the-us-by-medium/.

PHASE IV: CULTIVATING COURAGE AND POSITIVE RELATIONSHIPS TO THRIVE IN MIND, BODY, AND SPIRIT

1. Deepak Chopra, *The Book of Secrets: Unlocking the Hidden Dimensions* (New York: Random House, 2004).

Day 22: The Courage Solution

1. Osho, *The Book of Understanding: Creating Your Own Path to Freedom* (New York: Harmony Books, 2006).
2. Marianne Williamson, *A Return to Love: Reflections on the Principles of A Course in Miracles* (New York: HarperCollins, 1992).
3. Dan Millman, *Everyday Enlightenment* (New York: Warner Books, 1998).
4. To read more about fear, see Dean Burnett, "Phobias: The Rationale Behind Irrational Fears," *The Guardian*, June 28, 2013, www.theguardian.com/science/brain-flapping/2013/jun/28/phobias-rationale-irrational-fears, and Joseph Ledoux, "Searching the Brain for the Roots of Fear," *New York Times*, January 22, 2012, http://opinionator.blogs.nytimes.com/2012/01/22/anatomy-of-fear/?_r=0.
5. Ace Frehley, Joe Layden, and John Ostrosky, *No Regrets* (New York: Gallery Books, 2011).
6. For more information on how an imagined event can seem real, see Sandra Blakeslee, "Tracing the Brain's Pathways for Linking Emotion and Reason," *New York Times*, December 6, 1994, www.nytimes.com/1994/12/06/science/tracing-the-brain-s-pathways-for-linking-emotion-and-reason.html.
7. Carol S. Dweck, *Mindset: The New Psychology of Success* (New York: Ballantine Books, 2008).
8. To read more about Esther Earl, see Zakiya Jamal, "Meet Esther Earl, the Brave Girl Who Inspired *The Fault in Our Stars*," *People*, June 7, 2014, www.people.com/article/esther-earl-john-green-inspiration-fault-in-our-stars-book-movie and This Star Won't Go Out, "Esther's Story," http://tswgo.org/esthers-story.html.
9. See www.boxofficemojo.com/movies/?id=faultinourstars.htm.
10. Esther Earl, Lori Earl, and Wayne Earl, *This Star Won't Go Out: The Life and Words of Esther Grace Earl* (New York: Dutton Books, 2014).
11. David J. Schwartz, *The Magic of Thinking Big* (New York: Fireside, 1987).
12. For the full definition, see www.merriam-webster.com, s.v. "compass."
13. See www.goodreads.com/author/quotes/5627.Anthony_Robbins.
14. Eleanor Roosevelt, *You Learn by Living* (Louisville: Westminster John Knox Press, 1960).

15. For more information on how your body responds to fear, see Susanne Babbel, "Fear of Success," *Psychology Today*, January 3, 2011, www .psychologytoday.com/blog/somatic-psychology/201101/fear-success.

16. Elizabeth Gilbert, *Eat, Pray, Love: One Woman's Search for Everything Across Italy, India and Indonesia* (New York: Penguin Books, 2006).

Day 23: The Emotional Sobriety Solution

1. The term "emotional intelligence" was first coined by Peter Salovey but popularized by Daniel Goleman. See www.psychologytoday.com/articles /199709/the-unconventional-wisdom-emotional-intelligence.

2. Tian Dayton, "Signs of Emotional Sobriety," Tiandayton.com, October 15, 2013, www.tiandayton.com/signs-of-emotional-sobriety.

3. Victoria Balfour, "John Bradshaw," *People*, May 28, 1990, www.people .com/people/archive/article/0,,20117761,00.html. This source quotes recovery specialist John Bradshaw.

4. Only 47 percent of children reach the age of seven in an intact family. Patrick F. Fagan and Nicholas Zill, *The Second Annual Index of Family Belonging and Rejection* (Washington, DC: Marriage and Religion Research Institute, Family Research Council, November 17, 2011), http:// downloads.frc.org/EF/EF11K28.pdf.

5. According to the American Medical Association, 72 percent of American homes harbor someone with an addiction. www.theonion.com/articles/ dysfunctional-family-statistically-average,4699.

6. www.thework.com.

7. Ibid.

8. You can find a more detailed description of the steps of the process and a set of free downloadable worksheets to guide you in the process at www.thework.com. When you have time, after you complete the 30-day program, you might want to read Katie Byron, *Loving What Is: Four Questions That Can Change Your Life* (New York: Random House, 2002).

Day 24: The Meditation Solution

1. Eknath Easwaran, *Conquest of Mind: Take Charge of Your Thoughts & Reshape Your Life Through Meditation* (Tomales, CA: Nilgiri Press, 1988).

2. To read about some studies that talk about the benefits of meditation, see Robert Schneider, "Does Meditation Have Benefits for Mind and Body?" Medicalnewstoday.com, last modified February 26, 2014, www .medicalnewstoday.com/articles/272833.php.

3. To learn more about the history of meditation, see Robert Puff, "An Overview of Meditation: Its Origins and Traditions," *Psychology Today*,

July 7, 2013, www.psychologytoday.com/blog/meditation-modern-life /201307/overview-meditation-its-origins-and-traditions.

4. For an overall description of the study see M. B. Ospina, K. Bond, M. Karkhaneh, L. Tjosvold, B. Vandermeer, Y. Liang, L. Bialy, N. Hooton, N. Buscemi, D. M. Dryden, and T. P. Klassen, "Meditation Practices for Health: State of the Research," *Evidence Report/Technology Assessment* 155 (June 2007): 1–263, www.ncbi.nlm.nih.gov/pubmed/17764203.

5. Bill Phillips, *Transformation: The Mindset You Need, the Body You Want, the Life You Deserve* (Los Angeles: T-Media, 2010).

6. For more information on how meditation is an effective technique for those recovering from addiction, see "Meditation for Alcoholism and Drug Addiction Recovery," Elementsbehavioralhealth.com, July 6, 2014, www .elementsbehavioralhealth.com/featured/meditation-for-alcoholism-and-drug-addiction-recovery.

7. Phillips, *Transformation*.

8. To read about Dan Harris's experience and suggestions to make you happier, see Eric Barker, "Why You Should Meditate—and How to Do It," *Business Insider*, September 3, 2014, www.businessinsider.com /3-simple-things-that-will-make-you-10-happier-2014-8?nr_email_ referer=1&utm_source=Triggermail&utm_medium=email&utm_term= Business%20Insider%20Select&utm_campaign=BI%20Select%20 %2528Wednesday%20Friday%2529%202014-09-03&utm_content= emailshare.

9. To read the full article about the Seattle Seahawks and meditation, see Alyssa Roenigk, "Lotus Pose on Two," *ESPN the Magazine*, August 21, 2013, http://espn.go.com/nfl/story/_/id/9581925/seattle-seahawks-use-unusual-techniques-practice-espn-magazine%22%20%5Ct%20%22_ blank.

10. To read more about the benefits of mindfulness and meditation, see Dan Hurley, "Breathing In vs. Spacing Out," *New York Times Magazine*, January 14, 2014, www.nytimes.com/2014/01/19/magazine/breathing-in-vs-spacing-out.html.

11. To view Andy Puddicombe's TED Talk or to read the interactive transcript, see "Andy Puddicombe: All It Takes is 10 Mindful Minutes," Fall 2012, www.ted.com/talks/andy_puddicombe_all_it_takes_is_10_mindful_ minutes.

12. Sheff, *Clean*.

13. For more about ways that stress can affect your body, see "How Stress Affects the Body," Heartmath.com, 2010, www.heartmath.com/ infographics/how-stress-effects-the-body.

14. To read more about the impacts of stress, see Laura Garnett, "10 Signs Stress Is Ruining Your Performance," *Business Insider*, March 26, 2014, www.businessinsider.com/10-signs-stress-is-ruining-your-performance-2014-3?nr_email_referer=1&utm_source=Triggermail&utm_medium=email&utm_term=Business%20Insider%20Select&utm_campaign=BI%20Select%20%28Wednesday%20Friday%29%202014-03-26&utm_content=emailshare.

15. Blakeslee, "Placebos Prove So Powerful Even Experts Are Surprised."

16. To read more about stress hormones, see Sarah Klein, "Adrenaline, Cortisol, Norepinephrine: The Three Major Stress Hormones, Explained," Huffingtonpost.com, last modified April 19, 2013, www.huffingtonpost.com/2013/04/19/adrenaline-cortisol-stress-hormones_n_3112800.html.

17. Lipton, *Biology of Belief*.

18. For more uncommonly known facts about stress, see "What You Need to Know About Stress," Heartmath.com, March 25, 2014, www.heartmath.com/blog/health-well-being/what-you-need-to-know-about-stress.

19. To read more about alcohol and stress, see http://alcoholism.about.com/cs/alerts/l/blnaa32.htm.

20. To read more about hormones that can make you happy, see M. Farouk Radwan, "Hormones That Make You Happy," www.2knowmyself.com/Hormones_that_make_you_happy.

21. To read about other natural ways to increase serotonin in the brain, see Simon N. Young, "How to Increase Serotonin in the Human Brain Without Drugs," *Journal of Psychiatry & Neuroscience* 32, no. 6 (2007): 394–99, www.ncbi.nlm.nih.gov/pmc/articles/PMC2077351.

22. To read more about Dr. Andrew Weil's thoughts on breathing, see "Breathing: An Introduction," www.drweil.com/drw/u/ART00519/An-Introduction-to-Breathing.html.

23. To learn more about the 4-7-8 breath exercise, as well as other breathing exercises, see "Breathing: Three Exercises," www.drweil.com/drw/u/ART00521/three-breathing-exercises.html.

24. Matthieu Ricard, *Why Meditate? Working with Thoughts and Emotions* (Carlsbad, CA: Hay House, 2010).

25. Jon Kabat-Zinn, *Wherever You Go, There You Are* (New York: Hyperion, 1994).

26. See "Overcoming Addiction," www.chopra.com/overcoming-addiction.

27. See http://thinkexist.com/quotes/diana_robinson/.

Day 25: The Mind and Body Solution

1. See www.entheos.com/quotes/by_teacher/plato.

2. Harold Pollack, "Alcohol Is Still the Deadliest Drug in the United

States, and It's Not Even Close," *Washington Post Wonkblog*, August 19, 2014, www.washingtonpost.com/blogs/wonkblog/wp/2014/08/19 /alcohol-is-still-the-deadliest-drug-in-the-united-states-and-its-not-even-close.

3. To read more articles about alcohol and liver disease, see http:// alcoholism.about.com/od/liver.

4. To read more articles about alcohol and cirrhosis of the liver, see http:// alcoholism.about.com/od/cirrhosis.

5. To read more articles about alcohol and damage to the brain, see http:// alcoholism.about.com/od/brain.

6. To read more articles about alcohol and dementia, see http://alcoholism. about.com/od/dementia.

7. To read more about alcohol and blood pressure, see http://alcoholism. about.com/cs/heal/a/aa020722a.htm.

8. To read more about alcohol and an irregular heartbeat, see http:// alcoholism.about.com/od/health/a/bljama041011.htm.

9. To watch a video about how alcohol affects the body, see Samuel Ball, "Here's What Alcohol Does to Your Brain and Body," produced by Will Wei, *Business Insider*, May 28, 2014, www.businessinsider.com/alcohol-effects-brain-body-2014-5?nr_email_referer=1&utm_source=Triggermail&utm _medium=email&utm_term=Business%20Insider%20Select&utm_ campaign=BI%20Select%20%28Wednesday%20Friday%29%202014-05-28&utm_content=emailshare.

10. To read more articles on alcohol and cancer, see http://alcoholism.about .com/od/cancer.

11. To read more about how alcohol slows healing, see S. Guo and L. A. DiPietro, "Factors Affecting Wound Healing," *Journal of Dental Research* 89, no. 3 (2010): 219–29, doi:10.1177/0022034509359125.

12. US Department of Health and Human Services, National Institutes of Health, and National Institute on Alcohol Abuse and Alcoholism, "Alcohol's Damaging Effects on the Brain," *Alcohol Alert*, no. 63 (October 2004), http://pubs.niaaa.nih.gov/publications/aa63/aa63.htm.

13. For more information on alcohol related deaths, see Glenn Thomas and Tarik Jasarevic, "WHO Calls on Governments to Do More to Prevent Alcohol-Related Deaths and Diseases," *World Health Organization News Release*, May 12, 2014, www.who.int/mediacentre/news/releases/2014/ alcohol-related-deaths-prevention/en.

14. For more statistics on the consequences of alcohol use, see the following websites: www.niaaa.nih.gov/alcohol-health/overview-alcohol-consumption/alcohol-facts-and-statistics, www.alcoholism-and-drug-addiction-help.com/statistics-on-

alcoholism.html, and http://alcoholism.about.com/od/effect/a/alcohol_harm. htm?nl=1.

15. Cynthia Kuhn, Scott Swartzwelder, and Wilkie Wilson, *Buzzed: The Straight Facts About the Most Used & Abused Drugs* (New York: W. W. Norton, 2008).

16. To read more about this shocking statistic, see Alexandra Sifferlin, "Alcohol Kills 1 Person Every 10 Seconds, Report Says," Time.com, May 12, 2014, http://time.com/96082/alcohol-consumption-who.

17. For more information on the body's restorative capabilities, see Alan Goldhamer, "How Your Body Heals Itself," *T. Colin Campbell Center for Nutrition Studies Newsletter*, October 15, 1997, http://nutritionstudies.org /body-heals.

18. For more information about liver transplants and how the liver grows back, see http://uvahealth.com/services/digestive-health/conditions-and-treatments/liver-resection.

19. To read more about how old some body parts really are, see Angela Epstein, "Believe It or Not, Your Lungs Are Six Weeks Old—and Your Taste Buds Just Ten Days! So How Old Is the Rest of Your Body?" Dailymail.com, last modified October 13, 2009, www.dailymail.co.uk/health/article-1219995 /Believe-lungs-weeks-old—taste-buds-just-days-So-old-rest-body.html.

20. To read more about how the body regenerates, see Brent Atwater, "Time Schedule of Your Body's Cellular Regeneration," *Positive Attitudes for Health Challenges Blog*, July 28, 2012, http://positiveattitudesforhealthchallenges .blogspot.com/2012/07/time-schedule-of-your-bodys-cellular.html.

21. Karen Fischer, *The Healthy Skin Diet: Your Complete Guide to Beautiful Skin in Just 8 Weeks* (London: Rodale, 2009).

22. Joshua Rosenthal, *Integrative Nutrition* (New York: Integrative Nutrition Publishing, 2008).

23. We wish to thank Dr. Tony O'Donnell and Michael McCarthy for their guidance on nutrition and quitting drinking. We'll have more from them on the companion website for Day 25.

24. For more information about food allergies or intolerances, see Erik Ofgang, "Healthy Living: Allergy or Intolerance," *Connecticut Magazine*, May 2014, www.connecticutmag.com/Connecticut-Magazine/May-2014 /Healthy-Living-Allergy-or-Intolerance.

25. For more information about these nutrition basics, see "Nutrition Basics," www.cafebonappetit.com/wellness/nutrition-basics.

26. For more information about water, see F. Batmanghelidj, "You're Not Sick; You're Thirsty. Don't Treat Thirst with Medication," http://watercure .com.

27. F. Batmanghelidj, *Your Body's Many Cries for Water* (Falls Church, VA: Global Health Solutions, 1997).

28. For more information about why we prefer calorie-dense foods, see Katherine Harmon, "Addicted to Fat: Overeating May Alter the Brain as Much as Hard Drugs," *Scientific American*, March 28, 2010, www.scientificamerican.com/article/addicted-to-fat-eating.

29. For more statistics on obesity, see "Obesity and Overweight," *World Health Organization Fact Sheet*, No. 311, January 2015, www.who.int/mediacentre/factsheets/fs311/en.

30. Wendy C. Fries, "13 Ways to Fight Sugar Cravings," Webmd.com, June 22, 2011, www.webmd.com/diet/features/13-ways-to-fight-sugar-cravings.

31. Food Allergy Research and Education (FARE), "Facts and Statistics," www.foodallergy.org/facts-and-stats.

32. Nutritionist and fitness expert JJ Virgin has found that the seven most common allergies are to soy, corn, gluten (found in wheat, barley, and rye), dairy, sugar, artificial sweeteners (and alcohol!), eggs, and peanuts. For more information, see her book *The Virgin Diet: Drop 7 Foods, Lose 7 Pounds, Just 7 Days* (New York: Harlequin, 2012).

33. Lyn-Genet Recitas, *The Plan: Eliminate the Surprising "Healthy" Foods That Are Making You Fat—and Lose Weight Fast* (London: Orion, 2013).

Day 26: The Positive Addiction Solution

1. Glasser, *Positive Addiction*.

2. Veronica M. Hay and Deepak Chopra, "An Exclusive Interview by Veronica M. Hay with Deepak Chopra," *A Magazine of People and Possibilities*, www.peopleandpossibilities.com/chopra.html.

3. John Robbins, *Healthy at 100* (New York: Ballantine Books, 2007).

4. To learn more about the Research Society on Alcoholism (RSA), see www.rsoa.org.

5. To learn more about and read the RSA's study, see H. C. Karoly, C. J. Stevens, R. E. Thayer, R. E. Magnan, A. D. Bryan, and K. E. Hutchison, "Aerobic Exercise Moderates the Effect of Heavy Alcohol Consumption on White Matter Damage," *Alcoholism: Clinical and Experimental Research* 39, no. 9 (September 2013): 1508–515, doi:10.1111/acer.12135.

6. Shawn Achor, *The Happiness Advantage: The Seven Principles of Positive Psychology That Fuel Success and Performance at Work* (New York: Crown Business, 2010).

7. To read more about the release of endorphins and serotonin during exercise, see Jacqueline Stenson, "Getting High on Exercise: How Much Does It Take to Boost Mood?" MSNBC.com, September 18, 2007, www

.nbcnews.com/id/18043835/ns/health-fitness/t/getting-high-exercise/#
.VGzti_nF-So.

8. To read about other hidden benefits of exercise, see Mark Stibich, "The Hidden Benefits of Exercise," About.com, June 18, 2013, http://longevity .about.com/od/lifelongfitness/tp/Hidden-Benefits-of-Exercise.htm.

9. Brett Klinka and Chris Jordan, "High-Intensity Circuit Training Using Body Weight: Maximum Results with Minimal Investment," *ACSM'S Health & Fitness Journal* 17, no. 3 (May/June 2013): pp. 8–13, doi:10.1249 /FIT.0b013e31828cb1e8.

10. For more information about the 7-minute workout, see Gretchen Reynolds, "The Scientific 7-Minute Workout," *New York Times*, May 9, 2013, http://well.blogs.nytimes.com/2013/05/09/the-scientific-7-minute-workout/?_php=true&_type=blogs&_r=1.

11. To learn more about the benefits of being outside in nature, see Jessey Bernstein, Kirk Warren Brown, Louis Mastella, and Marylène Gagné, "Spending Time in Nature Makes People Feel More Alive, Study Shows," Rochester.edu, June 3, 2010, www.rochester.edu/news/show.php?id= 3639.

12. To learn more about beginning an exercise plan and the different types of exercise, see Brian D. Johnston, "Starting an Exercise Program," Merckmanuals.com, September 2014, www.merckmanuals.com/home/ fundamentals/exercise_and_fitness/starting_an_exercise_program.html.

13. See http://events.stanford.edu/events/324/32425.

14. To read more about the differences between aerobic and anaerobic exercise, see Sharon E. Griffin, "Aerobic vs. Anaerobic: What Is the Difference?" www.myfooddiary.com/resources/ask_the_expert/aerobic_vs_anaerobic .asp.

15. For more information on preventing the loss of muscle mass, see Laura Skladzinki, "How to Stay Strong and Prevent Muscle Loss," Greatist.com, May 24, 2012, http://greatist.com/fitness/how-stay-strong-and-prevent-muscle-loss.

16. To read more about muscle and fat, see Jennifer M. Regan, "One Pound of Fat Versus One Pound of Muscle: Clearing up the Misconceptions," *Bamboo Core Fitness Blog*, http://bamboocorefitness.com/one-pound-of-fat-versus-one-pound-of-muscle-clearing-up-the-misconception.

17. When starting to exercise after taking time off to recover from an injury, Jack found that Tony Horton's *10-Minute Trainer* DVDs provided him with a total body workout in just ten minutes first thing in the morning. You can learn more about it and order it at www.beachbody.com.

18. To read more about music releasing endorphins and increasing tolerance

for pain, see Robin Dunbar, Kostas Kaskatis, Ian MacDonald, and Vinnie Barra, "Performance of Music Elevates Pain Threshold and Positive Affect: Implications for the Evolutionary Function of Music," *Evolutionary Psychology* 10, no. 4, www.epjournal.net/articles/performance-of-music-elevates-pain-threshold-and-positive-affect-implications-for-the-evolutionary-function-of-music.

19. The US Marine Corps, *Run to Cadence with the US Marines*, vols. 1–3 (Documentary Recordings, 2002).

20. For more information on alcohol and sleep disorders, see Denise Mann, "Alcohol and a Good Night's Sleep Don't Mix," WebMD.com, January 22, 2013, www.webmd.com/sleep-disorders/news/20130118/alcohol-sleep.

21. To read more about alcohol's effect on sleep, see "Reviewing Alcohol's Effects on Normal Sleep," *Alcoholism: Clinical & Experimental Research*, January 22, 2013, www.sciencedaily.com/releases/2013/01/130122162236.htm.

22. To read more about the effects of alcohol on the body, especially when exercising, see Selene Yeager, "Drinking and Exercise: How Alcohol Affects Your Body: Do Drinking and Exercise Mix?" *Women's Health*, February 17, 2012, www.womenshealthmag.com/health/drinking-and-exercise.

23. Laura Entis, "How Much Sleep Do You Really Need?" *Entrepreneur*, April 4, 2014, www.entrepreneur.com/article/232784.

24. To read more about the ideal amount of sleep, see Laura Blue, "How Much Sleep Do You Really Need?" Time.com, June 6, 2008, http://content.time.com/time/health/article/0,8599,1812420,00.html.

25. To read more about the benefits of exercise and a good night's sleep, see "Exercise Helps Ready the Body for a Good Night's Sleep," Premierhealth.com, February 17, 2014, www.premierhealthnet.com/phndefault.aspx?id=78284.

26. To learn more about how naps can improve your performance, see Diana Rodriguez, "Why You Should Still Nap," Everydayhealth.com, February 14, 2011, www.everydayhealth.com/health-report/healthy-sleep/why-nap.aspx.

27. For a slideshow of some of these famous nappers, see "Famous Nappers: Historical Figures Known for Napping," Huffingtonpost.com, last modified November 17, 2011, www.huffingtonpost.com/2010/01/14/famous-nappers-historical_n_423279.html.

28. To read more about the health benefits of exercising for just five minutes, see Kevin Loria, "Running Just 5 Minutes a Day Could Add Years to Your Life," *Business Insider*, July 31, 2014, www.businessinsider.com/running-just-5-minutes-a-day-could-add-years-to-your-life-2014-7.

29. Glasser, *Positive Addiction.*

30. To read more about the frequency of daily laughter of children and adults, see Pamela Gerloff, "You're Not Laughing Enough, and That's No Joke," *Psychology Today*, June 21, 2011, www.psychologytoday.com/blog/ the-possibility-paradigm/201106/youre-not-laughing-enough-and-thats-no-joke.

31. To learn more about laughter yoga, see www.laughteryoga.org/english/ news/news_details/405.

32. To read more about the life-threatening dangers of stress, see Dr. Mercola, "Documentary Examines How Stress Kills," Mercola.com, July 5, 2014, http://articles.mercola.com/sites/articles/archive/2014/07/05/stress-effects.aspx, and "America's #1 Health Problem," The American Institute of Stress, www.stress.org/americas-1-health-problem.

33. For more information on the healing benefits of laughter, see Melinda Smith and Jeanne Segal, "Laughter Is the Best Medicine: The Health Benefits of Humor and Laughter," Helpguide.org, last modified February 2015, www.helpguide.org/articles/emotional-health/laughter-is-the-best-medicine.htm.

34. For more information about laughter and heart health, see Michelle Murray, "Laughter Is the Best Medicine for Your Heart," University of Maryland Medical Center News Release, July 2, 2013, http://umm.edu /news-and-events/news-releases/2009/laughter-is-the-best-medicine-for-your-heart.

35. Swayze and Niemi, *Time of My Life.*

Day 27: The Love and Relationship Solution

1. To read more about Bronnie Ware's experience and the top five regrets of the dying, see www.ariseindiaforum.org/nurse-reveals-the-top-5-regrets-people-make-on-their-deathbed.

2. See Deepak Chopra and David Simon, *Freedom from Addiction: The Chopra Center Method for Overcoming Destructive Habits* (Deerfield Beach, FL: Health Communications, 2007).

3. Glenn Plaskin, "Playboy Interview: Anthony (Tony) Robbins," Awaken .com, August 17, 2013, www.awaken.com/2013/08/playboy-interview-anthony-tony-robbins.

4. Alicia Dennis, "Tim McGraw: 'I Feel Better Than Ever,'" *People,* February 11, 2013, www.people.com/people/archive/article/0,,20674394,00.html.

5. Swayze and Niemi, *Time of My Life.*

6. Kathy Ehrich Dowd, "Michael J. Fox: I Was 'Drinking Heavily' Following

Parkinson's Diagnosis," *People*, September 26, 2013, www.people.com/people/article/0,,20739261,00.html.

7. Lawton Ursrey, "The Fastest Way to Life Success: Vulnerability," *Forbes*, July 20, 2014, www.forbes.com/sites/lawtonursrey/2014/07/20/the-fastest-way-to-life-success-vulnerability.

8. To read more quotes from Werner Erhard, see https://wernererhardquotes.wordpress.com/tag/erhard-seminars-training.

9. Rob Lowe, *Stories I Only Tell My Friends* (New York: Henry Holt, 2011).

10. To read more about Naomi Campbell, see Louise Gannon, "'I Didn't Think I Would Make It to 40. I'm Not Proud of What I've Done,' Naomi Campbell on Her Regrets," *Mail Online*, last modified March 21, 2010, www.dailymail.co.uk/home/moslive/article-1258631/Naomi-Campbell-I-didnt-think-I-make-40-Im-proud-Ive-done.html.

11. For more quotes by Anthony Robbins, see www.goodreads.com/author/quotes/5627.Anthony_Robbins.

Day 28: The Review Day and Bonus Solution

1. Deepak Chopra, *A Deepak Chopra Companion: Illuminations on Health and Human Consciousness* (New York: Three Rivers Press, 1999).

PHASE V: CREATING YOUR PERSONALIZED PLAN TO THRIVE IN LIFE

1. Covey, *7 Habits of Highly Effective People*.

Day 29: The Vision Solution

1. See http://yourstory.com/2014/05/dhirubhai-ambani-quotes.

2. Soren Gordhamer, "If the Buddha Used Twitter," *Huffington Post*, August 6, 2009, www.huffingtonpost.com/soren-gordhamer/if-the-buddha-used-twitte_b_224963.html.

3. Covey, *7 Habits of Highly Effective People*.

4. Swayze and Niemi, *Time of My Life*.

5. To read an article on finding your dream job and how to get it, see Laura Garnett, "5 Steps to Discover Your Dream Job," *Business Insider*, February 24, 2014, www.businessinsider.com/how-to-find-your-dream-job-2014-2?nr_email_referer=1&utm_source=Triggermail&utm_medium=email&utm_term=Business%20Insider%20Select&utm_campaign=BI%20Select%20Mondays%202014-02-24&utm_content=emailshare.

6. King, *On Writing*.

7. Hamilton, *Beyond Belief*.

8. Jim Loehr and Tony Schwartz, *The Power of Full Engagement: Managing*

Energy, Not Time, Is the Key to High Performance and Personal Renewal (New York: Free Press, 2003).

9. See www.people.com/people/archive/article/0,,20160692,00.html.

Day 30: The Sobriety for Life Solution

1. Millman, *Everyday Enlightenment*.
2. To read more about alternatives to abstinence and various studies, see Adi Jaffe, "Helping Addicts Get Their Lives Back," *Psychology Today*, www.psychologytoday.com/blog/all-about-addiction/201103/abstinence-is-not-the-only-option, and www.astrocyte-design.com/pseudoscience/alcoholism.html.
3. For the full definition, see www.thefreedictionary.com, s.v. "sobriety."
4. Clapton, *Clapton*.
5. Daniel Goleman, "Breaking Bad Habits: New Therapy Focuses on the Relapse," *New York Times*, December 27, 1988, www.nytimes.com/1988/12/27/science/breaking-bad-habits-new-therapy-focuses-on-the-relapse.html.
6. To read more about how abstinence is the best path for some people, see William J. Cromie, "Five Years Is Magic Number for Recovering Alcoholics: Attempts at Social Drinking Frequently Lead to Relapse," *Harvard University Gazette Archives*, March 14, 1996, http://news.harvard.edu/gazette/1996/03.14/FiveYearsIsMagi.html.
7. To read more about a survey that asked, "Did you once have a problem with drugs or alcohol, but no longer do?" see Josie Feliz, "Survey: Ten Percent of American Adults Report Being in Recovery from Substance Abuse or Addiction," Drugfree.org, March 6, 2012, www.drugfree.org/newsroom/survey-ten-percent-of-american-adults-report-being-in-recovery-from-substance-abuse-or-addiction.
8. To read and watch an interview with Audrey Kishline, see Dennis Murphy, "Road to Recovery," *Dateline*, Nbcnews.com, www.nbcnews.com/id/14627442/ns/dateline_nbc/t/road-recovery/#.VG6NJ_nF-Sp.
9. Agassi, *Open*.
10. *The Health Benefits of Volunteering: A Review of Recent Research* (Washington, DC: Corporation for National and Community Service, Office of Research and Policy Development, 2007), www.nationalservice.gov/sites/default/files/documents/07_0506_hbr.pdf?tbl_pr_id=687.
11. Millman, *Everyday Enlightenment*.
12. Wayne W. Dyer, *The Power of Intention* (Carlsbad, CA: Hay House, 2010).
13. "Samuel L. Jackson with 64 Movies to His Credit, Is Featured in 'Star Wars the Phantom Menace,'" *Jet,* June 7, 1999.

14. After a period of not being able to exercise for several months due to a back injury, Jack started back into exercise by using Tony Horton's *10-Minute Trainer* DVDs, produced and distributed by Beachbody. You can order the videos from amazon.com or beachbody.com. This is an easy way to get started. You just turn on the DVD and follow along.

15. See www.goodreads.com/author/quotes/399.Napoleon_Hill.

Index

ABOUT THE AUTHORS

Jack Canfield, known as America's #1 Success Coach, is a bestselling author, professional speaker, trainer, and entrepreneur. He is the founder and CEO of the Canfield Training Group, which provides training and multimedia programs on personal transformation, leadership, motivation, self-esteem, and peak performance, and how to accelerate the achievement of one's personal and professional goals. He has conducted live training for more than a million people in more than forty countries around the world. He holds two Guinness World Record titles and is a member of the National Speakers Association Speaker Hall of Fame.

Jack is the coauthor and editor of more than two hundred books, including *The Success Principles: How to Get from Where You Are to Where You Want to Be, The Success Principles for Teens, Tapping into Ultimate Success, Coaching for Breakthrough Success, The Success Secret, The Power of Focus, The Aladdin Factor, Jack Canfield's Key to Living the Law of Attraction*, and the Chicken Soup for the Soul® series, which includes forty *New York Times* bestsellers and has sold more than five hundred million copies in forty-seven languages around the world.

Jack is a featured teacher in the movie *The Secret*, and has appeared on more than a thousand radio and television shows, including *The Oprah Winfrey Show*, the *Today* show, *Fox & Friends, Larry King Live*, and the *NBC Nightly News* and the *CBS Evening News*.

Jack's coaches at Jack Canfield Coaching (www.canfieldcoaching .com) have provided one-on-one breakthrough success coaching to more than four thousand people in eighty countries.

Jack is the founder and chairman of the board of the Transformational Leadership Council, a professional association for owners of transformational training and coaching companies and thought leaders in the field of personal and organizational transformation.

To find out more about Jack's other books, audio programs, and live training, including his flagship Breakthrough to Success training and his Train the Trainer program, contact his office at:

The Canfield Training Group
PO Box 30880
Santa Barbara, CA 93130
www.jackcanfield.com
Phone: 805-563-2935
Email: info@jackcanfield.com
www.facebook.com/JackCanfieldFan
https://twitter.com/jackcanfield

Dave Andrews is an author, speaker, and sobriety coach who has been a featured "sobriety expert" on more than fifty national and international talk shows. After suffering for over a decade as an alcoholic, putting his work, his marriage, his hopes and dreams, and his life at risk, he was finally able to triumph over addiction. He is one of the world's leading experts in helping others recover, reclaim, and reinvent their lives without alcohol, freeing them to live a thriving life in sobriety.

As "America's #1 Sobriety Coach," Dave specializes in coaching people in early sobriety. With over six years of experience as a sobriety and life coach, Dave focuses on eliminating addictive behaviors and paving the way for positive change. He gets to the underlying causes of what holds people back, providing them with a road map for creating permanent breakthroughs.

Dave is a certified comprehensive positive psychology coach, a certified neurolinguistic programming (NLP) private practitioner Level 1, and a certified strategic intervention coach and marriage educator by the Robbins-Madanes Center for Strategic Intervention.

Dave is the CEO of The 30-Day Solution, LLC, and serves on the board of directors of the nonprofit organizations Young People in Recovery and Advocates for Recovery. He currently resides outside of Denver with his wife and two daughters, and has been sober for more than eight years.

To find out more about Dave's recovery resource offerings, including live training and speaking engagements, or to hire Dave as your personal sobriety coach, contact his office below.

To learn more about how you can help expand the reach of *The 30-Day Sobriety Solution*, including bringing *The 30-Day Sobriety Solution* Employee Assistance Program to your company, contact info@the-30daysolution.com or see more at http://30DayResources.com/eap.

The 30-Day Solution, LLC
6590 South Vine Street, Suite 112
Centennial, CO 80121
www.TheSobrietySolution.com
Phone: 1-844-My30Day (1-844-693-0329)
Email: info@thesobrietysolution.com
https://twitter.com/30daysolution
www.facebook.com/the30daysolution

to "test" drinking again, sometimes with just two or three drinks. After this experience, they realized that drinking wasn't a positive influence and returned to abstinence. If they were to follow standard AA guidelines, they would have to start over counting days, but we believe this isn't a fair representation of the changes they have made in their lives. It is critical that you don't judge your "testing the water" as an all-or-nothing event that somehow redefines the work you have done in the past as no longer applicable. If these 30-Day Graduates had treated their return to drinking as a complete failure requiring them to start all over, who knows if and when they would have become sober again.

Sometimes the information you get from "going back out there" can be invaluable. We are not saying you should drink again just to get that information, but if you decide to, then make sure you learn from the experience. As long as you practice some basic self-awareness and are honest with your feelings around the experience, it will be obvious whether or not you can maintain a healthy relationship with alcohol.

Thriving in Sobriety Through Abstinence

For most of you, abstinence is going to be the path that best serves you. And you are not alone.[6] Conservative estimates show that at least 23.5 million American adults are living in recovery from alcohol or drug abuse,[7] and this doesn't include all the teetotalers who just choose to not drink or use drugs in the first place.

Sometimes the real magic of thriving in sobriety comes when you actually decide you are done with drinking for good. When you know that door will never be opened again, you start to really understand your relationship to alcohol. The back and forth can be emotionally exhausting, and can take you away from doing the work you need to do. It goes back to the 100% Solution from Day 1—when you are not 100% committed to abstaining, you let the ongoing debate continue in your head.

However, when you decide you are never going back, the real